King Lear 'After' Auschwitz

King Lear 'After' Auschwitz

Shakespeare, Appropriation and Theatres of Catastrophe in Post-War British Drama

Richard Ashby

EDINBURGH
University Press

Edinburgh University Press is one of the leading university presses in the UK. We publish academic books and journals in our selected subject areas across the humanities and social sciences, combining cutting-edge scholarship with high editorial and production values to produce academic works of lasting importance. For more information visit our website: edinburghuniversitypress.com

© Richard Ashby, 2021, 2022

Edinburgh University Press Ltd
The Tun – Holyrood Road, 12(2f) Jackson's Entry, Edinburgh EH8 8PJ

First published in hardback by Edinburgh University Press 2021

Typeset in Sabon by
Servis Filmsetting Ltd, Stockport, Cheshire

A CIP record for this book is available from the British Library

ISBN 978 1 4744 7798 7 (hardback)
ISBN 978 1 4744 7799 4 (paperback)
ISBN 978 1 4744 7800 7 (webready PDF)
ISBN 978 1 4744 7801 4 (epub)

The right of Richard Ashby to be identified as the author of this work has been asserted in accordance with the Copyright, Designs and Patents Act 1988, and the Copyright and Related Rights Regulations 2003 (SI No. 2498).

Contents

Acknowledgements	vi
Introduction	1
1. 'After' Auschwitz	26
2. Why *King Lear*?	65
3. 'Strange mutations': The History of *King Lear* 'After' Auschwitz	96
4. 'The man without pity is mad': Edward Bond's *King Lears* and the Dialectic of Engagement	143
5. 'Rudkin I nothing am': Edgar, Exile and Self Re-authorship in David Rudkin's *Will's Way*	172
6. 'WHAT IS THIS GOOD?': The Ethics and Aesthetics of the 'Good Life' in Howard Barker's *Seven Lears*	203
7. 'Thought you were dead': Dover Cliff, Death and 'Ephemeral Life' in Sarah Kane's *Blasted*	234
Postscript: Writing and Performing from the Rubble: Forced Entertainment, *Five Day Lear* and *Table Top Shakespeare: The Complete Works*	264
8. 'And I was struck still . . .': Nature, the Sublime and Subjectivity in Dennis Kelly's *The Gods Weep*	276
Conclusion: 'Storm Still'	303
Bibliography	306
Index	329

Acknowledgements

This project began its life as a PhD. First and foremost, I owe huge thanks to my supervisor, Chris Megson, and advisor, Deana Rankin. My debt to them truly does make breath poor and speech unable. Thanks also to the AHRC for generous PhD funding and everyone involved in the TECHNE scheme.

I was fortunate enough to have as PhD examiners Karoline Gritzner and Eric Langley, who offered invaluable advice about turning the project into a monograph. I am also grateful to Karoline for sharing parts of her inspirational book on Adorno and modern theatre before it was published.

Deep thanks to Howard Barker and David Rudkin for taking the time to answer my questions – hearing what they had to say about Shakespeare, *King Lear* and the twentieth century was truly fascinating. I am particularly thankful to Howard for his generosity and hospitality. I am also indebted to Tim Etchells for his time and insights and to Maria Aberg for answering questions about *The Gods Weep*.

I am grateful to David Ian Rabey for some very inspiring conversations around the project and for so generously sharing materials from his personal Rudkin and Barker archives. The project has also benefited at various points from thought-provoking conversations with Kiernan Ryan, Ewan Fernie, Graham Saunders, Richard Wilson and John Joughin.

I would also like to thank the Drama Department at Royal Holloway for supporting the research for King Lear 'After' Auschwitz, and the English Department, where I have very much enjoyed teaching Shakespeare to the next generation of scholars. Particular thanks go to Harry Newman for his interest in the project and his support. Thanks also to Christie Carson for her thoughts on adaptation and appropriation and to Robert Eaglestone for reading recommendations and his advice on publishing.

I have met some wonderful researchers over the course of the project.

Sincere thanks to Jennifer Edwards, whose research and friendship has been an inspiration, and to Poppy Corbett, Chien-Cheng Chen, Jessica Chiba, Ursula Clayton and Timo Uotinen.

It has been a pleasure to work with Ersev Ersoy, whose guidance has been instrumental, and with everyone at Edinburgh University Press. I am also grateful to the staff at the British Library – particularly the indefatigable Helen Melody – for helping me to navigate the David Rudkin Archive, and to the staff at the Exeter Digital Archives. Thanks also to Donald Cooper at Photostage, Amberley Jamieson at DACS, and Michelle Morton at the RSC, for kindly helping to find (and granting rights to reproduce) the images I have used.

I want to thank my parents, Anne and David, for always being so supportive of me. I also want to thank my brother Paul and sister Holly, for being prepared to listen. Thanks too to Jean and Graham for all their encouragement.

My grandparents John, Emily and Eileen all sadly passed away while I was working on this project. They were all inspirational, larger-than-life figures and I can only hope I have inherited their selfless devotion to their loved ones and their incredible fortitude. They may come no more – but they will never be forgotten. This book is, in part, dedicated to their memory. We cannot forget the lessons of a generation that saw so much.

I also want to thank my partner, Sarah, to whom King Lear *'After' Auschwitz* is also dedicated. This book would not have been possible without her love and support.

And finally, to Rowan.

Introduction:
King Lear 'After' Auschwitz

Near the end of the 2010 Dennis Kelly play *The Gods Weep*, it suddenly and strangely begins to 'snow'. Under the fall, the protagonists, Colm and Barbara, come to a disturbing realisation:

>   *Suddenly it starts to snow. They look up.*
> **Barbara:** What?
>   *They hold their hands out.*
> **Colm:**   Snow? It's not cold.
>   *She rubs some in her hand.*
> **Barbara:** Ash.
> **Colm:**   Ash? Falling out of the sky? Someone must be burning something. It's not from near here. What do you think they're burning?
>   *They stand for a moment. They suddenly run into the shelter, away from the ash. They brush it off them, desperate to get it away from their bodies. They stare at each other. They watch the ash fall.*[1]

It is a shocking moment. Colm and Barbara seek cover from the snow because it is really ash – and the ash is coming from burnt human bodies. The image recalls the industrial incineration of corpses in the Holocaust, the degradation of millions of people into mere ash. *The Gods Weep* is a play that responds to the catastrophe of Auschwitz and the ongoing legacy of the camps.

It is also an appropriation of *King Lear*, its 'snow' derived from the stormy, 'strange' and 'out of season' weather of Shakespeare.[2] Kelly sets the action of Shakespeare in a vast transnational corporation, which

---

[1] Dennis Kelly, *The Gods Weep* (London: Oberon Books, 2010), p. 155. All references to *The Gods Weep* are from the Oberon edition and take the form of act, scene and page numbers.

[2] William Shakespeare, *King Lear*, ed. R. A. Foakes (London: Methuen, 1997), p. 173 and p. 224. I refer to the Arden edition of *King Lear* unless otherwise indicated. For more on the texts and textual history of *King Lear*, see below. All other references to Shakespeare are from William Shakespeare, *The Oxford*

the CEO, Colm, divides among his subordinates. Over the action of the play, the company collapses and, from its ruins, a full-scale war emerges. For most of the final act, Colm (the Lear figure) and Barbara (the Cordelia figure) are left stranded in a bleak, anti-pastoral world, while the rival factions continue the conflict. It soon becomes apparent that unimaginable atrocities are taking place, as witnessed by a sky inundated with human remains. Kelly appropriates *King Lear* for the purposes of a post-Auschwitz drama.

Kelly was largely condemned for his representation of atrocity and his supposed misuse of Shakespeare.[3] But his is far from the only play to use *King Lear* to respond to the catastrophes of modern times. Perhaps the most famous is the 1971 play *Lear*, by Edward Bond. Bond also appropriates *King Lear* in order to engage with the catastrophes of modernity. His unsparingly violent play – originally staged when the Vietnam War was raging, the Berlin Wall split East and West Berlin and the Cold War threatened a total nuclear apocalypse – reflects on the depth of ongoing, and the possibility of future, disasters.

The action of the play that caused (and continues to cause) the most upset are the scenes in which Lear is imprisoned, before he is perfunctorily blinded by an impassive sentry who uses a 'scientific device'.[4] The scene reimagines the blinding of Gloucester from Shakespeare:

Fourth Prisoner:	(*Produces a tool*): Here's a device I perfected on dogs for removing human eyes.
Lear:	No, no. You mustn't touch my eyes. I must have my eyes!
Fourth Prisoner:	With this device you extract the eye undamaged and then it can be put to good use. It's based on a scouting gadget I had as a boy.
Soldier N:	Get on, it's late.
Fourth Prisoner:	Understand, this isn't an instrument of torture, but a scientific device. See how it clips the lid back to leave it unmarked.
Lear:	No – no!
Fourth Prisoner:	Nice and steady (*He removes one of LEAR'S eyes*) [. . .]
Fourth Prisoner:	Note how the eye passes into the lower chamber and is received in a soothing formulation of formaldehyde crystals. One more, please (*He removes LEAR'S other eye*) [. . .] Perfect. (2.4.63)

Shakespeare: The Complete Works, 2nd edn, ed. Stanley Wells and Gary Taylor (Oxford: Oxford University Press, 2005).
[3] For more on the play and its negative reviews, see Chapter 8.
[4] Edward Bond, *Lear* (London: Methuen, 2009), p. 63. All references are to the Methuen edition and take the form of act, scene and page numbers.

The image grimly evokes the use of modern torture techniques and the pseudo-scientific 'investigations' performed on people in the Holocaust, with the disfigured Lear calling viscerally to mind images of 'victims of the Nazi concentration camps'.[5] William Gaskill, who directed the original production of the play at the London Royal Court, remarked that the scene was so 'reminiscent of Dachau' that it often provoked mass walkouts on the part of audiences.[6]

Since the Second World War, *King Lear* has emerged as the Shakespeare play that seems to speak most powerfully to modern catastrophe. From the fateful division of the kingdom that begins the play to the protracted death of Lear at its end as he cradles the dead body of his daughter Cordelia, the play insistently dramatises 'the disasters of the world' (I.i.175) and a vision of 'dark and deadly' (V.iii.288) devastation. By the close of the play only a few distraught survivors remain, and there is no sign that restitution is anywhere to be found on a blasted vista. Emily Sun writes that *King Lear* speaks with distinct urgency to audiences living in the continuing aftermath of 'genocidal horror and global total warfare'.[7] The increasing relevance of the play in post-war culture is reflected in both criticism and performance, where it has gained a now unparalleled status: R. A. Foakes convincingly shows that *King Lear* has come to displace the once ascendant *Hamlet* at the pinnacle of the Shakespeare canon.[8] Even with the war now fading from living memory, the 'play for the times is still *King Lear*' – and it is 'likely to remain so for the foreseeable future'.[9]

What has so far been neglected by critics, however, is the increased presence of *King Lear* in post-war playwriting. The play is not only vital for Kelly and Bond, but has been appropriated time and again in post-war writing for the stage by a host of playwrights and dramatists. These appropriations comprise variously conceived forms of creative intervention ranging from complete rewritings of the play to sequels and prequels, to re-visionings of single scenes or speeches, to the use of individual protagonists from the play, to allusions and citations,

---

[5] Peter Billingham, *Edward Bond: A Critical Study* (Basingstoke: Palgrave Macmillan, 2014), p. 50.
[6] William Gaskill, *A Sense of Direction: Life at the Royal Court* (New York: Limelight Editions, 1988), p. 123.
[7] Emily Sun, *Succeeding King Lear: Literature, Exposure and the Possibility of Politics* (New York: Fordham University Press, 2010), p. 14.
[8] R. A. Foakes, *Hamlet Versus Lear: Cultural Politics and Shakespeare's Art* (Cambridge: Cambridge University Press, 1993). See especially pp. 45–77.
[9] R. A. Foakes, '*King Lear* and the Displacement of *Hamlet*', *Huntington Library Quarterly*, 50:3 (1987), p. 275.

whether these are transient or more sustained. With plays that represent Shakespeare, there have also been appropriations of the iconic author of *King Lear* 'himself'.

This book analyses appropriations of *King Lear* in playwriting of the post-war period, concentrating on British drama, where appropriations of the play have been markedly dominant.[10] It will show that some of the most significant appropriations of the play – and vital trends in both post-war criticism and performance – can be situated historically and dramaturgically as responses to the catastrophes of modern times. Most of all, it is the catastrophe of the Holocaust – the systematic genocide of some six million European Jews, along with any other person or peoples deemed racially inferior, dangerous or degenerate, resulting in anything up to seventeen million deaths overall – that underpins and informs appropriations of *King Lear*.[11] Other catastrophes – Hiroshima and Nagasaki, genocides in Bosnia and Rwanda, the atomic fallout of Chernobyl and Fukushima, the events of 9/11, the global war against terrorism and climate change – are spectres that continue to haunt. Due to its unprecedented scale and the horrifying depredation it involved, however, the Holocaust retains a nightmarish place in the cultural imaginary, even becoming virtually metonymic of modern catastrophe.[12] Far from a more parochial concern with questions of national and cultural identity, British playwrights have appropriated *King Lear* to engage with a European (and indeed world) legacy of catastrophe, epitomised by the barbarity of the Holocaust.

King Lear is a play that has been used time and again to write the

---

[10] To be sure, there are appropriations of *King Lear* by international playwrights, including the 1976 play *Minetti* by the Austrian novelist and playwright Thomas Bernhard, the 1996 play *John Lear* by French playwright Michel Deutsch and the 1997 *Rey Lear* by Colombian writer and director Rodrigo García. Perhaps surprisingly, in German drama it is *Titus Andronicus* that has been more commonly appropriated to interrogate the Holocaust. See my *Comparative Drama* article '"Multidirectional" Shakespeare: Heiner Müller, *Anatomy Titus: Fall of Rome*, a Shakespeare Commentary, Postcolonialism and the Holocaust' (forthcoming). The 'tradition' of *King Lear* appropriations in British playwriting is far stronger. For more on British reactions to the Holocaust, see Caroline Sharples and Olaf Jensen (eds), *Britain and the Holocaust: Remembering and Representing War and Genocide* (Basingstoke: Palgrave Macmillan, 2013).

[11] For a survey of the Holocaust and the (estimated) number of victims involved, see The United States Holocaust Museum online, <https://encyclopedia.ushmm.org/content/en/article/documenting-numbers-of-victims-of-the-holocaust-and-nazi-persecution> (accessed 8 November 2019).

[12] This metonymic status does raise urgent historical, philosophical and ethical controversies. These are considered again in Chapter 1.

disaster.[13] This is not to say that post-war playwrights appropriate *King Lear* to write plays that directly or realistically depict the Holocaust and the dehumanising conditions of the concentration camps – though there have been 'documentary'-style Holocaust plays on the British stage.[14] The case I make has more to do with the status of the subject 'after' the Holocaust. For many artists and thinkers writing in its wake, the Holocaust is an event that represents the complete destruction of the human subject in modernity. Far from an autonomous agent shaping its own destiny, the concentration camps reveal the way subjects are degraded by modern systems of total social and political domination. These transform subjects into nothing more than objects, which may be systematically destroyed. This process of turning 'living' subjects into 'dead' objects reached a nadir in the Holocaust; but while the Holocaust represents the worst manifestation of European anti-Semitism and a catastrophe of unparalleled enormity and suffering, it also relates to the wider transformation of subjects into objects in post-Enlightenment cultural modernity. The possible outcome of that process is increasingly captured in a single word – Auschwitz, by some distance the largest Nazi concentration camp, where around 1.1 million people died.[15] Auschwitz is a unique place in the event known as the Holocaust, but so inhuman and debasing were its conditions that it has come to 'stand' for the Holocaust, and even the destruction of human beings in modernity, as a whole. I typically refer to Auschwitz, while also using the more common Holocaust and Shoah.[16]

---

[13] The idea of 'writing the disaster' is taken from Maurice Blanchot and his 1980 work *The Writing of the Disaster*, trans. Ann Smock (Lincoln and London: University of Nebraska Press, 1995). I return to the type of fragmentary writing demanded by the Holocaust in Chapter 1, though I do so through Theodor Adorno.

[14] These plays include – among others – *Kindertransport*, a 1984 play by Diane Samuels, and *Albert Speer*, a 2000 play by David Edgar. The plays I study are far less 'realist' in approach and realisation.

[15] For a short but powerful introduction to the camp, see Sybille Steinbacher, *Auschwitz: A History*, trans. Shaun Whiteside (London: Penguin, 2005).

[16] Auschwitz is sometimes preferred as a metonym for the Holocaust, as the word Holocaust has its roots in the Jewish practice of a sacrificial offering, which was burnt completely on an altar. The term is problematic in that it imputes a sacrificial status to the genocide of the European Jews – which may syncopate with Nazi ideology and its conception of the Final Solution as a necessary sacrifice in the name of Aryan racial purity. Timothy Snyder in *Black Earth: The Holocaust as History and Warning* (London: Penguin, 2015) contends that using Auschwitz metonymically is misleading, as it reduces the Holocaust to a single camp that was, in many ways, unrepresentative of the Holocaust as a whole (pp. 207–24).

If, as Elizabeth Sakellaridou has written, the 'iconography' of the Holocaust – ruined scenescapes, brutalising institutions of repression and torture, damaged and disfigured subjects, displacement and dislocation, desire and perverse eroticisation, destruction and death – haunts post-war playwriting, *King Lear* has obvious resonances for a post-Auschwitz historical and cultural imaginary.[17] This has seen the play develop into a vital intertext through which the degradation of the human subject – a bestialising process that would make humanity 'a worm' (IV.i.35) – might be written. The play has, perhaps unsurprisingly, been particularly pivotal in tragic playwriting 'after' Auschwitz. *King Lear* has enabled forms of tragic drama that would seek to represent, but also to contest, the devastating diminution of the modern human subject. These forms of post-Auschwitz tragedy have ranged from Beckettian absurdism to post-Brechtian political theatre and beyond. The play has been used in a variety of ways to (re)conceptualise both the subject and tragedy 'after' Auschwitz.

This book analyses plays by important post-war playwrights and theatre-makers, with case studies on Edward Bond, David Rudkin, Howard Barker, Sarah Kane, Forced Entertainment and Dennis Kelly – though it also considers other *King Lear* appropriations in Chapter 3. These playwrights and dramatists have, in a variety of ways, all engaged with and appropriated *King Lear*, using the play to produce newly conceived forms of tragic drama that seek to interrogate the catastrophe(s) of modernity. My case studies primarily consider the plays *Lear* (Bond, 1971), *Will's Way* (Rudkin, 1984), *Seven Lears* (Barker, 1989), *Blasted* (Kane, 1995), *Five Day Lear* (Forced Entertainment, 1999) and *The Gods Weep* (Kelly, 2010). I have principally used close reading to study these plays, considering the way playwrights intervene to appropriate and make intertextual changes to a prior work, but I also provide performance analysis to consider the way in which the post-Auschwitz tragic subject is theatrically embodied. I also draw on 'non-literary' and 'non-dramatic' writings by the playwrights under study – essays, critical articles, interviews, public addresses and so on; interviews I have conducted with some of the playwrights; and various archival materials and performance ephemera related to theatre history, from performance photographs to press reviews. *King Lear 'After' Auschwitz* is an

---

Nevertheless, due to its status in discourse around the Holocaust and modern catastrophe, I use Auschwitz metonymically.

[17] Elizabeth Sakellaridou, 'A Lover's Discourse – but Whose? Inversions of the Fascist Aesthetic in Howard Barker's *Und* and Other Recent English Plays', *European Journal of English Studies*, 7:1 (2003), p. 90.

interdisciplinary work combining Shakespeare studies, contemporary theatre studies, appropriation and adaptation studies and Holocaust studies. The criticism I engage with reflects that interdisciplinary scope, drawing on various areas of scholarly analysis to interpret *King Lear* appropriations.

Theatres of Catastrophe

To capture the range of theatrical forms that have been catalysed by *King Lear*, I use the phrase 'Theatres of Catastrophe'. This is a term I take from the playwright Howard Barker, who demarcates his self-styled conception of the 'Theatre of Catastrophe' in his 1989 artistic 'manifesto' *Arguments for a Theatre* – a vitally influential work of theatre and cultural criticism.[18] The 'Theatre of Catastrophe' (sometimes also 'Catastrophism') names a new form of tragic drama, which represents the autonomy the subject finds in moments of catastrophe. It is not simply that catastrophe is a destructive force in the Theatre of Catastrophe. On the contrary: catastrophe can also enable the subject. During times and spaces of disaster, the subject is suddenly emancipated from dominative social systems, which are left in ruins. This allows the subject to emerge 'anew' from the wreckage, refashioning him or herself out of the fragments of catastrophe. 'Catastrophe is also birth,' writes Barker: 'Out the ruins crawls the bloody *thing*, unrecognisable in the ripped rags of former life.'[19]

Catastrophe is not only a thematic concern for Barker, however; it is also formal. The Theatre of Catastrophe is a fragmentary form of tragedy that violates aesthetic closure. The upshot is a subject who retains his or her autonomy in a shattered world. Catastrophe is never brought to an end by the reinstatement of the status quo and the Catastrophist subject never reaches any form of reconciliation with the prevailing social and political order. There are no limits – aesthetic or ideological – placed on tragic subjectivity in Catastrophism.

Barker has situated his Theatre of Catastrophe as a response to the

---

[18] Howard Barker, *Arguments for a Theatre*, 3rd edn (Manchester and New York: Manchester University Press, 1997), p. 50. I place 'manifesto' in apostrophes as the fragments that make up the text do not constitute a systematic statement of intent. I touch on the formal properties of Catastrophism again in Chapter 6.

[19] Howard Barker, *Women Beware Women*, in Howard Barker, *Collected Plays: Volume 3* (London: Calder, 1986), p. 180.

degradation of the subject in modernity, which he relates to the Holocaust. His is a controversial post-Auschwitz aesthetic that is concerned to develop a new conception of tragic freedom. This is categorically not to say that the type of suffering that took place in the Holocaust can be seen as in any way 'liberating'. The idea is that catastrophic rupture may release the subject from repressive social and political systems, which otherwise tend to constrain and destroy human beings.

I want to make the case that the Theatre of Catastrophe has a wider relevance than Barker necessarily recognises. I do not contend that other playwrights are directly indebted to Barker – or indeed that Barker is writing under the influence of other playwrights in the post-war era – and nor do I contend that other playwrights would ever self-identify (as Barker has done) as 'Catastrophist'. The playwrights I analyse are, however, all engaged with the same constellation of ideas found in Barker around catastrophe, tragedy, subjectivity, human freedom and aesthetic form, which are interpreted in distinct ways. What unites the playwrights and theatre-makers I analyse are new forms of tragic drama and aesthetics that place a stress on the freedom of the human subject, even under the conditions of catastrophe. By applying catastrophe more widely than Barker intends, I aim to develop the possible critical usage of Catastrophism beyond Barker and his own distinctive definition(s). It is for that reason I prefer the plural 'Theatres of Catastrophe' over the 'Theatre of Catastrophe'. *King Lear* has played a vital role in a range of catastrophic theatres in post-war British playwriting and drama, which has been preoccupied with writing through and about disaster. When I refer specifically to Barker, I do so using the terms 'Catastrophism' and 'Catastrophist', applying the more generic 'catastrophic' to describe the theatre(s) of other playwrights.

The idea of various Theatres of Catastrophe will be developed through analyses of the work of the various figures I consider. But it will also mean drawing on the formative post-Auschwitz philosophy of self and aesthetics developed by the theorist Theodor Adorno, whose work continues to have a profound influence on post-war playwriting and drama.[20] Adorno, perhaps the foremost thinker of the Frankfurt School of critical theory, often uses the concept of catastrophe in his

---

[20] This has been eloquently demonstrated by Karoline Gritzner in her *Adorno and Modern Theatre: The Drama of the Damaged Self in Bond, Rudkin, Barker and Kane* (Basingstoke: Palgrave Macmillan, 2015). I aim to demonstrate the critical role *King Lear* has played in the development of post-Auschwitz Theatres of Catastrophe, whereas Gritzner tends to concentrate her analysis on the formative influence of Beckett and the ruined scenescapes of absurdism.

writing.²¹ It is, on the one hand, a descriptive historical category and is typically related to the total destruction of human subjectivity at Auschwitz, which Adorno understands as symptomatic of a supposedly 'enlightened' modernity and its paradoxical tendency towards disaster. On the other hand, catastrophe is also an aesthetic category, which Adorno relates to formally fragmented works of art.²² Adorno believes that catastrophic art, while not necessarily confined to a discrete era, is the aesthetic form *par excellence* in post-Auschwitz culture. Such artworks, by denying aesthetic harmony, implicitly reveal the catastrophic condition of modernity – its failure to embody its liberal ideals of harmony and progress. But at the same time, catastrophic art allows for the 'force of subjectivity'.²³ Through its violent ruptures and fissures, catastrophic art shatters formal coherence and closure. This opens a space for the representation of subjectivity beyond the parameters of conventional aesthetic form – a space, as Adorno understands it, of human possibility.

My analysis of catastrophic post-war playwriting and drama will consistently draw on and interrogate Adorno, as his work provides a powerful paradigm for analysing questions around modern catastrophe, subjectivity and aesthetics. Many of the same thematics are addressed in the writings of Hannah Arendt, Maurice Blanchot, Jean-François Lyotard, Jean-Pierre Dupuy and Giorgio Agamben – among others – whose work and writing I also consider in relation to *King Lear* in post-war playwriting and drama.²⁴ Adorno, however, remains a formative figure in the analysis (and critique) of society, cultural life and the self 'after' Auschwitz. His writings continue to inform understandings around the catastrophe of Auschwitz and the role that subjectivity and aesthetics might occupy in post-Auschwitz culture. He has also had a direct influence on many of the playwrights I study, particularly Barker.

---

²¹ For an introduction to the Frankfurt School, see Tom Bottomore, *The Frankfurt School and Its Critics* (London: Routledge, 2002).

²² This is particularly apparent in his observations in *Beethoven: The Philosophy of Music: Fragments and Texts*, ed. Rolf Tiedemann, trans. Edmund Jephcott (Cambridge: Polity, 1998). Adorno writes: 'The fragmented landscape is objective, while the light in which it grows alone is subjective. He does not bring about their harmonious synthesis. As a dissociative force, he tears them apart in time, perhaps in order to preserve them for the eternal. In the history of art, late works are the catastrophes' (p. 126).

²³ Ibid. p. 125.

²⁴ I pick up on the thoughts of some of these theorists again in Chapter 1 and in Chapters 2 and 5, particularly Lyotard and, via Michel Foucault, Agamben.

Periodising Catastrophe

This study analyses *King Lear* criticism, performance and appropriation over the period from 1939 to the 2010s. It is an era that begins with the outbreak of the Second World War and the Holocaust, then continues through the deepening tensions of the Cold War and the possibility of complete nuclear apocalypse, the fall of the Berlin Wall, the increasing dominance of modern consumer culture and the so-called 'End of History' as famously postulated by Francis Fukuyama, to the terrorist atrocities of 9/11 and 7/7, the 2008 worldwide crash and contemporary fears over the ecosphere and anthropogenic climate change.[25] This period of human history has in many ways been shaped – or indeed, unshaped – by catastrophic upheaval.

Post-war culture has seen many social and political transformations, but the most relevant for the present study is the seeming transition from modernity to postmodernity – as witnessed by the movement from industrial to post-industrial capitalism. To define that post-war shift, I use the phrase 'late capitalism'. My choice is partly influenced by Adorno, who tends to use late capitalism as a term for the developments in liberal, capitalist society after the Second World War.[26] But it is also influenced by theorist (and Holocaust survivor) Ernest Mandel, who popularised the phrase in his 1972 *Late Capitalism*.[27] Mandel predicted that the era of late capitalism would see the capitalist system become increasingly 'total', with the emergence of transnational corporations, globalised markets and labour, the fluidities of financial capital and a culture of mass consumption. He also predicted that post-industrial global capital, far from freeing people from repressive state administration and the inhumane depredations of the industrial system, would see the commodification – the 'industrialization' – of ever more inclusive areas of human life. He insisted that, far from 'representing a "post-industrial society"', late capitalism 'constitutes *generalized universal industrialization* for the first time in history'.[28] This means the supposed historical 'break' between an era of administered industrial capital and a

---

[25] Francis Fukuyama, *The End of History and the Last Man* (London: Penguin, 2012).

[26] See his 'Late Capitalism or Industrial Society?' in Theodor Adorno, *Can One Live After Auschwitz?*, ed. Rolf Tiedemann, trans. Rodney Livingstone et al. (Stanford: Stanford University Press, 2003), pp. 111–25.

[27] Ernest Mandel, *Late Capitalism* (London: Verso, 1998).

[28] Ibid. p. 387.

'freer', post-industrial capitalist system is not nearly as momentous as it appeared to be. Both forms, as Adorno similarly contests, tend to commodify ('industrialize') the world and everything before it – including people.[29]

My case studies begin in 1971 and end in 2010. Each case study provides specific historicisation around the play and the playwright under analysis. I also situate the plays in a wider critical and dramaturgical discourse around *King Lear* and the Holocaust, which can be genetically traced into the 1940s and the work of critics from John F. Danby to G. B. Harrison, and which continues to the present day.[30] I am, however, also concerned with catastrophic theatre as a post-Auschwitz aesthetic phenomenon and its relationship to late capital. By analysing appropriations of *King Lear* from the 1970s to the 2010s, I want to show that catastrophic theatre is also a response to late capitalist culture. It is a culture that has become increasingly total and that tends, as a result, to dominate and diminish the subject, whose autonomy is imperilled. Adorno, when using the phrase 'after Auschwitz', did so with the consciousness that there is no conclusive 'after': all the time subjects are reduced to nothing more than the objects of a totalised social system, the atrocities committed at Auschwitz remain a possibility that haunts both the present and the future. I have chosen to consistently place apostrophes around 'after' for the same reason – to adumbrate the historical continuity between Auschwitz and late 'liberal' capitalism, avoiding the idea of a definitive break that places the Holocaust safely in 'the past'.

Shakespeare and Appropriation

This book belongs within the wider analysis of Shakespeare and appropriation. It is a vast and still growing field of critical enquiry, covering everything from the appropriation of Shakespeare in ribald eighteenth-century political cartoons to 'YouTube Ophelias'.[31] This reflects a wider historical shift in Shakespeare studies from the meaning 'of' Shakespeare to the phenomenon of meaning 'by' Shakespeare, which abandons the

---

[29] For more on Adorno and late capital, see Chapter 1.
[30] See Chapter 3.
[31] For Shakespeare and political cartoons, see Jonathan Bate, *Shakespearean Constitutions: Politics, Theatre, Criticism 1730–1830* (Oxford: Clarendon Press, 1989), while a study of YouTube Ophelias can be found in Christy Desmet and Sujata Iyengar, 'Rebooting Ophelia: Social Media and the Rhetorics of Appropriation', in Kaara L. Peterson and Deanne Williams (eds), *The Afterlife of Ophelia* (New York: Palgrave Macmillan, 2012), pp. 59–78.

idea that there is any final, authoritative 'meaning' in Shakespeare for critics to decipher in favour of analysing the way Shakespeare is variously used to generate meaning(s) through the act of adaptation and/or appropriation.[32]

The artistic practice of 'appropriating' or 'adapting' Shakespeare, though of intense critical interest, remains a theoretically fraught topic – something reflected in ongoing debates about how the practice should be defined. What should artworks that are based on, or consciously rework and rewrite, previous works even be called? There is a 'problem of naming' – as Daniel Fischlin and Marker Fortier have called it – when it comes to defining artistic works that are based on or rework a prior work of art, causing a surfeit of possible descriptors, from 'offshoot' to 'version'.[33] Some particular terms are, however, more prominent than others and have tended to inform the theoretical and critical conversation around Shakespeare. Perhaps the most commonly used are intertextuality, adaptation and appropriation.

The theory of intertextuality is the most radical in its scope and implications, raising fundamental questions about ideas around the 'original', the 'author' and the integrity of the unique 'work'. Though usage has shifted in various ways, the word still tends to signify a series of endlessly unravelling relationships 'between' various texts.[34] The idea of intertextuality would have it that all texts, and not only consciously appropriative or adaptive texts, are made up of webs of allusions to – and transformations of – other texts. The 'meaning' of any work is ultimately produced by the interrelationship between it and various other texts, as opposed to being a unique product of the original work or the intentions of its author. Like much poststructuralist thought, intertextuality is suspicious of the supposed 'singularity' of the text and of the notion of the subject (author) as a unified centre of meaning.[35]

These very same features can, however, be problematic. The limitation of intertextuality is that, by concentrating on the general interplay of texts through space and time, it tends to elide the distinctiveness, or

---

[32] Terence Hawkes, *Meaning by Shakespeare* (London: Routledge, 1992).

[33] Daniel Fischlin and Mark Fortier (eds), *Adaptations of Shakespeare* (London and New York: Routledge, 2000), p. 2.

[34] See María Jesús Martínez Alfaro, 'Intertextuality: Origins and Development of the Concept', *Atlantis*, 18:1/2 (1996), pp. 268–85.

[35] See Roland Barthes, 'The Death of the Author', *Image Music Text*, trans. Stephen Heath (London: Fontana Press, 1977), pp. 142–8, and Michel Foucault, 'What Is an Author?', in James D. Faubion and Paul Rabinow (eds), *Michel Foucault: Aesthetics, Method, and Epistemology, Volume 2* (New York: The New Press, 1994), pp. 205–22.

alterity, of the textual and formal aspects that make up any specific text. By treating all texts as intertexts, intertextuality is ultimately inadequate for a study on the appropriations of a single play and, as a theory that posits a universal and ahistorical theory of the relation pertaining between all texts at all times, can also be blind to the reasons why a particular work might be prominent at a certain historical moment. Its stress on the so-called 'Death of the Author' is similarly problematic for the present study: implying as it does that the meaning and autonomy of the human subject is a chimera, intertextuality is in theoretical conflict with a study dealing with the total eradication of subjectivity at Auschwitz.[36] I will, at times, use the word 'intertext' to designate an appropriated work. But while I am interested in the relation between texts – and so 'intertexts' – that should not be taken to imply a simple endorsement of the theory of intertextuality.

The term 'adaptation' is increasingly used in criticism, as reflected by the formation of the International Association of Adaptation Studies in 2008, the same year the journal *Adaptation* was established. The etymology of adaptation sheds light on its usage. Derived from the Latin *adaptāre*, to make 'suitable' or 'fit', usually for a new purpose, adaptation has generally been concerned with the way in which a work from one medium is made to fit another – say the adaptation of a novel to film.[37] This is certainly the dominant meaning of adaptation for Linda Hutcheon.[38] But adaptation is not only used to designate the intermedial transformations of a work into another form; it has also been used in relation to intramedial works – as when an old play is adapted by another dramatist to make it 'fit' with a new milieu.[39] The problem with adaptation, however, is that it is potentially limiting in its scope. Due to its roots in intermedia transitions, adaptation tends to focus on the wholesale transformation of texts. This means that, when it comes to Shakespeare, adaptation has increasingly been used to designate complete rewritings of the 'original' adapted play. This does not necessarily leave room for other forms of artistic and cultural intervention in

---

[36] See also Sean Burke, *The Death and Return of the Author: Criticism and Subjectivity in Barthes, Foucault and Derrida*, 2nd edn (Edinburgh: Edinburgh University Press, 2008).

[37] 'adaptation, n.', <http://www.oed.com/view/Entry/2115?redirectedFrom=adaptation> (accessed 27 July 2017). See also Julie Sanders, *Adaptation and Appropriation* (Oxford: Routledge, 2006), p. 19.

[38] Linda Hutcheon, *A Theory of Adaptation*, 2nd edn (Oxford: Routledge, 2013).

[39] The way in which Nahum Tate adapts Shakespeare to 'fit' Restoration tastes is something I consider again below.

relation to Shakespeare – say the rewriting of a single scene or the use of a particular character.

I think that appropriation is wider in scope. The word appropriation has its etymological roots in the Latin *appropriāre* and tends to connote the seizure of 'property' belonging to another, to 'take to oneself' or 'make one's own'.[40] The word is most readily related in Shakespeare studies with cultural materialist criticism, which emerged in the 1980s and 1990s and remains a dominant approach to the question of Shakespeare and appropriation. Cultural materialist critics were (and are) generally concerned with the ways in which Shakespeare is appropriated and the ideological uses his plays and poetry are conscripted to serve. This has mostly meant interrogating the conservative use of Shakespeare in various forms; but, at the same time, critics have also sought to prioritise the redeployment of Shakespeare for politically and ideologically oppositional purposes. Such critics are particularly concerned with the way in which feminist, queer and postcolonial writers upend the patriarchal, heteronormative and imperialist ideologies that Shakespeare has been used to promulgate, in the service of 'marginalized, oppressed, and disenfranchised cultural voices'.[41] Such writers are seen to be appropriating the dominant, hegemonic culture – material belonging to the establishment – for themselves, interrogating the values attached to 'Shakespeare' while simultaneously repurposing him for new social and political aims.[42]

My own use of the word appropriation is less politicised than it is for cultural materialist criticism. Where appropriation has, in the past, often been used 'as a weapon in the struggle for supremacy between various ideologies' and 'various poetics', I am not as concerned with the way in which writers appropriate Shakespeare in the service of particular forms of (usually, identity) politics.[43] Such appropriations often work by

---

[40] 'appropriation, n.', <http://www.oed.com/view/Entry/9877?redirectedFrom=appropriation> (accessed 27 July 2017).

[41] Alexa Huang and Elizabeth Rivlin, 'Introduction', in Alexa Huang and Elizabeth Rivlin (eds), *Shakespeare and the Ethics of Appropriation* (London: Palgrave Macmillan, 2014), p. 1.

[42] The pathbreaking 1983 collection *Political Shakespeare: Essays in Cultural Materialism*, edited by Jonathon Dollimore and Alan Sinfield (Manchester: Manchester University Press, 1983), dedicated its second half (pp. 154–289) to analysing both conservative 'reproductions' of Shakespearean authority and radical 'appropriations' of it. I return to cultural materialism in Chapter 3.

[43] André Lefevere, 'Why Waste Our Time on Rewrites? The Trouble with Interpretation and the Role of Rewriting in an Alternative Paradigm', in Theo Hermans (ed.), *The Manipulation of Literature: Studies in Literary Translation* (Oxford: Routledge, 2014), p. 234.

representing a character marginalised in the 'original' play, with feminist rewritings of Shakespeare written from the untold perspective of Ophelia or Desdemona by no means unusual.[44] While I do not want to contest the political aspirations that underpin appropriation, cultural materialist criticism – in its search for oppositional meanings – has limited the scope of appropriation, which has been reduced to meaning nothing but 'a seizure of authority over the original in a way that appeals to contemporary sensibilities steeped in a politicized understanding of culture'.[45] This is hardly unjustified given the etymology of the word, but it has meant that other forms of appropriation have been overlooked. This is particularly true of some of the playwrights I consider – I am thinking mostly of Rudkin, Barker, Kane and Kelly, whose appropriations are not necessarily concerned with (and are even suspicious of) prescribed iterations of political identity and cultural belonging.

What I find useful about the word appropriation is that, far more strongly than intertextuality and adaptation, it implies an intentional subject doing the appropriating – an author. This reflects the 'proper' in 'appropriation', which means 'pertaining to a person' 'in particular, specific; distinctive, characteristic'.[46] Using appropriation creates space for authorial agency. This authorial aspect is – for Julie Sanders – 'inescapable' when thinking about the way a contemporary writer approaches and appropriates a prior text.[47] While appropriation may have its root in *propruis* – 'belonging to', the 'property of' – the 'a-' prefix denotes 'an approach towards'.[48] This conception of the 'approach' is open-ended; it does not necessitate a posture of antagonistically politicised hostility. The approach 'toward' property belonging to another may be more reverential – or simply more ambivalent – even if the desire of the author is to 'take' that property 'to oneself', to make it his or her 'own'. This may serve to make the relationship between the appropriator and the text more dialogic than antagonistic – a 'conversation' between writer and work, as Barker sometimes calls it, as opposed to the complete domination of the textual object by the appropriating authorial subject.[49]

---

[44] I refer to feminist appropriations of *King Lear* in Chapter 3.
[45] Fischlin and Fortier, *Adaptations of Shakespeare*, p. 3.
[46] 'appropriation, n.'.
[47] Sanders, *Adaptation and Appropriation*, p. 2.
[48] Christy Desmet and Sujata Iyengar, 'Adaptation, Appropriation, or What you Will', *Shakespeare*, 11:1 (2015), p. 14.
[49] In his *Arguments for a Theatre*, Barker stages a 'conversation' between himself and Thomas Middleton, pp. 25–8. This more open dynamic is also a vital aspect of Adornian thinking on the wider relationship between subject and object in post-Auschwitz life and culture.

The word appropriation can usefully serve to capture 'approaches' to past texts that are not necessarily constrained by questions of cultural and political identity. But it can also encompass several forms of artistic practice, in a way that is not so available to the more limited 'adaptation'. Where adaptation is increasingly identified with wholesale (and usually intermedial) transformations of a text, appropriation may be of a single speech or character, or even an unchanged quotation. This has been particularly useful in tracing the various ways in which *King Lear* is appropriated in post-war British playwriting. *King Lear* has been appropriated in many ways 'after' Auschwitz, from complete rewritings of the play (Bond and Kelly); to prequels and sequels (Barker); to the use of a vital scene (Kane); to adopting a particular character (Rudkin). By using appropriation, it is possible to bring various forms of practice into dialogue as part of a wider study into the way writers have used *King Lear*.

No single word can comprise all forms of intertextuality and, to a degree, all definitions will have limitations. It would be wrong, however, to take a 'What You Will' approach to the 'problem of naming': the theories of intertextuality, adaptation and appropriation, though in constant evolution, have underlying assumptions and critical genealogies. I have already given a rationale for using appropriation – but another part of its relevance has to do with *King Lear* itself, which from the beginning of its history has been a locus for interventions that evince the specifics of appropriation as an artistic and authorial act.

King Lear and Appropriation

King Lear has a long history of appropriations, (in)famously beginning in 1681 with Nahum Tate, who 'revived' the play, but with far-reaching 'alterations'.[50] The most telling change was to the ending: Tate replaced the cataclysmic finale of *King Lear* with a 'happy' ending, where Lear, after being restored to the throne by Cordelia and the King of France, retires to a 'cool Cell' for a life of monastic Christian contemplation.[51] The rationale for 'altering' *King Lear* was both aesthetic and political: the deaths of Cordelia and Lear violated formal closure and did not allow for the 'blest / Restauration' (V.95) of a legitimate sovereign,

---

[50] Quoted in Fischlin and Fortier, *Adaptations of Shakespeare*, p. 66.
[51] Nahum Tate, The *History of King Lear*, in Fischlin and Fortier, *Adaptations of Shakespeare*, p. 96. All references to the Tate *King Lear* are from the Fischlin and Fortier edition. Quotes from the play will be referenced using act and page numbers.

obviously a concern for Restoration playwrights and audiences. This version, however, far outlived its own historical moment: continuing moral disquiet about the action of the play and its radically irruptive form meant that the Shakespeare version of *King Lear* was not staged again until 1838, when William Charles Macready 'restored' the 'original' Shakespeare, most obviously the un-Tateified ending, in his famed production at the Covent Garden Theatre.[52]

Tate has been much maligned for his intervention and 'Tatification' has entered the language to describe an unnecessary and ill-advised re-visioning of a canonical work.[53] It is important to recognise, however, that Shakespeare is himself part of the long history of appropriation: his *King Lear* is in dialogue with, and consciously reworks, other 'King Lears' circulating in the early modern period (and before). The tale of King Lear (sometimes Leir, Ler or Llyr) was, for the early moderns, a part of ancient British history, recorded by Geoffrey of Monmouth in his twelfth-century *Historia Regum Britanniae*.[54] The story was retold in various ways in the sixteenth and seventeenth centuries, from the 1577 *Chronicles of England, Scotland, and Ireland* – where Raphael Holinshed gives a short retelling of the narrative which ends with the suicide of Cordelia when, after restoring Lear and succeeding to the throne, she is usurped by her nephews and imprisoned – to the 1574 *The Mirror for Magistrates*, where John Higgins has 'Cordila' (not Lear) recite her 'storie tragicall ech word'.[55] The Lear story also appears in Book Two of *The Faerie Queene* (1590) and *Albions England* (1586). For the Gloucester subplot, Shakespeare drew on the *New Arcadia* (1586) by Philip Sidney, where a legitimate son (Leonatus) is disowned by his father after being maligned by his illegitimate half-brother (Plexitrus) – a betrayal 'fit' enough 'to make the stage of any Tragodie'.[56]

The most obvious intertext for *King Lear* is the anonymous play

---

[52] See Emily Mullin, 'Macready's Triumph: The Restoration of *King Lear* to the Stage', *Penn History Review*, 18:1 (2010), pp. 17–35.

[53] David Crystal and Ben Crystal, *The Shakespeare Miscellany* (London: Penguin, 2005), p. 151.

[54] Geoffrey of Monmouth, *The History of the Kings of Britain*, trans. Lewis Thorpe (London: Penguin, 1966), pp. 81–7.

[55] John Higgins, *The first parte of the Mirour for magistrates* (London: 1574), <http://eebo.chadwyck.com.ezproxy01.rhul.ac.uk/search/fulltext?ACTION=ByID&ID=D20000998418730033&SOURCE=var_spell.cfg&DISPLAY-AUTHOR&WARN=N&FILE=../session/1501148434_13628> (accessed 27 July 2017).

[56] Philip Sidney, *The Countesse of Pembrokes Arcadia* (London: 1590), <https://data-historicaltexts-jisc-ac-uk.ezproxy01.rhul.ac.uk/view?pubId=eebo-ocm17202096e&terms=New%20Arcadia&pageTerms=New%20Arcadia&pageId=eebo-ocm17202096e-106206-1> (accessed 27 July 2017).

The True Chronicle History of King Leir, published in 1605 (and most likely originally performed in 1594). This play depicts the Lear story up until the moment the 'lawful king' Leir is restored to his throne, with the martial and political aid of Cordella (Cordelia) and Gallia (France) and an uprising by other nobles and the commons.[57] With Cordella and Leir 'firmly reconcil'd / In perfect love' (IV.iii.59–60) by the end of the action, the play conveys a socially and politically conservative moral steeped in Christian values, where the 'good' finally triumph: 'The perfect good indeed / Can never be corrupted by the bad' (V.iii.76–7) for 'the heav'ns are just and hate impiety' (V.ii.30). Where the story of Cordelia and her suicide is, in the early modern era, often portrayed in terms of 'tragedy', the anonymous author of *King Leir* precludes tragedy by ending his version in a more sentimental vein of reconciliation and restoration.

Even while the Lear story was sometimes related to tragedy, however, the change Shakespeare makes to the story is unprecedented. No other version has so catastrophic a finale, with Cordelia being hanged and Lear dying as he bewails her death. Shakespeare radically subverts both a conventional romantic ending, with Lear and Cordelia reconciled, and a more conventional tragic ending, which usually ends with the death of Cordelia and a moralistic dictum about the sin of suicide. His play violates aesthetic closure and containment, destabilising the meanings (social, political and moral) that are usually inscribed in the 'King Lear' story. It would not be stretching the point to say that Tate is not so much violating Shakespeare as he is restoring *King Lear* to some of its formal (and moral) shape.

It is not always the case that appropriation aims to 'repair' the damaged aesthetic of *King Lear*, however. Other playwrights have appropriated the play precisely because of its violation of the limits of tragic closure. This is a point made by the critic David Ian Rabey, whose own appropriations of *King Lear* in his sequels *The Back of Beyond* (1996) and *The Battle of Crows* (1998) are deeply influenced by the *Lear* plays of playwrights from Barker to Kane.[58] Rabey remarks in his 'On Being a Shakespearean Dramatist', which prefaces his *King Lear* plays, that through his appropriation of *King Leir* Shakespeare subverts a once-familiar story to prolong 'horror and uncertainty beyond the

---

[57] Anonymous, *King Leir*, ed. Tiffany Stern (London: Nick Hern Books, 2002), p. 92. All references are to the Nick Hern edition and take the form of act, scene and page numbers.

[58] David Ian Rabey, *The Wye Plays* (Bristol: Intellect Books, 2004). All references are from the Intellect edition, which I reference using act, scene and page numbers.

conventional generic markers of tragedy and drama'.[59] Rabey contends that, by appropriating a pre-existing play and subverting any resolution, Shakespeare (implicitly) authorises other writers to appropriate *King Lear* for the purposes of developing new – and catastrophic – forms of tragic drama and playwriting. It is in this sense that Rabey defines his appropriation as 'Shakespearean'. It is not that Rabey writes in slavish imitation or vainglorious hubris: it is that appropriating past works in the service of new forms of dramatic tragedy is a properly 'Shakespearean' undertaking.

Rabey provides a rationale for appropriating *King Lear* that resonates strongly with the playwrights under consideration, who also sometimes use the 'original' appropriation of *King Leir* to validate appropriating Shakespeare.[60] His allusion to *The True Chronicle History of King Leir*, however, also pays witness to various other 'Lear' texts in the early modern period – and beyond. This raises the problem of reference. What is the specific 'text' being referred to when a post-war (or any other) writer appropriates '*King Lear*'? Is it possible to identify a singular text which is being appropriated, or is it more appropriate to talk of various 'Lears'? This problem is even more acute when it comes to *King Lear*. The play exists in discrete 'versions', both of which seem reliably 'Shakespearean'. Should these be seen as distinct contributions to a wider Lear 'tradition'? Or is it possible to speak in the singular of a play called *King Lear* by Shakespeare? I want to address the controversy around the text(s) of *King Lear*, to make the case that the play can (and should) be seen as a singular textual and formal entity, even while it exists in varying versions. While the playwrights under study are part of a wider textual and historical Lear 'tradition', *King Lear* is – undeniably – the dominant intertext.

Which *King Lear*? The Textual Problem of *King Lear*

For any study of *King Lear*, the question inevitably arises – which *King Lear*? The play exists in the Quarto of 1608, originally entitled *The True Chronicle Historie of the life and death of King LEAR and his three Daughters*, and the 1623 Folio, called more simply *The Tragedie of King Lear*. On top of the titles and the generic shift from 'Historie' to

---

[59] Ibid. p. 6.
[60] Rabey does not cite Kane, but there are parallels, the most obvious of which is the 'ABRUPT MASSIVE SHATTERING EXPLOSION' (3.2.43) that concludes Act Three of his *The Back of Beyond*, which recalls *Blasted*.

'Tragedie', which indicates the roots of the Lear story and its reception as 'history' in early modern culture, there is a variety of both minor and more substantial textual variations between the versions of *King Lear*.

For most of its history, standard editorial practice has been to conflate the versions of *King Lear* and preserve as many aspects from both as possible, while negotiating the numerous textual variants either on aesthetic grounds or on the basis of a speculative reconstruction of printing history. The same practice, perhaps less controversially, has also been true of the play in performance. Directors have tended to work with a conflated text, even while the Folio has generally been considered to be the more amenable to the practicalities of theatrical realisation (Quarto- or Folio-only stagings remain something of a rarity).[61]

Over the mid-1980s, however, conflation began to be challenged. Under the influence of various articles and, most importantly, the landmark 1983 collection *The Division of the Kingdoms*, edited by Gary Taylor and Michael Warren, the distinct versions of *King Lear* were increasingly regarded as conceptually separate: closely related but appreciably distinct and authoritative treatments of the same basic content.[62] The idea that both versions are 'authoritative' derives from the notion that Shakespeare himself revised his play from Quarto to Folio.

Whatever the (ultimately unknowable) historical reasons for the existence of discrete texts, the view that Quarto and Folio can be read as distinct versions of the same play found favour in some quarters of Shakespeare studies. This reflected, in part, a growing interest in theatrical practices and the new brand of materially conscious, poststructuralist criticism that emerged in Shakespeare studies during the 1980s, which tended to question the precept of aesthetic 'unity' and engaged in deconstructive interrogations of textual gaps and ellipses, often with distinct political aims.[63] The Oxford *Complete Works* of 1985 printed the versions separately, and Quarto editions of the play were also published in 1994 and 2000.[64] René Weis published his parallel text edition

---

[61] In the 'Introduction' to his parallel text edition, René Weis notes that for his 1990 RSC production of the play Nicholas Hytner primarily used the Folio; yet even Hytner could not resist aspects of the Quarto, finally including the Quarto-only mock trial scene for III.vi. Weis concludes that the Folio could not '*automatically* carry the burden of performance', René Weis (ed.), *King Lear: A Parallel Text Edition*, 2nd edn (Oxford: Routledge, 2013), p. 31.

[62] Gary Taylor and Michael Warren (eds), *The Division of the Kingdoms: Shakespeare's Two Versions of King Lear* (Oxford: Oxford University Press, 1983).

[63] I return to the critical history around *King Lear* in Chapter 3.

[64] William Shakespeare, *The Oxford Shakespeare: The Complete Works*, Stanley Wells and Gary Taylor (Oxford: Oxford University Press, 1985); *The First Quarto*

of *King Lear* in 1993, which printed Quarto and Folio version side by side – though Weis, not unreasonably, remained unconvinced that the revisionist theory could ever be finally proved by scholars speculating about print history and conditions.⁶⁵

The revisionist theory is undeniably intriguing for a study on appropriations of *King Lear*, as it raises the prospect that Shakespeare adapted his own play. My own conviction, however, is that the distinctions between the texts, while no doubt important to recognise, have been overstated. I take the same position as Foakes, who, though he is persuaded by the revisionist stance on the Quarto and/or Folio debate, makes the case that the reworking of *King Lear* from Quarto to Folio is not so thorough as to mean that critics have to think of finally 'separate' plays.⁶⁶ Weis similarly insists on 'The Integral *King Lear*' and contends that the versions of the play tell a story of convergence, not divergence, while Richard Knowles concludes that 'if the F [Folio] *Lear* represents a new "concept" of the play, it is remarkably limited in its means of revision.'⁶⁷

Even in the wake of the bi-text controversy, *King Lear* can still be thought of as a formally and conceptually 'singular' work by Shakespeare – both in the world of Shakespeare studies and in the wider public cultural imaginary. With that in mind, I would make the case that contemporary appropriators of the play are confronting a single work. More practically for the purposes of the present study, it is worth remembering that the playwrights under analysis are precisely that – playwrights, not textual historians or academics concerned with the particulars of early modern print culture. My hunch is that, on the page, Bond, Rudkin and Barker would most likely have originally encountered *King Lear* in the popular, conflated 1952 Arden edition, edited by Kenneth Muir (reprinted in 1972). The edition Kane and more recent writers are most familiar with is harder to gauge – and it is worth pointing out that some of the 'unedited' editions that grew out of the revisionist controversy are readily available. Even so, I find it doubtful that questions around early modern book culture would represent a priority for most playwrights engaging with *King Lear*.

---

of *King Lear*, ed. Jay L. Halio (Cambridge: Cambridge University Press, 1994); *The History of King Lear*, ed. Stanley Wells (Oxford: Oxford University Press, 2000).

⁶⁵ Weis, 'Introduction', *King Lear: A Parallel Text Edition*, pp. 36–7.
⁶⁶ Foakes, *Hamlet Versus Lear*, p. 111.
⁶⁷ Weis, 'Introduction', *King Lear: A Parallel Text Edition*, p. 36; Richard Knowles, 'Two Lears? By Shakespeare?', in James Ogden and Arthur Scouten (eds), *Lear from Study to Stage: Essays in Criticism* (Madison and London: Associated University Presses, 1997), p. 64.

I do not want to ignore the distinction(s) between the texts of *King Lear* or insist that there is some 'definitive' version of the play. There are variations in the Quarto and Folio versions, and these variations can be relevant when a contemporary author intervenes to appropriate, or make textual changes to, the play. In the course of this study I touch on some of the textual and formal discrepancies between the versions of *King Lear* and pay attention to the varying ways appropriations may signify based on whether the Quarto or Folio is the 'appropriated' version under consideration. I also have cause to analyse some of the editorial interventions that have shaped the play, particularly around its (so-called) 'blasted heath'.[68] My emphasis, however, is on *King Lear* as a singular textual and formal entity, which has occupied an often central role in Theatres of Catastrophe. For the purposes of reference, I generally use the exemplary Arden 3rd edition of *King Lear*, edited by Foakes. This is a conflated text, but one that carefully draws attention to Folio and Quarto-only features. Where I consider the distinctions between the Quarto and Folio versions of *King Lear* more deeply, I do so using the 2nd Routledge edition of *King Lear: A Parallel Text Edition*, which usefully places the Folio and Quarto versions side by side on each page.

To underscore the textual 'integrity' of *King Lear* is not to say that playwrights engage in a direct and unmediated relationship with the text of *King Lear*, which is in some way hermetically sealed from 'outside' influence. Nor is it to say that *King Lear* has a singular textual 'meaning' that remains constant through time. There is obviously a wider historical, cultural and interpretive milieu around *King Lear* in the post-war era. Various interpretative formations have aggregated around the play over the period and, in some ways, determine its received 'meaning' in the wider imaginary. The playwrights under study are embedded in a wider cultural discourse around *King Lear* and, in both explicit and implicit ways, appropriations are always responsive to that discourse and not merely to the text 'itself'. There are, however, specific textual and formal features of *King Lear* which preoccupy the appropriators under consideration. These distinct authorial preoccupations serve to bring certain aspects of the play into focus, over and against those stressed in other interpretations in the post-war era – whether those are by scholars, practitioners or other playwrights.

Even while Shakespeare and appropriation grows as an area of critical enquiry, critics have (perhaps unexpectedly) not always been attentive to appropriations by modern playwrights, typically preferring intermedial

---

[68] For more on the heath, see Chapter 5.

appropriations (and adaptations) of Shakespeare as opposed to intramedial appropriations, reflecting the growth of new media.[69] It is only more recently that critics have attended to appropriations of Shakespeare by modern playwrights, as in the work of Graham Saunders and Sonya Freeman Loftis – though Ruby Cohn and Michael Scott do provide a precedent for analysing theatrical appropriations.[70]

This is not the only study dedicated to appropriations of *King Lear*. Emily Sun and Lynne Bradley have both recently analysed the cultural afterlife of the play, Sun considering the way the play 'generates a literary genealogy, or history of successors' by studying William Wordsworth and the James Agee and Walker Evans multimedia work *Let Us Now Praise Famous Men*, Bradley by analysing adaptations (by which she means wholesale rewritings) of *King Lear* from the Nahum Tate 'revival' of the play in 1681 to post-war plays from the twentieth century.[71] This is, however, the first study dedicated to *King Lear* appropriations in post-war British playwriting and the first to analyse the ongoing and powerful discourse around the play and the catastrophe of Auschwitz, which has shaped the way in which post-war playwrights have responded to and appropriated the play. By bringing appropriations of the play into a wider dialogue around Auschwitz, catastrophe and subjectivity, it offers new perspectives on *King Lear* and its place – and use – in modern culture.

Chapter Breakdown

King Lear 'After' Auschwitz begins with an analysis of Adorno. Chapter 1 considers his post-Holocaust philosophy and the profound impact the

---

[69] For instance, in Peter Erickson, *Rewriting Shakespeare, Rewriting Ourselves* (Berkeley: University of California Press, 1991), Jean I. Marsden (ed.), *The Appropriation of Shakespeare: Post-Renaissance Reconstructions of the Works and Myths* (Hemel Hempstead: Harvester Wheatsheaf, 1991) and Christy Desmet and Robert Sawyer (eds), *Shakespeare and Appropriation* (London and New York: Routledge, 1999), not a single playwright makes an appearance.

[70] Graham Saunders, *Elizabethan and Jacobean Reappropriation in Contemporary British Drama: 'Upstart Crows'* (Basingstoke: Palgrave Macmillan, 2018); Sonya Freeman Loftis, *Shakespeare's Surrogates: Rewriting Renaissance Drama* (London and New York: Palgrave Macmillan, 2013); Ruby Cohn, *Modern Shakespeare Offshoots* (Princeton: Princeton University Press, 1974); Michael Scott, *Shakespeare and the Modern Dramatist* (Basingstoke: The Macmillan Press, 1989).

[71] Sun, *Succeeding King Lear*; Lynne Bradley, *Adapting King Lear for the Stage* (Farnham and Burlington: Ashgate, 2010). Bradley considers Bond and Barker, but Rudkin, Kane, Forced Entertainment and Kelly are not mentioned.

concentration camps had on the way he conceptualised post-Enlightenment modernity, the subject, aesthetics and tragedy. I interrogate Adorno to show that, while he considered tragedy and tragic freedom redundant in the face of the Holocaust and its total destruction of the subject, his analysis of Auschwitz nevertheless implies a new aesthetic theory of post-Holocaust tragedy and subjectivity.

Chapter 2 draws on the reading of Auschwitz, subjectivity, aesthetics and tragedy provided in Chapter 1 to analyse the thematic and, most urgently, formal aspects of *King Lear* that have made it so pivotal an intertext in catastrophic playwriting. It shows that *King Lear* is a play occupied with catastrophe, modernity, subjectivity and tragic form in a way that makes it uniquely viable for post-Holocaust appropriation. This consideration of *King Lear* serves as a frame for Chapter 3, where I analyse the way these vital aspects of the play have been interpreted in criticism, performance and appropriation in the period from 1939 to the 2010s. This era saw significant shifts in the reception of *King Lear* and important developments in post-war society, from the outbreak of the Second World War to contemporary fears around ecocatastrophe and climate change. The chapter analyses a cultural discourse around *King Lear* and Auschwitz to show that the playwrights I consider are embedded in a wider post-war constellation of ideas around the play and modern catastrophe.

My case studies begin in Chapter 4, with an analysis of perhaps the most famous appropriation of *King Lear* in post-war British playwriting: *Lear*. It shows that Bond forms a critique of post-Auschwitz resignation in his appropriation of Shakespeare, which he aligns with absurdist theatre. *Lear* agitates for a socially and politically engaged subject in the wake of Auschwitz and other modern catastrophes, as opposed to apathetic resignation. I contend that Bond shares his analysis of modernity and disaster with other catastrophic playwrights, but that his tragic form remains reliant on ideals of progress and closure in a way that overdetermines the 'engaged' subject. This chapter also considers his more recent appropriations of *King Lear*, arguing that the approach Bond takes to the Holocaust remains contradictory.

In Chapter 5, I turn to David Rudkin, considering the vital role Edgar/Poor Tom plays in the way Rudkin conceptualises subjectivity – both on stage and in relation to his own process as an author. This revolves around the negative state of exile and the self-loss – and necessary self-reinvention – exile involves. I show that the tragic condition of exile is a state of autonomy from the repressive systems of contemporary society, contending that the stress Rudkin places on exile relates to his critique of the Holocaust and its degradation of the subject. This consideration of the 'outsider' figure continues into Chapter 6, with an analysis of post-Holocaust ethics and of the Barker play *Seven Lears*. I make the case that Barker appropriates *King Lear* to enact a profound interrogation of conventional understandings of the 'good life' after the catastrophe of Auschwitz. He undermines enlightened, humanist conceptions of 'the common good' and insists that the good life rests, not in sympathetic orientation with the ethical ends of the community as a whole, but in a state of tragic deviance from society. This analysis considers the way Barker radically refigures the storm scenes from *King Lear*, contesting the cultural-industrial overproduction of *King Lear* as a humanist play invested in normative conceptions of commonality and community.

Chapter 7 considers the Kane play *Blasted* and its appropriation of *King Lear*, showing that Kane interrogates the usual philosophical distinction between the material and the metaphysical by appropriating the infamous Dover 'cliff' scene from Shakespeare. I make the case that, through her appropriation, Kane creates a space for autonomy – for transcendence – in a totalised material world, drawing a relation between her critique of contemporary late capital, the Bosnian conflicts of the 1990s and the spectre of the Nazi concentration camps. The chapter ends with a short postscript on the theatre company Forced Entertainment, considering the 1999 performance piece *Five Day Lear* in relation to *Blasted* and the more recent 2016 Forced Entertainment series *Table Top Shakespeare: The Complete Works*. This postscript demonstrates that *King Lear* has enabled a post-Auschwitz performance style concerned with the representation (and interrogation) of catastrophe, as Forced Entertainment attempt to produce not passive spectators, but moral witnesses.

My final case study is on Kelly and his controversial 2010 play *The Gods Weep*, which I consider in Chapter 8. Through his appropriation of *King Lear*, Kelly draws parallels between the Holocaust, modern capitalist globalisation and anthropogenic climatic change, depicting a world of poverty, food insecurity, hunger and conflict. I argue that Kelly appropriates *King Lear* for the purposes of a post-Auschwitz tragic drama that represents the sublime plenitude of nature, in a way that undoes the commodifying approach to the natural world taken by the late capitalist system. By catalysing the freedom of nature from human ends, Kelly also aims to catalyse the freedom of the tragic subject. In the Conclusion, I return to these topics and set out the ongoing discourse around *King Lear* and catastrophe.

Chapter 1

'After' Auschwitz

> 'Millions of innocent people – to quote or haggle over the numbers is already inhumane – were systematically murdered. That cannot be dismissed by any living person as a superficial phenomenon, as an aberration of the course of history to be disregarded when compared to the great dynamic of progress, of enlightenment, of the supposed growth of humanitarianism.'
>
> Theodor Adorno[1]

'Auschwitz', observes Adorno, 'happened in the midst of the traditions of philosophy, of art, and of the enlightening sciences.'[2] It is that contradiction between the vaunted humanist 'traditions' of reason and progress embodied by the development of Enlightenment philosophy, art and the sciences and the overwhelming barbarity of the Holocaust that Adorno confronts when he thinks and writes about the wound of Auschwitz. Auschwitz represents a break in which the 'untruth' to be found in the previously unquestioned traditions of the Western Enlightenment had been revealed and after which profound transformations were necessary.[3] But while Auschwitz constitutes a breach in history, the conditions that had made it possible continue 'after' the Holocaust, raising the possibility that other catastrophes will take place in the future. Auschwitz had degraded human subjects to mere objects, to be processed and destroyed with systematic, industrial proficiency. This grievous reduction of subjects to objects is also true of post-war culture and its 'damaged' forms

---

[1] Theodor Adorno, 'Education After Auschwitz', in Theodor Adorno, *Can One Live After Auschwitz?*, ed. Rolf Tiedemann, trans. Rodney Livingstone et al. (Stanford: Stanford University Press, 2003), p. 20.

[2] Theodor Adorno, *Negative Dialectics*, trans. E. B. Ashton (London and New York: Continuum, 2007), p. 366.

[3] Ibid.

of subjectivity, making future disasters all too possible – even probable.[4] This underpins the 'new categorical imperative' imposed by the events of the Holocaust on 'an unfree mankind': that 'Auschwitz will not repeat itself', that 'nothing similar will happen'.[5]

It is in the 1944 *Dialectic of Enlightenment* that Adorno and his co-author, Max Horkheimer, begin to interrogate the seeming contradiction between modern Enlightenment progress and the atrocity of the Holocaust, making it vital 'for an understanding of the age'.[6] I begin by analysing *Dialectic of Enlightenment*, which proposes a deep-seated relationship between Auschwitz and the humanist philosophy of reason and freedom typified by the Enlightenment, before organising a constellatory dialogue around critical 'themes' from Adorno – subjectivity, aesthetics and tragedy – drawing on a range of vital works by Adorno and other theorists and thinkers. Auschwitz conditions the way in which Adorno interprets the fate of subjectivity, the aesthetic sphere and the genre of tragedy. These reflections have often had a direct influence on the writers and dramatists under study and form a particularly powerful paradigm for an understanding of the development of various Theatres of Catastrophe in the post-war era. This is not necessarily to say that Adorno would advocate a renewed form of tragedy 'after' Auschwitz; but while Adorno does not offer an overt theory (let alone a defence) of tragedy, his various insights on the Holocaust, modernity, subjectivity and aesthetics imply a theory of the post-Auschwitz tragic.[7]

Dialectic of Enlightenment

Though mostly written before the full scale of the atrocity was revealed, *Dialectic of Enlightenment* provides a formative analysis of the European

---

[4] Theodor Adorno, *Minima Moralia: Reflections on a Damaged Life*, trans. Edmund Jephcott (London: Verso, 2005).
[5] Adorno, *Negative Dialectics*, p. 365.
[6] Detlev Claussen, quoted in Rolf Tiedemann, 'Introduction', in Adorno, *Can One Live After Auschwitz?*, p. xiii.
[7] Other thinkers who consider Adorno and tragedy include Samir Gandesha, 'Enlightenment as Tragedy: Reflections on Adorno's Ethics', *Thesis Eleven*, 65:1 (2001), pp. 109–30; Markku Nivalainen, 'On Thinking the Tragic with Adorno', *The European Legacy*, 21:7 (2016), pp. 644–63; and Karoline Gritzner, *Adorno and Modern Theatre: The Drama of the Damaged Self in Bond, Rudkin, Barker and Kane* (Basingstoke: Palgrave Macmillan, 2015), pp. 163–81.

Enlightenment from the disconcerting vantage point of the Holocaust.[8] Adorno and Horkheimer write that 'in the most general sense of progressive thought, the Enlightenment has always aimed at liberating men'.[9] But seen from the disillusioned perspective of the Second World War, human freedom had degenerated into total domination and the 'earth radiates disaster triumphant'.[10]

It was the aim of the Enlightenment to free individual subjects from dogma by using reason to interrogate pre-modern, superstitious myths about fate and the non-human, divine forces imagined to shape the world, along with the autocratic institutions that perpetuate those myths – most obviously the monarchy and the church. This was supposed to usher in a new, modern era shaped by the progress of rational scientific beliefs and newly representative institutions that would enshrine human freedom, from democracy to the legal system. But for Adorno and Horkheimer, the Second World War obviously requires a newly reconfigured understanding of Enlightenment reason, progress and modernity. This is not simply because Enlightenment culture in some way 'failed' to redeem humanity from pre-modern myths and barbarity. More profoundly, Adorno and Horkheimer critique the Enlightenment for producing the very conditions that made Auschwitz possible. Far from viewing the Holocaust as an aberration – a violent deviation in the historical emancipation of an increasingly 'rational' and 'free' humanity over time – Auschwitz is closely related to Enlightenment progress itself, whereby 'the curse of irresistible progress is irresistible regression'.[11]

Dialectic of Enlightenment has at its centre a Nietzschean genealogical critique of the epistemological practices of Enlightenment philosophy and science. Adorno and Horkheimer make the case that enlightened, philosophical and scientific reason produces knowledge by separating the material world, and the objects that make it up, into abstract concepts or categories – say the taxonomic distinctions between various animal and plant species. These categories are understood to properly reflect the object of perception, where pre-modern dogma superstitiously mystifies it, usually by viewing the world as the product of divine fiat and fate. Through the use of reason, more and more objects are categorised, so that

---

[8] Theodor Adorno and Max Horkheimer, *Dialectic of Enlightenment*, trans. John Cumming (London: Verso, 2010). The text was republished in 1947 with a new chapter, 'Elements of Anti-Semitism', which was added once the extermination of European Jews in the Holocaust had become more widely known.
[9] Ibid. p. 3.
[10] Ibid.
[11] Ibid. p. 36.

the systematisation of the world is seen to be progressively complete – or 'total'. Over time, every 'thing' (and everything) is sublated under abstract categories of perception and utility, where the object is used as an instrument to serve the purposes of humanity, as it progressively dominates the material world for its own uses. It is that domination which underpins human freedom from nature and the rule of fate that prevails in myth.

Adorno and Horkheimer contend that Hegel represents the pinnacle of the Enlightenment and its theoretical and practical attempt to produce a unified totality of all human knowledge.[12] Hegel famously contests the Kantian 'block', the idea that the noumenal object – or as Kant calls it, the 'thing-in-itself' – is ultimately resistant to phenomenal human perception.[13] He insists that the objects of human experience can ultimately be seen to conform to human concepts – or 'conceptual cognition'.[14] By using concepts, it is possible for the subject to gain a complete perceptual understanding of the object, via a continuing process in which the subject 'negates the negation' – or the aspects of the object that seem to resist interpretation. This process is at the heart of the idea of dialectics – or the synthesis of thesis and anti-thesis. Hegel contends that the dialectic reaches its conclusion in the 'positive' synthesis of the subject (perception) and object (reality) in time. By virtue of reason, the subject comes to dominate a previously opaque and oppressive material world and, through its negation of a recalcitrant object, achieves full self-actualisation and self-determination. This allows Hegel to adopt a teleological view of history as the universal progress of reason and freedom over time. The perfected state of knowledge and autonomy to which humanity is progressing is the 'end of History', as Hegel called it.[15]

Hegel might represent the culmination of Enlightenment confidence in the unlimited powers of human reason, but for Adorno and Horkheimer, 'enlightenment' refers not only to the era known as the Enlightenment but to 'any intellectual and practical operations which are presented as demythologizing, secularizing or disenchanting some mythical, religious or magical representation of the world' through the power of 'modern' reasoning.[16] This is not necessarily restricted to the Enlightenment, but

---

[12] See in particular Georg Wilhelm Friedrich Hegel, *Phenomenology of Spirit*, trans. A. V. Miller (Oxford: Oxford University Press, 1977).

[13] For Hegel on the thing-in-itself, see John McCumber, *Understanding Hegel's Mature Critique of Kant* (Stanford: Stanford University Press, 2012), pp. 53–60.

[14] Georg Wilhelm Friedrich Hegel, *Philosophy of Mind*, ed. Michael Inwood, trans. W. Wallace and A. V. Miller (Oxford: Oxford University Press, 2007), p. 203.

[15] Georg Wilhelm Friedrich Hegel, *The Philosophy of History*, trans. J. Sibree (New York: Dover Publications, 2004), p. 103.

[16] Simon Jarvis, *Adorno: A Critical Introduction* (New York: Routledge, 1998), p. 24.

has its roots deep in European thought, with Adorno and Horkheimer making the case that the 'cunning' Odysseus displays in *The Odyssey* represents a disenchanted understanding of the mythic powers supposed to control human destiny.[17] The notion of a conceptual, systematic unity of knowledge, write Adorno and Horkheimer, remains 'the slogan from Parmenides to Russell'.[18]

Despite its central place in the history and development of European thought, for Adorno and Horkheimer there is a deep-seated problem with the conceptual 'unity' of knowledge supposedly provided by the powers of enlightenment reason. This has to do with the way enlightenment thinking ultimately reduces discrete objects to a conceptual category. By making various objects 'fit' into a predetermined epistemic class, the actual, specific uniqueness of the object under survey – its singularity – is lost to view. Every object becomes nothing more than a representative of the abstract category to which it has been consigned, 'without regard to distinctions'.[19] This causes Adorno and Horkheimer to critique enlightenment thought and perception as systematically misrepresenting reality by disregarding – or 'dissolving' – the singular qualities of the object that distinguish it from the category to which rational thought fatefully ascribes it.[20] What was once distinct is 'equalized':

> That is the verdict which critically determines the limits of possible experience. The identity of everything with everything else is paid for in that nothing may at the same time be identical with itself. Enlightenment dissolves the injustice of the old inequality – unmediated lordship and mastery – but at the same time perpetuates it in universal mediation, in the relation of any one existent to any other.[21]

Adorno would go on to use the term 'identity-thinking' to describe the process of categorical thought in enlightenment reasoning, which 'identifies' discrete objects with a preconceived category.[22]

The idea that a particular object can be subsumed within a general category without remainder leads to the idea that the conceptual realm has no outer boundary, that there is nothing it does not have the capacity

---

[17] Adorno and Horkheimer, *Dialectic of Enlightenment*, pp. 43–80. I capitalise Enlightenment for the era, using the uncapitalised enlightenment for the power of 'modern' reason in history more generally.
[18] Ibid. p. 8.
[19] Ibid.
[20] Ibid. p. 12.
[21] Ibid.
[22] Adorno, *Negative Dialectics*, pp. 4–6.

to identify. This means that the object becomes totally identical with the category under which it is sublated; but it also means that the whole of reality itself is necessarily subsumed within a single representational schema. It is for that reason Adorno and Horkheimer make the case that 'Enlightenment is totalitarian':[23] it produces a totalised system that cannot tolerate anything outside of itself, anything 'other'. This reversal is where the 'dialectic' of enlightenment becomes most obvious. By subsuming discrete objects into a totalised conceptual configuration and dispelling anything that does not fit, categorical reasoning institutes 'a law of perpetual sameness'.[24] Understood as identical with its representation in and by enlightened reason, reality comes to appear as heteronomous and unchanging, an immutable order that predetermines human perception and ultimately seems resistant to progressive intervention or transformation. Enlightenment thinking ends up reverting to the mythic state of fateful unfreedom it was understood to displace: 'Enlightenment is mythic fear turned radical.'[25] For the subject, the consequences are dire. Horkheimer writes that reason catalyses the elevation of reality to 'the status of the ideal', which 'confronts the subject as absolute, overpowering'.[26] The subject supposedly liberated by reason ends up totally conquered by it. This unfreedom reveals the way in which a philosophy of rational knowledge and self-determination dialectically reversed into domination – and even a social and political policy of genocide.

Enlightenment and Auschwitz

The question Adorno and Horkheimer address in *Dialectic of Enlightenment* is the way an enlightened, modern philosophy of rationality and freedom regressed into genocide on a unprecedented and industrial scale – or the recent 'course of European civilization'.[27] This involves combining a comprehensive deconstruction of the progress of reason with a Weberian analysis of disenchantment and administration. Adorno and Horkheimer contend that enlightened reason did not replace pre-modern traditions and institutions with enlightened civic and ethical values, which protect the freedom of the individual. On the

---

[23] Adorno and Horkheimer, *Dialectic of Enlightenment*, p. 6.
[24] Adorno, *Negative Dialectics*, p. 41.
[25] Adorno and Horkheimer, *Dialectic of Enlightenment*, p. 16.
[26] Max Horkheimer, *Eclipse of Reason* (London: Bloomsbury, 2013), p. 68.
[27] Adorno and Horkheimer, *Dialectic of Enlightenment*, p. 13.

contrary: the modern principles of systematic order and control have been applied to the total administration of society itself, so that subjects are increasingly bound in a repressive 'iron cage'.[28]

This process is reflected in the increasingly universal pervasiveness of systems of administration in modern societies. Adorno is deeply critical of the various systems of administrative organisation found in modernity, which operate by separating every subject into abstract classes or categories – most obviously on the basis of age, status, gender, sexuality and race, among other possible 'vectors' of identity that may be used for the purposes of categorisation. Just as categorical reason creates a totally organised system of knowledge, so the disenchanted process of rationalisation creates a totally organised social system, which similarly proceeds by administratively processing and dominating everything before it. Only where categorical thinking had previously been applied to objects – to brute material reality – rationalised social systems are now also practised on and through human subjects, who are deemed so much 'material' to be arbitrarily systematised and controlled as the dictates of the administration demand. 'For the rulers,' write Adorno and Horkheimer, 'men become material' – in the same way as 'nature as a whole is material for society':[29]

> Through the mediation of the total society which embraces all relations [. . .] men are once again made to be that against which the evolutionary law of society, the principle of self, had turned: mere species beings, exactly like one another.[30]

Through the rationalisation process, the modern subject becomes a cipher of the very same categorising reason it is supposed to practise and apply to the material world. Far from being emancipated, the modern subject is reified – or turned into an object, an object of reason.

This evinces the vital influence of György Lukács on *Dialectic of Enlightenment*. His analysis of reification in *History and Class Consciousness* uncovers the way in which a social and political system created by people comes to seem independent (and originally independent) of the very social actors who produce and reproduce it, so that 'the reified world' appears 'as the only possible world, the only conceptually accessible, comprehensible world vouchsafed to us humans'.[31] This occa-

---

[28] Max Weber, *Political Writings*, ed. Peter Lassman, trans. Ronald Speirs (Cambridge: Cambridge University Press, 1994), p. xvi.
[29] Adorno and Horkheimer, *Dialectic of Enlightenment*, p. 87.
[30] Ibid. p. 36.
[31] György Lukács, *History and Class Consciousness: Studies in Marxist Dialectics*

sions a profound reversal: subjects are turned into objects of the system, with the result that individuals are rendered passive or determined, while the system itself is understood as the active, determining agent – as a subject. This reversal means that subjects are transformed into little more than 'things' (the German word for reification, *Verdinglichung*, quite literally means 'thingification'). Adorno and Horkheimer contend that the dialectic of enlightenment is a reifying process, whereby the subject is transformed into an object of the 'reason' it is supposed to use for the purposes of self-reflexive thought and freedom and left 'without autonomy or substance of its own'.[32]

Under a system of administrative rationalisation, the subject comes to be completely identified with the category under which s/he has been placed, so the unique specificity of the individual subject is obscured – or as Adorno provocatively imagines it, 'liquidated'.[33] It is that depersonalising process that reached a horrifying apotheosis at Auschwitz, which represents the catastrophic nadir of a wider trend towards reification in post-Enlightenment society. The concentrationary universe, as Primo Levi calls it, following the work of French writer and fellow concentration camp survivor David Rousset, represents a total – and totally administered – social world, where subjects were ruthlessly 'processed' in a closed organisational system based on the categories to which they were consigned (Jew, Slav, Gypsy and so on).[34] This reduction of subjects to 'types' meant the individual was completely lost to view – and that whole masses of people could be systematically destroyed. It is not that the reifying process of administration inevitably ends in genocide, as its *telos*. But any process whereby subjects are reduced to the status of objects creates the conditions under which the events of Auschwitz were made possible. Adorno writes that the 'administrative murder of millions' that took place in the Holocaust resulted from a 'process of abstract integration' and is potentially 'in preparation wherever human beings are de-individualized'.[35] Through the camp, the social and political process of rationalisation has been 'refined' until subjects are 'literally exterminated' – but the camps are

(Pontypool: Merlin, 2010), p. 110. See 'Reification and the Consciousness of the Proletariat', pp. 82–222.

[32] Adorno, *Minima Moralia*, p. 15.
[33] Theodor Adorno, 'Trying to Understand *Endgame*', in Adorno, *Can One Live After Auschwitz?*, p. 286.
[34] Primo Levi, *The Drowned and the Saved* (London: Abacus Books, 2013), p. 7.
[35] Quoted in Gerhard Schweppenhäuser, *Theodor W. Adorno: An Introduction*, trans. James Rolleston (Durham, NC and London: Duke University Press, 2009), p. 67.

a consequence of the way modern society more widely liquidates the qualitative particularity of its subjects.[36]

This representation of the concentration camp does not mean Adorno and Horkheimer dodge or deny other explicatory causes for the Holocaust – not the least of which are European colonialism, the rise of nationalism, the development of pseudo-Darwinian racial sciences and the violent history of European Christian anti-Semitism, which culminates in the 'Final Solution to the Jewish Question', as that became urgent for the Nazi hierarchy with military collapse on the Eastern front a pressing concern after the defeat at Stalingrad.[37] Nor is it to deny the particularity of the Holocaust as a predominantly (though of course not singularly) Jewish experience.[38] The point Adorno makes by tying the Holocaust to the legacy of the Enlightenment is to deny that the events of Auschwitz represent an atavistic return of pre-modern barbarism in an era of civilised European progress. Adorno and Horkheimer also show that pre-modern religious myths about Jews can co-exist with – and even be strengthened by – a supposedly 'rational' age of modernity. The virulent anti-Semitism of European history is intensified by a modern social system shaped by a desire for regulated order and control. By virtue of not being fully 'integrated' into the state and the nation, the Jewish people appear unfixed – a part of society but also outside the 'whole'. This only deepens a mythic fear of the supposedly threatening 'other' – the Jews:[39]

> If [. . .] the concept encounters the particular only on an external plane, everything which stands for difference in society is threatened. Everyone is either a friend or an enemy [. . .] The lack of concern for the subject makes things easy for the administration. Ethnic groups are forced to move [. . .] individuals are branded as Jews and sent to the gas chamber.[40]

'The Fascists do not view the Jew as a minority' so much as 'the embodiment of the negative principle': there has 'always been an intimate link between anti-Semitism and totality'.[41] Peoples who are marginalised or 'other' are particularly vulnerable in a totalised society

---

[36] Ibid.
[37] See David Cesarani, *Final Solution: The Fate of the Jews 1933–49* (London: Macmillan, 2016), pp. 583–6.
[38] The Nazi theory of racial purity also classed Slavs and the Roma as 'inferior', though Jews were the main target of mass extermination.
[39] This is part of the explanation Adorno and Horkheimer offer in *Dialectic of Enlightenment*, in the chapter 'Elements of Anti-Semitism' (pp. 168–208).
[40] Ibid. p. 202.
[41] Ibid. p. 168 and p. 172.

– though Adorno remains suspicious of social and political claims to identity.

Auschwitz and Capitalism

Adorno and Horkheimer contend that the destruction of human subjectivity witnessed in the Second World War was not some sort of deviation but part of a wider practice of rationality based on a principle of absolute domination – of the world and the subjects that comprise it. This danger lies in the modern condition *per se*. 'It was', writes Zygmunt Bauman, 'the rational world of modern civilization that made the Holocaust thinkable.'[42] Auschwitz is imbricated in modernity – in identity-thinking, the process of categorisation, social rationalisation and the systemising practices of modern culture. Part of that modern condition is totalitarianism, from Nazi fascism to Soviet communism. But perhaps most provocatively, Adorno and Horkheimer also relate the atrocities committed under Nazism to the social and economic system that had seemed to prevail over fascism in Western Europe: liberal capitalism.

Drawing on a Marxist analysis of the commodity-form, Adorno and Horkheimer relate both epistemological and social systems based on identity-thinking to the way that capitalism, through the equalising process present in exchange-value, enables wholly unalike objects to be made commensurable and exchangeable.[43] The exchange-value of a commodity – the commodities it might be exchanged for in a trade or the price it fetches on the market – means that distinct objects become artificially commensurate, with the unique properties of the traded object obscured to understanding. It is not a historical coincidence that modern capitalism and the era of Enlightenment rationality converge in time. Latent in the law of identity-thinking is the commodity-form and vice versa. Categorical rationality and capitalist exchange are reciprocally informing historical developments that cannot be analysed in isolation.

The way in which Adorno and Horkheimer relate identity-thinking to capitalism means that the critique of Auschwitz and the history of reason also relates to pre- and post-war society. By incorporating everything into itself as a potentially exchangeable commodity, capitalism

---

[42] Zygmunt Bauman, *Modernity and the Holocaust* (Cambridge: Polity, 1989), p. 13.
[43] See also Andrew Bowie, *Adorno and the Ends of Philosophy* (Cambridge: Polity, 2013), p. 33.

is a universalising system, which produces a reified world of total fungibility. This is not a process the subject is able to escape – let alone determine. While it promotes a liberal and enlightened ideology of individual freedom, capitalist society ultimately reifies the subject – turning him or her into an object of a totalised social and economic process. This is typified by industrial capitalism, which, in its bid for uniform production, turns subjects (workers) into objects of a rationally administered process, so that it is not the free subject who rules, as people are 'degraded' into mere 'appendages' of the overall system and 'ultimately into ideology'.[44] Drawing parallels between industrial capital and the concentration camps, Enzo Traverso writes that Auschwitz operated 'as a factory, whose product was death', while the chimneys of the crematoria were uncannily reminiscent of perhaps the most common aspect of 'an industrial landscape'.[45] Adorno and Horkheimer are, however, also suspicious (perhaps even more keenly so) of rationalised systems of consumption in post-Auschwitz culture and life. It is not the case that the post-war transition from industrial (productive, Fordist) to post-industrial (consumer, late) capital represents a decisive shift in the standardising way that capitalism operates, with Adorno writing in his 'Late Capitalism or Industrial Society' that 'the dialectician, above all, should not let himself be forced into a clear-cut distinction between late capitalism or industrial society'.[46]

This continuity is most obvious in the devastating critique Adorno and Horkheimer mount against the so-called 'Culture Industry', a concept that relates to the mass production of cultural products in post-Auschwitz society.[47] Adorno and Horkheimer make the case that modern cultural life, far from being the product of a human subject concretising his or her creativity and freedom, has been brought under the ambit of the capitalist system, which 'impresses the same stamp on everything'.[48]

---

[44] Theodor Adorno, 'On Subject and Object', in Theodor Adorno, *Critical Models: Interventions and Catchwords*, trans. Henry W. Pickford (New York: Colombia University Press, 2005), p. 248.

[45] Enzo Traverso, *Understanding the Nazi Genocide: Marxism After the Holocaust*, trans. Peter Drucker (London: Pluto Press, 1999), p. 15. Dan Stone notes that the Nazis also adopted a policy of 'annihilation through labour'. See his *The Concentration Camp: A Short History* (Oxford: Oxford University Press, 2017), p. 47.

[46] Theodor Adorno, 'Late Capitalism or Industrial Society', in Adorno, *Can One Live After Auschwitz?*, p. 114.

[47] This appears in the chapter 'The Culture Industry: Enlightenment as Mass Deception', in Adorno and Horkheimer, *Dialectic of Enlightenment*, pp. 120–67.

[48] Ibid. p. 120.

Post-Auschwitz cultural production is akin to a factory rolling out standardised products – films, novels, plays, radio programmes, magazines and even astrology columns, all part of 'a system which is uniform as a whole and in every part'.[49] The result – once again – is that subjects (consumers) are integrated into a rationally administered system. The individual is transformed from a subject of cultural life to its object.

This is not to say that Adorno is in some way 'against' popular (or 'low') art, despite often being caricatured as a mandarin cultural elitist.[50] Adorno is aware that popular art can unleash politically oppositional and destabilising libidinal forces, and that popular art forms – and 'entertainment' – pre-date the Culture Industry, even while that industry is able to absorb that which is 'spontaneous' and not planned into 'planning'.[51] He is, however, profoundly critical of the 'repetitiveness, the self-sameness, and the ubiquity of modern mass culture', which tends to 'weaken the forces of individual resistance'.[52] Not unlike other modern forms of organisation, the Culture Industry incorporates subjects into a totalised world that degrades people into objects, abolishing individual particularity in favour of universal generality:

> The identity of the category forbids that of the individual cases [in] [. . .] the culture industry. Now any person signifies only those attributes by which he can replace anybody else: he is interchangeable, a copy. As an individual he is completely expendable and insignificant.[53]

Nowhere does Adorno simply collapse the qualitative distinction between consumer capitalism and the unmitigated horrors of Nazi fascism – though it is perhaps worth observing that Auschwitz operated as both a death camp and labour camp, with an industrial system of production and consumption that was exploited by private industry.[54] Adorno also remains conscious of the distinctions between capitalism and Stalinism, a totalitarian system which he often critiqued.[55] He does think, however, that capitalism, Nazi fascism and Stalinism are totalised

---

[49] Ibid.
[50] See in particular Robert Miklitsch, *Roll Over Adorno: Critical Theory, Popular Culture, Audiovisual Media* (New York: State University of New York Press, 2006).
[51] Adorno and Horkheimer, *Dialectic of Enlightenment*, p. 146.
[52] Theodor Adorno, 'How to Look at Television', in Theodor Adorno, *The Culture Industry*, ed. J. M. Bernstein (London: Routledge, 2001), p. 160.
[53] Adorno and Horkheimer, *Dialectic of Enlightenment*, pp. 145–6.
[54] See Sybille Steinbacher, *Auschwitz: A History*, trans. Shaun Whiteside (London: Penguin, 2005), pp. 51–3.
[55] See in particular 'Reconciliation under Duress', in Rodney Livingstone, Perry Anderson and Frances Mulhern (eds), *Aesthetics and Politics*, trans. various (London: Verso, 2007), pp. 151–76.

systems that can all be seen as iterations of rationalised modernity and identity-thinking. Adorno also makes the case that capitalism, in its reification of the subject, can slide into totalitarian fascism far more unresistingly than liberal thought would like to imagine ('whoever is not prepared to talk about capitalism', as Horkheimer once observed, 'should also remain silent about fascism').[56] These systems all produce widespread socialisation – or the 'total socialization' of society – and tend to disregard the particularity of the subject in the process.[57] While contemporary capitalist culture does not necessarily produce the same horrors as the concentration camp or the gulag, such catastrophes remain a disconcertingly live possibility. 'Auschwitz was possible', writes Adorno, 'and remains possible for the foreseeable future': its enabling conditions persist in a society that is marked by the 'permanent catastrophe' of a degraded human subject.[58]

The Actuality of Adorno

Adorno provides an undeniably bleak portrait of the transformation of modern freedom back into mythic oppression. He writes in his 1966 work *Negative Dialectics* that no 'universal history leads from savagery to humanitarianism, but there is one leading from the slingshot to the megaton bomb'.[59] While his ideas have been influential, however, there are inevitably criticisms of Adorno and his conceptualisation of modernity. These have ranged from the work of Jürgen Habermas – who critiques Adorno for being overly reliant on the subject–object relation, failing to consider the subject–subject relation and the possibility of rational communicative interaction between people through democratic systems – to Timothy Snyder, who makes a defence of the modern administrative state and its role in protecting Jews from the Nazis.[60] For the most part, however, criticisms of Adorno have been undertaken from

---

[56] Quoted in Peter Davies and Derek Lynch, *The Routledge Companion to Fascism and the Far Right* (London and New York: Routledge, 2002), p. 52.
[57] Adorno, *Negative Dialectics*, p. 346.
[58] Theodor Adorno, 'Is Art Lighthearted?', in Adorno, *Notes to Literature: Volume Two*, ed. Rolf Tiedemann, trans. Sherry Weber Nicholson (New York: Colombia University Press, 1992), p. 251; *Negative Dialectics*, p. 320.
[59] Adorno, *Negative Dialectics*, p. 320.
[60] See Deborah Cook, *Adorno, Habermas and the Search for a Rational Society* (London: Routledge, 2004) and Timothy Snyder, *Black Earth: The Holocaust as History and Warning* (London: Penguin, 2015), p. 340. I return to Habermas and intersubjectivity in Chapter 2.

a postmodern position. These are both philosophical and historical and tend to concentrate on the 'actuality' of critical theory in the (so-called) postmodern era.[61]

This critique of critical theory from a postmodern perspective largely begins with Lyotard, the foremost theorist of the postmodern, and his 1974 piece 'Adorno as the Devil' – an allusion to the 1947 Thomas Mann novel *Dr Faustus*, where Satan appears as Adorno and quotes the 1958 *Philosophy of Modern Music*.[62] I want to concentrate on Lyotard as his critique of Adorno rests on a changed understanding of the social and cultural shift from industrial to post-industrial capitalist society. Lyotard reiterates Adorno when he makes the case that modernity is shaped by totalising 'metanarratives' of reason and progress – overarching stories or systems of thought that seek to provide a total representation of the world and its development. He also critiques metanarratives as complicit with systems of domination that dissolve the heterogeneous. But where Lyotard ultimately parts with Adorno is with his more 'positive' representation of post-war society and his conception of postmodernity.

Lyotard makes the case that post-war society is not a total system, dominating subjects. He contends that metanarratives have been replaced by smaller, fragmented stories, which are conveyed in limited but pluralistic 'language-games' – a phrase he takes from Ludwig Wittgenstein.[63] This proliferation of language-games is a distinguishing feature of postmodern society, which breaks with the totalising conditions of modernity and embraces heterogeneity. This is not to say that Lyotard ignores the Holocaust. On the contrary: Auschwitz is a persistent theme for Lyotard in his conceptualisation of the postmodern, perhaps most obviously when he writes that Auschwitz is the 'crime opening postmodernity'.[64] Auschwitz signals the end of the metanarrative of reason and calls for the prioritisation of hybrid language-games over the rule of metanarratives. Lyotard insists that postmodernity ('after' Auschwitz) represents that historical shift from homogeneity towards plurality.[65]

---

[61] Theodor Adorno, 'The Actuality of Philosophy', *Telos*, 31 (1977), pp. 120–33. See also Max Pensky (ed.), *The Actuality of Adorno: Critical Essays on Adorno and the Postmodern* (New York: State University of New York Press, 1997).

[62] Jean-François Lyotard, 'Adorno as the Devil', *Telos*, 19 (1974), pp. 127–37.

[63] Jean-François Lyotard, *The Postmodern Condition*, trans. Geoff Bennington and Brian Massumi (Manchester: Manchester University Press, 1986), p. 10.

[64] Jean-François Lyotard, *The Postmodern Explained: Correspondence, 1982–1985*, trans. Julian Pefanis and Morgan Thomas (Minneapolis: University of Minnesota, 1997), p. 19.

[65] For more on postmodernity and the Holocaust, see Robert Eaglestone, *The Holocaust and the Postmodern* (Oxford: Oxford University Press, 2004).

Lyotard contends that the transition from modernity to postmodernity is a historical and cultural shift Adorno fails to perceive. This means the concept of totality is ultimately outmoded by the transition to postmodernity; but it also means that Adorno is retrogressively constrained by the very same universalising historical conditions he sets out to critique. Lyotard makes the case that Adorno provides a negative (or 'demonic') inversion that reiterates, albeit critically, precisely the same metanarrative he wants to undermine by prioritising the particular over the universal ('the slingshot to the megaton bomb').[66] This leads Adorno into various contradictions. Most of all, Adorno turns Auschwitz – a specific concentration camp and historical event, where real subjects lived and died – into an abstract category through which the whole historical metaprocess of modernity and reason is understood.[67] Adorno transforms the particular (Auschwitz) into the universal (dialectic of enlightenment).[68] This contradicts the singularity of the Holocaust itself, an event Lyotard sees as so far beyond reasonable comprehension that any undertaking to capture it in its totality is doomed to fail – and even to potentially rationalise the scale of human suffering it caused.[69]

The historical shift Lyotard considers also represents a shift in capitalisms. 'We have the advantage over Adorno', writes Lyotard of contemporary capitalist culture, of 'living in a capitalism that is more energetic, more cynical, less tragic', a system where 'the tragic gives way to the parodic' and where more open-ended and plural forms of subjectivity are 'catalysed'.[70] Lyotard, in his conceptualisation of the postmodern, is concerned with a shift away from industrial to post-industrial finance capital – which he sees as a less autocratic and authoritarian form of capitalism that releases more language-games, libidinal energies and

---

[66] See Lyotard, 'Adorno as the Devil'.

[67] This has parallels with the critique Habermas – the chief inheritor of critical theory – forms against Adorno, when he contends that his former mentor is guilty of a 'performative contradiction'. See his *The Philosophical Discourse of Modernity*, trans. Frederick Lawrence (Cambridge: Polity, 2007), p. 119.

[68] For more on the synecdochic usage of 'Auschwitz' in critical theory, see Mark J. Webber, 'Metaphorizing the Holocaust: The Ethics of Comparison', *Images*, 8:15/16 (2011), pp. 17–19.

[69] These are topics Lyotard develops in his *The Différend: Phrases in Dispute*, trans. George Van Den Abbeele (Minneapolis: University of Minnesota Press, 1998), in which he engages with Adorno and the notion of an 'after' Auschwitz, and – controversially – with the Holocaust denier Robert Faurisson. See pp. 87–91 and pp. 14–19.

[70] Lyotard, 'Adorno as the Devil', p. 128.

subjectivities.[71] Where industrial capitalism (Fordism) dominates and destroys the subject, for Lyotard post-industrial consumer capitalism unleashes a 'new spirit' of open-endedness and 'play'.[72] He even goes so far as to make the argument that, as opposed to being resisted, 'the dissolution of forms and individuals in the so-called "consumer society" should be *affirmed*'.[73]

The question, however, is whether the reifying conditions of modernity have truly been displaced by a new era of postmodernity and whether totality and catastrophe as critical concepts have, as a result, been historically and philosophically invalidated. Adorno would be suspicious of any belief that post-war capitalist culture represents a decisive shift away from totality towards the diverse. He writes in *Negative Dialectics* that for 'the time being a so-called pluralism would falsely deny the total structure of society'.[74] This is because 'total socialization objectively hatches its opposite' – the ostensible diversity of commodities and the lifestyles those commodities are supposed to represent.[75] This diversity is nothing but 'the anarchy of commodity production'.[76] Underlying the heterogeneous commodities of the market is the homogeneous totality of capitalist social relations, a paradox Adorno captures in his critique of the 'ever-changing sameness' of post-Auschwitz capitalist life.[77] Postmodern theory may tend to concentrate on the fragmentary and hybrid in its historico-philosophical speculations but it often does so by overlooking the enabling totality of capitalist hegemony. This oversight becomes even more obvious in an age of globalisation, which sees the market penetrate into every sphere of human existence around the world, intensifying the disastrous reification of subjectivity far into the post-war era.

Fredric Jameson famously makes the case that the seemingly fragmentary worlds of postmodernism are – paradoxically – the cultural 'logic' of an increasingly totalised capitalist system.[78] The phenomena of

---

[71] See *The Postmodern Condition* and *Libidinal Economy*, trans. Ian Hamilton Grant (London: Bloomsbury, 2015).
[72] I take the phrase 'new spirit' from Luc Boltanski and Eve Chiapello, *The New Spirit of Capitalism*, trans. Gregory Elliott (London: Verso, 2017).
[73] Quoted in Peter Dews, *Logics of Disintegration: Poststructuralist Thought and the Claims of Critical Theory* (London: Verso, 2007), p. 174.
[74] Adorno, *Negative Dialectics*, p. 346.
[75] Ibid.
[76] Theodor Adorno, *Aesthetic Theory*, trans. Robert Hullot-Kentor (London: Continuum, 2004), p. 281.
[77] Adorno, *Minima Moralia*, p. 238.
[78] Fredric Jameson, *Postmodernism, or, The Cultural Logic of Late Capitalism* (London: Verso, 1991).

post-industrialism and globalisation pay witness to the universalisation of capitalism, as opposed to its postmodern hybridisation. Jameson contends that postmodernity, far from representing a qualitative break with modern totality, is a continuation (even 'intensification') of it, writing that postmodernity is typified by an 'increasingly closed organization of the world into a seamless web'.[79] Jameson concludes that Adorno is not outdated by a shift into the new spirit of postmodernity, but on the contrary should be seen as the philosopher *par excellence* of the cultural and historical developments that took place over the post-war era and into our own contemporary moment:

> in which late capitalism has all but succeeded in eliminating the final loopholes of nature and the Unconscious, of subversion and the aesthetic, of individual and collective praxis alike, and, with a final fillip, in eliminating any memory trace of what thereby no longer existed in the henceforth postmodern landscape.[80]

Under the conditions of postmodern capitalism, the domination of the subject by totalising social and political systems has only increased; it is an era that 'calls forth a much degraded subject, one defined by much diminished capabilities for autonomy and agency, so crucial to the formation of human subjectivity'.[81] This degradation of subjectivity means that late capitalist culture is a potentially catastrophic dispensation: it continues the same depredation and destruction of human subjectivity that for Adorno found its nadir at Auschwitz.

Such pronouncements might seem fatally pessimistic. But there is a point to reviving the modernist concept of totality in the putatively postmodern epoch. Through the concept of totality, it once again becomes possible to conceptualise the tension between universal and particular, subject and object, which may otherwise be lost to view in the postmodern denial of totality. Jameson writes that Adorno underscores 'the relationship between the universal and particular', which is coincident with 'the objective' ('and specifically modernist') tension 'between the social totality and its subjects'.[82] This clash between subject and society,

---

[79] Fredric Jameson, 'Afterword', in Livingstone, Anderson and Mulhern (eds), *Aesthetics and Politics*, p. 208.

[80] Fredric Jameson, *Late Marxism: Adorno, or, the Persistence of the Dialectic* (London: Verso, 2007), p. 5. Timothy Bewes, though often critical of Jameson, similarly insists on understanding late capitalism through the concept of reification. See his *Reification, or, The Anxiety of Late Capitalism* (London: Verso, 2002).

[81] David Chandler and Julian Reid, *The Neoliberal Subject: Resilience, Adaptation and Vulnerability* (London and New York: Roman and Littlefield, 2016), p. 1.

[82] Jameson, *Late Marxism*, p. 245.

as I will go on to show, is the dynamic underlying tragic form, which Lyotard believes has been superseded by postmodernity. But in his writings, Adorno places the (tragic) tension between subject and totality at the forefront of his philosophy and cultural criticism.

Subjectivity

For the Frankfurt School, Auschwitz testifies to the liquidation of the subject in modernity. This liquidation necessitates a 'turn toward the subject', as Adorno often calls it, which entails a recovery of the subjective dimension and, critically, autonomy.[83] Adorno contends that the subject furnishes 'the only point of leverage' in a totalised social order which 'might indict it as such'.[84] Yet the theory of subjectivity Adorno develops is undeniably complicated and, for some, even seems to be flatly contradictory.[85] Adorno calls for a turn to the subject and insists on the possibility (and necessity) of subjective autonomy. This, however, runs parallel with a critique of the 'total' domination of the subject in post-Auschwitz culture. How can the subject realise even a shred of autonomy if it is totally dominated by a reifying social system?

The answer lies in the way that Adorno rewrites the history of the subject and revises the notion of autonomy itself. The turn to the subject does not herald a return of the humanist subject, who rationally interprets and controls the world. Adorno is suspicious of the humanist conception of autonomy, which is a form of subjectivity that cannot simply be left 'intact' post-Auschwitz.[86] This is not only because the subject has been liquidated; the humanist conception of subjectivity also plays its own vital role in the dialectic of enlightenment. The humanistic idea that the subject has total perceptual 'access' to the object means that reality is hypostasised: the various categories posited by the subject (reason) come to seem like the only possible – indeed the only real and factual – interpretation of the object and the world. This process ultimately rebounds on the subject. Precisely insofar as it reifies the world around it, the subject finally comes to be dominated by the very

---

[83] Theodor Adorno, 'Working Through the Past', in Adorno, *Can One Live After Auschwitz?*, p. 17.
[84] Rodney Livingstone, Perry Anderson and Frances Mulhern, 'Presentation IV', in Livingstone, Anderson and Mulhern (eds), *Aesthetics and Politics*, p. 147.
[85] See also Max Pensky, 'Introduction', in Pensky, *The Actuality of Adorno*, p. 14.
[86] Theodor Adorno, 'Adorno to Benjamin', in Livingstone, Anderson and Mulhern (eds), *Aesthetics and Politics*, pp. 118–19.

categories – and by the very object(s) – over which it seems to rule so imperiously. The subject, by hypostatising reality, finally capitulates 'before the alienated predominance of things':[87]

> world domination over nature turns against the thinking subject himself; nothing is left of him but that eternally same *I think* [...] What appears to be the triumph of subjective rationality, the subjection of all reality [...] is paid for by the obedient subjection of reason to [the] directly given.[88]

The philosophical and practical response Adorno provides in the teeth of such reification is typically dialectical. The way in which the humanist subject comes to be dominated by the reality it seems to perceptually organise around itself persuades Adorno to decentre the subject – to show it is not the all-knowing centre of the world. Adorno finds a fable of decentring in the 1957 Samuel Beckett play *Endgame*, where Hamm and Clov struggle to find the centre of the room where the play is set, having skirted its outermost edges in a (failed) quest for knowledge. 'Am I right in the centre?' enquires Hamm, as it becomes obvious that the centre cannot hold – or even be found.[89] The scene reveals 'the truth that expels man from the centre of creation': that the subject is not the master in its own house, but is dominated by a closed world of objects, which surrounds and penetrates it.[90]

This aspect of critical theory aligns Adorno with poststructuralist and deconstructionist thought and its representation of the subject as formed (and disciplined) by various forms of discourse.[91] But while Adorno seeks to decentre the subject, he does not completely dissolve it by prematurely proclaiming its 'death', which is to discard the 'whole notion of a subjective dimension itself'.[92] Far from abandoning the subject, Adorno proposes to use 'the strength of the subject to break through the fallacy of constitutive subjectivity'.[93] What that entails is producing a form of subjectivity that does not involve the subject arbitrarily 'constituting' the object of perception. By disabusing the subject of the fantasy that it constitutes the object world around it, Adorno aims to show that

---

[87] Adorno, *Minima Moralia*, p. 76.
[88] Adorno and Horkheimer, *Dialectic of Enlightenment*, p. 26.
[89] Samuel Beckett, *Endgame*, in Samuel Beckett, *The Complete Works of Samuel Beckett* (London: Faber and Faber, 2006), p. 104. All references to Beckett are taken from *The Complete Works*.
[90] Adorno, *Negative Dialectics*, p. 68.
[91] See also Dews, *Logics of Disintegration* for an analysis of Adorno and poststructuralist thought.
[92] Theodor Adorno, 'Portrait of Walter Benjamin', in Theodor Adorno, *Prisms*, trans. Samuel and Sherry Weber (Cambridge, MA: MIT Press, 1983), p. 235.
[93] Adorno, *Negative Dialectics*, p. xx.

the subject is itself constituted by the object and the reified categories through which it interprets the world. This would allow the subject to perceive that it is determined by the object, as opposed to being the determining agent. With that knowledge, a gap may open between subject and object, enabling the subject to recognise its imbrication in 'the supra-ordinated concept'.[94] Adorno purposes to free the subject from a reified world of objects and, critically, with society, to 'open up critical spaces' where the subject might 'think against' the world.[95] It is that gap between subject and object, subject and world, which Adorno calls non-identity. Over and against the 'positive' dialectics of Hegel, Adorno proposes his own 'negative' dialectics, which, far from positing the uniform identity of subject and object, strives to keep the antithetical tension – the non-identity – between subject and object in play.

Adorno contends that the subject is not always completely captured – or objectified – by the social process. Just as no object fits completely with the category under which it is placed, so the subject does not fit seamlessly with any of the conceptual categories that are used to identify it. This non-identity of the subject is something that Adorno also refers to as the subjective 'share' or 'surplus' – by which he means something that outstrips the identity of the categorising process.[96] Adorno writes that 'in the needs of even the people who are covered, who are administered, there reacts something in regard to which they are not fully covered – a surplus of the subjective share, which the system has not wholly mastered'.[97] Precisely because its uncanny 'superfluity' disengages the subject from the social totality, Adorno prioritises a non-identical subject – a subject that resists identity-thinking.

Adorno does not define the surplus in a strict way, stating that it is whatever 'stirs in a man' that 'contradicts his unity'.[98] But on occasion, Adorno does relate the surplus or share to experiences of social and political rupture – even disaster. Adorno is only too aware that crises and calamities are socially intermediated by – and can even be appropriated to serve – the 'total situation'.[99] But catastrophic rupture also contradicts the utopian idea that the subject and object have reached

---

[94] Ibid.
[95] David Sherman, *Sartre and Adorno: Dialectics of Subjectivity* (New York: State University of New York Press, 2007), p. 28.
[96] Adorno, *Negative Dialectics*, p. 41.
[97] Ibid. p. 92. Adorno also uses the phrase 'addendum' (ibid. pp. 226–30).
[98] Ibid. p. 277.
[99] See also Naomi Klein, *The Shock Doctrine: The Rise of Disaster Capitalism* (London: Penguin, 2007). I return to the idea of disaster capitalism when I consider *The Gods Weep*.

a congruent state of reconciled identity. Such experiences testify to a lack of fit between the subject and object and the conflicted state of a society that would otherwise seek to universalise itself by interpolating all subjects into the social totality.

This conceptualisation of the surplus speaks to the way that the word 'catastrophe' takes on a variety of potential meanings in critical theory.[100] Adorno makes the case that post-Auschwitz society is marked by permanent catastrophe – the continuing destruction of subjectivity in modernity, where the 'individual disappears before the apparatus'.[101] But catastrophe can also connote experiences of rupture – and particularly aesthetic rupture – in an otherwise closed social world that endlessly reproduces itself by reifying subjectivity. These disruptive experiences of crisis and upheaval – the sudden subversions of catastrophe – may serve to dislocate the subject from society, allowing for a critical, negative perspective on totality. These valences around the word catastrophe reveal the influence of Walter Benjamin, who writes in his 'Theses on the Philosophy of History' that the history of progress constitutes a 'single' unfolding 'catastrophe', but also forcefully insists on moments of profound catastrophic rupture that might 'blast' the subject out of 'the continuum of history'.[102]

This reinterpretation of subjectivity has profound implications for the notion of autonomy. Adorno does not imagine freedom as a 'positive' state, where the (humanist) subject freely determines itself as s/he wishes, realising its reason and free will in the world. He conceives of autonomy negatively, as the power of refusal. Jameson provides an eloquent synopsis of the type of autonomy Adorno means, writing in his *Marxism and Form* that

> wherever the concept of freedom is once more understood, it always comes as the awakening of dissatisfaction in the midst of all that is – at one, that is, with the birth of the negative itself: never a state that is enjoyed, or a mental construction that is contemplated, but rather an ontological impatience in which the constraining situation is for the first time perceived in the very moment in which it is refused [. . .] It is not too much to say that the concept of freedom permits us to transcend [. . .] the most fundamental contradictions in modern existence.[103]

---

[100] I discuss the meaning(s) of catastrophe again in Chapter 2.
[101] Adorno and Horkheimer, *Dialectic of Enlightenment*, p. xiv.
[102] Walter Benjamin, 'Theses on the Philosophy of History', in Walter Benjamin, *Illuminations*, ed. Hannah Arendt, trans. Harry Zorn (London: Pimlico, 1999), p. 249 and p. 254.
[103] Fredric Jameson, *Marxism and Form* (Princeton: Princeton University Press, 1971), pp. 84–5.

Freedom is coincident with the 'birth of the negative', the dissatisfaction with – and resistance to – the social totality with which the subject is confronted. Adorno writes in *Negative Dialectics* that freedom turns concrete 'in negation only, corresponding to the concrete form of a specific unfreedom'.[104] The basis of Adornian non-identity and freedom is the deep, totalising system Adorno equates with Auschwitz and post-Auschwitz rationality. To gain freedom it is up to the subject to continually break the grip of identity-categories that 'circulate within the (now globalized) capitalist life-world, be it in the rather abstract domains of philosophy, or in the repetitive and recombinant practices of the "culture industry"'.[105]

Identity Politics

The idea of the 'reified identities that circulate in the capitalist life-world' brings up the fraught question of the relationship between identity-thinking and modern identity politics – a form of political thought and action which, as I set out in the Introduction, has often conditioned (and been conditioned by) particular approaches to appropriation. I do not want to deny the social and political gains of various movements motivated by identity and nor do I want to downplay the reactionary forces that have contested the representation of marginalised peoples, not least in the wake of the #MeToo and the Black Lives Matter movements – and the resistance both have met from right-wing and fascist agitation.[106] But from a Frankfurt School perspective, there is a question as to whether identity politics truly challenges identity-thinking and the desubjectifying process of modernity.

For present purposes, the concept of identity politics can be defined as a tendency for those belonging to a specific (and usually marginalised) gender, sexuality, race or religion to form ideological coalitions and social movements to strive for political representation, based on shared but usually disregarded experiences.[107] This form of political identity can be historicised as part of a wider shift away from humanist notions

---

[104] Adorno, *Negative Dialectics*, p. 231.
[105] Bradley J. McDonald, 'Theodor Adorno, Alterglobalization, and Non-identity Politics', *New Political Science*, 34:3 (2012), p. 328.
[106] For a compelling study of contemporary identity politics, see Asad Haider, *Mistaken Identity: Race and Class in the Age of Trump* (London: Verso, 2018).
[107] See also Cressida Hayes, 'Identity Politics', <https://plato.stanford.edu/archives/sum2016/entries/identity-politics/> (accessed 24 April 2017).

of the subject – which shape white, patriarchal European Enlightenment thought – to a more socially and politically diverse postmodern society, with its transition from reifying Western metanarratives to fragmented language-games. Such politicised conceptions of subjectivity show that the metanarrative of the human subject is phallo-, hetero-, Euro- and ethnocentric. This has meant challenging the non-representational status of post-Enlightenment social and political institutions, which build themselves around (putatively) 'universal' humanist principles of freedom and equality.

Adorno does not deny that the autonomous, humanist subject of enlightened rationality has historically been gendered – not to say sexualised and racialised, culminating in the Nazi vision of the racially and sexually 'pure' masculinity of the blue-eyed, blonde-haired Aryan. This means, as Adorno writes in *Minima Moralia*, that historically women have borne the 'the negative imprint of domination', while Adorno is similarly aware of the way in which other oppressed or marginalised sections of society bear the negative imprint of domination – not least European Jews.[108] There is a deep-seated relationship between totality and various forms of social injustice.

For the most part, however, critics are not necessarily wrong to insist that gender, sexuality and race do not always represent a political or theoretical priority for Adorno, as reflected in the rift between Adorno and the radical student and social movements that emerged over the 1960s.[109] Despite its emancipatory aims, identity politics can itself be seen as a variety of identity-thinking, whereby the (particular) subject is understood as representative of a (universal) category. The problem with identity politics is that it risks reiterating the form of reasoning found in 'the administered world', where the subject is subsumed under various conceptual categories (man/woman, heterosexual/homosexual, black/white and so on) – however intersectionally these identities may be imagined.[110] The danger is that totalising appeals about the meaning

---

[108] Adorno, *Minima Moralia*, p. 95.

[109] See John Abromeit, 'Limits of Praxis: The Social-Psychological Foundations of Theodor Adorno's and Herbert Marcuse's Interpretations of the 1960s Protest Movements', in Belinda Davis et al. (eds), *Changing the World, Changing Oneself* (New York and Oxford: Berghahn Books, 2012), pp. 13–40.

[110] Adorno, 'Education After Auschwitz', in Adorno, *Can One Live After Auschwitz?*, p. 21. For more on Adorno and feminism, see Renee J. Heberle (ed.), *Feminist Interpretations of Theodor Adorno* (Pennsylvania: Pennsylvania University Press, 2006). See also Rei Terada, *Looking Away: Phenomenality and Dissatisfaction, Kant to Adorno* (Cambridge, MA: Harvard University Press, 2009) for a queer Adorno. For work dealing with Adorno and postcolonialism,

of politically laden experiences to diverse people risks obscuring the singularity of the subject supposed to be 'representative', even reinforcing categories that have often been pre-established by instrumental reason.[111] What is required for Adorno is not an identity politics, but a non-identity politics. The political aspect of the subject lies precisely in its refusal to wholly identify with any prescribed categorisation. The political emerges as the capacity to reflect and contest.

It may even be the case that, in its less disruptively radical social and political forms, the concern with identity has been co-opted by the totalisation of the commodity-form under late global capital – a point that has also been made by Alexandra Chasin.[112] Moishe Postone echoes Jameson on the nature of postmodernity when he writes of identity:

> The contemporary hypostatization of difference, heterogeneity, and hybridity, does not necessarily point beyond capitalism, but can serve to veil and legitimate a new global form that combines decentralization and heterogeneity of production and consumption with increasing centralization of control and underlying homogeneity.[113]

The stress that Adorno lays on the non-identity of the subject, over and above its possible identifications, is perhaps more and not less relevant in the culturally diverse milieu of capitalist globalisation. It is a provocative thesis, but if the non-identity of the subject relies on its ability to resist the identities that 'circulate within the (now globalized) capitalist life-world', identity politics might be thought of as inhibiting, as opposed to enabling, the autonomy of the subject. Such freedom is for Adorno crucially reliant on a realm of human experience and creativity that, despite the Culture Industry, retains some negative force – the aesthetic sphere.

---

see Robert Spencer, 'Thoughts from Abroad: Theodor Adorno as Postcolonial Theorist', *Culture, Theory and Critique*, 51:3 (2010), pp. 207–21.

[111] Anthony Appiah, 'Identity, Authenticity, Survival: Multicultural Societies and Social Reproduction', in Amy Gutmann and Charles Taylor (eds), *Multiculturalism* (Princeton: Princeton University Press, 1994), pp. 149–64. Dvora Yanow has analysed the questions around political activism based on a pre-established, externally imposed categorisation. See her *Constructing 'Race' and 'Ethnicity' in America: Category Making in Public Policy and Administration* (Oxford: Routledge, 2015).

[112] See Alexandra Chasin, *Selling Out: The Gay and Lesbian Movement Goes to Market* (Basingstoke and New York: Palgrave Macmillan, 2001).

[113] Moishe Postone, 'Theorizing the Contemporary World: Robert Brenner, Giovanni Arrighi, David Harvey', in Robert Albritton, Robert Jessop and Richard Westra (eds), *Political Economy and Global Capitalism: The 21st Century, Present and Future* (London: Anthem Press, 2007), p. 22.

Aesthetics

Despite his often-quoted proclamation that 'To write poetry after Auschwitz is barbaric' – a formulation he would revise and partially refute due to the confusion it seemed to cause – no twentieth-century philosopher reflected as deeply about the implications of the catastrophe of Auschwitz for aesthetics than Adorno, whose magnum opus, *Aesthetic Theory*, was posthumously published in 1970.[114] Adorno states that, in 'the wake of the European catastrophes', the ostensibly 'apolitical' world of aesthetics and the artwork it interprets is undergoing 'a crisis'.[115] Most of all, Auschwitz problematises the priorities of Enlightenment aesthetics – represented most powerfully by Kant and Hegel – which are no longer valid.

Adorno observes that aesthetics has traditionally prioritised notions of unity and harmony in its reflections on beauty. This harmony is usually understood through the relation of 'whole' and 'part'. For most Enlightenment philosophies, the more 'beautiful' artworks are those which harmoniously unify the various parts that make up the work into a sensuously pleasing whole, with artworks becoming more and more 'beautiful' throughout human history. The progress of art over time reflects a wider faith in the possibility of human development. Through its harmonious reconciliation of its parts, art concretises universal history, adumbrating a more 'ideal' realm where particular and universal find synthesis.

Adorno contends that a harmonious aesthetic relation between whole and part is no longer possible (or desirable) 'after' Auschwitz. With the totalised system of the concentration camp in mind, Adorno is suspicious of any system – social or aesthetic – that subsumes the part (particular) under the whole (universal). Adorno believes that a form which prioritises the universal risks destroying the particular in its drive for ever-closer integration. By making the case that aesthetic unity amounts to the identity of particular and universal, Adorno contends that the 'task of aesthetics today' is nothing short of the 'historical suspension of aesthetic harmony altogether'.[116] This allows for a more nuanced understanding of the so-called 'barbarity' of poetry after Auschwitz. Adorno is not saying that all art – all *poesies* – is compromised by Auschwitz. His

---

[114] Theodor Adorno, 'Cultural Criticism and Society', in Adorno, *Prisms*, p. 34. Adorno clarifies his point in *Negative Dialectics*, pp. 362–3.
[115] Adorno, *Aesthetic Theory*, p. 239.
[116] Ibid. p. 170 and p. 145.

argument relates to the 'traditional concept of the poetic' as 'something categorically higher and sacred' – the idea that art mimics in its form a perfected ideal realm where particular and universal find harmonious synthesis.[117] Auschwitz renders such art – 'before' and 'after' the catastrophe – 'barbaric':

> The mistake of traditional aesthetics is that it exalts the relationship of the whole to the parts to one of entire wholeness, to totality, and hoists it in triumph over the heterogeneous as a banner of illusory positivity [...] The dubiousness of the closed society applies equally to that of the closed artwork.[118]

After the unprecedented catastrophes of post-Enlightenment modernity, 'art that makes the highest claim compels itself beyond form as totality and into the fragmentary'.[119] This 'claim' has to do with the way that fragmented artworks allow for the aesthetic release of the particular – the part – from the whole, from the 'spell' of identity. These works disallow the unified harmony envisaged in previous conceptions of aesthetics and, by virtue of fragmentation, invalidate the idea that art provides a semblance of the historical synthesis of subject and object. 'What appears in art is no longer the ideal, no longer harmony', writes Adorno: 'the locus of its power of resolution is now exclusively in the contradictory and the dissonant'.[120]

Works of art cannot 'return to peace and order' post-Auschwitz, to 'affirmative replication and harmony'.[121] What is required is 'a radically darkened art'.[122] This is not to say that, to reflect harrowing events, art should be depressing, or even more banally, 'sad'.[123] It is to say, however, that the artwork should follow the 'necessity of going to the extreme'.[124] It can only do so by violating its own formal closure, by refusing resolution and insisting on contradiction. Through formal closure, the various contradictions to be found in a work of art are artificially resolved, a displaced echo of the social violence that typifies modernity. Adorno prioritises artworks that disavow every last possible trace of reconciliation, where 'form tends to dissociate unity', drawing a distinction

---

[117] Ibid. pp. 21–2.
[118] Ibid. p. 206.
[119] Ibid. p. 193.
[120] Ibid. p. 111.
[121] Ibid. p. 338.
[122] Ibid. p. 50.
[123] See also Adorno, 'Is Art Lighthearted?', in Adorno, *Notes to Literature: Volume Two*, pp. 247–53.
[124] Adorno, *Aesthetic Theory*, p. 44.

between 'open' (authentic) and 'closed' (inauthentic) aesthetic forms.[125] Where closed forms reflect a closed society by enforcing integration, open forms – which eschew resolution – indict both closed aesthetic forms and the notion of harmonious integration itself. The open form retains the unreconciled antagonism of the universal and particular, so that 'art takes into itself the impossibility of the unity of the one and the many' – an insight relevant to post-Auschwitz tragedy, where the clash between subject and society ('the one and the many') goes unresolved.[126]

Adorno contends that 'explosion' is one of the 'invariants' of open forms, writing that open works have 'blasted away the overarching form' through which part and whole otherwise 'cohere' and where it is 'the catastrophic instant that destroys temporal continuity'.[127] What Adorno privileges in his analysis of post-Auschwitz art is an aesthetic of catastrophe, which shatters formal harmony. Unity 'dissolves in a catastrophe', writes Adorno, which is bound up with the impossibility of bringing antagonisms into 'equilibrium': the catastrophic 'negation of synthesis' becomes in post-Holocaust artworks 'a principle of form'.[128] These catastrophic aesthetic forms also lay the ground for the 'social explosiveness' of art.[129] Adorno contends that the formally fragmented artwork resists not only the false totality of closed aesthetic form, but its own inscription into the wider social totality. Through its dissonant form, the artwork unleashes 'the fleeting, the ephemeral and the transitory in a form that is immune to reification'.[130] This means that authentic works provide a negative, inverse image of a social system that seeks everywhere to unify whole and part, universal and particular, object and subject. The work of art stands critically opposed to a homogeneous social world that perpetuates itself by reducing everything to identity.

This is where the 'autonomy' of the aesthetic resides.[131] The idea of aesthetic autonomy requires clarification. Adorno does not believe that the artwork subsists in some sort of rarefied sphere 'beyond' society. He concedes that artworks are material products of society informed by the cultural specificities of time and place. He also recognises that 'aesthetics' as a branch of thought has a specific historical genealogy, as evidenced by the (relatively late) usage of the word in relation to

---

[125] Ibid. p. 108 and p. 206.
[126] Ibid. p. 245.
[127] Ibid. p. 29, p. 142 and p. 29.
[128] Ibid. p. 112 and p. 203.
[129] Ibid. p. 298.
[130] Ibid. p. 286.
[131] Ibid. p. 1.

modern art theory.¹³² But that is not to say that the artwork or the aesthetic sphere is completely reducible to the determinations of society and history. The artwork has a relation to wider society analogous to that of the subject: it is a product of society, but it is also able to realise its autonomy by negating society, which it does through its fragmentary form. This negation of totality underpins the 'metaphysics of art', as Adorno calls it – its partial transcendence of the immanent material and social world.[133]

The notion that artworks open a perspective beyond the social totality persuades Adorno to dismiss those artworks that reflect social reality – or the world as it is. Adorno denounces 'dull-minded doctrines of aesthetic realism' that would strive to reflect (and reflect on) topical social and historical events, as opposed to challenging totality through aesthetic form.[134] This notion also (and relatedly) prompts Adorno to dismiss artworks that are socially and politically 'engaged', or that seek to promulgate a social and political 'message' – something Adorno accuses Brechtian theatre of doing.[135] 'The view of art as politically engaged or didactic', contends Adorno, 'integrates art into the reality it opposes'.[136] This compromises the autonomy of the aesthetic and sinks art into a social world characterised by total fungibility, as the singularity of the work of art is compromised by turning it into an iteration of something else, a political proposition. This paradoxically aligns politically engaged art with the Culture Industry, which similarly integrates the subject into the social totality.

This critique of politically engaged art does not mean that Adorno conceives of works of art as apolitical. He insists that art does have distinct social and political ramifications. This, however, arises from its fragmented form, not from its content. 'Art is not a matter of pointing up alternatives' writes Adorno, 'but rather of resisting, solely through artistic form, the course of the world, which continues to hold a pistol to the heads of human beings.'[137] Precisely by virtue of its refusal to 'engage', the artwork negates a social and political world that has become totalised. This goes some way to clarifying why Adorno similarly refused to adopt a clear-cut position on political action. It also sheds light on his decision

---

[132] Adorno reflects primarily on the development of art theory in relation to the idea of natural beauty (ibid. p. 81).
[133] Ibid. p. 173.
[134] Ibid. p. 120.
[135] Ibid. pp. 316–17.
[136] Ibid. p. 114.
[137] Theodor Adorno, 'Commitment', in Adorno, *Can One Live after Auschwitz?*, p. 244.

to deploy a fragmented and aphoristic writing style (*Darstellung*) in his own philosophical reflections. His sometimes fractured, sometimes dense style is intended to be resistant to integration and the pitfalls of a holistic philosophical 'system', where discrete observations all serve to underwrite a binding whole.[138] Lyotard famously calls it a 'writing of the ruins' – a form of writing that responds to the destruction wrought in the Second World War while also embracing fragmentation.[139]

The disconcerting irony of politically committed art is that it integrates subjects into the society it sets out to critique. This is precisely the opposite of authentic aesthetic experience, as Adorno understands it. Adorno makes the case that aesthetic experience is ecstatic and individuating, that it momentarily throws the subject beside him or herself and outside of the collective parameters of the social totality. This – once again – results from the way the artwork fragments itself. By denying reconciliatory synthesis, the artwork releases its parts from an overarching whole. This means that 'in art one experiences something singular, something particular in its necessity'.[140] The fragmented work of art cannot be reduced to a totalising concept; it is up to the viewer to self-reflexively interpret the work without recourse to the shared categories of understanding derived from the social totality. This severs the subject from a reified world of conceptual identity, so the subject 'becomes aware of itself as a negativity', which 'no fiction of a positive community can abolish'.[141]

The autonomy of the aesthetic serves to catalyse the autonomy of the subject. This form of aesthetic response sometimes goes under the enigmatic name of 'the shudder'.[142] It is a phrase Adorno uses to try and capture the disequilibrium caused by artworks that cannot be determined by the usual categories of identity-thinking. By challenging the subject with something that cannot be rationally determined, the fragmented artwork occasions a more ambiguous reaction, which pushes the shuddering subject (however fractionally) out of the wider conceptual order. The shudder, writes Adorno in *Aesthetic Theory*, is a form of affect that is 'radically opposed to the conventional idea of experience'; 'it is the

---

[138] See also Steven Helmling, *Adorno's Poetics of Critique* (London: Continuum, 2009).

[139] Jean-François Lyotard, *Heidegger and 'the jews'*, trans. Andreas Michel and Mark Roberts (Minneapolis: University of Minnesota Press, 1988), p. 43.

[140] Bowie, *Adorno and the Ends of Philosophy*, p. 164.

[141] Theodor Adorno, 'Parataxis: On Hölderlin's Late Poetry', in Adorno, *Notes to Literature: Volume Two*, p. 127.

[142] Adorno, *Aesthetic Theory*, p. 418. Adorno writes that 'aesthetic comportment is to be defined as the capacity to shudder' (ibid).

moment of being shaken': 'Consciousness without shudder is reified consciousness'.[143] James Hellings has called it *'the shock of the unintelligible'*, which 'finally emancipates the subjectivity of the spectator'.[144] It has to be said, however, that Adorno does not empirically 'evidence' his claims about aesthetic response. His imagined aesthetic subject is more of an exemplar or ideal, arising from his conception of formal disunity and fragmentation.

Late Modernism

These reflections on the disintegration of aesthetic form occasion a 'turn' to the friable and fragmentary forms of modernist art, which Adorno tends to favour in his writings – most notably in the atonal and dissonant works of Kafka, Beckett, Schoenberg and Picasso. Adorno laments the dwindling of the modernist tradition and complains of the 'loss of tension in post-war art, much of which goes slack the moment it appears'.[145] To historically and philosophically 'place' Adorno, I use the category 'late modernism'. I understand late modernism as an iteration of modernism that was made possible by the critical retheorisation of modernism in the post-war period – or 'after' Auschwitz.[146] Where 'high' (or as Jameson sometimes calls it, 'classic') pre-war modernism often embraced mythic ideas around national 'unity' with a simultaneous investment in the possibility of social and scientific progress, late modernism brings those values into question in the face of the catastrophe of the Second World War and Nazism. This precipitates a shift towards aesthetic disintegration, as opposed to the unity and coherence of form concomitant with classic modernism.

This transition obviously has parallels with postmodern aesthetics, which is similarly understood in terms of fragmentation, disallowing metanarratives and the totalisation of whole and part.[147] Jameson con-

---

[143] Ibid. p. 319, p. 318 and p. 418.
[144] James Hellings, *Adorno and Art: Aesthetic Theory Contra Critical Theory* (Basingstoke: Palgrave Macmillan, 2014), p. 103 and p. 104.
[145] Adorno, *Aesthetic Theory*, p. 240.
[146] My choice of late modernism is partly inspired by Fredric Jameson and his *A Singular Modernity* (London: Verso, 2012) – though Jameson uses the phrase more critically than I do. See especially pp. 161–79. Adorno also uses the phrase 'late modernism' in *Aesthetic Theory*, though he does so to make a distinct point about unity versus fragmentation (p. 135).
[147] For a classic take on postmodern (anti-)aesthetics and its relation to modernism, see Hal Foster (ed.), *Postmodern Culture* (London: Pluto Press, 1985).

tends that postmodernism is epitomised by the collapse of the traditional distinction between 'high' and 'low' culture, techniques of pastiche and parody, the cannibalisation of past styles, the play of random stylistic allusion, and a loss of the feeling of social alienation and a more schizophrenic consciousness, which embraces the synchronic understanding of time and space in modern consumer capitalism.[148]

But late modernism and postmodernism are also qualitatively distinct. The problem with postmodern aesthetics is that it risks formally reiterating the total reification of historical and cultural life in post-Auschwitz society. Jameson makes the case that, precisely by virtue of its collapse of all sorts of qualitative distinctions, postmodern aesthetics reflects and enables the system of universal equivalence that reigns in the totalised world of late capitalism. He contends that the cultural practice of postmodernism concretises a field of stylistic and discursive heterogeneity that ultimately obscures an underlying homogeneity – the social totality. This, critically, leaves little room for formulations of subjectivity and autonomy. This is no doubt consistent with a postmodernist and poststructuralist worldview that would seek to deny the idea that the subject (or indeed the artwork) is an autonomous entity, but is composed of heteroglot discourses (language-games) which collapse the modernist subject–object dialectic. But the denial of the subjective dimension in postmodern aesthetics also tends to foreclose the possibility of resisting a reified totality which, more often than not, postmodern theory disavows.

This is where late modernism might be seen as a potential 'corrective' to postmodernism. Unlike postmodernism, late modernist aesthetics remains suspicious of mass society and culture and, as a consequence, seeks to retain the autonomy of the aesthetic and the subject in post-Auschwitz life.[149] This formalisation of the autonomy of the subject over and against society means that late modernism has obvious parallels with tragic form. Christopher Butler writes that 'modernism has a close affinity to the conflicts of the tragic tradition', as modernist art prioritises a subjectivity that is opposed to 'any political or institutional forces'.[150] Despite that status, however, Adorno is wary of the notion of post-war tragedy, which 'after' Auschwitz he understands to be a historically invalid form.

---

[148] See in particular Jameson, *Postmodernism, or, The Cultural Logic of Late Capitalism*.

[149] See also Robert Genter, *Late Modernism: Art, Culture, and Politics in Cold War America* (Philadelphia: University of Pennsylvania Press, 2010).

[150] Christopher Butler, *Modernism: A Very Short Introduction* (Oxford: Oxford University Press, 2010), p. 44 and p. 66.

Tragedy

The idea of post-Auschwitz tragedy may, for Adorno, be something of an oxymoron. Adorno contends that Auschwitz renders tragedy problematic because, historically, tragic form relies on a tension between the subject (individual) and object (society) which is increasingly being nullified in post-Auschwitz culture. Auschwitz testifies to the reification of subjectivity in modernity and, as such, similarly testifies to the possible 'death' of tragedy as a viable idiom.[151] 'This liquidation of tragedy', write Adorno and Horkheimer, 'confirms the abolition of the individual.'[152]

Adorno clarifies his theory concerning the negative relation between artwork and society by analysing the dialectic between the content and form of classical tragedy. It might be that Greek tragedy depicted, as its thematic content, the same violent events that took place in society; but the deeper relation between society and tragedy is adumbrated by its form:

> It is possible to argue over how much Attic tragedy, including those by Euripides, took part in the violent social conflicts of the epoch; however, the basic tendency of tragic form, in contrast to its mythical subjects, the dissolution of the spell of fate and the birth of subjectivity, bears witness as much to social emancipation from feudal familial ties as, in the collision between mythical law and subjectivity, to the antagonism between fateful domination and a humanity awakening to maturity. That this antagonism, as well as the historicophilosophical tendency, became an *a priori* of form rather than being treated simply as thematic material, endowed tragedy with its social substantiality.[153]

The social 'substance' of tragedy, as captured in its form, is the opposition between subject and society, where 'mythical law and subjectivity' and 'the antagonism between fateful domination and a humanity awakening to maturity' is concretised in the clash between conflicting social forces. The language recalls that of the *Dialectic of Enlightenment*. It is vital to recall, however, that 'enlightenment' is not a strictly historical category in Adornian thinking, to be identified with the era known as the

---

[151] *Dialectic of Enlightenment*, p. 154. George Steiner also insists that tragedy is a defunct form – though for him the death of tragedy is a result of the historical rise of 'positive' ideologies like Christianity and Marxism. See his *The Death of Tragedy* (New Haven: Yale University Press, 1996) and, for a reconsideration, '"Tragedy", Reconsidered', *New Literary History*, 35:1 (2005), pp. 1–15.
[152] Adorno and Horkheimer, *Dialectic of Enlightenment*, p. 154.
[153] Adorno, *Aesthetic Theory*, p. 303.

Enlightenment, but a tendency with deep roots in Western civilisation. Greek tragedy formalises the collision between the fateful domination of the object world (society) and the autonomy of the tragic protagonist (subject) – a clash that becomes increasingly pronounced in modern European society and its art. The collision between subject and society is for Adorno 'the basic tendency' of Western tragic drama from the Greeks onwards and is an *a priori* of the form *per se*, similarly discernible in subsequent iterations of tragic form – including the tragedies of Shakespeare.[154]

This is not to say that Adorno collapses the historical distance between Greek and Shakespearean tragedy, or that he proposes a universal concept of the tragic that might sublate its particular historical and formal iterations – a form of identity-thinking. Adorno gives due consideration to the historical conditions inflecting tragedy over time while retaining a consciousness of the ideational ties between discrete forms. While a universal theory of the tragic cannot be formulated, there are nevertheless similarities – or as Terry Eagleton puts it, 'family resemblances' – that pertain over time.[155] The split between subject and society is something that Adorno takes to be an integral aspect of tragic form in its various historical guises – so much so that 'tragedy' is impossible, or abolished, without it.

While he insists that the dialectic between subject and society is the driving principle of tragic form, Adorno is under no illusions about the usual result of that clash. Adorno is aware that tragic drama frequently ends with the demise of the tragic 'hero', whose death results from hubristically transgressing the inherited norms and values of the community. This vision of the tragic is confirmed in tragic theory – most obviously as it is found in German Idealism. Peter Szondi observes that the philosophy of the tragic in German thought more or less coincides with the Enlightenment era. Szondi contends that tragedy provides Enlightenment philosophers with a formal paradigm for the dialectical synthesis of forces which are otherwise in contradiction – namely subject and society.[156] It is an understanding of tragedy partly built on Aristotle.

---

[154] See also Garrett Sullivan, 'Tragic Subjectivities', in Emma Smith and Garrett Sullivan (eds), *The Cambridge Companion to English Renaissance Tragedy* (Cambridge: Cambridge University Press, 2010), pp. 73–85. Sullivan writes: 'Early modern tragic subjectivity is created out of the collision between the individual and the social order' (p. 73).

[155] Terry Eagleton, *Sweet Violence: The Idea of the Tragic* (Oxford: Blackwell, 2003), p. 3.

[156] Peter Szondi, *An Essay on The Tragic*, trans. Paul Fleming (Stanford: Stanford University Press, 2002).

Though perhaps most famous for his notion of catharsis, where tragic incidents arousing pity and fear allow for the safe 'purgation' of anti-social feelings, Aristotle also provides an analysis of tragic form. He makes the case that tragedy should depict the downfall of the tragic hero, who – via a process of revelation and recognition (*anagnorisis*) about the dominant powers of fate or the divine – undergoes a change 'from ignorance to awareness'.[157] It is not always necessary for the hero to die in a tragedy; but if the hero does survive, there should be a resolution in which the hero recognises and reconciles him or herself to prevailing forces beyond intervention.

Hegel, writing in the *Phenomenology of Spirit*, draws on Aristotle to contend that tragic form depicts the clash between civic and ethical society – represented by the Chorus – and the individual, represented by the tragic protagonist.[158] Where the institutions of the state represent and enshrine the freedoms of all, the tragic protagonist – by pursuing a particular claim over and above the state – privileges his/her individual freedom. Either the tragic hero recognises the predominant claim of the state and reconciliation between the subject (individual) and object (society) is formalised, or the individual is destroyed. 'Life proceeds to negation and its grief', insists Hegel: 'Only by the cancellation of such negation in itself does life become affirmative' and 'it is true that if it remains in mere contradiction, without resolving it, then on contradiction it is wrecked'.[159] The universal ultimately must prevail over the particular if contradiction is to be overcome.[160]

The idealist reading of tragedy which insists on formal reconciliation and resolution is deeply suspicious for Adorno and the rest of the Frankfurt School. The idea that the tragic hero (particular) is finally integrated in, or destroyed by, society (universal) is no doubt consistent for a philosophy which posits that historical progress proceeds via the 'negation of the negation'. Such a reading has, however, become problematic 'after' the event of Auschwitz, where the progress of reason led – not to the final synthesis of subject and object – but to the Final

---

[157] Aristotle, *Poetics*, trans. Gerald Franck Else (Ann Arbor: University of Michigan Press, 1967), p. 21.
[158] See Hegel, *Phenomenology of Spirit*, pp. 439–53.
[159] Georg Wilhelm Friedrich Hegel, *Aesthetics: Volume One*, trans. T. M. Knox (Oxford: Oxford University Press, 1975), p. 97.
[160] See also Martin Thibodeau, *Hegel and Greek Tragedy*, trans. Hans Jakob Wilhelm (New York and Plymouth: Lexington Books, 2013), particularly pp. 160–3.

Solution and the complete 'liquidation' of subjectivity. 'The annihilation of the individual', as Adorno contends, 'is no longer transcended positivity.'[161]

The historical fate of the subject and tragedy 'after' Auschwitz is for Adorno most powerfully revealed in the plays of his favourite playwright, Beckett. Adorno contends that the damaged and incapacitated characters found in Beckett testify to the liquidation of subjectivity – and so the impossibility of tragedy – in post-Auschwitz life.[162] Adorno makes the case that Beckett 'writes the comedy of the tragic'.[163] His plays represent the complete collapse of the tragic subject, who is transformed into a useless and reviled comic figure. This diminution of the voluntaristic subject of tragedy into a clownish failure is reflected in the way *Endgame* reduces the name 'Hamlet' to the porcine 'Hamm' – though Beckett disagreed with that reading and was frustrated when Adorno chose to pursue it publicly.[164] Adorno contends that, where *Hamlet* has been understood as witnessing 'the birth of the subject' – the 'nominalistic Shakespearean breakthrough into mortal and infinitely rich individuality' – Hamm reveals the mutilating damage that has been done to the subject, its reduction to thing-like, consumable status.[165] Through Hamm, Beckett forms a post-Holocaust response to Shakespeare that centres on the degradation of the tragic subject.

It is not simply that tragedy has 'disappeared' from post-Auschwitz life, however: it has also been misappropriated by the Culture Industry. Adorno and Horkheimer make the case that the Culture Industry does not necessarily shrink from the representation of 'tragic' suffering. What it does, however, is present that suffering as a 'fate' to which the subject falls when it flouts prevailing norms and values, to which the subject must adapt for its own self-preservation.[166] This means that tragedy becomes an institution for moral improvement and that catharsis – *à la* Aristotle – catalyses the controlled purgation of anti-social feelings: 'The doctrine of catharsis imputes to art the principle that ultimately the culture industry appropriates and administers.'[167] It is an understand-

---

[161] Adorno, *Aesthetic Theory*, p. 259.
[162] He writes: 'the catastrophes that inspire *Endgame* have shattered the individual' ('Trying to Understand *Endgame*', in Adorno, *Can One Live After Auschwitz?*, p. 267).
[163] Adorno, *Aesthetic Theory*, p. 259.
[164] See Andrea Oppo, *Philosophical Aesthetics and Samuel Beckett* (Oxford: Peter Lang, 2008), p. 136.
[165] Adorno, *Aesthetic Theory*, p. 279.
[166] Adorno and Horkheimer, *Dialectic of Enlightenment*, p. 152.
[167] Adorno, *Aesthetic Theory*, p. 311.

ing of tragic 'inevitability' that has some parallels with Brecht and his critique of conventional tragic form – though for Brecht tragedy resembles fate only because the solitary tragic hero cannot possibly oppose society alone: meaningful social and political change can only take place through concerted collective action.[168]

There is a contradiction in the way Adorno thinks about modern tragedy. On the one hand, Adorno praises Beckett for his representation of an incapacitated subject and the 'death' of tragedy. On the other, Adorno provides a profoundly sceptical reading of the representation of tragic suffering in the Culture Industry. What both forms share, however, is a denial of the properly negative, subjective dimension of tragic form. Adorno vies that Beckett represents the only adequate dramaturgical response to the Holocaust, as his plays portray the total reification of the subject – and the death of tragedy. This 'unprotesting depiction of ubiquitous regression' is perceived by Adorno as 'a protest against a state of the world that so accommodates the law of regression that it no longer has anything to hold up against it'.[169] Though purposefully paradoxical, it is not necessarily a convincing argument: it is hard to see that Beckettian drama is likely to provoke 'protest' if the very (tragic) subject required for negative critique is no longer able to contest its reification. It may be that Beckettian drama, in the same vein as the Culture Industry, transforms tragic suffering into 'fate' – an irresistible social and historical necessity to which subjects must resign or adapt.

This contradiction causes Adorno (albeit occasionally) to provide analyses of subjectivity and totality that would seem to undermine his otherwise consistent valorisation of Beckettian drama as the post-Auschwitz form *par excellence*. Adorno writes suspiciously in *Negative Dialectics* of any philosophy (or, indeed, of any work of art) that might 'confirm the sense of impotence' that typifies post-Auschwitz culture, which can only serve to reinforce 'the spell of fate'.[170] With words that could form a critique of Beckettian silence, Adorno contends that a denial of the subjective dimension can be seen to be 'directly abetting speechless domination and barbarism', precluding the negativity of the subject in 'a gesture of self-imposed muteness and vanishing'.[171] This

---

[168] This is a conception of the tragic I will return to in Chapter 4, where I discuss Bond and his *Lear*. John Gray writes of Brecht that, 'in all his dealings with tragedy, concern for the whole supresses his concern for the individual', quoted in Gritzner, *Adorno and Modern Theatre*, p. 171.
[169] Adorno, 'Trying to Understand *Endgame*', p. 266.
[170] Adorno, *Negative Dialectics*, p. 68 and p. 216.
[171] Adorno, *Aesthetic Theory*, p. 273.

undermines the possibility of even the 'tiniest bit of self-reflection by a subject pondering upon itself and its real captivity'.[172] What the reification of subjectivity in post-Auschwitz culture requires is tragic form and its split between subject and society, which recognises the suffering, and freedom, of the subject.

Despite the absence of a fully articulated tragic theory in his writings, tragedy and autonomy, both subjective and aesthetic, are deeply intertwined in Adornian thinking. Adorno makes the (admittedly speculative) case that tragedy 'may have been the origin of the idea of aesthetic autonomy'.[173] This originating status lies in the way that tragedy can be seen as 'an afterimage of cultic acts'.[174] The cultic acts Adorno refers to are sacrificial. Adorno contends that, in pre-modern, myth-based societies, ritualised sacrifice was seen as performing the role of appeasing otherwise uncontrollable divine forces and ensuring the continued survival of the community as a whole. This scapegoating continues into tragedy, only now the 'sacrifice' is of the tragic hero, who transgresses the ethical norms of the body politic and threatens the survival of the *polis*. The eventual 'sacrifice' – or failing that, reintegration – of the hero is necessary if the social whole and the civic life of the *polis* is to be preserved. Part of the problem with post-Auschwitz culture is that it demands 'the introversion of sacrifice', as Adorno and Horkheimer call it, where the individual actively 'sacrifices' aspects of his or her self that do not conform to society.[175] This disallows non-identity from the outset: the opposition between subject and society is pre-empted and tragedy thwarted.

Adorno contends that sacrifice generates a dialectical relation between subject and object, particular and universal. On the one hand, the sacrifice is a cipher for the community as a whole – a sort of 'stand-in' to expiate the wrongs of the politic. On the other hand, the sacrifice is uniquely singular, an entity nothing else can take the place of in the ritual. The sacrifice is both exchangeable and non-exchangeable; or, perhaps more precisely, the sacrifice becomes non-exchangeable even in the act of its exchange. The sacrifice exhibits the 'non-specifty of the example' and so conforms to the norms of categorical reason; but it also embodies the uniqueness of the 'chosen one', which 'marks it off' and makes it 'unfit for exchange'.[176]

The notion of sacrifice is vital for Adorno because it allows for a

---

[172] Adorno, *Negative Dialectics*, p. 68.
[173] Adorno, *Aesthetic Theory*, p. 8.
[174] Ibid.
[175] Adorno and Horkheimer, *Dialectic of Enlightenment*, p. 55.
[176] Ibid. p. 10.

properly social and historical understanding of autonomy. The sacrifice, for Adorno, is social by its opposition to society.[177] This dialectic continues into tragedy, which formalises the autonomy of the subject, its release from the domination of society – even if that autonomy is revoked by his or her sacrificial death. It also lays the foundations for the autonomy of the aesthetic, whereby 'the emancipation of the subject in art is the emancipation of the autonomy of art'.[178] Though not always stated explicitly, the alignment between tragedy, subjectivity, aesthetics and autonomy is critical to Adorno: tragedy originates the autonomy, not only of the subject, but also the aesthetic, which might resist the totalisations of modern social and political life.

The critique of conventional tragic synthesis – and indeed, aesthetic resolution *per se* – and the introversion of sacrifice serves to adumbrate a conception of tragedy in which the antagonism between subject and society remains intact, as opposed to being nullified by formal closure. Far from upholding reconciliation, a conception of the tragic informed (though not necessarily advocated) by Adorno would refuse the sacrificial process of resolution, keeping the tension between the tragic 'hero' and society unresolved by insisting on a subject who refuses the need to identify, to reconcile with the collective. This would mean a tragic subject who violates aesthetic closure, instantiating precisely the type of open-ended aesthetic form Adorno calls for in response to post-Auschwitz totality. Where aesthetic fragmentation occasions the autonomy of the viewer, the tragic hero who upends resolution can even be thought of as catalysing subjective freedom – a point I return to throughout the case studies. It is such a form of tragic drama that I have described as 'catastrophic'.

Conclusion

Adorno may not make a case for a post-Auschwitz tragic, but his writings still adumbrate a conception of tragedy. Tragedy prioritises – and for Adorno, is partly historically responsible for – freedom, the autonomy of the subject and the aesthetic. But the critique of conventional tragic synthesis – and indeed, aesthetic resolution *per se* – along with his conception of negative dialectics, non-identity and the introversion of sacrifice all signify that a post-Auschwitz tragic should avoid reconciliation

---

[177] I take the phrase from *Aesthetic Theory*, where Adorno uses it about the artwork (p. 296).
[178] Ibid. p. 257.

and remain formally open-ended, as opposed to providing a 'concealed meaning in the sense of redemption or closure'.[179] No final synthesis (or final solution) between whole and part, universal and particular, object and subject can be realised. This post-Auschwitz conception of the tragic preserves a dramaturgy and discourse of the subject, whose suffering (and indeed freedom) cannot be 'positively' negated by the process of closure, which – as Adorno understands it – obscures the individual in favour of the general, formally reiterating the idealist progress of history towards its *telos*.

'To save the tragic from the limits set to it by a redundant dramatic form', contends Marku Nivalainen, 'it is necessary to find the modern locus of the tragic outside the traditional forms of tragic art.'[180] The idea that the canonical Shakespeare has been the 'locus' where tragedy has been refigured outside 'traditional forms of tragic art' may initially seem perverse. Yet the play has been used over and again for the purposes of post-Auschwitz tragedy. Chapter 2 provides some preliminary answers to the question – why *King Lear*?

---

[179] Nivalainen, 'On Thinking the Tragic with Adorno', p. 655.
[180] Ibid.

Chapter 2

Why *King Lear*?

Introduction

Why is it that *King Lear* has emerged as the canonical Shakespeare play 'after' the atrocity of Auschwitz? Why has the play been so prominent in post-war British drama and its theatres of catastrophe? This chapter begins to address these questions by considering the thematic and, perhaps most importantly, formal aspects of the play that have made it critical for various playwrights writing in the wake of mass disaster. By providing a close reading of the play and by drawing on relevant criticism, I contend that *King Lear* is a play concerned with catastrophe, social and cultural modernity, subjectivity and the limits of tragic resolution, in a way that makes it – perhaps uniquely – open to intervention and appropriation 'after' Auschwitz.

I begin by showing that *King Lear* thematises catastrophe. The play consistently portrays disaster and its impact on subjectivity, whereby catastrophe brutalises the human individual and occasions a degenerative reversal into a form of 'base life'. I proceed to analyse the way catastrophe is understood by the protagonists of the play itself. These interpretations adumbrate the emergence of a new humanist and rationalist ethos that, *pace* the dialectic of enlightenment, ultimately reifies subjectivity. By providing a close reading of Edgar and his transformation into Poor Tom, I go on to analyse the way subjectivity implicitly emerges as a site of non-identity – most obviously in those moments of crisis and upheaval that fissure totality. I finally consider the aesthetics of catastrophe in *King Lear*. Drawing on early modern dramatic theory, as derived from Aelius Donatus, I show that *King Lear* violates formal closure – or, as early modern usage would have it, 'the catastrophe'.

Catastrophe in *King Lear*

King Lear is a play that piles disaster upon disaster. Its unremitting catastrophes seem to 'top extremity' (V.iii.206) and 'amplify too much' (V.iii.205) to allow for respite or reprieve, as humanity is 'left darkling' (I.iv.208) in a desolate world of 'ruinous disorders' (I.ii.113–14). 'Who is't can say "I am at the worst"?', reflects Edgar, in a speech that epitomises the 'sequent' (I.ii.106) movement of ever-worsening 'terrors' (II.ii.479) in the play, 'I am worse than e'er I was' (IV.i.27–8): 'And worse I may be yet' (IV.i.29). So cataclysmic are the events of the play that Gloucester believes the 'great world / Shall so wear out to naught' (IV.vi.130–1) – perhaps an apocalyptic consummation devoutly to be wished, as humanity cannot 'carry / Th'affliction, nor the fear' (III.ii.48–9) of the devastation that begins to 'mar' (I.iv.32) it.

The sheer 'extremity' (III.iv.100) of the ruin depicted in *King Lear* occasions a reversion of the human subject into its 'worst estate' (V.iii.208) – a 'worse than brutish' (I.ii.77) condition of degradation. This reduction of people to a form of 'base life' (II.iv.212) is most obvious in the storm scenes, which dominate Act Three of the play. 'Is man no more than this?' (III.iv.101) wonders Lear, as he gazes upon 'Poor Tom', the 'basest' (II.ii.178) form of humanity that Edgar can imagine. Poor Tom, as far as Lear sees, is 'the thing itself': 'Unaccommodated man is no more but such a poor, bare forked animal as thou art' (III.iv.104–6).

'Is man no more than this?': for some Holocaust survivors and scholars, the question, along with other images of human deprivation in *King Lear*, takes on new urgency 'after' Auschwitz.[1] The words are even echoed in *If This Is a Man* – the title which Primo Levi gave his autobiographical reflections on his internment at Auschwitz.[2] 'Consider if this is a man', writes Levi, 'Who works in the mud / Who does not know peace / Who fights for a scrap of bread / Who dies because of a yes or a no'.[3] 'Consider him well' (III.iv.101) declares Lear, importuning Kent and the Fool to reconsider the status of the human in conditions of catastrophe.

The question – and, indeed, the word – that *King Lear* time and again

---

[1] See especially Edward Alexander, *The Holocaust: History and the War of Ideas* (New Brunswick and London: Transaction Publishers, 1994), p. 141, and Berel Lang, *The Future of the Holocaust: Between History and Memory* (Ithaca and London: Cornell University Press, 1999), p. 38.

[2] Primo Levi, *If This Is a Man/The Truce* (London: Abacus, 2013).

[3] Ibid. p. 11.

invokes, however, is the 'cause' (III.iv.151). What (or perhaps who) is 'guilty of our disasters' (I.ii.120)? The play itself provides a variety of interpretations. The most consistently realised can be designated as the reactionary/traditionalist response and the nihilistic/absurdist response. The traditionalist response would have it that catastrophe inevitably results from the collapse of a providentially ordained, hierarchical world order, which is embodied by the sovereign; the nihilistic interpretation of events, however, would have it that catastrophe simply is the lot of a wretched humanity, which suffers humiliating (yet also grotesquely comic) depredations through the agency of arbitrary forces that are beyond appeal and intervention.

I want – briefly – to trace both interpretations of disaster. Both have been influential in important post-war readings, stagings and appropriations of *King Lear*, which I analyse in Chapter 3. Both also serve to adumbrate a social and historical shift depicted in the play towards a more obviously modern, proto-Enlightenment worldview that, in the same dialectical reversal analysed by the Frankfurt School, precipitates catastrophe. The reactionary conservative stance is the ideology against which a proto-modern, rationalist discourse emerges; while the constant apostrophes to a violent universe beyond human reckoning (whether driven by fate, fortune, or the gods) unwittingly reveal the way in which the protagonists of the play have become trapped in – and dominated by – impersonal forms of power and control.[4] By analysing the way catastrophe is interpreted in the play, I want to show that *King Lear* both ideationally and rhetorically frames the emergence of an incipiently modern subject–object split, which portends the brute reification of all human life.

Understanding Catastrophe in *King Lear*

The opening scene of *King Lear* famously depicts the division of the kingdom, where the ageing Lear seeks to split his kingdom between his daughters (and, more to the point in his patriarchal world, his current and prospective sons-in-law) so 'that future strife / May be prevented now' (I.i.43–4). Lear, as part of the wider public ceremony, sets up a 'love-test':

---

[4] See also Hugh Grady, *Shakespeare's Universal Wolf: Studies in Early Modern Reification* (Oxford: Clarendon Press, 1996), p. 31, for an analysis of the relationship between the apostrophe and catastrophe.

> Tell me, my daughters –
> Since now we will divest us both of rule,
> Interest of territory, cares of state –
> Which of you shall we say doth love us most,
> That we our largest bounty may extend
> Where nature doth with merit challenge. (I.i.48–53)

Goneril and Regan instantly comply and 'profess' (I.i.72) to love Lear 'Beyond what can be valued' (I.i.57). Cordelia, however, refuses the rhetorical inflation, insisting that 'I love your majesty / According to my bond, no more nor less' (I.i.92–3). She tells Lear that she has 'Nothing' (I.i.89) to add to the words of her sisters. '[N]othing will come of nothing' (I.i.92) replies Lear:

> Thy truth then be thy dower,
> For by the sacred radiance of the sun,
> The mysteries of Hecate and the night,
> By the operation of the orbs
> From whom we do exist and cease to be,
> Here I disclaim all my paternal care,
> Propinquity and property of blood,
> And as a stranger to my heart and me
> Hold thee from this forever. The barbarous Scythian,
> Or he that makes his generation messes
> To gorge his appetite, shall to my bosom
> Be as well neighboured, pitied and relieved,
> As thou my sometime daughter. (I.i.109–21)

Loving Cordelia 'most' (I.i.124) and having intended to set his 'rest / On her kind nursery' (I.i.124–5), Lear vents his wrath and banishes Cordelia, leaving Albany and Cornwall to 'digest' (I.i.129) her portion of the kingdom. Lear goes on to 'invest' Albany and Cornwall with his 'power' (I.i.131) but intends to 'retain / The name, and all th'addition to a king' (I.i.136–7).

Kent admonishes Lear for banishing Cordelia after she refuses to 'heave' (I.i.91) her heart into her mouth and produce the 'glib and oily' (I.i.226) rhetoric Lear demands. 'Thy youngest daughter does not love thee least', Kent tells Lear, apparently seeing the mistake Lear makes in trusting the 'large speeches' (I.i.184) of Goneril and Regan, 'Nor are those empty-hearted, whose low sounds / Reverberate no hollowness' (I.i.153–5). But it is not simply that Lear has placed his faith in the 'wrong' and least trustworthy children: Kent insists that to break the social order apart is, in and of itself, catastrophic, as it risks unleashing mere anarchy into the world. Though undertaken with the aim of preventing rivalrous power-struggles in the future, Kent believes that for Lear to 'unstate' (I.ii.99) himself and destroy the prevailing social and political hierarchy is a disastrously 'rash' act that can only result in complete chaos. 'Reserve thy state', Kent pronounces boldly to Lear, 'And in thy best consideration check / This hideous rashness' (I.i.150–2): 'thou dost evil' (I.i.167).

Kent is so alarmed because the order he so steadfastly valorises – 'Kent, on thy life, no more' (I.i.155) – is not only social and political; it is also inscribed in 'nature' (I.ii.111) and the 'divine' (I.ii.126) and part of 'Heaven and earth' (I.ii.97). By abdicating the throne, dividing the kingdom and disowning Cordelia, Lear not only ruptures the order of both state and family: he also threatens the orderly system of hierarchy that obtains in the world of nature and the cosmos. When Lear invokes the 'mysteries' (I.i.111) of the natural world and the cosmic 'orbs' (I.i.112) that ordain human life, Kent chastises him for swearing 'thy gods in vain' (I.i.162): Lear has violated the providentially ordained natural and cosmic order the sovereign is supposed to embody. Kent implies as much when he states that the 'madness' of Lear allows him to break with the usual customs of decorum and openly indict the actions of his wayward monarch: 'be Kent unmannerly / When Lear is mad' (I.i.146–7). The 'unmannerly' intervention adumbrates the wider collapse of patriarchal and providential world order, allowing Kent to addresses the supposedly 'divine' figure of the king as 'old man' (I.i.147).

For the arch-traditionalist Kent, the division of the kingdom violates a divinely ordered social and political world. With the breaking of that world order, 'evil' ensues. This conservative understanding of catastrophe is also taken up by Gloucester. Gloucester similarly fears that the division of the kingdom heralds 'death, dearth, dissolutions of ancient amities' (I.ii.145–6) – or the collapse of the old ('ancient') order and various unifying relationships and fealties between individuals ('amities'). Gloucester believes that unusual natural and astrological events are intimately related to the emergent social and political chaos. He frets:

> These late eclipses of the sun and moon portend no good to us. Though the wisdom of Nature can reason it thus and thus, yet nature finds itself scourged by the sequent effects. Love cools, friendship falls off, brothers divide: in cities, mutinies; in countries, discord; in palaces, treason [. . .] We have seen the best of our time, machinations, hollowness, treachery and all ruinous disorders follow us disquietly to our graves. (I.ii.103–14)

What the speech reveals is the way in which the social and political order is part of a wider system that occurs in nature and the cosmos. There is, as Gloucester understands it, a relationship between volatile, uncommon cosmic events and the break-up of society. The 'late eclipses' Gloucester worries over portend the collapse (the 'falling off') of social and political order, the subversion of its natural and divine 'bonds'. These turn from order into 'discord'. 'We have seen', laments Gloucester, 'the best of our time': the whole universe is falling to pieces.[5]

Gloucester is reacting to the 'plot' against his life formed by his 'legitimate' (I.ii.19) son, Edgar – a plot, in reality, cooked up by his bastard 'whoreson' (I.i.22) Edmund, who has designs on the land he cannot inherit. The plot, as far as Gloucester is concerned, is testament to the collapse of hierarchical relationships and civilised – or as Lear imagines it, 'sophisticated' (III.iv.104) – social life. This unleashes a self-interested, individualist ethos which propagates 'hollowness' and 'treachery'. The collapse of all social values seemingly presaged by late eclipses raises the prospect of a *bellum omnium contra omnes* – a war of all against all where, as the Duke of Albany states, 'Humanity must perforce prey on itself / Like monsters of the deep' (IV.ii.50–1) in a state of appetitive *homo homini lupus*. It is the same nightmare Thomas Hobbes would go on to imagine: humanity in a cruelly anarchic 'State of Nature', from which traditional social authority and constraint is the only possible salvation.[6]

The pagan world of *King Lear* obviously pre-dates the Incarnation and the advent of Christianity. It is 'the gods' and not 'God' who appear in the rhetoric of the play – and those gods named individually are all drawn from classical myth: 'Hecate' (I.i.111), 'Apollo' (I.i.161) and even 'blind Cupid' (IV.vi.134). But the providential order represented in the play, and the social world it permeates and sanctions, is by no means incompatible with the stratified universe found in early modern theocentric political thought – not least as propagated by James I. This is the 'world picture' (as E. M. Tillyard famously called it) of a hierarchically ordered Christian universe, in which every aspect of reality and the universe partakes.[7] This would similarly have it that the subversion of

---

[5] The word 'disaster' is etymologically related to a calamity brought about by the evil influence of a star or planet: 'disaster, n.', <http://www.oed.com/view/Entry/53561?rskey=0OAKY4&result=1> (accessed 26 April 2018). See also Alexandra Walsham, 'Deciphering Divine Wrath and Displaying Godly Sorrow: Providentialism and Emotion in Early Modern England', in Jennifer Spinks and Charles Zika (eds), *Disaster, Death and the Emotions in the Shadow of the Apocalypse, 1400–1700* (Basingstoke: Palgrave Macmillan, 2016), p. 23.

[6] For a recent interpretation of the intersection between Hobbes and Shakespearean drama see Andrew Moore, *Shakespeare between Machiavelli and Hobbes: Dead Body Politics* (New York and London: Lexington Books, 2016), pp. 63–82.

[7] For more on the so-called Elizabeth world picture, see E. M. Tillyard and his

social and political order is a violation of godly precepts, which can only result in unmitigated disaster for humanity. It is a vision that preaches stability and condemns factious power-seeking and the universal anarchy to which it leads.[8]

Over the action of the play, however, the idea that disaster results from the violation of a providentially sanctioned world order is transformed into something even more pessimistic – that catastrophe simply is the 'lot' of a degraded humanity, which is prey to arbitrary forces beyond its ken. This would have it that the 'gods' do not truly exist – or do exist, but are irredeemably cruel. Perhaps ironically, it is Gloucester who, after being viciously blinded by Cornwall and Regan, provides the most trenchant statement of that despair, when he insists that 'As flies to wanton boys are we to the gods / They kill us for their sport' (IV.i.38–9). Lear provides a similarly nihilistic image of the human condition, which is both tragic and, at the same time, absurdly comic – a stage of fools. 'When we are born, we cry that we are come', he states in Act Four, 'To this great stage of fools' (IV.vi.178–9).

This nihilistic interpretation of catastrophe leaves little room for meaningful human agency. Lear preaches 'patien[ce]' (IV.vi.174) to Gloucester in the face of tragicomic absurdity – a reaction echoed by Edgar when he tells Gloucester that 'Men must endure' (V.ii.9) as, finally, 'Ripeness is all' (V.ii.11). These responses would have it that resigned endurance is the only response to an inherently catastrophic world, which, far from an immanently meaningful cosmological order, appears as a torturously 'tough rack' (V.iii.313) on which human subjects are stretched, broken to pieces and finally destroyed – for no reason whatsoever.

Neither interpretation of catastrophe is, however, adequate. On the one hand, the conservative reading exculpates a hierarchical order that itself is obviously liable to produce disaster. Lear may act rashly in dividing the kingdom – but his rashness is, as Goneril and Regan so piercingly observe, a 'long-engrafted condition' (I.i.298). His rashness has been socially and culturally 'conditioned' by the 'long-engrafted' (or artificially implanted) autocratic power and authority that devolves to the king.[9] Perhaps more urgently, as the play progresses Lear also begins to

---

The Elizabethan World Picture: A Study of the Idea of Order in the Age of Shakespeare, Donne and Milton (London: Chatto and Windus, 1943).

[8] Leonard Tennenhouse contends that the original purpose of *King Lear* was the exemplary torture of a royal miscreant who, by splitting his kingdom and renouncing his divinely sanctioned position, has violated the taboos that safeguard the mystique of sovereignty. See his *Power on Display: The Politics of Shakespeare's Genres* (London: Routledge, 2005), pp. 102–46.

[9] The word 'engrafting' relates to horticulture and the artificial grafting of plants.

see that hierarchical 'authority' (IV.vi.154) as such is politically suspect and socially unjust. Not only is the 'great image of authority' that a 'dog' is 'obeyed in office' (IV.vi.154–5), but – as Lear perceives – 'Through tattered clothes great vices do appear; / Robes and furred gowns hide all' (IV.vi.160–1). These sentiments leave little room for the backward-looking, conservative nostalgia evinced by Kent and Gloucester. On the other hand, the nihilistic interpretation provided by Gloucester (and, at other times, by Lear and others) would serve to release humanity from any responsibility whatsoever for disaster, implying as it does that people are at the mercy of implacable forces beyond intervention. Both Lear and Gloucester are culpable for the disaster that overtakes the kingdom: Lear for dividing the kingdom and trusting to the sincerity of Goneril and Regan, disinheriting Cordelia and banishing Kent, and Gloucester for his own utterly insensitive treatment of Edmund, treatment itself authorised by the system of primogeniture and its 'order of law' (I.i.18).[10]

But while the traditionalist and nihilistic interpretations are both flawed, neither should be dismissed outright. Both frame the emergence and experience of new and potentially catastrophic 'disposition[s]' (IV.ii.32): humanist reason and capitalist self-interest – those irruptive social and historical phenomena commonly understood as modernity. Through the 'images of revolt and flying off' (II.ii.279) that suffuse the play, *King Lear* conveys the 'great decay' (V.iii.296) of a mystified hierarchical system as it gives way to a disenchanted, capitalist worldview, a rapacious ideology that, once set in motion, seems divorced from human control. Perhaps more than any other character, it is Edmund who embodies the newly emergent, modern view of the world and its reversal into reifying domination.

Modernity and Catastrophe

It is often observed that *King Lear* depicts a historical transition from a pre-modern (feudal) to a more recognisably modern (capitalist) society.[11] The 'old' order is based on hierarchy, embodied by the figure of the sovereign, and is characterised by superstitious beliefs about nature

---

[10] Gloucester says that the 'whoreson' – by which he means son of a whore – 'must be acknowledged' (I.i.22–3). Gloucester is less than discreet when talking about Edmund and his mother: he even boasts to Kent about his sexual 'sport' (I.i.22) in front of Edmund.

[11] See in particular Paul Delaney, '*King Lear* and the Decline of Feudalism', in Ivo

and the cosmos, most obviously in the gods/God and other non-human entities that determine human life (whether beneficently or cruelly). The 'new' order is less hierarchical and more individualistic, with a developing set of scientific, rational beliefs that overturn the more superstitious ideas inherited from the past. The old order is largely represented by the older characters: Lear, Gloucester, Kent and, though in a perhaps more complicated way, the Fool.[12] The new order is represented by a younger and more 'hard-hearted' generation – Goneril, Regan, Cornwall, Edmund and that 'brazen-faced varlet' (II.ii.26) Oswald. The reactionary interpretations of catastrophe provided by Kent and Gloucester evince a pre-modern, mythical worldview, where a hierarchical society is understood to manifest a deific order – an order Lear refers to as the 'mystery of things' (V.iii.16). But the play also depicts a modern, disenchanted worldview that interrogates the type of mystified thinking other characters cleave to in the midst of catastrophe. This iconoclastic worldview is epitomised by Edmund.

During his reading of astrological signs, Gloucester contests the 'wisdom of Nature' – by which he means the type of scientific 'reason' (I.ii.104–5) that would seek to provide a more 'naturalistic' interpretation of the material world and its many mysteries. This is precisely the type of thinking that Edmund embraces when he gleefully ironises his credulous father:

> This is the excellent foppery of the world that when we are sick in fortune – often the surfeit of our own behaviour – we make guilty of our disasters the sun, the moon, and the stars, as if we were villains by necessity, fools by heavenly compulsion, knaves, thieves, and treachers by spherical predominance, drunkards, liars, and adulterers by an enforced obedience of planetary influence, and all that we are evil in by a divine thrusting-on. (I.ii.118–26)

Edmund echoes the contemporaneous English thinker and philosopher Francis Bacon, whose proto-scientific critique of 'wild astrology' and 'celestial magic' in favour of 'a man acquainted with nature' opens the analysis of enlightenment in *Dialectic of Enlightenment*.[13] Far from being providentially ordained, the disasters which trouble the world have, as Edmund perceives it, a human cause. Edmund also refers to the 'goatish disposition' (I.ii.127) of humanity, recalling the meaning of tragedy – 'goat song'. Edmund is saying that the 'tragic' (catastrophic)

Kamps (ed.), *Materialist Shakespeare: A History* (London: Verso, 1995), pp. 20–38.
[12] I return to the ambiguous figure of the Fool in Chapter 6.
[13] Theodor Adorno and Max Horkheimer, *Dialectic of Enlightenment*, trans. John Cumming (London: Verso, 2010), pp. 3–7.

disposition of humanity is of its own making. This is a humanistic shift in perception. Where for Gloucester humanity is dominated ('compelled') by deterministic forces ('spherical dominance') beyond its control, for Edmund the individual subject is free to act on the world as he or she wishes – which also comprises the choice to be 'evil'. This turns the world and the various phenomena that constitute it into an instrument of the willed purposes – or as Edmund notably calls it, 'business' (I.ii.180) – of a rationally intervening and self-fashioning human subject. Edmund boasts that, for him, everything is 'meet that I can fashion fit' (I.ii.182). Edmund, armed as he is with modern understanding, is able to 'fashion', to frame, the world and himself in a way that suits (is 'meet' with) his own ends.

Edmund introduces a split between subject and object, between the individual and the world s/he inhabits, which allows him to interpret and dominate a once opaque reality.[14] Using reason allows Edmund to overturn the belief that humanity is prey to divine forces beyond its understanding; but he also pours scorn on the hierarchical society which that cosmic order is supposed to sanction. For him, traditional social and political authority is nothing but convention, less a divine order than a human creation that has simply taken on the appearance of being absolute. Edmund, in the soliloquy that opens Act One, Scene Two, states:

> Thou, Nature, art my goddess; to thy law
> My services are bound. Wherefore should I
> Stand in the plague of custom, and permit
> The curiosity of nations to deprive me?
> For that I am some twelve or fourteen moon-shines
> Lag of a brother? Why bastard? Wherefore base?
> When my dimensions are as well compact,
> My mind as generous, and my shape as true,
> As honest madam's issue? Why brand they us
> With base? With baseness, bastardy? Base, base?
> Who, in the lusty stealth of nature, take

[14] Some cultural historicist critics have revised the modern, humanist subject–object split when it comes to pre-Cartesian early modern period texts. See in particular Gail Kern Paster, '"Minded Like the Weather": The Tragic Body and Its Passions', in Michael Neill and David Schalkwyk (eds), *The Oxford Handbook to Shakespearean Tragedy* (Oxford: Oxford University Press, 2016), pp. 202–17. Paster contends that, in *King Lear*, the subject is corporeally embedded in a mutually interpenetrating cosmological order. Paster, however, has to more or less dismiss Edmund, who questions the sort of cosmological order his (ignorant) father posits. My own conviction is that the play does open out a more modern conception of the subject–object split.

More composition and fierce quality
Than doth, within a dull, stale, tired bed,
Go to the creating of a whole tribe of fops,
Got 'tween asleep and wake? Well, then,
Legitimate Edgar, I must have your land.
Our father's love is to the bastard Edmund
As to the legitimate. Fine word, legitimate!
Well, my legitimate, if this letter speed,
And my invention thrive, Edmund the base
Shall top the legitimate. I grow, I prosper:
Now gods stand up for bastards! (I.ii.1–22)

Edmund provides a deeply sceptical, rationalistic critique of the 'plague of custom' and the 'curiosity of nations', which have no obvious basis in 'nature' or the cosmos, but are only human inventions. These customs mean that he – as an illegitimate bastard – is cruelly marginalised from civilised social discourse and barred from inheriting land. His is a form of (as he calls it) 'base' life – life that is lived outside of received social and political legitimacy and meaning. His response, in an ironic, even quasi-satirical twist, is to make all human life 'base'.

Through his quest for self-promotion, Edmund turns the customary order into nothing more than an instrument of his own willed designs, where his falsified 'conspiracy' manipulates the disavowed, intergenerational tensions that are produced by the patriarchal system of primogeniture. 'I have heard him oft maintain it to be fit', Edmund reports to Gloucester, as he informs against Edgar, 'that, sons at perfect age and fathers declined, the father should be as ward to the son' (I.ii.71–3). This desacralising instrumentalisation of the social order also means the desacralising instrumentalisation of the subjects who make it up. By virtue of his demystification of superstitious beliefs and traditional social forms, Edmund makes supposedly 'legitimate' subjects 'illegitimate' – most obviously his father and brother, who are transformed into the means by which Edmund can achieve his own nefarious ends.

This process occasions a profound reversal. Without the legitimacy conferred by the social order, Edmund makes it so that potentially any and all subjects are rendered 'base' – are not afforded the authority and even protection that a 'lawful' place in the hierarchy should otherwise underwrite. So when he ironically calls upon the gods to stand up for bastards, Edmund is not only inverting the usual order by claiming grace for those outside the social and cosmic hierarchy. He is also saying that now, with everybody reduced to the illegitimate status of baseness, all subjects are 'bastards' and will need divine favour – which he knows, from his own life, does not exist. Edmund, as part of his humanistic perspective on the world, ends up delegitimising all human life. His rationalist critique reveals the way in which the 'sovereignty, knowledge and reason' (I.iv.223–4) purposed with freeing the subject from traditional authority can reify people – and even degenerate into 'slaughter' (I.iv.312). Edmund embodies the dialectic of enlightenment: the human 'reason' that should make humanity the 'paragon of animals' produces people who are worth so much 'dust' (*Hamlet*, II.ii.309–10).

The word 'business' – and its relationship to the universalisation of base life – is also important. Edmund is not only depicted in the play as a proto-humanist figure; he is also a nascent, self-interestedly acquisitive capitalist, who seeks for his own advancement in the world, as typified by his use of the word 'prosper'. There is an obvious relation in *King Lear* between humanist reason and the emergent commodity-form. By making all life base, Edmund collapses any and all qualitative distinctions between individuals, creating a world of total fungibility that brings about the transvaluation of all values. 'Fine word, legitimate', as Edmund says – but perhaps only a word and open to transformation. This makes the subject (potentially) interchangeable – a 'base' commodity with no obvious inherent value or meaning. Through his rationalistic deconstruction of hierarchy, Edmund plans – quite literally – to exchange himself for his brother, whose own life is (as far as Edmund is concerned) no more sacrosanct than his own form of base ('illegitimate') life. The rhetoric of disenchantment and the rhetoric of reification are symbiotic in *King Lear*: proto-humanist rationality and proto-capitalist commodity fetishism cannot be neatly parcelled out in the play.

What the speech also reveals is the ideational and rhetorical tie between scientific reason and the natural world it is meant properly to interpret and dominate. Edmund, in a statement that might seem to contradict his status as a rational humanist, cites 'Nature' as his 'goddess', proclaiming the 'lusty stealth of nature' over and above the type of civilised cultural relations epitomised by 'lawful' primogeniture. This is deeply paradoxical. Edmund uses his reason to undermine the 'naturalness' of the prevailing social and political order, part of his bid for freedom. But his reason ends up creating conditions that once again take on the semblance of 'nature' and to which subjects must subscribe for the sake of self-preservation. Edmund thinks that dog-eat-dog competition is simply the way of the world – 'natural'. This, however, is not the natural state of humanity at all; it is a state produced by the new order of capitalist reason Edmund represents. The freedom that reason is supposed to provide ultimately relapses into a new form of heteronomy, into conditions that take on the appearance of 'a law of nature'. This reversal sheds light on the oft-repeated apostrophes to 'nature' (and the 'gods') in the play. The appeals to various inhuman agencies in

King Lear reveal the way in which reason takes on an autotelic life of its own, apparently beyond the control of the individuals it is supposed to serve. The representation of 'Nature' as a detached, ravening system reflects the reign of capitalist reason run wild: images of beast-like life evince, not humanity in 'a state of nature', but its brutalisation by a reified rationality.

The notion that reason brutalises the subject – and produces inhumanly cold and rapacious individuals – is particularly relevant to Goneril and Regan, who are variously described as 'Tigers' (IV.ii.41) and 'wolvish' (I.iv.300). These epithets, and the absence of any characterisation that may offer some orientation in telling 'one o'the pairings' (I.iv.179) from the other, has been critiqued as misogynistic – a misogyny that is most obvious when Lear talks of the vagina as a place of 'hell' and 'darkness' (IV.vi.123–4). But the seeming absence of any distinction between Goneril and Regan may also be read as symptomatic of the type of depersonalised subjects produced by 'a reified power'.[15] Goneril and Regan are depicted as typical of the depersonalised 'automaton-like subjects' to be found 'in the new system of nothing'.[16] It would also be wrong to solely identify that 'new system' with Goneril and Regan (or even Edmund and Cornwall): its ascendancy is apparent even in the opening scene of the play, where the abstract quality of love is turned into the quantity of land to be (prematurely) inherited by the next generation. During the division of the kingdom, Lear describes the resistant Cordelia as 'untender' (I.i.107). He means that she is emotionally hard-hearted (quite literally, un-tenderised). But the word 'tender' also signifies her refusal to engage in the system of exchange (tendering) that Lear institutes through the love-test. Lear tells the king of France that, as a result, 'her price is fallen' (I.i.198).[17] The emergent dispensations represented in *King Lear* cannot be isolated to a single 'immoral' character, even if Edmund is the most eloquent rhetorician of base life found in the play. The historical and ideological shift the play depicts ultimately debases the whole of society.[18]

This debasement of the subject and his or her traditional cultural life

---

[15] Grady, *Shakespeare's Universal Wolf*, p. 154.
[16] Ibid. p. 155.
[17] On the other hand, France attests that nothing can 'buy' (I.i.261) Cordelia from him; paradoxically, she becomes precious and priceless to him precisely by virtue of her banishment and debasement. This may speak to the paradoxically sacred status of those profane and abject entities that do not circulate on the market. For more on *King Lear*, the sacred and the abject, see the Rudkin chapter, where I discuss the relation between exile and abjection.
[18] This vision of wholesale, sweeping social and historical change is reflected in the

is revealed in other, critical moments of the play. Perhaps most obvious is Act Two, Scene Two, where Goneril and Regan seek to 'mingle reason' with the 'passion' (II.ii.423) and 'rash mood' (II.ii.358) of an increasingly irate Lear. This is the scene in which Goneril and Regan take a united front to insist that Lear, as Goneril puts it in Act One, 'disquantity' his 'train' (I.iv.240) – to reduce the large company of knights he stipulates as part of the division of the kingdom.

Much of the way the scene is understood depends on the representation of the knights – whether they are, as Lear insists, 'men of choice and rarest parts' (I.vi.255) or the 'debauched' (I.iv.233) mob prone to 'Epicureanism and lust' (I.iv.235) Goneril laments, a description that would lend credence to the complaints voiced by Goneril about whether it is truly 'politic and safe' (I.iv.316) to allow Lear such 'scope' (I.iv.284).[19] Less open to interpretation, however, is the way Goneril and Regan rationalise. 'What need one?' (II.ii.452) reasons Regan, when she tells Lear that his needs may be met by those servants already attendant on her and her sister: 'What should you need of more?' (II.ii.427). 'O, reason not the need!' (II.ii.453) is the defiant (and till now, atypically philosophical) response given by Lear: 'Our basest beggars / Are in the poorest things superfluous' (II.ii.453–4):

> Allow not nature more than nature needs,
> Man's life is cheap as beast's. Thou art a lady:
> If only to go warm were gorgeous,
> Why, nature needs not what thou gorgeous wear'st
> Which scarcely keeps thee warm. (II.ii.455–9)

Whatever the superficial interpretive ambiguities of the scene, the struggle over the knights reveals the way in which reason can debase the subject by reductively stripping away every part of his or her cultural life: 'What need you five and twenty? Ten? Or five?' (II.ii.450). The 'need' (II.ii.453) to which Lear refers cannot be so easily quantified – his knights are, for him, necessary insofar as his train symbolises his royal authority and his quasi-divine status, a reflection of his (increasingly redundant) mythical-religious worldview. This qualitative way of seeing the world is – for Goneril and Regan – simply not rational: Lear is cleaving to values that appear as so much misty sentiment, ideology and outmoded myths of a bygone time. Not unlike Edmund, Goneril and Regan have

---

use of a subplot that extends the action beyond a single family. It is worth noting that *King Lear* is the only Shakespearean tragedy with a subplot.

[19] For his 1962 production of the play, Peter Brook staged knights who were every bit as violent and disruptive as Goneril complains.

seen through conventions and customs that define life in a hierarchy and all the pomp and regalia that attends the figure of the sovereign.

It is a process which may have anything but the 'wholesome end' (II.ii.333) Regan so blandly imagines. Lear denounces the rationality of his daughters as portending a vision of 'base life' (II.ii.404) where, as he by no means unjustly intuits, human life is 'as cheap as beast's'. Lear is not far wrong. The scene dramatises, in the words of Peter Holbrook, 'the ruthless demolition' of individual human 'experience and consciousness'.[20] The sort of rationalistic worldview propagated by Goneril and Regan has no time for the individual experience and consciousness of the subject or his or her inherited cultural life, but reifies human life, turning the subject into little more than a cipher for a brutalising rationalist ethos.

This reification of the subject reaches its nadir in a scene that never seems to lose its ability to shock – the blinding of Gloucester. With one eye already gouged out, Regan states that 'One side will mock another – th'other too' (III.vii.70). Though obviously and purposefully cruel, the scene evinces the same mindset portrayed in Act Two, Scene Two: the type of subtractive, rationalistic thinking that debases the subject – almost as if the human body has been transformed into nothing more than an equation, in need of 'balancing'. If the 'subject quakes' (IV.vi.107) in *King Lear* it is, as a disabused Lear comes to recognise, not in the awesome, divine presence of the monarch, but before a cruelly dehumanising rationality.

King Lear and the Camp

Foakes observes that, of all the plays by Shakespeare, *King Lear* speaks most directly to a late capitalist culture that appears to place ultimate ideological importance on 'individual expression and fulfilment, on the freedom and autonomy of the individual' and its actual material 'diminution of the subject to a nobody', another 'entry in the systems of the government, banks, police and advertisers, marking the social, economic and political insignificance of each person in a mass society'.[21] *King Lear*, as Foakes understands it, represents nothing short of a prophetic indictment of a (still developing) culture of abstract capitalist rationality.

---

[20] Peter Holbrook, 'The Left and *King Lear*', *Textual Practice*, 14:2 (2000), p. 348.
[21] R. A. Foakes, *Hamlet Versus Lear: Cultural Politics and Shakespeare's Art* (Cambridge: Cambridge University Press, 1993), p. 213.

It is a boldly stated argument – but Foakes does not pursue it as far as he might.

If the play portrays the total reification of the subject, the action of *King Lear* can also be seen to portend the 'future strife' (I.i.43) and 'the image and horror' (I.ii.173) of the concentration camps, where human life truly did become vanishingly 'base' and 'cheap'.[22] What Edmund (and other characters) institute through the reduction of the human being to a form of base life is a world of biopolitics, as Michel Foucault and Giorgio Agamben call it.[23] Foucault and Agamben use the phrase 'bare life' to name forms of human life that are in some way forced to subsist 'outside' of or beyond cultural legitimacy. Agamben contends that, in early modern culture, the sovereign establishes his power through the production of a social and political order based on the exclusion of bare, human life – or the 'poor, bare forked animal' of *King Lear*. He does so by enacting 'exceptions' in which the law is suspended, withdrawn from the individual human being, who is cast out beyond the usual limits of society. With the transition to modernity, however, totalising social and political systems begin to produce bare life as a 'generalized' condition, where 'a "biopolitics" of the human race' emerges.[24] When he searches for a paradigm of the modern bio-political regime, Agamben alights on the Nazi concentration camps, which he calls 'the *nomos* of the modern' – or 'the space that is opened up when the state of exception begins to become the rule'.[25]

The opening scene of *King Lear* depicts a world where who is allowed to participate in legitimate cultural life and its rights is a decision taken by the sovereign (the 'yes or no' Levi writes about): when Cordelia tells Lear that she has 'nothing' to add to the protestations of love produced by her sisters in Act One, Lear banishes her. He turns her into a 'stranger' – an exile. So when Lear calls on Burgundy and France to see if

---

[22] Margot Heinemann writes that the blinding of Gloucester qualifies Cornwall as nothing less than 'a Nazi-type brute'. See her 'Demystifying the Mystery of State: *King Lear* and the World Turned Upside Down', in Stanley Wells (ed.), *Shakespeare Survey: Volume 44* (Cambridge: Cambridge University Press, 1992), p. 80.

[23] See Michel Foucault, *The Birth of Biopolitics: Lectures at the Collège de France, 1978–1979*, ed. Michel Sellenart, trans. Graham Burchell (Basingstoke: Palgrave Macmillan, 2008) and Giorgio Agamben, *Homo Sacer: Sovereign Power and Bare Life*, trans. Daniel Heller-Roazen (Stanford: Stanford University Press, 1998).

[24] Michel Foucault, *'Society Must Be Defended': Lectures at the Collège de France, 1975–1976*, ed. Mauro Bertani and Alessandro Fontana, trans. David Macey (London: Penguin, 2004), p. 243.

[25] Agamben, *Homo Sacer*, p. 166 and p. 169.

either still intend to marry Cordelia, he tells them that all she now has is her 'little-seeming substance' (I.i.199) – by which he means her physical body, her substance, her bare life. She no longer has a dowry because she no longer has a 'place' in the system of hierarchy and she can no longer be considered a daughter to a king, as Lear has 'disclaim[ed]' (I.i.114) her – cast her out of society, precisely as Edmund is 'outside' legitimate society due to his status as a mere bastard (as indeed is the banished Kent). Edmund, however, produces bare life, not as an 'exceptional' status, but as a universal condition, which may feasibly apply to anyone at any time. This – as Agamben understands it – is the modern condition, the condition of the camps, where politics has been transformed 'into the realm of bare life' – 'that is, into a camp'.[26]

The concept of bio-power is undeniably relevant to *King Lear*, but it does not necessarily allow for the possibility of tragic freedom. This obscures some of the more vital aspects of the play. For while *King Lear* depicts the often disastrous outcomes of modern rationality, it also presents catastrophe as potentially generative – a paradox captured in the storm-flung imagery of Act Three, when Lear calls out for the end of the world, desiring that the storm 'crack' the 'moulds' through which 'Nature' produces and reproduces its many forms, so that 'all germens spill at once' (III.ii.8). It is an image of catastrophic destruction that, at the same time, raises the prospect of anarchic (re)creation, which takes place without being determined by the forms and shapes ('moulds') that have obtained before. The play comprises the diverse meanings of catastrophe analysed in the Introduction and in Chapter 1: modernity as a form of permanent catastrophe, a 'general woe' (V.iii.318) that reduces human subjects to mere ciphers, to be cruelly disposed of at will; and catastrophe as potentially emancipatory, a disastrous upheaval that 'blasts' the subject from reifying social and political systems and forces. To analyse the relationship between catastrophe and subjectivity in *King Lear*, I consider Edgar, who begins the play typical of the nondescript 'tribe of fops' (I.ii.14) Edmund rails against, but in catastrophe also discovers new forms of subjectivity – even freedom.

Catastrophe and Subjectivity

Despite the violent terrors it represents, *King Lear* also evinces a paradoxical 'openness to change and catastrophe'.[27] It is in moments of

---

[26] Ibid. p. 129.
[27] Steven Mentz, '"Strange Weather" in *King Lear*', *Shakespeare*, 6:2 (2010), p. 147.

disruption and crisis – in moments when, to quote Lear, 'We are not ourselves' (II.ii.296) – that new possibilities for subjective experience and autonomy might be actualised. This is typified by Edgar. When, in Act Two, Edgar is exiled and shorn from his inherited social and political identity, he is forced to reinvent himself as the raving Bedlamite Poor Tom, a (non)identity that cedes to a host of others as Edgar embodies a whole variety of other 'selves' over the play. 'Edgar I nothing am', states 'Edgar', as he 'rebirths' himself, 'poor Tom, / That's something yet' (II.ii.191–2). It is a speech (and process) I return to in Chapter 5, when I consider the drama of David Rudkin.

Hugh Grady states that Edgar is a 'consummate figure of human indeterminacy and potential', who confirms through his self-transformations the open-ended 'possibility of human change', defying absorption into 'ready-made signifying systems'.[28] Edgar does not necessarily apostrophise against the social and political totality or even form a coherent critique of the type of all-consuming, modern *ratio* which arises in the play. But his protean transformations testify to the way in which subjectivity implicitly emerges as a space of resistance to a reifying modernity. Edgar retains a form of autonomy, of freedom from totality.

The importance of Edgar and his non-identical subjectivity is underscored by the Quarto version of the play, which, after advertising the 'True Chronicle History of the life and death of King Lear' also features 'the unfortunate life of Edgar, son and heir to the Earl of Gloucester and his sullen and assumed humour of Tom of Bedlam'.[29] The words 'assumed' and 'sullen' are significant. The word 'assumed' obviously means more than that Edgar simply 'pretends' to be Poor Tom: the Latin *adsumere*, meaning 'to take to oneself', implies that Edgar takes another identity to himself in his time of crisis; while the word 'sullen' is, as the *OED* notes, derived from the Anglo-Norman 'solein' or 'solain', from the Latin *solitaneus*, meaning 'sole, solitary, alone', or 'singular'.[30] By taking up the figure of Poor Tom, Edgar testifies to the tragic non-identity of subject (the one) and society (the many) in *King Lear*. Edgar takes it upon himself to become a singular figure in – and non-identical with – his social world.

Grady develops an interpretation of modernity that is informed by

---

[28] Grady, *Shakespeare's Universal Wolf*, p. 178, p. 168 and p. 158.
[29] Quoted in the 'Introduction' to René Weis (ed.), *King Lear: A Parallel Text Edition*, 2nd edn (Oxford: Routledge, 2013), p. 4. I have modernised spelling.
[30] 'assume, v.', <http://www.oed.com/view/Entry/12036?redirectedFrom=assume>; 'sullen, adj., adv., and n.', <http://www.oed.com/view/Entry/193784?rskey=PoH4SH&result=1> (accessed 30 May 2017).

Habermas and the idea of consensual intersubjectivity.[31] He makes the case that modern, reifying 'systems' in the play should be set against the resistance provided by customary 'lifeworlds' that have yet to be fully incorporated into a dominative social totality.[32] Where systems tend to reify the subject, lifeworlds foster the possibility of mutual understanding.[33] Grady is drawn to a subaltern, plebeian culture of communal solidarity that he finds in the play – a world Edgar comes to be identified with in his (initial) transformation into the impoverished Poor Tom. Grady picks out the servant who so bravely tries to intervene to stop his master Cornwall from blinding Gloucester – 'A peasant stand up thus?' (III.vii.79) is the incredulous response given by Regan, while Cornwall orders the body of the dead 'slave' to be cast on a 'dunghill' (III.vii.95–6); the servants who, in the Quarto, tend to the blinded Gloucester – bringing 'flax and the whites of eggs / To apply to his bleeding face' (III.vii.105–6); and the Old Man who leads Gloucester to Poor Tom and (apparent) safety and brings him 'the best 'pparel that I have' (IV.i.52).

The most stunning political identification with a subaltern life-world, however, takes place in the storm scenes of Act Three. Lear, after suffering the onslaught of the storm without any material comfort, makes a famous 'prayer' to the destitute masses he has neglected:

> Poor naked wretches, whereso'er you are,
> That bide the pelting of this pitiless storm,
> How shall your houseless heads and unfed sides,
> Your looped and windowed raggedness, defend you
> From seasons such as these? Oh, I have ta'en
> Too little care of this! Take physic, pomp,
> Expose thyself to feel what wretches feel,
> That thou mayst shake the superflux to them. (III.iv.28–35)

Through his own suffering, Lear comes to learn about and empathise with the suffering of others. He will even attempt to assert his common identity with 'unaccommodated man' by removing his royal erminc – 'Off, off, you lendings: come unbutton' (III.iv.105–6). Lear postulates a new form of sociality where the 'superflux' – the surplus wealth and property owned by the ruling classes – comes to be distributed to the

---

[31] My own take on intersubjectivity in Shakespeare is far less consensual than that proposed by Grady, via Habermas. See my 'Face-Off: Defacement, Ethics and the "Neighbour" in *The Comedy of Errors*', *Textual Practice*, 32:8 (2018), pp. 1255–75.
[32] Grady, *Shakespeare's Universal Wolf*, p. 22.
[33] Ibid. p. 138.

poor, overturning the social injustice that obtains in the kingdom. This more consensual relationship between self and others means that Grady perceives 'utopian alternatives to reification within the debris of *King Lear*'.[34] There is, as Grady understands it, hope that self and society can synthesise in *King Lear*. This collective unity represents for Grady the main agent of resistance against the impersonal power of the new regimes of modernity. It is an interpretation that recalls previous humanist, Christian and indeed Marxist readings of *King Lear*, which I analyse more fully in Chapter 3. These readings of the play similarly concentrate on the storm scenes and the idea that through his suffering Lear attains some form of moral (and indeed social) redemption.

This is where a catastrophic interpretation of *King Lear* parts ways with Grady. I do not deny the play depicts powerful moments of empathy and solidarity that contradict the cruelly reductive, depersonalising form of modern reasoning implemented by (and, indeed, through) Edmund, Cornwall, Goneril and Regan. Nor do I contest the political aspirations which underpin the desire to find utopian alternatives to a totalising autotelic *ratio*. The problem with the type of reading pursued by Grady is that, by insisting on the possibility of reconciliation between subject and society, he is guilty of ignoring the form of the play, its violation of aesthetic closure. The reconciliatory movement Grady identifies in *King Lear* is obviously dashed at the end of the drama, which denies the sort of *telos* he wants to trace. The prospect of some sort of sort of dialectical synthesis of subject and society seems remote by the end of a play which, as Ewan Fernie writes, insists on a 'tearing tension' between 'the gored state' (V.iii.319) and an 'equally wounded and deformed subject'.[35] Subject and society, as Fernie observes, remain in an unreconciled state at the close of *King Lear*. This fragmentary, catastrophic form, with its irruptive violation of closure and the possibility of resolution, means that *King Lear* is a play that 'Cannot be bordered certain in itself' (IV. ii.34).

'Is this the promised end?': *King Lear* and the Aesthetics of Catastrophe

My analysis of *King Lear* so far has tended to use the word 'catastrophe' as more or less equivalent with 'disaster', so that catastrophe can be

---

[34] Ibid. p. 56.
[35] Ewan Fernie, *Shakespeare for Freedom: Why the Plays Matter* (Cambridge: Cambridge University Press, 2017), p. 214.

understood as 'terrible event'. This was not necessarily the dominant meaning of the word in the early modern era, however, as 'catastrophe' did not begin to be more readily identified with 'sudden disaster' (or 'an event producing a subversion of order or system') until towards the end of the seventeenth century.[36] When *King Lear* was composed, catastrophe was a term that related to dramatic form.

For early moderns, catastrophe meant the resolution of a play or simply the end or conclusion of something more generally, as evidenced by Thomas Cooper in his 1565 *Thesaurus Linguae Romanae et Britannicae*, where catastrophe is defined as 'the latter end of a comedie, the ende of any thing', a definition reflecting the Greek καταστροφή, which connotes 'overturning, sudden turn, conclusion'.[37] Samuel Johnson (whose own famed reaction to the death of Cordelia – and Lear – will be touched upon again) similarly defines catastrophe as the 'change or revolution which produces the conclusion or final event of a dramatic piece' – though his definition conspicuously widens the potential generic scope of catastrophe beyond comedy to any 'dramatic piece', so that catastrophe might apply beyond comedy.[38]

The early modern usage derived largely from the reception of the writings of fourth-century Roman rhetorician Aelius Donatus via his commentary on Terence and his comedy *The Andrian*, published in the fifteenth century.[39] Donatus separated drama into the *prologue*, followed by the *protasis* ('the beginning of the drama'), the *epitasis* ('the development and enlargement of the conflict and, as it were, the knot of all error') and, finally, *catastrophe* – 'the resolution of the events' in comedy 'so that there is a happy ending which is made evident to all by the recognition of past events'.[40] By tying up the *epitasis* in a moment of recognition – or *anagnorisis* – catastrophe strongly denotes a resolution of conflict. The catastrophe, as a sudden transformation, may for Donatus be an event, but it may equally be a character that intervenes

---

[36] 'catastrophe, n.'.
[37] Quoted in Franz Mauelshagen, 'Defining Catastrophe', in Katharina Gerstenberger and Tanja Nusser (eds), *Catastrophe and Catharsis: Perspectives on Disasters and Redemption* (Rochester, NY: Camden House, 2015), p. 174.
[38] 'catastrophe, n.'.
[39] For the reception of Donatus in Renaissance Europe and England, see Howard B. Norland, *Drama in Early Tudor Britain, 1485–1558* (Lincoln and London: University of Nebraska Press, 1995), pp. 65–83.
[40] Quoted in David Galbraith, 'Theories of Comedy', in Alexander Leggatt (ed), *The Cambridge Companion to Shakespearean Comedy* (Cambridge: Cambridge University Press, 2002), p. 9.

from 'outside' of the plot to resolve the conflicts which the action of the play has generated – a sort of non-narrative *persona ex machina*.[41]

Leo Salingar makes the case that, in his reading of Terentian comedy, Donatus shifts an Aristotelian interpretation of tragic form onto comic drama.[42] Not unlike Aristotle, Donatus stresses the formal necessity of resolving conflicts and confusions – a reading of tragic form which, as I set out previously, is critical for Hegel and his conception of dialectics. While early modern thought tends to classify catastrophe in terms of comic drama, the word, particularly insofar as it implies formal resolution, might be understood to transcend genre.[43]

Kenneth Muir posits that catastrophe is a word Shakespeare derived from the John Florio translation of Montaigne, where catastrophe is understood in Donathusian terms as 'the conclusion or shutting up of a comedie or any thing else'.[44] On the rare occasions when he uses the word, Shakespeare tends to do so in an ironic vein, as typified by *Henry IV Part Two*, where Page tells Mistress Quickly that he will 'tickle' her 'catastrophe' (II.i.62) – by which he means beat her backside (her 'end', her 'catastrophe'). The same comic-ironic tone appears in *King Lear*, when Edmund uses the word (which, *pace* Donatus, he relates to comic form) to describe the entrance of his brother, against whom, moments previously, he had been plotting. 'Pat he comes', Edmund quips, 'like the catastrophe of the old comedy' (I.ii.134). The superficial point is that Edgar, like the character of the catastrophe in both Old and New Comedy, has arrived right on 'cue' (I.ii.135). This implies the total authorial control Edmund seems to have over (even 'chance') events. He has trapped his brother in a pre-scripted plot of his devising and Edgar arrives, *ex machina*, on cue and on time.

But the allusion also self-reflexively ironises the artificiality of the catastrophe as a formal device – and indeed the overdetermined conventions of dramatic resolution more widely. It is telling that *King Lear* is the only tragedy where there is a citation of the catastrophe. The allusion to dramatic theory, as Alan Rosen has convincingly shown, invites attention to the wider violation of formal closure in *King Lear*, its (as

---

[41] See also Alan Rosen, *Dislocating the End: Climax, Closure, and the Invention of Genre* (Oxford: Peter Lang, 2001), p. 8.
[42] Leo Salingar, *Shakespeare and the Traditions of Comedy* (Cambridge: Cambridge University Press, 1974), p. 84.
[43] See also T. W. Baldwin, *Shakespeare's Five-Act Structure: Shakespeare's Early Plays on the Background of Renaissance Theories of Five-Act Structure from 1470* (Urbana: University of Illinois Press, 1947), pp. 252–311.
[44] Kenneth Muir, *Shakespeare's Sources: Comedies and Tragedies* (Oxford: Routledge, 2005), p. 161.

Rosen calls it) anti-formalist 'shape'.⁴⁵ The catastrophe, conventionally supposed to take place at the end of a drama and resolve its outstanding conflicts and confusions, makes a 'displaced' appearance in Act One of *King Lear* – almost as if the rest of the play were a grotesquely elongated catastrophe. Through its untimely allusion to the catastrophe and early modern dramatic theory, *King Lear* self-consciously reveals its own violent transgression of 'due resolution' (I.ii.100).

Perhaps the most astute interpreter of the anti-form of *King Lear* is Stephen Booth, who provides a particularly insightful reading of the way in which *King Lear* constantly transgresses its own formal limits.⁴⁶ Booth analyses a range of closure-defying techniques. These range from the way Shakespeare draws repetitively on a constellation of words – 'fool', 'kind', 'nature', 'fate', 'nothing', 'something' and so on – but with diverse possible meanings, so that repeated words are constantly and 'arbitrarily redefined'.⁴⁷ This serves to forestall any final 'meaning' – any closure. The same can be said for the way Shakespeare uses words that are 'densely resistant to verse articulation' – 'tender-hefted' (II.ii.360), 'sea-monster' (I.iv.253), 'Sepulchring' (II.ii.321), 'head-lugged' (IV.ii.43) – which adumbrate the 'operation of some dangerously unregulable power, something not quite contained by the procedures that seek to organize it'.⁴⁸ The failure of formal closure also relates to the representation of space and time. The main characters spend most of the play wandering about in (literally) unbounded outside spaces, without any obvious 'conclusive' destination. This dilates the onward progress of time itself, which, far from obeying conventional linearity towards a teleological end, is often suspended. The same can be said of the representation of death in the play, where characters that, to all intents and purposes, seem 'dead' might also and at the same time be 'alive' – an idea also discussed in the analysis of *Blasted* in Chapter 7.

This violation of formal limits pertains most obviously to the end of the play, which subverts the usual Lear/Leir narrative. Over the action of Act Five, the play seems to be resolving the 'complications' that characterise the *epitasis* and working towards the catastrophe, 'the resolution of the events' and 'recognition'. The plot against the life of

---

⁴⁵ Rosen, *Dislocating the End*, pp. 6–26.
⁴⁶ Stephen Booth, *King Lear, Macbeth, Indefinition and Tragedy* (New Haven: Yale University Press, 1983). David Ian Rabey was taught by Stephen Booth while he was working on *Indefinition and Tragedy*. The way in which Rabey understands catastrophic theatre owes, I believe, a debt to Booth and his reading of *King Lear*.
⁴⁷ Ibid. p. 40.
⁴⁸ Michael Goldman, '*King Lear*: Acting and Feeling', in Laurence Danson (ed.), *On King Lear* (Princeton: Princeton University Press, 1981), p. 33.

Albany is revealed (V.iii.71–90); Edgar defeats Edmund in single combat (V.iii.160–71); the sisters who have vied for marriage to Edmund both die, Goneril killing Regan with poison (V.iii.105) before she kills herself (V.iii.222–6); and Albany and Edgar both give moralising speeches that are typical of the end of a play – of the catastrophe – with Edgar stating 'the gods are just and of our pleasant vices / Make instruments to plague us' (V.iii.168–9).

But while the play seems to be enacting a formalised 'catastrophe' that will, by the end of the action, have 'concluded all' (IV.vii.42), it soon becomes apparent that, as Booth contends, *King Lear* only appears to be formally concluding 'while its substance is still in urgent progress'.[49] The precise whereabouts of Lear and Cordelia towards the end of the play have been overlooked: 'Great things of us forgot!' (V.iii.235). No sooner has Edmund repented and revealed his 'commission' (V.iii.250) on the lives of Lear and Cordelia than Lear re-enters the stage – carrying the dead Cordelia in his arms: 'Howl, howl, howl, howl!' (V.iii.255). Booth writes that, in having both Lear and Cordelia finally die, Shakespeare presents the 'final action of the play *after* the story is over', so that *King Lear* transgresses the 'generic promise inherent in its story'.[50] *King Lear* outstrips the formal containment it seems to be observing, creating a sense of uncertainty and irresolution at precisely the moment it should be providing closure. The play has violently subverted its own catastrophe.

This uncertainty and irresolution spills over into the speeches that take place after the deaths of Lear and Cordelia. I quote from the Folio version of the play – for reasons I will develop shortly:

Lear: No, no, no life.
Why should a dog, a horse, a rat have life
And thou no breath at all? Thou'lt come no more.
Never, never, never, never, never.
Pray you, undo this button. Thank you, sir.
Do you see this? Look on her, look, her lips.
Look there, look there.   *He dies.*
Edgar: He faints. My lord, my lord.
Kent: Break, heart, I prithee break.
Edgar: Look up, my lord.
Kent: Vex not his ghost. O let him pass. He hates him
That would upon the rack of this tough world
Stretch him out longer.
Edgar: He is gone indeed.

---

[49] Booth, *King Lear, Macbeth, Indefinition and Tragedy*, p. 22.
[50] Ibid. p. 28.

>   The wonder is he hath endured so long.
>   He but usurped his life.
> **Albany:** Bear them from hence. Our present business
>   Is general woe. [*To Edgar and Kent*] Friends of my soul,
>   you twain
>   Rule in this realm, and the gored state sustain.
> **Kent:** I have a journey, sir, shortly to go;
>   My master calls me, I must not say no.
> **Edgar:** The weight of this sad time we must obey,
>   Speak what we feel, not what we ought to say.
>   The oldest hath borne most; we that are young
>   Shall never see so much, nor live so long.
>
> *Exeunt with a dead march.*[51]

The final action and speeches of *King Lear* are deeply ambiguous, from the final state of Lear (rapturous about the seeming survival of Cordelia, or completely deluded?) to the precise intentions of Kent (does 'shortly to go' indicate his suicide, or simply that he will shortly die of old age?). Perhaps most uncertain, however, is the political situation, which remains unresolved. Albany is the socially superior of the survivors and should be the obvious heir to the throne; however, he instantly passes the crown to Kent and Edgar, as he had previously tried to 'resign' it back to the 'old majesty' (V.iii.298): Lear. Kent, however, implies that he must follow Lear into death, meaning that the crown (if the resignation of the state to Kent and Edgar 'twain' still obtains after Kent has stated his apparent intention to commit suicide) seemingly falls to Edgar. But his ascension to the place of king is not stated unambiguously: Edgar (or in the Quarto, Albany) is provided with a truly obscure quatrain which leaves both the political situation and the play disconcertingly 'unfixed'.[52] The final speech offers 'no strongly felt reassurance that the world is now once more firmly the right way up'.[53]

The ending of *King Lear* departs from the other tragedies of Shakespeare, *Hamlet*, *Macbeth* and *Othello*, which portray the imminent reinstitution of the social and political order. Hamlet dies importuning Horatio to tell his 'story' (V.ii.301) and formally gives his 'dying voice' (V.ii.308) to 'th'election' (V.ii.307) of the questing and 'warlike' (V.ii.304) Fortinbras, whose newfound status as *de facto* king of Denmark is signalled by his delivery of the final speech of the play,

---

[51] Quoted in Weis, *King Lear: A Parallel Text Edition*, p. 339.
[52] Booth, *King Lear, Macbeth, Indefinition and Tragedy*, p. 65.
[53] Heinemann, 'Demystifying the Mystery of State', p. 80. Heinemann writes that, in *King Lear*, 'no single dominant ideology or consensus is capable of holding the society together' (p. 76).

where he commands that the body of Hamlet be borne 'like a soldier to the stage' (V.ii.350). The same formality – and the restoration of a broken social and political order – is found in *Macbeth*. With the death of the 'tyrant' (V.viii.1) Macbeth, the true heir to Duncan, Malcolm, is restored to the throne of Scotland – and is duly given the climatic speech of the play, proclaiming his coronation by inviting his thanes 'to see us crowned at Scone' (V.xi.41). The ending of *Othello* does not repeat the ritual state ceremonies of *Hamlet* and *Macbeth*, but Othello is given a final, climatic speech, where a distracted Lear is not, in which he asks others to 'relate' (V.ii.350) his story, kissing Desdemona during his suicide (V.ii.368–9). Lodovico appears to consent, settling the new political organisation of Cyprus before he states his intention to return to Venice and 'relate' the tragic events, 'straight aboard, and to the state / This heavy act with heavy heart relate' (V.i.380–1).[54]

I have quoted the Folio version of *King Lear* because the Quarto provides even less in the way of resolution. This version has no stage direction indicating when (if?) Lear finally dies and is also missing the rapt words found in the Folio, where Lear seems to die in the belief that Cordelia lives (the discrepancy has prompted some critics to observe that the Quarto is the 'bleaker' version of the play).[55] Albany (not Edgar) is given the final quatrain of the play (which appears unchanged) – but, as in the Folio, Albany has already resigned the crown and the care of the 'gored state'. Though he is given the final speech, the precise status of Albany (and that of the state itself) remains unclear. The Quarto is also missing the direction '*Exeunt with a dead march*', which is found in the Folio, a processional, funeral ritual proper to the ending of a tragedy.[56] But as Booth shows, even the '*dead march*' of the Folio is ambiguous: *King Lear* is the only Shakespeare tragedy in which the final speeches do not point to an immediate offstage location to which the bodies (and the survivors) are meant to repair. Albany, Kent and Edgar are left to simply walk off the stage – seemingly to nowhere.[57]

This failure to restore communal social and political relations at the end of *King Lear* is reflected in the (relative) absence of collective

---

[54] The total ruin depicted in *King Lear* arguably resonates more strongly with the sonnets than it does with the other tragedies. Drawing on Derrida and his conception of total nuclear war, Tom Muir has made the case that the sonnets are shaped by a vision of 'remainderless destruction'. See his 'Without Remainder: Ruins and Tombs in Shakespeare's Sonnets', *Textual Practice*, 24:1 (2009), pp. 21–49.
[55] See the Introduction for more on the texts of *King Lear*.
[56] See Brian Cummings, '"Dead March": Liturgy and Mimesis in Shakespeare's Funerals', *Shakespeare*, 8:4 (2010), pp. 368–85.
[57] Booth, *King Lear, Macbeth, Indefinition and Tragedy*, p. 28.

pronouns in its final speeches. Kent refers to himself, using 'I', while 'thou' and 'you' are used on five occasions, cognates of 'him'/'her' on ten. The distant (and distancing) 'them' is used once, while 'we' only occurs in the final quatrain. The referent is, however, unclear. '[W]e that are young' would presumably disqualify Kent (who roundly declares himself to be in his late forties in Act Two) and potentially also Albany, so that the collective imperative ('we must obey'/'speak what we feel') does not have any obvious onstage addressee(s). It may be that Edgar delivers the final speech directly to the audience, turning the final quatrain into a sort of quasi-epilogue. But if so, the demands the play/Edgar is making on that collective entity ('we') 'remains enigmatic'.[58] There is an irreconcilable contradiction implicit in the appeal. Edgar insists on the need to pay full witness to experience, speaking feelingly (and so truthfully) about everything that has been seen. But at the same time, the survivors will 'never see so much' as those who have 'borne most'. It is up to the survivors to speak about, to bear witness to, events and experiences that defy comprehension, violating the limits of understanding. This paradox is as liable to make 'breath poor and speech unable' (I.i.60) as it is to encourage 'us' to speak 'feelingly' (IV.vi.145). It is precisely the same contradiction that, for survivors and those who 'come after', besets Auschwitz, the un-narratable event: paying witness to the unwitnessable, speaking the unspeakable.[59] Edgar does not go on to say anything at all, let alone speak from the 'heart' (I.i.105). The type of response *King Lear* calls for remains open-ended.

This contradiction means the shared, collective response Edgar calls for cannot be made operative. Some of the other Shakespeare tragedies – most obviously *Hamlet* and *Othello* – place an emphasis on 'relating', on telling a story around which society can, once again, unify. But the scale of the catastrophe in *King Lear*, the devastation of witnessing so much, would seem to prevent narration – or relation. The end of the play invalidates all of its morally trite but shareable 'conclusions' – 'the gods are just'/ 'the wheel is come full circle' – and so does very little to 'approve the common saw' (II.ii.158). This inability to relate adumbrates a wider failure of relationships as such – the possibility of shared social meaning and being. Even while Edgar calls for a collective response, the

---

[58] Foakes, 'Introduction', in Shakespeare, *King Lear*, ed. Foakes, p. 79.

[59] The contradiction around Holocaust testimony – of speaking the unspeakable, representing the unrepresentable – has, as Sara Horowitz writes, become the central paradox of Holocaust literature. See her 'Literature', in Peter Hayes and John K. Roth (eds), *The Oxford Handbook of Holocaust Studies* (Oxford: Oxford University Press, 2010), p. 430.

play leaves individuals adrift; it does not allow for the social relation(s) that may enable a 'wholesome end' (II.ii.333).

It is its shocking violation of formal coherence and resolution that has preoccupied critics of *King Lear* throughout its history. There is an in-depth analysis of the critical reception of *King Lear* in Chapter 3, where I concentrate on its post-Auschwitz 'afterlife'; but I also want to provide a brief survey of pre-Holocaust criticism, to show the way in which the fragmentation of the play can take on new meanings in discrete cultural moments.

King Lear and Catastrophe in Criticism

In his reflections on *King Lear*, Samuel Johnson famously bewailed the death of Cordelia, which, he confessed, left him so shocked he did not reread the final scenes until he 'undertook to revise them as editor'.[60] Johnson laments the end of *King Lear*, which violates 'poetic justice':

> Shakespeare has suffered the virtue of Cordelia to perish in a just cause, contrary to the natural ideas of justice [...] and, what is yet more strange, to the faith of the chronicles [...]. I cannot be easily persuaded that the observation of justice makes a play worse; or that [...] the audience will not always rise better pleased from the final triumph of persecuted virtue.
> In the present case the public has decided. Cordelia, from the time of Tate, has always retired with victory and felicity.[61]

By transgressing the formalised convention of the final recovery (and 'felicity') of Lear and Cordelia – however temporary that recovery is even in other versions of the story – Shakespeare, as far as Johnson is concerned, upends both formal resolution and the 'form of justice' (III.vii.25) supposedly enshrined in that closure: that the morally 'good' finally prevail. Though Johnson also provides some criticism of Tate in his remarks on *King Lear* – 'blaming' him for some aspects of his 'alteration' – he ultimately endorses the horrified 'sensations' which (for his era) still make the Tate version more popular with the theatre-going 'public'.[62]

The concerns articulated by both Tate and Johnson with regard to the 'ruinous disorders' (I.ii.113–14) of *King Lear* reflect an increasingly 'enlightened' emphasis on aesthetic order and ethical decorum in the Restoration era and beyond, against which the disintegration and

---

[60] Quoted in John Joughin, 'Lear's Afterlife', *Shakespeare Survey: Volume 55*, ed. Peter Holland (Cambridge: Cambridge University Press, 2002), p. 70.
[61] Ibid.
[62] Ibid.

disorder of *King Lear* as it shatters into 'a hundred thousand flaws' (II. ii.474) seems out of place. But for the Romantics, the unbounded aesthetic overflow of *King Lear* was testament to its sublimity, which poets from Coleridge to Keats usually tied to its representation of an awesome and (in the words of Coleridge) 'convulsed Nature' that escapes arbitrary human categories and cannot be compassed by the 'little world of man' (III.i.10).[63] Even Coleridge, however, finally critiqued *King Lear* for its failure fully to 'harmonize' – though it was the blinding of Gloucester that he seems to have found most excessive, despite his (somewhat Bardolatrous) 'reluctance' to 'find Shakespeare wrong' in his choices for the action of the play.[64]

The absence of harmonious aesthetic resolution became even more apparent in the nineteenth century, particularly after 1838, when William Charles Macready ditched the Tate version of the play for the Shakespeare *King Lear* (albeit still in a cut and altered version). Algernon Swinburne observed that the 'tragic fatalism' of *King Lear* denied 'atonement' and the usual tragic 'pledge of reconciliation' – an insight reiterated by George Bernard Shaw, who, observing its failure to instate resolution, remarked on 'the blasphemous despair of Lear'.[65] Such thoughts were also on the mind of the perhaps most influential of early twentieth-century Shakespeare critics, A. C. Bradley. Though Bradley was concerned to try and make the action of *King Lear* fit a providential schema that relies on generic closure, he also laments, in words that recall Donatus, the 'unexpected catastrophe' of the deaths of Lear and Cordelia.[66] This ending (or indeed non-ending) takes place 'outside the dramatic nexus', writes Bradley, as if it were a sort of grotesque outgrowth – 'or embossed carbuncle' (II.ii.413) – that 'monsters' (I.i.221) closure.[67]

Though it has often been criticised or even negated entirely through the act of appropriation, the violation of closure – of the catastrophe – in *King Lear* takes on shifting meanings in discrete historical moments. Lawrence L. Langer writes in *Preempting the Holocaust* that *King Lear* 'may be a singular exception' in tragic drama in that it does not allow for a 'cathartic resolution' or for aesthetic closure.[68] This uniquely qualifies the play, Langer contends, as an intertext for 'working through'

---

[63] Quoted in Joan Fitzpatrick, 'The Critical Backstory', in Andrew Hiscock and Lisa Hopkins (eds), *King Lear: A Critical Guide* (London: Continuum, 2011), p. 33.
[64] Ibid. pp. 33–4.
[65] Ibid. p. 40.
[66] A. C. Bradley, *Shakespearean Tragedy* (London: Penguin, 1991), p. 252.
[67] Ibid. p. 233.
[68] Lawrence L. Langer, *Preempting the Holocaust* (New Haven and London: Yale University Press, 1998), p. xvi.

questions around tragedy, subjectivity and meaning after the Holocaust, an event that for Langer (as for Adorno) clearly disallows the type of formal resolution that tragedy conventionally necessitates.[69] Rosen, who is also a Holocaust scholar, makes an analogous case, writing that 'historical catastrophes' (by which Rosen principally means Auschwitz) 'intersect with and alter the formal properties of catastrophe' and that 'formal violations of endings play a key role in the invention of genre' – a pertinent point for the way *King Lear* has been used in new forms of tragic drama.[70]

These ideas have also been picked up by John Joughin. Joughin insists on the necessity of situating the (non-)ending of *King Lear* in relation to post-Auschwitz culture. The ongoing cultural and historical 'afterlife' of the play in late modernity is related to its deep-seated formal disintegration. Joughin makes the case that *King Lear* is remarkable for its aesthetics of 'irruptive excess' – something Joughin (*à la* Booth) sees being epitomised by the final deaths of Cordelia and Lear, which happens 'outside an *a priori* grid of expectations' and refuses 'generic and ideological foreclosure'.[71] This makes *King Lear* the exemplary Shakespeare play 'after' Auschwitz. By virtue of its failure to resolve – by being 'constitutively incomplete and unfulfillable in its very failure to reconcile' – the play obviates the cumulative, 'harmonious' synthesis of part and whole, individual and universal, subject and object, instantiating the more fragmentary aesthetic that Adorno calls for 'after' the Holocaust.[72]

This aesthetic also catalyses an 'excessive affect', where the 'viewing subject experiences a sense of ungrounding and disorientation'.[73] The play occasions a type of uncanny, shuddering disequilibrium that challenges our interpretive capacities. Edgar (or Albany) might call for a form of collective response at the end of the play, but *King Lear* cannot ultimately be experienced through any unifying generic categories of 'meaningful interpretation' or 'reasonable explanation'.[74] By virtue of its violation of aesthetic resolution and the shallow moral 'saws' provided by Edgar and Albany, *King Lear* does not offer any consensual interpretive frame through which to contain the action, so displacing the subject 'outside' of a totalising conceptual system and occasioning

---

[69] Ibid.
[70] Rosen, *Dislocating the End*, p. 3.
[71] Joughin, '*Lear's* Afterlife', p. 70.
[72] Ibid. p. 78.
[73] Ibid. p. 71.
[74] Ibid. p. 67.

a more reflexive, individual response. There is no straightforward sense in which *King Lear* underwrites 'a form of restoration', states Joughin.[75] The play opens up 'a form of inexplicable alterity or otherness', rather than providing us with 'the grounded repleteness of a "meaningful" solution'.[76]

Conclusion

My analysis of the anti-form of *King Lear* is not to say that the play can be considered uncomplicatedly 'catastrophic', or that it depicts the type of ideologically illimitable subjects found in catastrophic post-war tragedy. The play is, however, obviously concerned with questions around catastrophe, modernity, subjectivity and tragic form in a way that makes it uniquely 'open' to post-Auschwitz appropriation. This chapter has shown that *King Lear* thematises catastrophe and its impact on human subjectivity; that the play depicts a historical shift to a rationalist ethos that precipitates disaster; that, in the throes of a systematically totalising *ratio*, subjectivity implicitly emerges in the play as a force of non-identity; and that, through its violation of the formalised dramatic convention of the catastrophe, *King Lear* subverts tragic resolution. This is not a comprehensive reading of *King Lear*; the aim has been to identify facets of the play that have made it so vital an intertext for various theatres of catastrophe.

Chapter 3 analyses the history of *King Lear* in the post-war era, considering the way in which a range of critics, practitioners and playwrights have interpreted its representation of catastrophe, modernity, subjectivity and its aesthetic form 'after' Auschwitz.

---

[75] Ibid. p. 78.
[76] Ibid. p. 67.

Chapter 3

'Strange mutations': The History of *King Lear* 'After' Auschwitz

Introduction

Few plays have been so widely and varyingly read, staged and appropriated as *King Lear*. The play has drawn an array of critical and artistic interpretations, even becoming 'an exemplary site of contention' between the dominant paradigms of 'contemporary criticism'.[1] This chapter will analyse the critical, performance and appropriation history of *King Lear* in the post-war era. The aim is to provide a newly conceived history of the play, revealing the vital role *King Lear* has played in shifting ideational and dramaturgical responses to modern catastrophe. This is most obviously marked by the deep and ongoing tie between *King Lear* and the Holocaust. The spectre of Auschwitz continues to haunt the discourse surrounding the play: it is an event that underscores the contemporary relevance of *King Lear* and its vision of disaster, while *King Lear* has also become a drama through which seemingly incomprehensible atrocities may be interpreted and understood.

This analysis of the post-war history of *King Lear*, while wide-ranging, cannot be all-inclusive. To gain a wider historical understanding of *King Lear*, I have identified for analysis some of the more important interpretations, stagings and appropriations of the play, which emblematise developments in its reception over the post-war era. By analysing the modern history of *King Lear*, I want to demonstrate that the playwrights I study are embedded in a wider constellation of ideas around the play and modern mass disaster. This constellation comprises various conceptions of catastrophe, the modern subject and tragic aesthetics, as critics,

---

[1] Kiernan Ryan, '*King Lear*: A Retrospective, 1980–2000', *Shakespeare Survey: Volume 55*, ed. Peter Holland (Cambridge: Cambridge University Press, 2002), p. 1.

directors and playwrights developed changing and often competing responses to a play that came to be seen as the Shakespearean drama for 'our times'. It is not always the case that playwrights who appropriate *King Lear* are responding directly to other interpretations or stagings of the play in the post-war era. But if *King Lear* 'has entered the fabric of artistic and critical discourse as a play somehow capable of shedding light on catastrophe, of providing illumination in the wake – and the midst – of disaster', appropriations should be seen as part, if a distinct part, of that wider artistic and cultural 'fabric'.[2]

This analysis traces changing responses to *King Lear* from 1939 to the 2010s, from the outbreak of the Second World War up until the contemporary moment, trailing catastrophe from the outbreak of total war and the Holocaust to globalisation, the calamity of the 2008 crash and climate change. The chapter is split into sections on the 1940s and 1950s, the 1960s and 1970s, the 1980s and 1990s, and the 2000s and 2010s. Each section will analyse *King Lear* in criticism before going on to consider the play in performance and any dramatic appropriations, drawing out some of the relationships between these various forms of interpretive intervention. This approach is not to say that new understandings of *King Lear* displace previous interpretations as the decades go by. On the contrary: it is often the case that an interpretation of the play lives far beyond its originary moment and continues to influence its cultural reception, even as new paradigms emerge over time. These periods do, however, represent important changes in the post-war history of *King Lear* and the way the play has been understood.

The 1940s and 1950s: The Christian Consensus and the Perils of Modernity, or 'the gods are just'

King Lear in Criticism

Over the period of the Second World War and its direct aftermath, the action of *King Lear* was predominantly understood to reproduce the Christian morality play tradition. Though set in a pre-Christian, pagan world, the play, as Christian readings would have it, depicts a proud and sinful king who, through his purgatorial suffering in the storm, ultimately achieves salvation as he undergoes a Christian pilgrimage through

---

[2] Emily Sun, *Succeeding King Lear: Literature, Exposure and the Possibility of Politics* (New York: Fordham University Press, 2010), p. 14.

'sin-suffering-redemption'.³ These religiously inclined readings of *King Lear* (and Lear) were unwaveringly common: R.W. Chambers, Irving Ribner, R. B. Heilman and Kenneth Muir are only a few of the critics to make the case that *King Lear* is nothing short of a 'sublime morality play', with Muir observing that, while Lear may lose the world, through his revelatory night in the storm he 'gains his soul'.⁴

This interpretation pays witness to the profound influence of A. C. Bradley on post-war Shakespeare criticism. Bradley had concentrated his analysis of *King Lear* most acutely on the storm scenes, where Lear, after being pushed out into the wilderness and stripped of his status and even his clothes, reaches through suffering 'the power of moral perception and reflection' as a result of a 'process of purification'.⁵ This redemptionist reading even took in the final, catastrophic *dénouement*, where Lear hunches over the corpse of Cordelia and repeats his hopeless, echoing 'Never, never, never, never, never' (V.iii.307). Bradley takes Lear at his word when he states the survival of Cordelia would 'redeem all sorrows / That ever I have felt' (V.vii.264–5). His sudden (Folio only) 'Look on her: look, her lips' (V.iii.309) before he dies signifies that Lear (if not those around him, or indeed the audience) does believe Cordelia is alive and so passes 'redeemed' from his doubtful 'sorrows'. This prompts Bradley famously to make the case that the play might be retitled *The Redemption of King Lear*, with Lear dying in an ecstasy, not of unredeemed agony, but unbearable '*joy*'.⁶

Bradley does not necessarily make the case that *King Lear* is a Christian play, but his stress on redemption implies a Christian interpretation that would universalise *King Lear* into a morality tale on the suffering of 'Man' (or Everyman) on his 'quest' to find deliverance from sin.⁷ There are moments in his analysis of *King Lear* where Bradley seems to contradict his own case – not least when stating that the end of

---

³ I take the phrase 'sin-suffering-redemption' from William Elton and his *King Lear and the Gods* (Lexington: The University Press of Kentucky, 1966), p. 337. I touch on Elton again when analysing *King Lear* criticism in the 1960s.

⁴ O.J. Campbell, 'The Salvation of Lear', *English Literary History*, 15 (1948), p. 94; Kenneth Muir, 'Introduction', in William Shakespeare, *King Lear*, ed. Kenneth Muir (London: Methuen, 1952), p. lix. See also R. W. Chambers, *King Lear*, W. P. Ker Memorial Lecture, 1939 (Glasgow: Jackson Son and Co., 1940); Irving Ribner, '"The Gods are Just": A Reading of *King Lear*', *Tulane Drama Review*, 2:3 (1958), pp. 34–54; Robert B. Heilman, 'The Unity of "*King Lear*"', *The Sewanee Review*, 56:1 (1948), pp. 58–68.

⁵ A. C. Bradley, *Shakespearean Tragedy* (London: Penguin, 1991), p. 263 and p. 266.

⁶ Ibid. p. 262 and p. 269.

⁷ Ibid. p. 261.

the play appears to be 'a dramatic mistake' and that disaster has to be contained within 'certain limits in tragic art'.[8] The implication is that *King Lear* does not necessarily observe the traditional limits of tragic art. These doubts were not, however, recognised by the Christian critics that emerged in the post-war period.

The prominence given in Christian readings to the 'final victory' of the good over and against a 'poisonous evil' concerned with conquest and power had an obvious attraction during and after the Second World War.[9] William French has made the case that, where the rise of Nazism in Germany and Europe had represented 'a mortal threat' to the very survival of traditional 'British Christian civilization', for wartime and post-war critics the Bradleyean notion of redemption proved to be 'an irresistible temptation'.[10] This concern with the inherited values of traditional 'Christian civilization' preoccupied no few critics, from Theodore Spencer to Edwin Muir. These critics would have it that *King Lear* depicts the rise of modern, disenchanted ideologies and social systems concerned with total power, which are pitted against a pre-modern, Christian cultural world based on the values of patriarchy and fealty. This was often understood in terms of a clash between 'natural' and 'unnatural' forms of society, with Muir claiming that Lear and others embody 'an order of society so obviously springing from the nature and needs of man that it can be called natural'.[11] But the idea that *King Lear* represents an epochal schism found its most eloquent interpreter in John F. Danby, who also interpreted the play as developing shifting conceptions of 'nature' and the 'natural'.

Danby contends that *King Lear* depicts a seismic shift from a traditional, Christian world that has its basis in a conception of nature as benignant order of patriarchal relationships, to a more recognisably modern conception of nature as competition, where inherited relationships are overturned.[12] Danby writes that, through its representation of epochal change, *King Lear* presages 'the new age of scientific enquiry,

---

[8] Ibid. p. 235 and p. 297. Bradley also writes that Shakespearean tragedy should 'be a self-contained whole with a catastrophe' (p. 256) – by which he means formal closure.

[9] Chambers, *King Lear*, p. 25.

[10] William W. French, 'A Kind of Courage: *King Lear* at the Old Vic, London, 1940', *Theatre Topics*, 3:1 (1993), p. 52 and p. 53.

[11] Edwin Muir, 'The Politics of *King Lear*', W. P. Ker Memorial Lecture, 1946 (Glasgow: Glasgow University Publications, 1947), p. 49. See also Theodore Spencer, *Shakespeare and the Nature of Man* (New York: Macmillan, 1942).

[12] John F. Danby, *Shakespeare's Doctrine of Nature: A Study of King Lear* (London: Faber, 1949). The text was reprinted in 1951, 1958 and 1961.

of industrial development, of bureaucratic organisation and social regimentation'.[13] This nascent era of Weberian disenchantment is, in its capitalistic iteration, epitomised by the 'New Man' Edmund, who spurns traditional social relationships in his individualistic 'impulse to acquire'.[14] But it can also be seen in other characters. When an irate Lear casts Cordelia out for refusing to quantify her love in the gross conditions he demands – 'Which of you shall we say doth love us most / That we our largest bounty may extend' (I.i.51–2) – he falls foul of the same instrumentalising rationality seen in Edmund. This causes Danby to make the case that Cordelia – in her commitment to the 'natural' 'bond[s]' (I.i.93) of familial and national fealty, which are at threat of being displaced – is representative of 'the perfection of truth, justice, charity'.[15] If in his dark night of the soul Lear gains new moral perception, for Danby that 'redemption' is not merely personal, but also implies a return to the ties of traditional society.[16] Danby believes that Lear is 'redeemed' from nothing less than the 'New Age' of disenchanted, secular rationality, as represented by his tearful reconciliation with Cordelia in Act Four.

The critique Danby mounts in his analysis of *King Lear* is predominantly against the 'New Man' of the capitalist revolution. But when Danby makes the (frankly startling) observation that the 'prison' (V.iii.9) to which Lear and Cordelia are led away towards the end of the play 'points to the continuing possibility of [the] concentration camp', it becomes obvious that, in his interpretation of *King Lear* as a conservative Christian drama, his critique relates not only to capitalism but to modernity and – in its most horrifying manifestation – fascism and the Holocaust.[17] Edmund presages not only the fallen world of capital, but also the world of the camp, a world where people become mere ciphers for an unconstrained, total power – though perhaps oddly, Danby seems blind to the way the Nazis combined modernity with dark myths about a traditional 'organic' community, invalidating any idea of 'good-natured patriarchy'.[18]

Geoffrey Bickersteth, writing on Edmund ('Yet if Edmunds exist, Cordelias must perish') in 1946, remarks on the 'close resemblance' of

---

[13] Ibid. p. 46.

[14] Ibid. p. 41.

[15] Ibid. p. 138.

[16] See also R. A. Foakes, *Hamlet Versus Lear: Cultural Politics and Shakespeare's Art* (Cambridge: Cambridge University Press, 1993), p. 53.

[17] Danby, *Shakespeare's Doctrine of Nature*, p. 194.

[18] Theodor Adorno, 'Reflections on Class Theory', in Theodor Adorno, *Can One Live After Auschwitz?*, ed. Rolf Tiedemann, trans. Rodney Livingstone et al. (Stanford: Stanford University Press, 2003), p. 93.

King Lear to 'the world as experienced by countless millions of human beings at the present time' – a world that is 'characterised above all by the fact it suffers'.[19] He quotes Caroline Spurgeon to identify the central image of the play as

> 'a human body in anguished movement, tugged, wrenched, beaten, pierced, stung, scourged, dislocated, flayed, gashed, scalded, tortured and, finally, broken on the rack' – the image, in short, of a German concentration camp, a Belsen or Dachau expanded to include the whole human race, its Hitlers and Himmlers the very gods themselves, wantonly killing us like flies.[20]

This same analogy – or perhaps genealogy – between Edmund and Nazism is posited by Benjamin Spencer, who, in his 1944 piece '*King Lear*: A Prophetic Tragedy', makes the case that Edmund – by overturning the traditional 'bonds of family and society' – has a surprising 'lineal descendant' in 'the Nazi spokesman, Dr Hans Frank', the Governor-General of occupied Poland in the Second World War, who instituted a reign of terror against the civilian population and became directly involved in the mass murder of Jews.[21] *King Lear* is 'prophetic' because Shakespeare not only sensed 'the tragic vulnerability and the potential barbarism' that were 'implicit in the individualism and in the social relationships of the emergent Renaissance culture' but also 'presaged something of the character of a succeeding era'.[22] G. B. Harrison writes: '*Lear* was written by a man who had seen a vision of absolute evil such as was given to those who sat through the Nuremberg trials, or who first entered Dachau or Belsen in 1945 – a world in which good, however pure and refined, is overwhelmed by evil.'[23]

Danby contends that *King Lear* represents the catastrophic eruption of modernity and a less disenchanted time when subject and object, individual and society, word and feeling, and even mind and body were not – as Gloucester imagines it – 'crack'd' (I.ii.105) but part of a harmoniously unified form of life, which is ordered by traditional

---

[19] Geoffrey Bickersteth, 'The Golden World of *King Lear*', *British Academy Annual Shakespeare Lectures, 1946–1951* (London: Geoffrey Cumberlege Amen House, 1951), p. 19 and p. 13.

[20] Ibid. p. 13.

[21] Benjamin Spencer, '*King Lear*: A Prophetic Tragedy', *College English*, 5:6 (1944), p. 305. For more on Hans Frank and his role in the Holocaust, see Martyn Housden, *Hans Frank: Lebensraum and the Holocaust* (Basingstoke: Palgrave Macmillan, 2003). Frank was found guilty of war crimes in 1946 and hanged.

[22] Spencer, '*King Lear*: A Prophetic Tragedy', p. 306.

[23] G. B. Harrison, *Shakespeare's Tragedies* (London: Routledge, 1951), p. 159.

values.[24] The inherent desirability of that more traditional cultural world is, as Danby sees it, the 'final outcome' of the 'achieved insights' of Shakespeare and 'the wisdom the tragic period establishes', where tragedy is identified with the ruinous breakdown of society but also its final reinstitution.[25] These ideas around organic 'unity' also inform the way Danby understands aesthetic form.[26] Danby views *King Lear* as a unified aesthetic whole that progresses towards closure. While it depicts the catastrophe of modernity, *King Lear* ultimately enacts formal resolution, which Danby sees as embodied by Edgar, his chivalric victory over Edmund and his rise to the throne.[27] The play for Danby is as formally unified as the idealised world it represents, progressing as it does towards a morally and artistically coherent outcome.

For many critics in the 1940s and 1950s, Edmund, Goneril and Regan typify modernity and even, in the words of Muir, 'the rise of Fascism', while Lear, Cordelia and Edgar represent an imperilled but finally triumphant 'communal tradition'.[28] This interpretation represents a desire to find within 'an idealized British culture the basis for regeneration into a desired post-war redemptive utopia, in the wake of the Gonerils and Regans of Nazism'.[29] This same desire can also be seen in the performance history of *King Lear* over the period and, perhaps most powerfully, in the 1940 production of the play at the Old Vic.

King Lear in Performance

John Gielgud took up the role of the ageing King Lear in the 1940 Old Vic production, a staging nominally directed by Lewis Casson but, in reality, dominated by the ideas and presence of Harley Granville-Barker.[30] While the choice of Shakespeare for a wartime production was not unusual, with *Henry V* often used for the purposes of wartime propaganda, the choice

---

[24] See also Foakes, *Hamlet Versus Lear*, p. 54.
[25] Danby, *Shakespeare's Doctrine of Nature*, p. 189.
[26] Ibid. p. 169. See also Hugh Grady, *The Modernist Shakespeare: Critical Texts in a Material World* (Oxford: Clarendon Press, 1991) for the high modernist concept of aesthetic unity.
[27] Danby, *Shakespeare's Doctrine of Nature*, p. 191.
[28] Quoted in Foakes, 'Introduction', in Shakespeare, *King Lear*, ed. Foakes, p. 44.
[29] Hugh Grady, *Shakespeare's Universal Wolf: Studies in Early Modern Reification* (Oxford: Clarendon Press, 1996), p. 161.
[30] See Jonathan Croall, *Performing King Lear: Gielgud to Russell Beale* (London: Bloomsbury, 2015), pp. 22–5. Granville-Barker sets out his (largely Christian redemptionist) reading of *King Lear* in his *Preface to King Lear*, originally published in 1927 (London: Nick Hern Books, 1993).

of *King Lear* was: in 1940 the play was 'not part of the Shakespeare canon that dominated the English theatre' and, perhaps more to the point, a play that depicts a foreign army invading Britain – with the aid of collaborators who, in the form of Kent and Gloucester, conspire with foreign forces – 'may not have seemed a wise choice at the time'.[31]

King Lear, as viewed by Gielgud and Granville-Barker, is representative of the traditional values that were under threat from modernity: the choice of the play at the outset of the war reflected, on the parts of both Granville-Barker and Gielgud, an 'idealistic view of the social role of theatre' converging with a 'sense of the Nazi threat to civilized values'.[32] 'Nothing but a mighty work like *King Lear* could have kept one so concentrated', reflected Gielgud, 'with such a holocaust going on around us' – his use of the (un-capitalised) word 'holocaust' signifying the war generally, as opposed to the Shoah.[33] The play was to be used to unify audiences around British and Christian ideals in a period of wartime suffering and deepening social and political distress. 'Our fight has been a fight for the future of Christian civilization', stated Granville-Barker after the war, 'and it was bound to be won.'[34]

The collective address ('our fight') was reflected in the spatial arrangements of the Old Vic stage, recorded in the copious notes of Hallam Fordham.[35] During the storm, Gielgud occupied the front of the stage and physically knelt during his 'prayer' to the suffering, the 'poor naked wretches'. When the prayer ended – 'And show the heavens more just' (III.iv.36) – Gielgud 'dropped his hands in front of him, palms outward, in a gesture of complete supplicatory resignation to suffering'.[36] This posture signified that his struggle had been resolved, as suffering evoked – not rage and egoistic pride – but patience and compassion.[37] By bringing Lear out of the picture-frame of the proscenium arch and onto the apron during the scenes in the storm, Gielgud and Granville-Barker catalysed deeper identification with the suffering of Lear, bringing Gielgud closer to the audience with the aim of 'empowering them with

---

[31] French, 'A Kind of Courage', p. 47.
[32] Ibid. p. 46.
[33] John Gielgud, *Sir John Gielgud: A Life in Letters*, ed. Richard Mangan (New York: Arcade Publishing, 2004), p. 59.
[34] Harley Granville-Barker, *The Use of the Drama* (Princeton: Princeton University Press, 1945), p. 88.
[35] These can be found in the Folger Shakespeare Library, but Alexander Leggatt provides some analysis in his *Shakespeare in Performance: King Lear*, 2nd edn (Manchester: Manchester University Press, 2005), pp. 25–40.
[36] French, 'A Kind of Courage', p. 52.
[37] Ibid.

the mythic collective power' of the 'Christian' and national values Lear 'embodied'.[38] The play ended with formalised gestures of mourning, implying an end to the violence and the final restitution of a divinely sanctioned, Christian religious and social order.[39]

French astutely observes that the 'positive', Christian interpretation of *King Lear* in the 1940 production seemed more plausible at a time 'before bombs fell upon London, before the first Nazi rockets whistled in, before Auschwitz had become a household word for horror, before Hiroshima was incinerated'.[40] Chambers betrays the ideological and historical limits of the Christian interpretation of *King Lear* when he considers other versions of the Lear story, in which Cordelia gives in to despair and commits suicide, and the Shakespeare *King Lear*, in relation to the concentration camps. Chambers makes the case that:

> in our days the communication has been smuggled out of Concentration Camps: 'You will be told that I committed suicide: it will not be true.' The sender of the communication has wished to save his reputation from what he feels would be a slur upon it.[41]

Shakespeare does not allow Cordelia to do the 'unbearable', which is to give in to the newly emergent forces of modernity (represented by Edmund and others) and commit self-slaughter, because 'the feeling of Christendom, and often that of the pagan world also, has been that men and women may not kill themselves to avoid the torture or the tedium of imprisonment or sickness'.[42] Chambers is writing in 1939, before the Final Solution and the revelation of the full horrors of the death camps, which entailed far more suffering and degradation than the mere 'tedium' of imprisonment or even simply 'torture'. These revelations would severely undermine the idea that Christian belief – and the stoic fortitude of martyrdom – may be enough to challenge the destructive social and political systems of modernity.

Even so, the conservative interpretation of *King Lear* as a parable of Christian redemption still held sway both in criticism and on the stage for most of the 1940s and 1950s.[43] It was not until the 1960s that the Christian consensus began seriously to be challenged.

---

[38] Ibid. p. 51.
[39] Leggatt, *Shakespeare in Performance: King Lear*, p. 34.
[40] French, 'A Kind of Courage', p. 54.
[41] Chambers, *King Lear*, pp. 22–3. I have not been able to trace the source of the quote, which Chambers does not reference. It may be his invention.
[42] Ibid. p. 22.
[43] One exception is the experimental 1955 Gielgud/George Devine production, which included futuristic sets and costumes by the American-Japanese designer

The 1960s and the 1970s: From the Absurd to the Political, or 'as flies to wanton boys'?

King Lear in Criticism

Over the 1940s and 1950s, *King Lear* was typically read 'positively' as a story of Christian redemption, even being conscripted as a bulwark of traditional social and moral values in the face of a catastrophic modernity, represented most disturbingly by the camp system and Auschwitz. But in the 1960s, the play began to be read 'negatively', as violating the type of schematic Christian worldview that would finally see Lear redeemed through his sufferings.

This newly negative tone was set by Barbara Everett in her pathbreaking 1960 piece 'The New *King Lear*', in which she contests the Christian readings of *King Lear* that had dominated Shakespeare criticism – and the recent performance history of the play.[44] She does so by squaring in on the ongoing legacy of Bradley. Everett makes the case that Christian interpretations had overstated the aspects of Bradley that imply a Christian understanding of *King Lear*, obscuring his 'honest doubt' about the play and the purported 'redemption' of Lear.[45] Everett writes that, while Lear may make a variety of tragic 'discoveries' over the play, it remains more than 'hard to accept that the moral weight of these discoveries presents some kind of counterpoint to the sufferings he has undergone'.[46] William Elton similarly sets out to challenge the 'widespread view' of previous critics that *King Lear* is 'an optimistically Christian drama', in the sense that the redemptive suffering of Lear is indicative of 'a cosmically derived plan, which somehow gives providential significance to the events of the tragedy'.[47] Elton insists that – crucially – 'no evidence exists to show that Lear arrives finally at "salvation", "regeneration" or "redemption"', meaning the benevolent providence ascribed to the play 'cannot be shown to be operative'.[48] He even goes as far as to say that the ending of the play 'shatters, more violently than any earlier apostasy may have done, the very foundations of Christian faith itself'.[49] J. Stampfer echoes Everett and Elton when

---

Isamu Noguchi. The production caused a furore, perhaps indicting the depth of cultural investment in a Christian conception of *King Lear*.
[44] Barbara Everett, 'The New *King Lear*', *Critical Quarterly*, 2 (1960), pp. 325–39.
[45] Ibid. p. 335.
[46] Ibid. p. 336.
[47] Elton, *King Lear and the Gods*, p. 3.
[48] Ibid. p. 336.
[49] Ibid. p. 337.

he writes that the 'purgation' and 'spiritual regeneration' of Lear take place not at the end of the play, but in Acts Three and Four, while Act Five only serves to confirm 'the worst fear' – that humanity inhabits 'an imbecile universe'.[50] The agonised questions that Lear poses over the corpse of Cordelia – 'Why should a dog, a horse, a rat have life / And thou no breath at all?' (V.iii.305–6) – reverberate unanswered, in a cosmic void.

Far from revealing a providentially ordained world order, which is shattered by modernity but still finally restored, the 'new' understanding of *King Lear* that emerged in the 1960s insists that the play depicts a godless cosmos which is resistant to meaning and understanding. This interpretation of *King Lear* involves a radically changed understanding of its aesthetic form. Danby and other Christian interpreters had made the case that *King Lear* progresses towards a morally Christian ending – something that Heilman had described in 1948 as 'The Unity of "*King Lear*"'.[51] But the play as read by Everett, Stampfer and Elton violates the aesthetic closure imputed to it by previous critics. Lear may achieve some form of salvation in Act Four – but the play violently rolls into Act Five, which transgresses 'the promised end' of Christian redemption. The play is remarkable less for its aesthetic 'unity' than its irruptive aesthetic deformity, which has 'no relish of salvation in't' (*Hamlet*, III. iii.92). Dennis Kennedy, tying the aesthetic form of *King Lear* to contemporary catastrophes, remarked in 1976 that, after the cataclysm of 'the death camps, and the daily threat of whimsical world-annihilation, the ending of *King Lear* seems not only appropriate but necessary'.[52] 'What the history of our century has allowed us to do', Kennedy forcefully concludes, 'is to face squarely the terrifying implications of the final scene, the possibility that "Truth and Vertue" may be rewarded with the same cosmic indifference as treachery and evil.'[53]

Foakes makes the case that the challenge mounted to the Christian interpretation of *King Lear* in the early years of the 1960s can (and should) be read in direct relation to contemporaneous global social and political events – most obviously the deepening tensions of the Cold War and the threat of nuclear apocalypse. Foakes observes that the hydrogen bomb was tested in 1956, the Berlin Wall built in 1961, the Cuban crisis

---

[50] J. Stampfer, 'The Catharsis in *King Lear*', *Shakespeare Survey: Volume 13*, ed. Allardyce Nicoll (Cambridge: Cambridge University Press, 1966), p. 10.
[51] See Heilman, 'The Unity of "*King Lear*"'.
[52] Dennis Kennedy, '"*King Lear*" and the Theatre', *Educational Theatre Journal*, 28:1 (1976), p. 40.
[53] Ibid. p. 41.

played out over 1961–2, and the US involvement in and commitment to the Vietnam War continued over the period of the 1960s before eventual withdrawal (and the fall of Saigon) in the 1970s.[54] But shifting responses to the play also reflected the growth of public and political consciousness about the Holocaust. It was only in the 1960s and the 1970s that the full scale of the atrocities committed during the Second World War began to be more widely known. The Adolf Eichmann trial in 1961, famously covered by Hannah Arendt in *Eichmann in Jerusalem*, and the Frankfurt Auschwitz trials of 1963–5 increased public awareness about the unparalleled suffering and degradation of the Nazi camps.[55] The scale of destruction unleashed in the Holocaust – along with the prospect of total nuclear warfare – profoundly challenged the idea that history has any providential meaning or that salvation from a fallen world is possible, inaugurating a new conception of human life as inherently absurd. Under the horrifying conditions of 'arbitrary servitude and extermination', writes George Steiner in 1971, 'our prognostication must be that of Edgar in *King Lear*: "And worse I may be yet"'.[56]

The novelist Rosamond Lehmann had remarked in 1946 that 'This is the time, the age, to take in *Lear*': 'It seemed prophetic for our age – the gigantic moral anarchy – every word true', even comparing the final image of the dead Cordelia to a female inmate at Bergen-Belsen 'thrown away on a concentration camp rubbish heap'.[57] But where in the 1940s and 1950s the cultural and moral anarchy represented in *King Lear* finally gave way to the hope of Christian redemption, by the 1960s Christian consolation was being challenged and the contemporariness of the play aligned with its unrelieved, nightmare vision of a world without any meaning. Writing in his 1965 *King Lear in Our Time*, Maynard Mack contends that 'after the World Wars and Auschwitz', the violence of *King Lear* – 'its sadism, madness and processional of deaths' – 'resonates more powerfully' than it had done for pre-war and even wartime audiences.[58] Other critics similarly observed that *King*

---

[54] Foakes, *Hamlet Versus Lear*, p. 58 and p. 71.
[55] For more on the Holocaust and international public awareness, see the exemplary David S. Wyman (ed.), *The World Reacts to the Holocaust* (Baltimore and London: The Johns Hopkins University Press, 1996). I return to Arendt in Chapter 4.
[56] George Steiner, *In Bluebeard's Castle: Some Notes Towards the Redefinition of Culture* (New Haven: Yale University Press, 1971), p. 69.
[57] Quoted in Terry Coleman, *Olivier: The Authorised Biography* (London: Bloomsbury, 2005), p. 189.
[58] Maynard Mack, *'King Lear' in Our Time* (Berkeley and Los Angeles: University of California Press, 1965), p. 25.

Lear 'is above all others the Shakespearean play of our time', as its 'holocaust vision accommodates the horrors of the twentieth century more adequately than the moody introspection of *Hamlet*', with L. C. Knights writing in 1960 that *King Lear* is the play in which 'the age most finds itself'.[59]

By far the most powerful voice proclaiming the modern 'resonance' of *King Lear* (and Shakespeare) in the 1960s was Jan Kott, whose influential *Shakespeare Our Contemporary* was published in 1964.[60] Kott – a Pole from a Jewish background who had lived through Nazi occupation, the Holocaust and the social and political regressions of Soviet communism – insists on reading *King Lear* through the prism of disastrous modern events, which comprised:

> modern war in all its destructiveness, occupation by invading armies, life in bombed out cities, the *univers concentrationnaire* – that whole Dante-esque inferno of concentration camps, gas chambers, genocide – and the world of ghettos and [...] systematic destruction.[61]

These catastrophic events revealed that human life, far from inhering to the type of immanently meaningful providential schema Christian critics had found represented in *King Lear*, is absurd – that its 'sole meaning is its meaninglessness'.[62] 'Auschwitz is no exception, but the rule', writes Kott: 'History is a sequence of Auschwitzes.'[63] The concentration camps have, Kott contends, revealed the meaningless absurdity of the human condition, which obtains throughout history. This is precisely the vision found in *King Lear*: Kott remarks that, in the damaged and despairing world that Shakespeare portrays in *King Lear*, 'there is neither Christian heaven, nor the heaven predicted and believed in by humanists' – precisely the utopian endpoints that had been imagined in recent interpretations of the play:

> *King Lear* makes a tragic mockery of all eschatologies: of the heaven promised on earth, and the heaven promised after death; of both Christian and secular theodicies; of cosmogony and of the rational view of history; of the gods and natural goodness, of man made in the 'image and likeness'.[64]

---

[59] Ibid. p. 87; Herbert Coursen, *Reading Shakespeare on Stage* (London: Associated University Presses, 1995), p. 134; L. C. Knights, *Some Shakespearean Themes: And An Approach to 'Hamlet'* (Stanford: Stanford University Press, 1950), p. 153.
[60] Jan Kott, *Shakespeare Our Contemporary* (New York: Norton, 1974).
[61] Martin Esslin, 'Introduction', in Kott, *Shakespeare Our Contemporary*, p. xiii.
[62] Ibid. p. xx.
[63] Jan Kott, *The Theatre of Essence* (Evanston: Northwestern University Press, 1985), p. 177.
[64] Kott, *Shakespeare Our Contemporary*, p. 147.

Kott stresses the contemporaneity of *King Lear* by drawing parallels between its hopeless vision of an imbecile universe and the drama of Beckett. *King Lear*, as Kott understands it, is less of a conventional tragedy than it is a presciently absurdist play. This is typified by the representation of the tragic subject in the play. Kott contends that in *King Lear* the individual, far from being free, finds him or herself trapped in degrading but inescapable situations – a reading that, as discussed in Chapter 7, relies on his reading of the scene at Dover 'cliff'. This stress on closed systems reflects the apparent absence of any wider metaphysical schema that provides history and tragedy with meaning – or, as Kott calls it, 'the Auschwitz experience'.[65] With the collapse of any transcendent value, human life is deprived of tragic worth and grandeur, as the subject is reduced to grotesque clowning and arbitrary violence. *King Lear* represents a 'great stage of fools' (IV.vi.179) in a world where humanity has been abandoned and left 'darkling' (I.iv.208). Unable to pursue self-realisation, all the tragic subject can do is stoically endure the depredations of an absurd cosmos. The action of *King Lear*, Kott pronounces, leaves no room for 'freedom of choice.'[66]

The Kott reading of *King Lear* as paradigmatic work of the Theatre of the Absurd gave, in the words of Foakes, 'powerful currency' to 'a bleak reading' of *King Lear* that stressed its 'supreme tragic horror'.[67] But some more positive, politically informed understandings of *King Lear* were also beginning to emerge in Shakespeare studies over the 1960s into the 1970s. If the play truly did presage a rent world of violence and even the concentration camps, for Marxist critics the response that disaster called for is not resignation to events, but revolutionary social and political action, to overturn the reifying conditions that produce catastrophe. This required a new conception of the subject and tragedy. Where the absurdist interpretation provided by Kott denied the possibility of human agency, political interpretations of *King Lear* called upon a 'heroic' subject able to act meaningfully on the world. This tragic heroism was often understood to be embodied by Lear himself.

Arnold Kettle set the priorities for political readings of *King Lear* in his 1964 piece 'From Hamlet to Lear'.[68] Kettle contends that, in its representation of a transition from a feudal to a bourgeois social order, a more radically egalitarian socialist ethos is also incipient in *King Lear*

---

[65] Ibid. p. 92.
[66] Ibid. p. 132.
[67] Foakes, *Hamlet Versus Lear*, p. 59.
[68] Arnold Kettle, 'From Hamlet to Lear', in Arnold Kettle (ed.), *Shakespeare in a Changing World* (London: Laurence and Wishart, 1964), pp. 146–71.

– not least in the scenes in the storm and on the heath, where Lear identifies with the poor and promises to act against social inequality. Kettle sees the rampant individualism of Goneril, Regan and Edmund as being already outmoded by a more humane dispensation the play is prefiguring in the midst of images of historical strife and ruin. This dispensation is, as Kettle reads the play, embodied by Lear, whom Kettle sees as a tragic 'hero' – by which he means someone who, though ultimately destroyed by the dominant forces of history, bears 'something of the actual aspirations of humanity in its struggle to advance its condition'.[69]

The revolutionary spirit of the late 1960s is perhaps most apparent in the words of H. A. Mason, who writes in his 1970 work *Shakespeare's Tragedies of Love* that Lear dies not in a rhapsody of Christian hope or in nihilistic despair but as 'an obstinately unreconstructed rebel' – as if Lear died 'most rebel-like' (IV.iii.14) with a Molotov cocktail in his hand.[70] The same idea is pursued by S. L. Goldberg in his 1974 *An Essay on King Lear*, where Goldberg echoes Kettle and makes the case that Lear can be seen as a 'heroic' figure who discovers the impulse to act 'energetically in and on the world'.[71] Lear, as Goldberg reads the play, recognises 'the need both to realize an essential capacity of the self and to make "justice" an objective reality'.[72] The 'true need' of humanity is for nothing less than concerted 'action and justice'.[73] Lear and Cordelia may die, but Lear fights to the end, even killing the soldier who hangs Cordelia.

These readings were obviously informed by the radical political interventions of 1968, which saw student unrest and protests break out across Europe and other parts of the world. The uprisings were inspired by the prospect of a radically changed future society, which broke with the capitalist system; but protests were also about a reckoning with the catastrophic fallout of recent history. Moshie Postone and Eric Santner observe that 'the student revolts in the 1960s are generally held to be a crucial breakthrough in the history of responses to the Holocaust', which often 'took shape within the frame of critiques of capitalism'.[74] It was not unusual for the movements of the time to 'discern a continuity

---

[69] Quoted in Kiernan Ryan (ed.), *King Lear: Contemporary Critical Essays* (Basingstoke: Macmillan, 1993), p. 29.
[70] H. A. Mason, *Shakespeare's Tragedies of Love* (London: Chatto and Windus, 1970), p. 226.
[71] S. L. Goldberg, *An Essay on King Lear* (Cambridge: Cambridge University Press, 1974), p. 117.
[72] Ibid.
[73] Ibid.
[74] Moshie Postone and Eric Santner, *Catastrophe and Meaning: The Holocaust and the Twentieth Century* (Chicago: University of Chicago Press, 2003), p. 5.

of the societal relations characteristic of National Socialism and those of post-Auschwitz Western liberal democracies in capitalism'.[75] 'The world today', as Herbert Marcuse writes in his 1964 *One-Dimensional Man*, which is sometimes thought of as the 'bible' of the student movement and 1960s activism, 'is still that of the gas chambers and concentration camps': 'Auschwitz continues to haunt.'[76] Kettle, who fought in the Second World War, does not necessarily align *King Lear* with the Holocaust, but he does write in his analysis of the poetry of W. H. Auden of the unavoidable 'necessity of politics' and of 'human solidarity' of precisely the type that he finds in *King Lear* when faced, not only with the inhumane 'corruption' of contemporary capitalist culture, but also with 'the Nazi concentration camps and the crosses in the War Cemeteries spread out beneath the skies of Europe'.[77] This convergence of a desire for revolutionary action and a critique of the unprecedented scale of modern catastrophe is perhaps most obvious in the drama of Edward Bond, as discussed in Chapter 4.

The divergence between absurdist and political interpretations of *King Lear* (and, indeed, the Holocaust) also relates to the performance history of the play over the 1960s and 1970s, as exemplified by the 1962 Peter Brook production and the 1974 Buzz Goodbody *Lear*.

King Lear in Performance

Shakespeare Our Contemporary did not appear in English until 1964, but Peter Brook – whose production of *Titus Andronicus*, with Laurence Olivier as Titus, Kott had seen in Warsaw in 1957 – read the French edition in the early 1960s.[78] His 1962 RSC production of *King Lear* at Stratford, with Paul Scofield taking the title role, was famously influenced by the absurdist reading pioneered by Kott, which changed the way Brook thought about Shakespeare, tragedy and modernity.[79] Through

---

[75] Erik Vogt, '"The Useless Residue of the Western Idea of Art": Adorno and Lacouc-Labarthe Concerning Art "After" Auschwitz', in Ryan Crawford and Erik Vogt (eds), *Adorno and the Concept of Genocide* (Leiden and Boston: Brill Rodopi, 2014), p. 34.

[76] Hebert Marcuse, *One-Dimensional Man: Studies in the Ideology of Advanced Industrial Society*, trans. Douglas Kellner (Oxford: Routledge, 2002), p. 185 and p. 252.

[77] Arnold Kettle, *Literature and Liberation: Selected Essays*, ed. Graham Martin and W. R. Owens (Manchester: Manchester University Press, 1988), p. 108.

[78] See Leanore Leiblein, 'Jan Kott, Peter Brook and *King Lear*', *Journal of Dramatic Theory and Criticism*, 1:2 (1987), pp. 39–49.

[79] Ibid.

Kott, Brook had come to view *King Lear* as a prototypically absurdist drama and a play that had a distinct relevance for post-Holocaust audiences – even resembling something akin to the 'concentration camp document' *The Deputy*, the controversial Rolf Hochhuth drama Brook would stage in 1963, directly after *King Lear*.[80]

Brook chose a stage aesthetic that reflected the cataclysmic, disenchanted fallout of recent European and world history – or the metaphysical 'abyss of Auschwitz', as Brook called it.[81] His stage was virtually bare, while the few props Brook did use were in a state of ruinous disintegration – as in the rusty thunder-sheets that visibly descended from the flies to rumble ominously in the storm scenes.[82] This bare space was meant to signify a vacant and godless universe, a pitiless void in which human life is drained of any meaning or purpose, leaving individuals bereft of hope and unable to act. 'The emptiness was metaphysical, as well as "actual",' writes Marvin Rosenberg: 'The fierce illumination banished any shadows of divinity, mystery or superstition.'[83] Alexander Leggatt writes that the empty space, with no more than 'tall, coarse-textured off-white screens' serving as a backdrop, adumbrated a 'tiny humanity dwarfed by a vast, bleak universe' – an impression augmented by the way Brook used the full width and depth of the vast Royal Shakespeare Theatre stage, which was usually reduced by using a back-wall placed closer to the audience.[84]

By treating *King Lear* as the 'prime example of the Theatre of the Absurd' – 'from which everything good in modern drama has been drawn' – Brook also stressed the grotesque violence of the play.[85] This meant cutting any moments that might relieve the brutality, from the servants who tend to Gloucester after he is blinded to the final, doomed attempt of Edgar to do 'Some good' (V.iii.241) and reprieve Cordelia and Lear from his death sentence. By intensifying the violence, Brook disallowed the redemptive consolation found in Christian interpretations of *King Lear*. This was epitomised by the ending (such as it was) of the production. Where the 1940 Gielgud production ended with formal acts of mourning, adumbrating the return of some form of Christian metaphysical order, in his production Brook had the actor playing

---

[80] Peter Brook, *The Empty Space* (London: Penguin, 2003), p. 82.
[81] Quoted in John Courtney Trewin, *Peter Brook: A Biography* (London: Penguin, 1971), p. 138.
[82] Leggatt, *Shakespeare in Performance: King Lear*, p. 44.
[83] Marvin Rosenberg, *The Masks of King Lear* (London: Associated University Press, 1975), p. 34.
[84] Leggatt, *Shakespeare in Performance: King Lear*, p. 44.
[85] Ibid. p. 55.

Edgar unceremoniously drag the corpse of his vanquished brother off stage, while somewhere in the distance the low, portentous growl of thunder that had presaged the storm scenes was heard again.[86] This not only forestalled any possibility of resolution; it also intimated that there would soon be another outbreak of catastrophic violence. The *dénouement* (once again) drew on Kott, who in his image of the 'Grand Mechanism' observed that, in Shakespeare, characters are mere 'cogs' in the self-perpetuating and repetitive cycles of history, which does not admit of any transcendent meaning.[87]

Writing in a *Scene* review tellingly entitled 'Waiting for Scofield', Tom Stoppard remarked on the Beckettian imagery and form of the Brook production. Stoppard praised Brook for capitalising on 'the deformity of structure' in *King Lear* – most obviously its failure to reach any form of recognisable *dénouement*, as in the failed suicide of Gloucester.[88] This transformed the play from a Christian parable into an absurdist play of meaningless *Godot*-like postponement and failure – something that would influence Stoppard in his own creative responses to Shakespeare. His 1966 play *Rosencrantz and Guildenstern Are Dead* was originally conceived by Stoppard as *Rosencrantz and Guildenstern Meet King Lear*, a one-act playlet that premiered at the 1964 Edinburgh Festival Fringe.[89] The tragicomic absurdism Stoppard would bring to his celebrated appropriation of *Hamlet* can be seen to have had its origins in the 'New' *King Lear* and the Beckettian images of Brook.

Even while acknowledging that Kott set the 'dark', post-Auschwitz tone of his production, Brook self-consciously drew on an array of Continental stylistic influences and theories: Kott, Beckett, Ionesco, Artaud and Brecht.[90] The use of Brechtian dramaturgy in 1962 was most obvious in its use of the distancing *Verfremdungseffekt* ('alienation effect' or 'distancing effect'). Whereas past productions (as in Gielgud-Barker in 1940) sought to promote empathetic identification with Lear,

---

[86] Ibid. pp. 54–5.
[87] Kott, *Shakespeare Our Contemporary*, p. 10.
[88] Quoted in Charles Joseph Del Dotto, 'Engaging and Evading the Bard: Shakespeare, Nationalism, and British Theatrical Modernism, 1900–1964', PhD (Duke University, 2010), p. 191.
[89] For more on the genesis of *Rosencrantz and Guildenstern Are Dead*, see Jeffrey Kahan, 'Introduction', in Jeffrey Kahan (ed.), *King Lear, New Critical Essays* (New York and Oxford: Routledge, 2008), p. 81.
[90] For more on the self-consciously hybrid stylistic influences informing the 1962 production, see Brook, *The Empty Space*, especially 'The Rough Theatre', pp. 65–97.

Brook wanted to 'detach' the audience.[91] This was evident in the storm scenes, where the thunder-sheets hanging over the stage served as a constant reminder of the aesthetic unreality of the events Lear is (ostensibly) struggling through on his path to 'redemptive' self-realisation.

Brook also drew on Artaud, whose Theatre of Cruelty aims less at rational disinterest and more at puncturing the subconscious of the spectator through remorseless sensory agitation.[92] This informed the way in which Brook chose to stage the blinding of Gloucester. Brook purposefully contradicted the way the scene was usually staged. It had been customary for the blinding to be staged after the interval, so that anyone in the audience unwilling to watch the violence could prudently postpone his or her re-entrance. Brook not only placed the blinding before the interval, forcing the audience to watch, but also 'cruelly' raised the house-lights, intensifying the visceral impact of the scene on a stunned audience.[93]

The 1962 production remains, in the words of Jay Halio, 'undeniably the most influential post-war production of the play'.[94] Perhaps the most important contribution of the Brook production was to 'de-Englishize or de-nationalize *King Lear* and Shakespeare'.[95] Where in the 1940s and 1950s the play was understood as positive reminder of British Christian civilisation, over and against the destructive threat of 'unnatural' forms of Continental modernity, Brook used the play for the purposes of a far less insular engagement with the catastrophes of twentieth-century Europe and to reflect on the shared experience of living through Stalinism, Nazism and, most harrowingly, the Holocaust. Brook brought Shakespeare and *King Lear* into dialogue with a variety of European, late modernist dramaturgies as these developed in the wake of Auschwitz, from Beckett to Brecht. This set the scene for other, post-Auschwitz interpreters of the play – not least Edward Bond and Buzz Goodbody.

Buzz Goodbody was, as Elizabeth Schafer has remarked, citing Colin Chambers, influenced by Brook.[96] Her 1974 RSC production of *King*

---

[91] See Leggatt, *Shakespeare in Performance: King Lear*, p. 52.

[92] See Antonin Artaud, *The Theatre and Its Double*, trans. Victor Corti (London: OneWorld Classics, 2010).

[93] Leggatt, *Shakespeare in Performance: King Lear*, p. 45.

[94] Jay Halio, 'Introduction', in William Shakespeare, *The Tragedy of King Lear*, ed. Jay Halio (Cambridge: Cambridge University Press, 2005), p. 47.

[95] Zoltan Markus, 'Kott in the West', in Hugh Grady (ed.), *Great Shakespeareans, Volume Thirteen: Empson, Wilson Knight, Barber, Kott* (London: Continuum, 2012), p. 158.

[96] Elizabeth Schafer, *Ms-Directing Shakespeare: Women Direct Shakespeare* (New York: St Martin's Press, 2000), p. 234.

Lear drew on the same empty aesthetic Brook had used, with a *mise-en-scène* that was, for the most part, 'uncluttered' by props.[97] But her version was far more consciously politicised, offering a vision of the play that was 'forcefully directed towards social change'.[98] This production, which has been viewed as the most important re-evaluation of *King Lear* since 1962, was the first production at The Other Place, the smaller studio space Goodbody opened in 1974 with the intention of staging more politically and artistically *avant-garde* productions than were possible at the main Royal Shakespeare Theatre.[99]

Goodbody cut the play drastically and concentrated her interpretation of its action around the poor and the disenfranchised, revealed to Lear when he confronts Poor Tom. Dympna Callaghan observes that, over the action, the gulf between rich and poor was powerfully shown in the simple distinction between 'being clothed and going naked'.[100] Goodbody sought to underscore the way in which the modern capitalist system reduces the masses to a form of naked – 'unaccommodated' – bare life. She would go as far as to include a controversial prologue – spoken in unison by Lear (Tony Church) and Edgar (Mike Gwilym) – that drew parallels between the condition of the iterant poor in the early modern era and that of the industrial working classes of the 1970s.[101] The aim was to indict 'the capitalist order' and its 'cultural apparatus' in its 'totality'.[102] It is an order which debases and – quite literally – denudes subjects. The moment when Lear chances on Poor Tom and 'unbuttons', as he promises to pass the 'superflux' to the naked masses, became the centre for a revolutionary Marxist-socialist staging of the play that stressed the necessity of social and political action. Lear gained a heroically 'oppositional consciousness' over the production, becoming a radical critic of the social injustice he had blindly presided over during his reign.[103]

By showing the subject reduced to a form of bare 'naked' life,

---

[97] Ibid.
[98] Dympna Callaghan, 'Buzz Goodbody: Directing for Change', in Jean Marsden (ed.), *The Appropriation of Shakespeare: Post-Renaissance Reconstructions of the Works and Myths* (Hemel Hempstead: Harvester Wheatsheaf, 1991), p. 177.
[99] See Alycia Smith-Howard, *Studio Shakespeare: The Royal Shakespeare Company at The Other Place* (Aldershot: Ashgate Publishing, 2006), pp. 1–3. For a reading of the 1974 *(King) Lear*, see pp. 35–42.
[100] Callaghan, 'Buzz Goodbody: Directing for Change', p. 172.
[101] See Smith-Howard, *Studio Shakespeare*, p. 37 and Callaghan, 'Buzz Goodbody: Directing for Change', p. 171.
[102] Callaghan, 'Buzz Goodbody: Directing for Change', p. 177.
[103] Ibid.

Goodbody revealed that her social and political conception of modern capitalism was implicitly informed by Auschwitz and the production of 'unaccommodated man' in the concentration camps. This was not necessarily unusual in post-1968 critiques of capitalism. But it also revealed her specific debt to Bond. Goodbody, evincing the influence of Bond, shortened the title of *King Lear* to *Lear* – precisely as Bond had done for his 1971 appropriation of the play. Her understanding of *King Lear* and its relevance for modern capitalist society was informed by Bond and his post-Auschwitz version of Shakespeare, which views *King Lear* as 'a play where people are getting on and off trains with a lot of luggage' – an image that recalls the mass transportation of Jews to the camps and the appropriation of Jewish property by the Nazis.[104]

Goodbody was both a Marxist and a feminist.[105] Her production concentrated on Lear and his nascent understanding of social injustice. But it also sought to provide a critique of patriarchal culture by showing 'how much the "bad" sisters had to put up with'.[106] This desire to fashion new perspectives on the play, from institutionally and politically 'marginal' spaces, would become an important aspect of Shakespeare criticism over the 1980s and 1990s.

The 1980s and 1990s: Identity Politics and Postmodernity, or 'unaccommodated man'?

King Lear in Criticism

The transformation in Shakespeare studies over the 1980s and 1990s can, for Kiernan Ryan, be summed up in a single word: 'politics'.[107] For many Shakespeare critics in the 1980s and beyond, even the 'political' readings of *King Lear* that had emerged after the Second World War were deaf to political struggle as it related to the plight of marginalised and oppressed sections of society – from homosexuals to Black and Asian men and women. Over the 1980s and 1990s, Shakespeare critics increasingly sought to secure the representation and social and political freedom of specific constituencies marginalised in society – and indeed in Shakespearean drama – challenging oppressive discourses of identity

---

[104] Quoted in Susannah Carson (ed.), *Shakespeare and Me* (London: OneWorld Classics, 2013), p. 54.
[105] See Callaghan, 'Buzz Goodbody: Directing for Change', pp. 163–7.
[106] Ibid. p. 171.
[107] Kiernan Ryan, 'Introduction', in Ryan, *King Lear: Contemporary Critical Essays*, p. 3.

and subjectivity in the dominant culture and its cherished canonical plays. This political agenda was perhaps most obvious in the work of cultural materialist critics.

Most problematic for cultural materialist critics was the humanist conception of the subject to be found in Shakespearean tragedy, which for Catherine Belsey is the white, heterosexual, male subject of European Enlightenment modernity, emergent in the early modern Renaissance culture of Shakespeare and his contemporaries.[108] This conception of the tragic subject is, as Belsey understands it, exclusive of other forms of subjectivity and identity – non-male, non-white, non-heterosexual – and not universally intelligible or meaningful at all.

Jonathan Dollimore, writing in his 1984 *Radical Tragedy*, similarly critiques humanist understandings of Shakespeare and *King Lear*. He remarks that, by overcoming the Christian and absurdist takes on the play, the humanist view of *King Lear* has become 'culturally dominant'.[109] Dollimore alludes to the influential writings of Clifford Leech, Wilbur Sanders, Philip Brockbank and G. K. Hunter, all of whom adopt humanist takes on *King Lear*.[110] These critics would have it that Lear comes to question otherwise ingrained, pre-modern mythic ideas around the divinity of the sovereign and, by discovering his humanity in the storm, realises that any hope for progress and dignity rests in human reason and action, not in fate or the stars, where the possibility of grace is 'not in heaven, but in nature, and especially in human nature, and it cannot be rooted out'.[111] For humanist interpreters, *King Lear* is a play that invests its hope not in God but in humanity, so that if 'man' is 'to be redeemed at all, he must redeem himself'.[112] The 'modern' view of *King Lear*, writes Hunter, is that the play is:

> seen as the greatest of tragedies because it not only strips and reduces and assaults human dignity, but because it also shows with the greatest force [. . .] the process of restoration by which humanity can recover from degradation.[113]

---

[108] Catherine Belsey, *The Subject of Tragedy: Identity and Difference in English Renaissance Drama* (London: Methuen, 1985), p. 2.

[109] Jonathan Dollimore, *Radical Tragedy: Religion, Ideology and Power in the Drama of Shakespeare and his Contemporaries*, 3rd edn (Basingstoke: Palgrave Macmillan, 2010), p. 189.

[110] Ibid. pp. 189–91.

[111] Wilbur Sanders, *The Dramatist and the Received Idea: Studies in Shakespeare* (Cambridge: Cambridge University Press, 1968), p. 336.

[112] Dollimore, *Radical Tragedy*, p. 189.

[113] G. K. Hunter, *Dramatic Identities and Cultural Tradition: Studies in Shakespeare and His Contemporaries* (Liverpool: Liverpool University Press, 1979), p. 251.

The problem with the way in which humanist critics valorise *King Lear*, however, is that the vision of the human which the play promotes is by no means 'universal', but marked by ideological bias.

The humanist take on *King Lear* is – as far as Dollimore is concerned – nothing more than a secularisation of the Christian reading and its interpretation of the 'redemption' of Lear. Where the Christian reading places God at the centre of a providential universe, the humanist reading places the tragic subject (Lear) at the centre of meaning and action, as through 'kindness and shared vulnerability human kind redeems itself'.[114] The same constraining humanism is visible in politically Marxist readings of the play, which also centre on the redemption of Lear and his identification with the suffering masses. It can even be seen in absurdist interpretations, which would have it that life without the human subject as the centre of meaning is barely imaginable – and hardly worth living. Dollimore makes the case that previous readings are guilty of an 'essentializing humanism' which ignores that *King Lear* is 'above all, a play about property, power and inheritance'.[115] The vision of the 'human' promulgated by the play is – as Dollimore sees it – socially and politically exclusive. The human comes to be identified with the white, patriarchal figure of a king – Lear – whose identification of himself with 'unaccommodated man' (or 'Man') in the shape of Poor Tom obliterates class, sexual and racial distinctions and, paradoxically, endorses the status quo and the systems of marginalisation and oppression perpetuated through the inequitable division of 'property, power and inheritance'.

This politicised reconsideration of the humanism of *King Lear* was also (and perhaps most powerfully) reflected in feminist interpretations of the play. Kathleen McLuskie in her 1984 critique of 'The Patriarchal Bard' contends that the subject of tragedy, far from being simply 'human', is explicitly and misogynistically gendered as male, while the female characters in the play are marginalised in a repressive, patriarchal world. This world insists on heterosexual relations in which the woman is subordinated, with any figures contesting that social and familial organisation deemed disruptively 'monstrous' or 'unnatural' and in dire need of containment – as Goneril and Regan consistently are by Lear and, indeed, by Cordelia.[116] Feminist interpretations of the play are also advanced in the nuanced psychoanalytic readings of critics Coppélia

---

[114] Dollimore, *Radical Tragedy*, p. 189.
[115] Ibid. p. 197.
[116] Kathleen McLuskie, 'The Patriarchal Bard: A Reading of *King Lear*', in Ryan, *King Lear: Contemporary Critical Essays*, pp. 48–59.

Kahn and Janet Adelman. Both attended to the strangely 'missing' wife/ mother figure from the play, with Adelman observing

> King Lear has no wife, his daughters no mother; nor, apparently, have they ever had one: Queen Lear goes unmentioned, except for those characteristic moments when Lear invokes her to cast doubt on his paternity.[117]

Adleman and Khan both read the absence of any mother figure from the play as part of a wider homosocial desire to supress the debilitating memory of maternal origin and disavow an uncontrollably sexualised female presence – a fear reflected in the anxiety-ridden speeches of Lear, where he refers to the vagina as a 'sulphurous pit' (IV.vi.130) and to the 'riotous appetite' of women: 'Down from the waist they are centaurs, though women all above' (IV.vi.121–2). 'O, how this mother swells toward my heart', yelps a 'hysterical' Lear, '*Hysterica passio*, down, thou climbing sorrow / Thy element's below!' (II.ii.246–8). Harry Berger similarly undercuts the 'heroic' image of Lear, concentrating his psycho-analytic reading of the play on the storm scenes, when Lear declaims against 'crimes / Unwhipped of justice':

> Tremble, thou wretch,
> That hast within thee undivulged crimes
> Unwhipped of justice. Hide thee, thou bloody hand,
> Thou perjured, and thou similar of virtue
> That art incestuous. (III.ii.51–5)

Berger makes the case that Lear is alluding to his own 'pent-up guilts' (III.ii.57) and that he himself is 'unwhipped', the Lear 'family romance' an otherwise untold story of incestuous rape.[118]

Less common were readings that contested the perceived heteronormative or racist aspects of the play – though as Keith Linley observes, the 'lust' that Lear bewails was often understood in the early modern era to comprise all 'unclean thoughts and unclean acts, involving unnatural desires like bestiality, incest and homosexuality', so that the rage against female lust might (albeit spectrally) include a variety of possible and unspecified sexual acts.[119] Benjamin Minor and Ayanna Thompson also

---

[117] Janet Adelman, *Suffocating Mothers: Fantasies of Maternal Origin in Shakespeare's Plays, Hamlet to The Tempest* (London: Routledge, 1992), p. 104; Coppélia Kahn, 'The Absent Mother in *King Lear*', in Ryan, *King Lear: Contemporary Critical Essays*, pp. 92–113.

[118] Harry Berger, Jr., '"*King Lear*": The Lear Family Romance', *The Centennial Review*, 23:4 (1979), pp. 348–76.

[119] Keith Linley, *King Lear in Context: The Cultural Background* (London and New York: Anthem Press, 2015), p. 57.

draw attention to the early modern ideational tie between diabolic possession and the figure of 'the Moor', so that – in his ostensible possession by and flight from demonic forces – Poor Tom can be said to be haunted by a figure against which the Eurocentric norm of the civilised white Christian male was formed and became recognisable.[120] Minor and Thompson do not make the argument, but the implication is that, in identifying with the figure of Poor Tom, the common human identity Lear avows in the storm is a white, Europeanised identity pathologically haunted by the devilish 'black' figure it would seek to disavow and (quite literally) exorcise – if it only could.

By bringing the various subjectivities marginalised or oppressed in the play back to the fore, many Shakespeare critics were concerned to show that the 'tragic' discourse of subjectivity in *King Lear* is not universal, but reveals the need for 'dissident politics of class, race, gender and sexual orientation, both within texts and in the role those texts play in culture'.[121] This often involved a self-consciously deconstructive hermeneutic practice which concentrated on the gaps, omissions and ellipses in the play (the missing mother, the absent 'back-stories' of Goneril and Regan, the disappearance of the Fool and so on). These various 'gaps', along with the newly acknowledged divergences between Quarto and Folio versions of *King Lear*, provided critics with the opportunity to interrogate the play and its investment in suspicious ideological and aesthetic values. It was the work of criticism to reveal the lie of aesthetic unity and read the play against the grain of its superficial 'meaning' by analysing its disavowed absences and interstices – though that often meant simply accepting that *King Lear* is the unified aesthetic phenomena previous (most usually Christian) critics had found. This failure to give proper consideration to aesthetic form would ultimately undermine much political criticism over the period, as both John Joughin and Hugh Grady have contended.[122] Most political interpretations of *King Lear*

---

[120] Benjamin Minor and Ayanna Thompson, '"Edgar I nothing am": Blackface in *King Lear*', in Rory Loughnane and Edel Semple (eds), *Staged Transgression in Shakespeare's England* (New York and London: Palgrave Macmillan, 2013), p. 155.

[121] Alan Sinfield, *Faultlines: Cultural Materialism and the Politics of Dissident Reading* (Berkeley, Los Angeles, Oxford: University of California Press, 1992), p. 10.

[122] John Joughin, 'Shakespeare, Modernity, and the Aesthetic: Art, Truth and Judgement in *The Winter's Tale*', in Hugh Grady (ed.), *Shakespeare and Modernity: Early Modern to Millennium* (London: Routledge, 2000), pp. 61–84; Hugh Grady, *Shakespeare and Impure Aesthetics* (Cambridge: Cambridge University Press, 2009), pp. 1–5.

treated the idea of aesthetic form with suspicion, insisting that the play – far from being in any way 'above' or 'beyond' society – is ultimately made up of ideological discourses that ought to be interrogated by critics.[123]

On the one hand, Shakespeare critics in the 1980s were obviously and openly responding to previous readings of *King Lear* as a Christian, humanist or absurdist play – a response informed by growing social movements from the 1960s onwards and by the reception of Continental theory via cultural studies. On the other hand, the politicisation of Shakespeare studies in the 1980s and 1990s is also a response to the rise of the so-called New Right, as represented by the election victories of Margaret Thatcher in 1979 and Ronald Reagan in 1981. The New Right stressed conservative ('British') values that were exclusive of precisely those marginalised peoples and identities which the cultural materialists were keen to defend and promote. The wide range of social and religious concerns (abortion, education, gay rights) around which the New Right organised itself were disproportionately damaging for sections of the community that did not seem to fit into the ideological vision of traditional (male, white, heteronormative) values, while cuts also impacted already marginal communities.[124]

But the development of cultural materialism can, as Grady has shown, also be seen as indicative of a shift from modernism to postmodernism – and from industrialism to post-industrialism – in culture and theory over the 1980s and 1990s.[125] Previous Christian, absurdist and political readings of *King Lear* were, if in various ways, all responsive to the reification of the subject by modern totalised systems. But with its new preoccupation with pluralist discourses of the subject, Shakespeare studies reflected the transition to post-industrial society, where the heterogeneously postmodern worlds of globalised capitalism and consumer culture made more hybrid forms of identity newly intelligible. These social developments were – ironically – largely brought about by the reform of economic policy wrought by the New Right, even as its social policy promoted a return to 'traditional' 'Victorian values'.

With the movement from modernist reification to postmodern identity politics, the ideational tie with Auschwitz begins to weaken in the critical discourse surrounding *King Lear*. Where in previous readings Auschwitz is seen as the nadir of modernity, in the politically radical

---

[123] Grady, *Shakespeare and Impure Aesthetics*, pp. 1–5.
[124] See in particular Sylvia Bashevkin, *Women on the Defensive: Living through Conservative Times* (London and Chicago: University of Chicago Press, 1998).
[125] See the final chapter of Grady, *The Modernist Shakespeare*, 'Towards the Postmodern Shakespeare: Contemporary Critical Trends', pp. 191–245.

criticism of the 1980s and 1990s the Holocaust largely falls from view. There is no allusion to the event that – in many ways – had led to the unrivalled supremacy of *King Lear* in the Shakespeare canon in the pathbreaking 1984 collection *Political Shakespeare: Essays in Cultural Materialism*. It is also absent from *The Subject of Tragedy* and a host of other vital works of Shakespeare criticism that deal with *King Lear*, including *Radical Tragedy*.[126] Postmodernism – as I set out in Chapter 1 – has been theorised as a critical response to the Holocaust.[127] But the near-total absence of Auschwitz from critical analyses of *King Lear* is telling: it is indicative of a paradigm shift away from a concern with desubjectification in totalised, modern society and towards the articulation of various forms of political identity in fragmented, postmodern society, comprising feminist, postcolonial and queer intersections.

One of the few critics to address the relationship between *King Lear* and Auschwitz over the period of the 1980s and 1990s is Terence Hawkes, who in his 1995 study of the play contests the idea that there is an '"original", essential, unchanging' *King Lear* for critics to decipher, stating that 'Instead of a Masterpiece' there is a series of interpretations of *King Lear* – or a series of *King Lears* – that are entirely determined by the historical and cultural moment of its reception.[128] 'It is surely questionable', writes Hawkes, 'whether any human enterprise can operate beyond limitations of culture and history, factors which shape all human activity'.[129] Hawkes writes that the canonical place *King Lear* gained over the post-war era is due the destruction of the Second World War and its 'shattering of worlds'.[130] This

> was no ordinary conflict but one which raised for the first time the possibility of universal cataclysm by means of nuclear weapons [and] it had seen, in the discovery of the Nazi concentration camps, evidence of a Holocaust which signalled the destruction, not only of European Jewish life, but any idea that European civilization itself might present something of a permanent value in the world. The horrors revealed in 1944–1945 indicated the persistence of barbarism.[131]

---

[126] Terry Eagleton does refer to Auschwitz in his Foreword to the third (2010) edition (p. x) and Dollimore takes up the challenge in his new 'Introduction' (p. xxv and p. xxvii).
[127] See Chapter 1.
[128] Terence Hawkes, *William Shakespeare: King Lear* (Plymouth: Northcote House Publishers, 1995), p. 61, p. 58.
[129] Ibid. p. 58.
[130] Ibid. p. 63.
[131] Ibid.

The atrocities of the war may seem to have imbued *King Lear* with 'universal' relevance for humanity – but that relevance cannot necessarily survive as history changes over time or in new cultural conditions. The implication is that, while *King Lear* may seem to have acquired canonical validity due to the unparalleled destruction of the Second World War, it does not necessarily resonate in the same way 'in our society', where new values of 'pluralism' are at hand and critics set out to contest 'principles of subordination and marginalization' in culture.[132] *King Lear* signifies in a new way (if at all) in a post-Cold War, postmodern world – as a deeply reactionary play, the tragic action of which fosters a limited conception of the human.

Even if it is true that *King Lear* can in no way be thought of as an autonomous work of art, the case might be made that Hawkes, in consigning Auschwitz to 'the past', is more than a little complacent, as if history – and 'our society' – has moved resolutely on from a previous period of modernity and its catastrophes. This is all the more perplexing considering that a genocidal war was raging in the divided kingdom of the former Yugoslavia at the time Hawkes was writing, while the mass slaughter of the Rwandan genocide had only taken place in 1994. These disastrous European and world events may have led Hawkes to pause for thought before casting *King Lear* onto the scrapheap of literary and cultural history.

Cultural materialist criticism set out to critique both *King Lear* and its critical reception, which had tended to universalise the play. But it also critiqued the meanings produced by both past and contemporary stagings. These were often seen as inadequate and caught up in institutional forms of power that did not represent the marginalised and oppressed.

King Lear in Performance

It would be wrong to say that stagings of *King Lear* over the 1980s and 1990s were 'apolitical'. But it would also be wrong to say that productions of the play pursued the social and political questions that were relevant to the anti-hegemonic priorities of Shakespeare criticism. Productions of *King Lear* were predominantly shaped, on the one hand, by the discourse of Christian or humanist redemption and, on the other, by the discourse of absurdism – precisely the universalising interpretations of the play critics were placing under scrutiny.

For his 1982 production, Adrian Noble directed *King Lear* in repertoire with *Lear* (*King Lear* was played on the main stage, *Lear* at

---

[132] Ibid. p. 66.

The Other Place). The decision reflected a desire to produce a political interpretation of the play that drew on Brecht; but Noble also drew on Kott and, as he put it, sought to stress 'the savage cruelty and the sense of the absurd' found in 'a vengeful, godless universe'.[133] Precisely the same vision informed the 1997 Peter Hall production at the Old Vic: fresh from having directed the same company in a production of *Waiting for Godot,* Hall made the case that *King Lear* conveys a 'Sophoclean – almost a post-Beckett – recognition of the awful meaninglessness and randomness of life,' with director, company and reviewers playing up – perhaps unavoidably – the 'unmistakable echoes between these plays'.[134] Nicholas Hytner similarly refuted 'the idea of the tragic hero ennobled and achieving wisdom through suffering' and in his 1990 staging insisted that *King Lear* is 'a brutal play which offers no consolation' for the unmitigated 'catastrophe' that Lear 'unleashes'.[135]

It is perhaps not surprising to find that David Hare – former Royal Court playwright-in-residence in 1971–2 and a co-founder of the politically radical Joint Stock Theatre Company – found the Kott reading of Shakespeare as 'an unknowing forerunner of Beckett' and *King Lear* as a prototypical work of the Theatre of the Absurd 'nonsense' – even though it was his attendance at the 1962 Brook production that had originally inspired Hare to become a playwright.[136] Hare had alluded to *King Lear* in his play *The Great Exhibition* (Hampstead Theatre, 1972) – a satirical anatomy of the self-enclosed middle-class world of the political elite as typified by the temperamentally aloof Labour MP Charlie Hammet. The epigraph to the play is the 'unaccommodated man' speech from *King Lear,* placed alongside statistics concerning the 'Distribution of Private Property: Percentage of total net private capital in relation to percentage of total population'.[137] Maud Hammet – the Tory wife of Charlie – is the casting director in an amateur production of *King Lear* and ends up playing Cordelia in a performance that is deemed a failure. Even more of a failure, however, is the way Charlie meets his mistress, Catriona. Charlie publicly exposes (or 'exhibits') himself to Catriona on Hampstead Heath. She fails to respond, rendering Charlie impotent. The whole scene, with its parodic inversion of the heath scenes

---

[133] Croall, *Performing King Lear*, p. 56 and p. 57.
[134] Ibid. p. 88 and p. 89.
[135] Ibid. p. 100.
[136] Ibid. pp. 218–19.
[137] See Scott Fraser, *A Politic Theatre: The Drama of David Hare* (Amsterdam and Atlanta: Rodopi, 1996), pp. 33–40. This obviously has parallels with the prologue Goodbody used in her 1974 production.

from *King Lear*, is indicative of the way the ostensibly radical Charlie fails to live up to and properly 'perform' socialist politics – the politics of the heath.[138] His interest lies less in distribution undoing excess than tawdry self-display and illicit affairs. Charlie does nothing to advance the condition of the working classes.

Hare might be accused of the same type of political failure. Hare directed *King Lear* at the National Theatre in 1986 – the first time he had directed Shakespeare and the first time the play had appeared at the National.[139] He stated that *King Lear* is a play 'about' 'Family, religion, politics, madness, sex'.[140] Whereas in the 1970s 'politics' may have been paramount, by the 1980s 'politics' had been displaced by a concentration on family and religion, fading into the distance with 'madness' and 'sex'. This division served to artificially separate areas of social life from 'politics', rendering family, religion, madness and sex ostensibly 'above' or 'beyond' material cultural and historical specificity. Carol Homden contends that Hare produced a humanist *King Lear* that was 'incompatible with a supposed genesis within a tradition of political theatre', where the 'mystery is no longer merely political, it is eternally human' – a sense of the 'eternal' formalised by the Brook-influenced bare stage Hare used.[141]

Perhaps the most openly 'political' staging of *King Lear* in the 1990s was the Max Stafford-Clark production at the Royal Court in 1993. For reviewer Paul Taylor, 'tremors of contemporaneity' were stirred in images of a disintegrating state that echoed the break-up of Yugoslavia – not least in the final act, where cowed refugees were seen hurrying with meagre worldly goods bundled into supermarket trolleys while artillery fire sounded in the distance.[142] Such images would return to the Royal Court with the *1995 Blasted* (I analyse some of the overlaps in Chapter 7). But for most reviewers and critics, the most remarkable aspect of the production was the 'drag-queen' Fool, played by Andy Serkis.[143] The sexually indeterminate Fool underscored the misogyny of Lear, even as he disrupted and undermined the performative nature

---

[138] Ibid. p. 37.
[139] See Croall, *Performing King Lear*, p. 218.
[140] Quoted in Carol Homden, *The Plays of David Hare* (Cambridge: Cambridge University Press, 1995), p. 231.
[141] Ibid.
[142] Paul Taylor, 'The Woman Question', <https://www.independent.co.uk/arts-entertainment/theatre-the-woman-question-paul-taylor-reviews-max-stafford-clarks-production-of-king-lear-at-the-1480290.html> (accessed 19 April 2019).
[143] Ibid. See also Peter Holland, *English Shakespeares: Shakespeare on the English Stage in the 1990s* (Cambridge: Cambridge University Press, 1997), p. 154.

of the gender binaries on which that misogyny rests. This aspect of the production was applauded for its feminist and queer credentials and its reconsideration of the 'heroic' Lear, who in the opening scenes was seen bending over while the Fool pretended to ride him, whipping the monarch with his own crop.[144] But the politically radical feminist/queer aspects of the production were – for some – ultimately diminished by the way in which Lear underwent 'a late-flowering recognition of social injustice', where a universalising humanism restated the image of 'unaccommodated "Man"'.[145]

For the most part, the production history of *King Lear* in the 1980s and 1990s did little to progress the sort of interrogatory political agenda being advanced in the world of Shakespeare studies. Susan Bennett takes an irrevocably dim view of the prominence of *King Lear* on stage in the 1980s (and beyond). Bennett contends that the cultural-industrial 'over-production' and unceasing 'proliferation' of the play over the 1980s and 1990s served to perform 'a nostalgic identification with greatness – of the text, of Shakespeare'.[146] She sees productions of the play as relying on a narrow set of design, acting and conceptual choices which did little to shift the dominant interpretations that had been formed by previous stagings. This is most apparent in the persistent ideational tie between the play and Beckettian absurdism and Christian-humanist redemption, both of which restate the 'transcendent' cultural value of the play through time. These choices leave little room for the cultural representation of marginalised peoples, which Bennett sees as politically urgent.

This cultural homogenisation of *King Lear* is portrayed in the Caryl Churchill satire *Serious Money* (Royal Court, 1987), which represents the machinations of the London International Financial Futures and Options Exchange. One of the more rapacious traders in the play, Billy Corman, is elected to the board of the National Theatre and uses the cultural capital his new position affords him to burnish his own self and public image and to make contacts that augment his various business and political interests. Earlier in the action, Corman had met the Tory cabinet minister Gleason during an intermission at the National, which is used for the purposes of a consultation. The play on offer is *King Lear* – but while Gleason perfunctorily deems the production to be 'excellent *of course*', he also admits to bouts of sleep that are spasmodically

---

[144] Taylor, 'The Woman Question'.
[145] See Croall, *Performing King Lear*, p. 181.
[146] Susan Bennett, *Performing Nostalgia: Shifting Shakespeare and the Contemporary Past* (London: Routledge, 1996), p. 77.

interrupted by the 'shouting' onstage, while he also confuses both Goneril and Regan with Ophelia from *Hamlet*.[147] This brief interlude reflects the commodification of Shakespeare in the market-driven world of the 1980s and the privileged canonical status given to *King Lear* as a piece of 'high' national and cultural capital – even while that position remains haunted by the memory of the once ascendant *Hamlet*. The implication is that *King Lear* has become a cultural 'experience' to be consumed by philistine audiences in a state of post-work stupor – a situation akin to the commodification of 'leisure time' critiqued by Adorno and the growing role of the Culture Industry in post-Auschwitz life.[148]

It is the increasing cultural homogenisation of Shakespeare that underpins calls for appropriation in politically radical readings of Shakespeare – the arrogation and transformation of property that belongs to the establishment in the service of politically oppositional meanings. Providing an analysis of *Lear's Daughters* (1987) and *King of England* (1988) shows that some writers have appropriated *King Lear* to represent the culturally marginalised.

King Lear and Appropriation

For the most part, cultural materialist criticism addressed itself to the conservative social and political ideologies Shakespeare is appropriated to serve. But for Dollimore and Sinfield, writing in *Political Shakespeare*, 'appropriation could work the other way: subordinate, marginal or dissident elements could appropriate dominant discourses' – even while, for Francis Barker, it would take 'a massive re-writing' to make the action of *King Lear* 'radical'.[149] This reflects a wider prioritising of acts of so-called 'creative vandalism' in Shakespeare studies over the 1980s and 1990s.[150] Cultural materialist critics called on artists (and other critics) to engage in acts of artistic and political sabotage against Shakespeare,

---

[147] Caryl Churchill, *Serious Money*, ed. Bill Naismith (London: Methuen, 2013), p. 102 (emphasis added).

[148] See in particular the essay 'Free Time' in Theodor Adorno, *The Culture Industry*, ed. J. M. Bernstein (London: Routledge, 2001). pp. 187–97.

[149] Jonathon Dollimore, 'Shakespeare, Cultural Materialism and the New Historicism', in Jonathon Dollimore and Alan Sinfield (eds), *Political Shakespeare: Essays in Cultural Materialism* (Manchester: Manchester University Press, 1983), p. 12; Francis Barker, *The Culture of Violence: Essays on Tragedy and History* (Manchester: Manchester University Press, 1993), p. 49.

[150] Jonathon Dollimore, 'Shakespeare Understudies: The Sodomite, The Prostitute, The Transvestite and Their Critics', in Dollimore and Sinfield, *Political Shakespeare*, p. 144.

often through the use of ironic postmodern aesthetic strategies, including pastiche and parody. Such vandalism was to be undertaken with the aim of deconstructing the 'original' play and allowing the space for marginalised subjectivities to (re)appear in an exclusionary dramatic work.

This 'creative vandalism' is typified by the 1987 play *Lear's Daughters* – originally written by Elaine Feinstein, but heavily and collaboratively rewritten by the Women's Theatre Group (WTG).[151] Joan Ure had produced a feminist appropriation of *King Lear* in her short 1971 play *Something in it for Cordelia* – originally staged alongside *Something in it for Ophelia* – but for Lizbeth Goodman, *Lear's Daughters* represents 'a landmark in feminist "re-inventing" of Shakespeare', the play a 'her-story' prequel that deconstructs the moralistic 'fairy-tale structure of *King Lear*' and its simplistic binary of 'good' and 'bad' daughters.[152] Over a series of fifteen short, non-linear scenes, *Lear's Daughters* depicts the early lives of Goneril, Regan and Cordelia – with a Nanny and an androgynous ('a woman or a man?') Serkis-like Fool, who acts as a morally ambiguous narrator, in tow.[153] The play fills out the back-stories of the daughters to show that all are victims of psychological and sexual abuse on the part of Lear. *Lear's Daughters* omits Lear from the stage completely, indicative of its deep-seated interrogation of the Lear figure, his perceived moral 'progression' and his misogyny.

This shift from a humanist (phallocentric) narrative of moral progress and tragic recognition to the marginalised subjectivities of Goneril, Regan and Cordelia is typified by the way the play subverts the word 'unbutton'. Lear 'unbuttons' in *King Lear* to assert his identity with the poor and suffering – with 'man' in its most basic, denuded state – but in *Lear's Daughters* Goneril remembers Lear 'unbuttoning' (8.224) as a prelude to incestuous rape. 'I don't remember everything', admits Cordelia, 'but when I do I remember *exactly*' (5.222) – a form of self-narration that witnesses a traumatised history. The non-linear form of the play allows for a more open-ended, exploratory dramatisation of

---

[151] See Daniel Fischler and Mark Fortier, 'Introduction' to The Women's Theatre Group and Elaine Feinstein, *Lear's Daughters*, in Daniel Fischlin and Mark Fortier (eds), *Adaptations of Shakespeare* (London and New York: Routledge, 2000), p. 215.

[152] Lizbeth Goodman, 'Women's Alternative Shakespeares and Women's Alternatives to Shakespeare in Contemporary British Theater', in Marianne Novy (ed.), *Cross-Cultural Performances: Difference in Women's Re-Visions of Shakespeare* (Urbana and Chicago: University of Illinois, 1993), p. 220.

[153] WTG and Feinstein, *Lear's Daughters*, p. 226. All references to the text are from Fischlin and Fortier, *Adaptations of Shakespeare*, where I indicate scene and page number.

the damaged subjectivities of the daughters, all of whom are individualised in a more compelling way than in *King Lear*. The Nanny even provides 'fairy tale' stories about the daughters, recalling that Cordelia conveys her history through 'words', Goneril through 'colours' and Regan through 'touch' and 'shape' (1.217–18).

The absence of the 'missing mother', Queen Lear, is also clarified in the play, though she never appears onstage. Lear, in his patriarchal desire for a male heir (as the Nanny remembers) constantly 'whined on at [the Queen] to let him fuck her' (10.228). This, however, results in a string of miscarriages which eventually kills the Queen; any memory of her is subsequently repressed and her plight is understood as nothing short of biological destiny: 'It's what we're here for. To marry and breed' (12.229). But while the play depicts the oppressive patriarchal ideology that reduces women to 'daughters, wives and mothers', it also insists on the possibility of female empowerment and liberation. Despite her death, the Nanny remembers that the Queen was 'important' to Lear: 'Yes. She *was* important to him. She organised the budget. Looked after his interests. Night after night when he wasn't with her, adding and subtracting' (10.228). The idea that Queen Lear would make a more responsible and morally upright ruler in view of the chaos presided over by Lear – 'He'll have to manage on his own now,' as Goneril plaintively puts it (8.224) – is similarly broached by Barker in his *Seven Lears*, while the play also stages something akin to the opening scene of *Seven Lears*, where the 'poor' – 'begging for food' (9.226) – plead hopelessly with those in power:

> Bars. As I walked past, these hands came from out of them, clawing and scratching. Nanny. There were people in there. Shut in [. . .] He's the King. He must know that they're there? (10.228)

These parallels aside, Barker eschews the type of overt political meanings developed at the end of *Lear's Daughters*: the final image of the play shows the crown that once belonged to Lear being thrown unceremoniously into the air before it is caught by Goneril, Regan and Cordelia simultaneously – an unambiguous image of collective female self-empowerment and sovereignty that undoes the perceived misogyny of Shakespeare in the action of *King Lear*.[154]

With his play *King of England* (1988) – staged at the London Theatre Royal in the ethnically diverse community of Stratford – Barrie Keefe produced a 'racialised' *King Lear*, which used the play to dramatise the contradictions and intergenerational conflicts that shape the racial and class identity of succeeding generations of Black Caribbean migrants.

---

[154] Goodman, 'Women's Alternative Shakespeares', pp. 222–3.

The play transforms 'King' Lear into the black Trinidadian tube driver Mr King, who on his retirement decides to leave his (now mortgage-free) council home in Forest Gate to his daughters, Susan (Cordelia) and Linda (Goneril and Regan) and relocate back 'home' to Trinidad, after the recent death of his wife (the 'missing' mother) – Malvina. Both daughters are sceptical – and, in the case of Linda, downright resentful – of the social and political conservativism of King. King is a monarchist and he also upbraids Susan for her 'un-ladylike' criticism of Thatcher, who – for King – necessarily demands respect because she is prime minister: 'I find such sentiments particularly astonishing coming from a woman.'[155] During an *'intimate family occasion'* (1.1.12) of a restaurant dinner to mark his retirement, King waxes lyrical about the 'Mother Country' (by which he means England) and insists that his daughters drink a toast to the nation – which both abhor: 'England – some bloody mother!' (1.1.23).

King recalls how, 'after the war', he thought he would be 'welcome home to England, the Mother Country' as a 'hero' (2.3.35) – a statement of post-war optimism in the type of social justice *King Lear* has often been thought of as envisioning. King even seems to see the dream of home ownership (as expedited by the Thatcherite right-to-buy policy) as a natural extension of the 'better things' (2.2.35) promised after the war. Susan, however, disabuses her father of his 'fantasy' (1.1.23) with a more clear-eyed view of Thatcherism. 'Thatcher is butchering the NHS,' observes Susan, who provides her Cordelia-like 'kind nursery' (I.i.125) as an NHS nurse. 'England is going to rack and ruin' (1.1.12): 'This country now, does not care about its weak, or its poor or its ill. Not really care. Because that costs money' (1.1.24).

Keefe uses *King Lear* to reflect on the 'shame' and the 'tragedy' (2.1.30) of the disproportionate impact New Right policy had on marginalised and oppressed sections of society – as typified by the inadequate care the missing mother Malvina receives in her struggle against breast cancer, the disease that finally kills her (2.4). Keefe does not necessarily 'interrogate' the humanist, redemptive understanding of *King Lear* in *King of England*. The play even restores the 'happy ending' of the original Lear myth, as King and Susan reconcile before his return to Trinidad, with the Bob Marley score that accompanies the play shifting to *'Redemption Song'* (2.4.37) in the final scene. Keefe does, however, appropriate the play to represent otherwise marginalised subjectivities. He even provides some ideologically suspicious demystification of *King*

---

[155] Barrie Keefe, *King of England and Bastard Angel: Two Plays* (London: Methuen, 1988), p. 14. All references to the text are from the Methuen edition, where I indicate act, scene and page numbers.

Lear in his reworking of the storm scenes. When he meets a former tube worker called Jimmy – now a homeless alcoholic after being made redundant – in a scrapyard, King engages in some Lear-like rhetoric about his apparent loss, and rediscovery, of 'humanity': 'I am a man!' (2.1.26). The partial character of that ascription 'man' is betrayed by Jimmy, whose repugnant homophobic rhetoric reveals the ideological and cultural limits inscribed in patriarchal ideals of masculinity.

Both *Lear's Daughters* and *King of England* represent the type of appropriation cultural materialist critics thought necessary to 'radicalise' Shakespeare and allow *King Lear* to represent culturally marginalised peoples. But in more recent times, the notion that *King Lear* is a contemporary play that speaks directly to modern catastrophes, as opposed to being an outmoded drama marked by its misogyny and racism, has once again come to the fore.

The 2000s and 2010s: *King Lear* and the Anthropocene, or 'the terrors of the earth'

King Lear in Criticism

The most recent critical paradigm to emerge around *King Lear* – perhaps paradoxically – requires a return to an otherwise unfashionable critical voice: John F. Danby. Danby – as I set out above – makes the case that *King Lear* depicts a culturally unified civilisation that has become imperilled by the disastrous irruption of a disenchanted modernity. This clash, as far as Danby sees it, is primarily conveyed by the competing conceptions of nature that arise in the play: '*King Lear* can be regarded as a play dramatising the meanings of the single word, "Nature"'.[156] Danby contends that 'traditional' society – embodied by Lear, Gloucester and Edgar, among others – has a benign view of nature as a divinely ordained system, in which humanity must strive to 'fit' and preserve. 'He that has and a little tiny wit', sings the Fool, 'With hey, ho, the wind and the rain, / Must make content with his fortunes fit, / Though the rain it raineth every day' (III.ii.74–7). For the characters who embrace the nascent modern revolution, however, nature is less a place of imminent divine order than it is a godless wilderness where competitive anarchy reigns. This, writes Danby, is more familiar to 'a post-Darwinian age'.[157] He also makes the case that, since Hiroshima and the splitting of the

---

[156] Danby, *Shakespeare's Doctrine of Nature*, p. 15.
[157] Ibid. p. 32.

atom, nature has inevitably come to appear 'as a cruel and dangerously explosive force'.[158]

This concern with the representation and meaning(s) of nature in *King Lear* has re-emerged in the 2000s and 2010s with the advent of ecocriticism – a form of criticism that, arising out of the ecological movement, prioritises the representation of the environment and 'nature'.[159] *King Lear*, as Jennifer Mae Hamilton has recently observed, has been taken up as a vital, even 'canonical', play for (as she calls it) 'the ecological turn' in contemporary criticism.[160] The play is remarkable for its 'more-than-human features', whether that is its abiding concern with disturbing climatic conditions – most obviously the storm with its wind, 'sheets' of thunder (III.ii.46) and rain, though the play also variously alludes to volcanoes and earthquakes – its representation of land and landscape, and its incredibly biodiverse imaginary, which takes in non-human animal life from the lowliest worm to ravenous tigers, not to say a cast of mythological creatures, from dragons to various other prodigal monsters.[161] *King Lear* is deeply concerned with the environment – and the human place within it.

This ecocritical paradigm obviously reflects a rising concern with climate change, environmental degradation and the catastrophic collapse of biodiversity over the period of industrial and post-industrial capitalist modernity – or the Anthropocene, as it has come to be called.[162] The answer to the question 'What is the cause of thunder?' (III.vi.151) has become: 'humanity'. What new forms of ecocriticism share with cultural materialism (and related forms of new historicism)

---

[158] Ibid. p. 20.

[159] For more on Shakespeare and green criticism, see Gabriel Egan, *Green Shakespeare: From Ecopolitics to Ecocriticism* (London: Routledge, 2006) and Lynne Bruckner and Dan Brayton (eds), *Ecocritical Shakespeare* (London: Routledge, 2011).

[160] Jennifer Mae Hamilton, *This Contentious Storm: An Ecocritical and Performance History of King Lear* (London: Bloomsbury, 2017), p. 74.

[161] Ibid. For the storm, see Steven Mentz, '"Strange Weather" in *King Lear*', *Shakespeare*, 6:2 (2010) and Gwilym Jones, *Shakespeare's Storms* (Manchester: Manchester University Press, 2015), pp. 59–78; for land and landscape, see Stuart Eldon, 'The Geopolitics of *King Lear*: Territory, Land, Earth', *Law & Literature*, 25:2 (2013), pp. 147–65 and Jayne Elisabeth Archer, Richard Marggraf Turley and Howard Thomas, 'The Autumn King: Remembering the Land in *King Lear*', *Shakespeare Quarterly*, 63:4 (2012), pp. 518–43; and for animals, see Laurie Shannon, *The Accommodated Animal: Cosmopolity in Shakespearean Locales* (London and Chicago: University of Chicago Press, 2012), pp. 127–65.

[162] For an astute introduction see Erle C. Ellis, *Anthropocene: A Very Short Introduction* (Oxford: Oxford University Press, 2018), especially pp. 144–60.

is a suspicious critique of the enlightened, humanist subject, which is deemed to be anthropocentric: the (white, male, heterosexual) subject bases his 'sovereign' freedom on the conquest and utilisation of the natural world – and indeed the peoples considered to be in a 'state of nature'. Only where cultural materialist critics tended to read *King Lear* (and Shakespearean tragedy more widely) as developing and valorising a nascent vision of the humanist subject, ecocritics have been more ready to take the position that *King Lear* undermines that very same subject. This speaks to a new conception of materialist criticism around *King Lear*: where cultural materialist critique often deems that all material human 'activity' (to quote Hawkes) is self-created – is cultural – for ecocriticism that is to ignore the brute material reality of nature and the cosmos, which is finally beyond human intentionality.[163] This allows for a recuperation of tragic form and its representation of the clash between subject (individual) and object (nature): the aesthetic deformity of *King Lear* – not least the storm that rages uncontrolled over no fewer than seven scene-breaks – adumbrates a material reality that cannot be conceptually or aesthetically limited, something that aligns contemporary ecocritical interpretations of *King Lear* with Romantic conceptions of the sublime.[164] Ecocriticism has largely contended that, in his representation of Lear, Shakespeare stages a subject who, though once deluded about his own sovereignty over both nature and other people, comes to accept his limiting finitude in the face of the overwhelming power of the storm. Lear realises that, far from being 'everything' – an all-encompassing centre of agency and meaning – he is no more than a fragile body:

> To say 'ay' and 'no' to everything that I said 'ay' and 'no' to was no good divinity. When the rain came to wet me once, and the wind to make me chatter, when the thunder would not peace at my bidding—there I found 'em, there I smelt 'em out [. . .] I am not ague-proof. (IV.vi.98–104)

Lear is transformed from 'everything' into little more than a piece of nature – and a 'ruined piece of nature' (IV.vi.130) at that: not above or beyond the natural world at all, but a precarious and suffering part of it. This is not necessarily to deny the subject or to eradicate the notion of autonomy – something that, as discussed in Chapter 1, has sometimes been the case in poststructuralist discourse-critique. On the contrary: to

---

[163] See also the collection *New Materialisms: Ontology, Agency, and Politics*, ed. Diana Coole and Samantha Frost (Durham, NC and London: Duke University Press, 2010).
[164] For *King Lear* and the sublime, see Chapters 2 and 8.

free nature from instrumental rationality may also be to free the human subject.

Simon C. Estok, Laurie Shannon and Hamilton have all variously argued that *King Lear* critiques 'environmental degradation by virtue of its timely criticism of the human hierarchies'.[165] So when he searches for a vision of human finitude that may serve to undercut the pretensions of the Enlightenment self in an era of climate change, it should not be surprising to see that philosopher Jean-Pierre Dupuy also alights on *King Lear*. Dupuy writes that, in his representation of the storm and its impact, Shakespeare presages the way humanity is now at the mercy of violent natural forces beyond the aims and intentions of the self. He even adapts 'As flies to wanton boys' to serve, not an absurdist, but an ecocritical ethos.[166]

Anthony Parr has observed that after the unimaginable atrocities of the Second World War *King Lear* came to be seen as 'the drama that most urgently addressed the concerns of contemporary civilization', a world of 'nuclear nightmares and totalitarian repression'.[167] But for him, 'the threat of environmental catastrophe is not only as immediate as the nuclear annihilation promised by the Cold War' but also 'more in tune with the intimations of apocalypse in *King Lear* than were the global confrontations of the recent past'.[168] It may be the case that *King Lear* is more obviously concerned with strange weather events than it is with the prospect of nuclear catastrophe or terrorism. But environmental collapse and the other catastrophic phenomena of the twentieth and twenty-first centuries are by no means unrelated: there is a relationship between the reification of subjects and the reification of nature, which has brought about the collapse of the environment.

The environmental movement that emerged during the Cold War often went hand in hand with anti-militarism – whether that related to the destruction of nature caused by nuclear weapons or the use of Agent Orange in Vietnam. At the same time, modern concerns over climate change have been more and more centred on the increased chances of mass violence – even genocide – that may be caused by conflicts over

---

[165] Hamilton, *This Contentious Storm*, p. 176. Simon C. Estok, *Ecocriticism and Shakespeare: Reading Ecophopbia* (Basingstoke: Palgrave Macmillan, 2011), pp. 19–32; Shannon, *The Accommodated Animal*, p. 132.

[166] Jean-Pierre Dupuy, *A Short Treatise on the Metaphysics of Tsunamis*, trans. M. B. DeBevoise (East Lansing: Michigan State University Press, 2015), p. 30.

[167] Anthony Parr, '"The Wisdom of Nature": Ecological Perspectives on *King Lear*', in Andrew Hiscock and Lisa Hopkins (eds), *King Lear: A Critical Guide* (London: Continuum, 2011), p. 118.

[168] Ibid.

dwindling natural reserves and the possibility that environmental degradation may be met with new forms of authoritarian power.[169] It is also clearly the case that, though a global phenomenon, climate change does not impact all equally: the poor, the subaltern and other peoples unable to evade or avoid environmental shifts are not only disproportionately impacted, but more at risk of falling victim to a (potentially genocidal) rationality, where provisions from shelter to food are distributed unequally across human populations.[170] Timothy Snyder is only the most recent historian who, writing from the perspective of contemporary concerns over climate change, reminds us that the Nazi invasion of the East and the Holocaust were born out of a pseudo-Darwinian conception of a struggle between races over scant natural resources.[171]

These interactions between climate and other, apparently more historically distant disasters have not always been at the forefront of ecocriticism on *King Lear*. But there is scope for reading *King Lear* in a way that shows the continuities between the reification of subjects (Auschwitz) and environmental collapse (climate change) – a relationship also pursued by Dupuy.[172] What many of the ecocritical interpretations of *King Lear* share is a reconsideration of the storm. It has become a critical (and theatrical) commonplace that the storm should be thought of in the abstract, as a metaphor for the psychological collapse of Lear and the social and political disruption brought about by his quasi-abdication. Lear, however, is 'minded like the weather' (III.i.2): the weather, nature, is primary; it is not 'minded like Lear' and it does not emanate from him or his 'mind' – indeed Lear rages, in a remarkable phrase, that the storm is 'thought-executing' (III.ii.4). Far from being interpreted as a pathetic fallacy, ecocriticism has insisted on understanding the storm and its 'impetuous blasts' (III.i.8) as a material event, which 'invades' the people unfortunate enough to be stranded in it to 'the skin' (III.iv.7). Leslie Thomson writes that 'it *is* only a storm', not some philosophical abstraction – though it is only the more powerful and damaging for that.[173]

This reinterpretation of the storm opens the way to reconsider the

---

[169] See Alex Alvarez, *Unstable Ground: Climate Change, Conflict, and Genocide* (London: Rowman and Littlefield, 2017).

[170] See Henry Shue, *Climate Justice: Vulnerability and Protection* (Oxford: Oxford University Press, 2014).

[171] See his *Black Earth: The Holocaust as History and Warning* (London: Penguin, 2015), particularly pp. 194–5.

[172] See his *A Short Treatise on the Metaphysics of Tsunamis*, pp. 38–50.

[173] Leslie Thomson, 'The Meaning of "Thunder and Lightning": Stage Directions and Audience Expectations', *Early Theatre*, 2 (1999), p. 11.

'poor, naked wretches' that abide the 'pelting' of the 'pitiless storm' and are forced to contend with 'the fretful elements' (III.i.4) without clothes, shelter or food. These 'wretches', seen through the prism of climate change and environmental collapse, may almost be analogues for contemporary climate refugees or indeed any people forced to endure the vicissitudes of climate catastrophe without the forms of material and cultural support that the 'sophisticated' take for granted. The reification of subjects and the reification of nature are – once again – intimately related: mass social and political violence cannot be parcelled out from climatic change. Cheryl Lousley writes of 'the representational challenge that ecocriticism faces'.[174] This is not 'the representation of nature, but the politicization of environment'; or, making 'complex socio-ecological interactions socially visible as political concerns'.[175] *King Lear* is clearly a play that foregrounds social and ecological interactions in the storm.

King Lear in Performance

When he famously observed that *King Lear* is a play that 'cannot be acted', it was the storm scenes that Charles Lamb had principally in mind. Lamb makes the argument that, to see Lear acted,

> to see an old man tottering about the stage with a walking-stick, turned out of doors by his daughters in a rainy night, has nothing in it but what is painful and disgusting [. . .]
> On the stage we see nothing but corporal infirmities and weakness, the impotence of rage; while we read it, we see not Lear, but we are Lear – we are in his mind, we are sustained by a grandeur which baffles the malice of daughters and storms.[176]

For Lamb, the stage inevitably betrays the 'greatness' of *King Lear* precisely because the storm is not really (or at least not only) a storm; it is an emanation from the mind of Lear: 'It is his mind which is laid bare.'[177] To see Lear physically reduced to a frail, corporeal body in nature – precisely the type of 'infirmities and weakness' valorised in

---

[174] Cheryl Lousley, 'Ecocriticism and the Politics of Representation', in Greg Garrard (ed.), *The Oxford Handbook of Ecocriticism* (Oxford: Oxford University Press, 2014), p. 156.
[175] Ibid.
[176] Quoted in Grace Ioppolo (ed.), *A Routledge Literary Sourcebook on William Shakespeare's King Lear* (London: Routledge, 2003), p. 51.
[177] Ibid.

recent ecocriticism – can only be 'painful and disgusting' and indeed a betrayal of the ultimate meaning of *King Lear*.

Despite the qualms set out by Lamb, recent performances of *King Lear* have tended, in the same vein as modern ecocriticism, to underscore the brute materiality of the storm. This has principally meant drowning Lear (and the stage) in vast quantities of water – something that, as Hamilton observes, was very rare in past productions.[178] Performances that have used water to materially represent the storm range from the 2008 Rupert Gould production at the Liverpool Everyman Theatre to the 2018 Jonathan Munby production at the London Duke of York Theatre. But perhaps the most remarkable of the productions to 'let fall' (III.ii.18) water for the storm scenes is the 2010 RSC production at the Courtyard Theatre, Stratford.

Through his production of *King Lear*, director David Farr set out to 'critique the dominant political class in a changing climate'.[179] The *mise-en-scène*, using the 'barn-like' space of the Courtyard with its visible scaffolding, evoked a post-industrial world, so that the kingdom Lear (Greg Hicks) intended to bequeath to his daughters was less reminiscent of 'the shadowy forests and with champains riched' and 'plenteous rivers and wide-skirted meads' (I.i.64–5) Lear imagines than a disused factory – a site of industrial, capitalist production as opposed to Edenic nature.[180] Though it initially appeared a hermetically sealed space, cut off from anything 'outside' it, over the action of the play the factory disintegrated, as the space began to crumble, not only under the pressure of social and political upheaval, but also under the stress caused by the 'fretful elements' – the howling wind, thunder and lightning and, most disastrously, vast quantities of rain, which fell throughout the storm scenes. This progressive erosion or weathering of the *mise-en-scène* indicted modern industrial capital for its damaging impact on the environment and, at the same time, showed that the humanly created world is all too precarious, unable to withstand the 'terrors of the earth' (II.ii.471) unleashed by climate change. Kate Rumbold saw 'a despairing, post-industrial vision of modernity itself in decline'.[181] This precarity was also signalled by Lear: though he began the play as an imperious despot – a king who, in the words of Coen Heijes, desired

---

[178] Hamilton, *This Contentious Storm*, pp. 127–66.
[179] Ibid. p. 186.
[180] See also Kate Rumbold, 'Review of Shakespeare's *King Lear* (directed by David Farr for the Royal Shakespeare Company) at the Courtyard Theatre, Stratford-upon-Avon, 30 March 2010', *Shakespeare*, 7:2 (2010), p. 218.
[181] Ibid. p. 219.

to be 'in absolute control' – Lear was ultimately reduced to a shivering wreck, as he initially attempted to contest the storm, before succumbing to its onslaught.[182]

What has troubled some critics about the Farr production, however, is that Lear was 'singled out' in the storm: the rain fell in a solitary 'shaft' on a raging Lear, while the other characters remained untouched. This image of Lear alone in the rain potentially reinforces the idea of a one-to-one relationship between Lear and the storm, reducing it from a tangible material event to the fantasy of a disturbed mind.[183] But the singling out of Lear can also be interpreted as part of the wider decision taken by Farr to use *King Lear* to critique the 'dominant political class in a changing climate'. By showing the rain falling solely on Lear, Farr ensured that Lear was indicted directly for unleashing unpredictable and violent climatic events. Lear, as the acme of the political and industrial elite, was forced to realise that suffering and mass violence were caused not only by his past negligence or his decision to divide the kingdom, but also by his principal role in producing a rapidly changing ecosphere.

For many Shakespeare critics writing from a cultural materialist perspective, the ongoing influence of the Brook production – with its Beckettian images of existential absurdity – has been seen as politically retrogressive, an interpretation of Shakespeare that fails to interrogate problems that arise out of a distinct cultural time and place in favour of a universalising interpretation of human suffering as inherent to a cruelly meaningless universe. It is perhaps more than serendipitous, however, that the Brook production debuted in 1962 – the same year that Rachel Carson published *Silent Spring*, a seminal work of the ecological movement that documented the adverse environmental impacts caused by the indiscriminate use of pesticides.[184] Brook may have avoided literally representing the weather in favour of a more Brechtian approach to the storm, but his bare stage, along with the primitively crude clothing and implements used by the cast, connoted an apocalyptic post-nuclear winter, in which nature has been compromised, as much as a pre-modern, Neolithic world.

The changing valences of the Brook production in an era of climate catastrophe are perhaps most powerfully disclosed by the 2016 RSC production of *King Lear* directed by Gregory Doran, with Antony Sher as Lear. This production began with Lear – 'enthroned like a secular

---

[182] Coen Heijes, 'Reviews: *King Lear* by David Farr; *Antony and Cleopatra* by Michael Boyd', *Shakespeare Bulletin*, 28:4 (2010), p. 532.
[183] See Rumbold, 'Review of Shakespeare's *King Lear*', p. 219.
[184] Rachel Carson, *Silent Spring* (Boston: Houghton Mifflin, 1962).

Figure 3.1 Edgar (Oliver Johnstone) sits on a blackened, ashy wasteland, contemplating the sky and a world apparently without rain. (2016: The Royal Shakespeare Theatre, dir. Gregory Doran. Photograph: Ellie Kurtz. © RSC)

god' – in an elevated Plexiglas box, physically (and, it would seem, emotionally) insulated from any contact with his family or with the natural world.[185] This Plexiglas box was replaced by (or perhaps expanded to) a full white-box production, with a *Godot*-like blasted tree appearing at the back of the stage. This visually recalled the Brook production and its famously empty space. The aim was not only to adumbrate an empty, meaningless cosmos in which subjects are cruelly trapped, but also to signify a closed, totally human world in which nature, the horizon and any sense of non-human otherness has been violently wiped out. The gnarled, dead tree was matched by blackened, ashy earth, from which nothing grew (Figure 3.1).

Mark Shenton revealed the increasingly common use of water to literalise the storm when he complained that, in the Doran production, the storm scenes were 'underwhelming, created only with lighting, a noisy soundtrack and a large plastic sheet, but no actual rainfall'.[186]

---

[185] Michael Billington, '*King Lear* review – Sher shores up his place in Shakespeare royalty', <https://www.theguardian.com/stage/2016/sep/02/king-lear-review-royal-antony-sher> (accessed 30 October 2019).

[186] Mark Shenton, 'Antony Sher in *King Lear*, Royal Shakespeare Theatre Review – "Physically Subdued"', <https://www.thestage.co.uk/reviews/2016/antony-sher-

While Doran decided against using actual water for the storm, however, his use of distinctly Beckettian images and his visual allusions to the Brook production were designed to secrete an ecocritical awareness, using *King Lear* and its images of death and dearth to interrogate the human destruction of the environment and biodiversity. Sher, writing in his *Year of the Mad King: The Lear Diaries*, observes that Doran viewed *King Lear* as a Beckettian play with pressing resonance for those living after the Second World War and 'a Holocaust of unimaginable cruelty and suffering'; but he also refers to 'harvest failures' and the way *King Lear* imagines a world of acute 'food shortage'.[187] The image of Edgar, naked apart from a rough shawl, as he sat forlornly on the blackened earth looking up to a sky without the generative power of the rain, revealed that the destruction of the environment and the destruction of humanity are of a piece, calamities that cannot be disentangled.

Edgar was not alone, however: the poor naked wretches Lear prays to in the storm and that Edgar draws on for his Poor Tom disguise were not merely an imaginary abstraction in the Doran production, but often materially present on stage, struggling through the same elemental upheaval as the former king. Peter Smith recalls that, as the audience entered the theatre for the Doran production, the 'stage was set with a dozen or so refugees, cowled in rags and kneeling, facing upstage'.[188] These reminded Smith of 'so many asylum seekers or those left dispossessed by the current conflict in Syria'; but the ideational and visual parallel between the 'poor, naked wretches' and Poor Tom, left cast out into a violent but also desolate environment, also implied climate refugees, who were reliant on food handouts from the wealthy, as the natural world seemed unable to provide the conditions necessary for human life.[189] Unlike the Farr production, Doran undermined the centrality of Lear, training the attention of the audience onto the unfed and unclothed bodies of those peoples forced to suffer changeable and inclement weather without any material provision.

---

as-king-lear-review-royal-shakespeare-theatre-physically-subdued/> (accessed 16 October 2019).

[187] Antony Sher, *Year of the Mad King: The Lear Diaries* (London: Nick Hern Books, 2018), p. 172 and p. 185.
[188] Peter Smith, 'Play Review: *King Lear*, directed by Gregory Doran for RSC, Royal Shakespeare Theatre', *Cahiers Élisabéthains*, 92:1 (2017), p. 102.
[189] Ibid. p. 103.

Conclusion

Over the period of the post-war to contemporary eras, *King Lear* has undergone a variety of transformations – or strange mutations: from a play that, while set in a pagan culture, can be interpreted as a Christian drama about sin, suffering and redemption; to a Beckettian, absurdist nightmare *avant la lettre* in which there is no God, and human action – and tragedy – has been rendered meaningless; to a play about the importance of concerted political action in a profoundly inequitable world; to a progressive, humanist parable that portrays an enlightened triumph over mythic superstition; to a politically patriarchal and heteronormative drama that reveals the conservative institutional investment in Shakespeare and the canon, which must be contested; to a play that radically predicts the 'strange weather' of the era of the Anthropocene and the impact of human action on the environment.

These interpretations – while undeniably divergent – can all be seen as part of an ongoing response to the catastrophes of modernity, whether that evinces a reactionary desire for a more culturally unified time, as in the Christian reading provided by Danby, or interrogates the relationship between climate change and mass social and political violence, as in more recent ecocritical interpretations of the play. This relationship between *King Lear* and modern catastrophe is perhaps most powerfully disclosed by the continuing ideational tie between the play and the Holocaust, which (albeit controversially) remains a symbol of modern disaster – of the reification and destruction of human subjects. From the period of the Second World War, *King Lear* has emerged as a play through which the Auschwitz experience – the total destruction of the subject by modern social systems – has been interpreted.

The various appropriations of *King Lear* in post-war British playwriting and drama should be situated in the community of discourse that has aggregated around the play and modern catastrophe. Bond, Rudkin, Barker, Kane, Forced Entertainment and Kelly are all part of a far wider conversation around *King Lear*, catastrophe and ongoing legacy of Auschwitz. It is also important to situate the act of appropriation around recent (particularly cultural materialist) debates in Shakespeare studies. There are some obvious parallels between the politically informed understanding of appropriation advanced by cultural materialist critics and the theatres of catastrophe under analysis. These playwrights (in various ways) all repudiate traditional interpretations of *King Lear* and are suspicious of the investments of institutional power. Bond, Rudkin, Barker, Kane, Forced Entertainment and Kelly are also deeply suspicious of the growing role of various Culture (including 'Shakespearean') Industries in society and the totalisation of late capitalist culture. Where there is divergence between catastrophic theatre and cultural materialist criticism, however, is in the stress placed on the autonomy of the tragic subject, who cannot be finally constrained by any form of identity, and on aesthetic autonomy – categories that have been treated with suspicion (if not scorn) in cultural materialism.

This concern with the agency and autonomy of the tragic subject evinces a form of theatre that is less preoccupied with political conceptions of identity than it is with the destruction of subjectivity as such in the totalised social systems of modern culture, so that a late modernist critique of totality is continued into the postmodern epoch. This situates catastrophic theatre in an ongoing discourse around *King Lear*, modernity and the Holocaust that stretches back into the early to mid-1940s. *King Lear* becomes a vehicle through which contemporary playwrights can interrogate the destruction of the subject in post-Auschwitz life and insist on the autonomy of the tragic subject, who (re)fashions him or herself out of disaster.

Chapter 4

'The man without pity is mad': Edward Bond's *King Lears* and the Dialectic of Engagement

Introduction

'[I]nstead of being used as useful imaginative experience', observes Edward Bond of Shakespeare, his plays and poetry have been 'reified as some holy script' by the institutions of criticism and performance, with the 'sublime action' of *King Lear* the ultimate image of rarefied 'high [...] culture'.[1] Bond, perhaps the foremost British dramatist of the post-war era and a committed Marxist socialist, has made repeated and wide-ranging use of *King Lear* throughout his dramaturgy, poetry and discursive writings, not as 'some reified holy script' from the past, but as valuable 'imaginative experience' that may be used to reflect on and interrogate the problems of modern society. Bond lived through the London Blitz, with its 'sublime ruins' and 'dust dust dust', and viscerally recollects seeing images of Nazi concentration camps at the end of the Second World War – images that have remained with him and continue to inform his playwriting and drama.[2] The problem of modern society is ultimately the problem of Auschwitz, the reduction of subjects to nothing more than objects of rationalised systems, which degrade human values – and lives. Bond makes the case that 'the last century is the century of darkness and the darkness is still in us': 'it created the place of absolute nihilism: Auschwitz'.[3] Bond poses the question: 'By the time

---

[1] Edward Bond, *Edward Bond: Letters Volume 4*, ed. Ian Stuart (Amsterdam: Harwood Academic Publishers, 1998), p. 25; Edward Bond, *Lear*, Programme Note, quoted in Jenny S. Spencer and Jane Spencer, *Dramatic Strategies in the Plays of Edward Bond* (Cambridge: Cambridge University Press, 1992), p. 81.

[2] Edward Bond, *Edward Bond: The Playwright Speaks*, ed. David Tuaillon (London: Bloomsbury Methuen, 2015), pp. 16–18.

[3] Edward Bond, 'The Third Crisis: The State of Future Drama', <http://www.edwardbond.org/Comment/comment.html> (accessed 3 May 2018).

of the century of Auschwitz society had created vast new resources of knowledge and power. Its philosophy was progress. How did it become the most destructive and regressive of all times?'[4] These are the contradictions and questions under which *King Lear* 'has lasting value'.[5]

This chapter will analyse the way Bond has used *King Lear* to confront the contradiction of modernity and write the disaster of Auschwitz. It will primarily analyse his famed appropriation of Shakespeare in his 1971 play *Lear*, but it will also analyse the 1973 play *Bingo* and other, more recent engagements with *King Lear* in his poetry and imaginative writing, which – though often critically neglected – reflect developments in his post-Auschwitz theory of the self and dramaturgy.[6] I will show that Bond has an ongoing relationship with *King Lear*; but I will also show that his engagements with and appropriations of the play for the purposes of a post-Auschwitz subject and aesthetic are beset by a deep-seated contradiction. Bond aims for a tragic dramaturgy that places emphasis on the suffering but also freedom of the individual subject, who acts against a system that precipitates catastrophe. Despite his critique of Auschwitz and the dialectic of enlightenment, however, Bond remains thematically and formally reliant on a Marxist-humanist conception of the historical process, which is conditioned by a rationalistic faith in the possibility of moral and social 'progress' over time.[7] This creates a tragic form that paradoxically reifies the very subject it strives to represent and emancipate, as that subject is required to act in a historically prescribed way. This contradiction I call the dialectic of engagement.

Lear

'[C]oldness, the basic principle [. . .] without which there could have been no Auschwitz'

Theodor Adorno[8]

---

[4] Ibid.
[5] Edward Bond, *Edward Bond: Letters Volume 3*, ed. Ian Stuart (London: Routledge, 2003), p. 83.
[6] Though still widely studied, Bond has seen his reputation within the UK theatre establishment fall – though his work is still recognised and performed in Continental Europe. This, in part, has to do with his own self-imposed exile from UK theatre, which he deems to be in crisis – if not dead. See Graham Saunders, 'Edward Bond and The Celebrity of Exile', *Theatre Research International*, 29:3 (2004), pp. 256–66. I return to the topic of exile in Chapter 5.
[7] See Spencer, *Dramatic Strategies in the Plays of Edward Bond*, pp. 1–12.
[8] Theodor Adorno, *Negative Dialectics*, trans. E. B. Ashton (London and New York: Continuum, 2007), p. 363.

'Once the wall is built, it takes almost a miracle to break through it'
Max Horkheimer[9]

Lear has been described as a 'landmark' in British theatre and is perhaps the most famous appropriation of *King Lear* – and possibly Shakespeare more widely – by a post-war British playwright.[10] The play, originally staged at the Royal Court Theatre in 1971, is a wholesale rewriting of *King Lear* that makes sweeping formal and textual changes to the Shakespearean 'original'.[11] The action of the play, which reduces the five acts of *King Lear* into a more condensed three-act form, centres on the construction and attempted destruction of a Wall, which Lear is building in order to keep out the (largely imagined) enemies of his kingdom. His daughters, Bodice and Fontanelle (Goneril and Regan), secretly conspire to marry the Duke of Cornwall and Duke of North – the very same enemies Lear opposes. Lear soon finds himself in conflict with his daughters and, by the end of Act One, is defeated and made a refugee. Cordelia appears in the play as an anonymous woman whose husband gives the outcast Lear temporary haven. Cordelia is subsequently raped and widowed in an act of state terror. Prompted by motives of vengeance to take up arms against the daughters and the dukes, Cordelia adopts the role of revolutionary utopian ideologue, subduing Bodice and Fontanelle and taking over the state by the end of Act Two. Far from instituting a promised utopian society, Cordelia repeats the depravations of the previous regimes and begins a reign of revolutionary terror, symbolised by the rebuilt Wall. Lear, who escapes from prison, is haunted by a ghost from his past, who in Act Three tries to tempt Lear away from politics into an idyllic, pastoral fantasy. Lear resists the ghost and confronts Cordelia: 'Our lives are awkward and fragile and we have only one thing to keep us sane: pity, and the man without pity is mad' (3.3.84). Lear, however, fails to make Cordelia 'pregnant to good pity' (*King Lear*, IV.vi.219). His only recourse is a final, doomed gesture: the play ends with Lear scaling the Wall and attempting to dig it up, before he is shot dead.

The ominous Wall around which the action of *Lear* revolves obviously alludes to the Berlin Wall and the retrogression of the Soviet

---

[9] Max Horkheimer, *Critique of Instrumental Reason*, trans. Matthew Jay O'Connell et al. (London: Verso, 2012), p. 116.

[10] Peter Billingham, *Edward Bond: A Critical Study* (Basingstoke: Palgrave Macmillan, 2014), p. 37. The possible exception is *Rosencrantz and Guildenstern Are Dead* by Tom Stoppard – a play that, as I set out previously, began its life as *Rosencrantz and Guildenstern Meet King Lear*.

[11] For production details, see Patricia Hern, 'Commentary', in Bond, *Lear*, pp. lxvii–lxviii and pp. 103–8.

revolution, with Bond openly stating that the specific event informing the play (and the representation of the despotic Lear) was Stalinism.[12] But the representation of the Wall is also informed by the catastrophes of the twentieth century more widely, epitomised by the Holocaust and the totally reified world of Auschwitz.[13] 'Art has always looked at the atrocities of the age in which it was created,' states Bond – and for Bond, Auschwitz is emblematic of the atrocities committed in modern societies and the continuing crisis of instrumental rationality, which fatally limits the freedom and imagination of the subject.[14] Bond appropriates *King Lear* in response to that crisis.

Through his appropriation of *King Lear*, Bond critiques a posture of complete resignation to events. Bond considers resignation to be the 'moral' *King Lear* promotes in response to catastrophe – something that aligns the play with the absurdist drama that emerged in the 1950s and 1960s, most obviously through Beckett. Bond intends to replace the passivity of *King Lear* with a version of the play that insists on concerted social and political engagement in and with the world, which is necessary to bring about change towards a more humane society. Not unlike other Marxist interpretations of the play in the 1970s, Bond sees absurdist resignation as politically retrogressive.[15] His version of *King Lear* represents 'heroic' action against a reified and reifying world that destroys individuality – the world not only of the Nazi concentration camps, but also of Stalinist Russia and late Western capitalism.

The notion that drama should both represent and catalyse action against a dehumanising social system evinces the profound influence of Brecht. Bond had seen the Berliner Ensemble in 1956 and, under the influence of Royal Court directors George Devine and William Gaskill, had begun to formally investigate and utilise Brechtian techniques by

---

[12] Edward Bond, *Edward Bond: Letters Volume 5*, ed. Ian Stuart (London: Routledge, 2001), p. 149. This critique of Stalinism was partly pragmatic, as well as ideological. Bond states: 'I needed to distance myself from Stalinism because that was having a propaganda block to socialism in the West,' quoted in David L. Hirst, *Edward Bond* (Basingstoke: Macmillan, 1985), p. 140.

[13] Chien-Cheng Chen writes that Bond is more concerned 'with the rational logic at the heart of modernity' – epitomised by Auschwitz – 'than with any specific historical events or social phenomena'. See his 'On Edward Bond's Dramaturgy of Crisis in *The Chair* Plays: The Dystopian Imagination and the Imagination in Dystopia', *Platform*, 10:2 (2016), p. 33.

[14] Edward Bond, 'Introduction', *The Fool*, in Edward Bond, *Plays 3: Bingo, The Fool, The Woman, Stone* (London: Bloomsbury Methuen, 1999), p. 79.

[15] See Chapter 3.

the time that he turned to his appropriation of *King Lear*. Prior to drafting *Lear* in 1969, Bond had also collaborated with Keith Hack on an abortive translation of *Roundheads and Peakheads* (itself an adapted version of *Measure for Measure*) reflecting his own impressions of the Berliner Ensemble as 'Shakespearean'. 'I recognized his importance then as I'd only done with one other writer', as Bond observes of Brecht: 'Shakespeare'.[16] *Lear* is usually regarded as a pivotal moment in the development of post-Brechtian, Epic political theatre in British playwriting, while also representing a decisive shift from the more socially realist plays set in working-class south London that had made Bond (in)famous, not least with the censor.[17]

This is not, however, to ignore the critical controversy around the 'debt' that Bond owes to Brecht. Bond has increasingly come to distance himself from Brecht. He has even accused Brechtian theatre of being 'the theatre of Auschwitz'.[18] This critique has to do with the perceived acquiescence of Brecht with the East German Soviet regime ('his answer to Auschwitz is the Gulag') and to the idea that the *Verfremdungseffekt* 'creates the psychology of the death-camp' – by which Bond means an overly detached form of subjective consciousness (or as Adorno calls it, 'coldness').[19] Brecht intends for his *Verfremdungseffekt* to distance the audience from emotional, empathetic engagement with onstage characters, encouraging the audience to adopt a properly critical, 'scientific' understanding of a play and its historical materialist analysis of

---

[16] Quoted in Janelle Reinelt, *After Brecht: British Epic Theater* (Ann Arbor: The University of Michigan Press, 1994), p. 51.

[17] See in particular James C. Bulman, 'Bond, Shakespeare and the Absurd', *Modern Drama*, 29:1 (1986), p. 62. For a broader study dealing with the complex reception and re-evaluation of Brechtian dramaturgy and theory in post-war British drama, see *After Brecht*. Bond made legal history with his debut *Saved* (1965): it was the last play successfully prosecuted by the Lord Chamberlain before his powers of censorship were rescinded to parliament.

[18] Edward Bond, *The Hidden Plot: Notes on Theatre and the State* (London: Methuen Drama, 1999), p. 169. See also Kate Katafiasz, 'Alienation is the Theatre of Auschwitz: An Exploration of Form in Edward Bond's Theatre', in David Davis (ed.), *Edward Bond and the Dramatic Child: Edward Bond's Plays for Young People* (Trentham Books: Stoke-on-Trent, 2005), pp. 25–48.

[19] Bond, 'The Third Crisis: The State of Future Drama'. The notion of coldness in Adorno is important: by stating that it is a vital part of the conditions under which Auschwitz became possible, Adorno obviously underscores that similar catastrophes were more than possible in the period of the Cold War. For a fine reading of coldness in Adorno, see Simon Mussell, '"Pervaded by a chill": The Dialectic of Coldness in Adorno's Social Theory', *Thesis Eleven*, 117:1 (2013), pp. 55–67. Mussell notes that, before he suddenly died in 1969, Adorno was planning a work called *Kälte* – 'Cold' (p. 57).

inequitable social conditions. But for Bond, Brechtian detachment does not do enough to incite committed sympathetic engagement, fostering an aesthetically distanced response that can be considered comparable to the silent passivity of those who failed to resist (or colluded in) the Final Solution.[20] 'To say that empathy is all is foolish', remarks Bond, 'but it is also foolish to say that we need no empathy. The soldiers shot the Jews at Babi Yar – the Nazis gassed the Jews at Auschwitz – because they had no empathy with them. Auschwitz is the theatre of the A-Effect.'[21]

This is not necessarily the place to analyse the value of the critique Bond has formed against Brecht. What is at stake, however, is the notion of engagement – of concerted social and political action. This underpins the critique Bond has mounted against Shakespearean, Beckettian and, since around the mid-1990s, Brechtian drama. Bond critiques all of these playwrights for a perceived failure to depict and elicit imaginative social and political engagement. These writers are all attentive to suffering and catastrophe, but ultimately fail to catalyse the engaged subject that Bond sees as vital for change 'after' the calamity of Auschwitz.

Bond, Shakespeare and *King Lear*

Bond has a conspicuously split understanding of *King Lear*. He praises *King Lear* for its piercing insight into social and political injustice, stating that 'Shakespeare created Lear, who is the most radical of all social critics.'[22] Bond bases his interpretation of the social and political radicalism of *King Lear* (and Lear) on the storm scenes and the scenes on the heath, in which Lear rails against the inequality of society in his 'Poor naked wretches' (III.iv.28) speech and forms a devastating critique of all forms of authority and injustice. These scenes – which in previous performances from the 1940s provided the basis for a Christianised, redemptionist reading of the play – are secularised by Bond and interpreted from a radical Marxist-humanist perspective, in which Lear is transformed into the most powerful critic of inequality in the play, insisting on a reformed world where 'distribution should undo excess' (IV.i.73).

---

[20] Kate Katafiasz, 'Quarrelling with Brecht: Understanding Bond's Post-structuralist Political Aesthetic', *Studies in Theatre and Performance*, 28:3 (2008), p. 247.
[21] Bond, *The Hidden Plot*, p. 169.
[22] Edward Bond, 'Introduction', *Bingo*, in Bond, *Plays 3*, p. 4.

Bond ultimately finds *King Lear* dissatisfying, however: while Shakespeare endows his protagonist with acute insight, he finally allows Lear to escape into a private fantasy in which the possibility of engagement is slowly drained. This fantasy of escape constellates around Cordelia, with whom Lear famously wishes to share the remainder of his days in prison:

> No, no, no, no! Come, let's away to prison.
> We two alone will sing like birds i' th' cage.
> When thou dost ask me blessing, I'll kneel down
> And ask of thee forgiveness. So we'll live,
> And pray, and sing, and tell old tales, and laugh
> At gilded butterflies, and hear poor rogues
> Talk of court news, and we'll talk with them too—
> Who loses and who wins, who's in, who's out—
> And take upon's the mystery of things
> As if we were God's spies. And we'll wear out
> In a walled prison packs and sects of great ones
> That ebb and flow by the moon. (V.iii.8–19)

The problem with the private fantasies Lear withdraws into is that he finally accepts suffering and injustice as inevitable, the product of an absurd universe which is resistant to intervention. Lear turns a contingent, materially determined situation into metaphysical fate, which is as inevitable as it is irresistible, akin to the 'ebb and flow of the moon'. The problems dramatised in *King Lear* are, states Bond, irrevocably 'political' – but 'the solution given isn't'.[23] Brecht, also writing on tragic fate and the notion of the Shakespearean 'hero', observes:

> great solitary figures, bearing on their breast the star of their fate, carry through with irresistible force their futile and deadly outbursts; they prepare their own downfall; life, not death, becomes obscene as they collapse; the catastrophe is beyond criticism. Human sacrifices all round! Barbaric delights![24]

---

[23] Quoted in Hern, 'Commentary', *Lear*, p. xxvi. Bond, perhaps oddly, seems unconvinced by the anti-hierarchical, engaged resistance provided by the servant who tries to stop his master Cornwall from blinding Gloucester. Bond states:

> Servants don't do that – that's a feudal myth he's going back to. [Shakespeare] wants very much to believe that sort of thing, and it's not true. If the man's paid to stand by, he will stand by – there's nothing else he can do. (Quoted in Malcolm Hay and Philip Roberts, *Edward Bond: A Companion to the Plays* (London: TQ Publications, 1978), p. 60)

These words reflect the passivity of those who 'stood by' in the Holocaust.

[24] Bertolt Brecht, *Brecht on Theatre*, ed. Marc Silberman, Tom Kuhn and Steve Giles, trans. various (London: Bloomsbury, 2019), p. 282.

The determinism of tragic fate forestalls any 'criticism' of catastrophe, which is understood as inevitable, so as long as 'the stars of his fate hang over King Lear'.[25] It is a view Brecht challenges by implicitly aligning the heavenly stars alluded to in *King Lear* with the stars the Nazis forced Jews to wear when in public spaces (which were also borne on the chest). Whether the idea of tragic fate is viable after the Holocaust is pertinent for both Brecht and Bond.

Not unlike Kott and Brook, Bond aligns *King Lear* with the Theatre of the Absurd. Only where Kott praises Shakespeare for his prescient anticipation of absurdism, Bond critiques Shakespeare for failing to advocate for changes in the social and political conditions that lead to disaster and suffering.[26] 'I don't like the absurdists,' reflects Bond; 'I am an optimist. I believe in the survival of mankind. I don't believe in an *Endgame* or *Waiting for Godot*.'[27] Bond accepts that Beckettian drama has been read 'optimistically' as revealing the power of the human spirit, but it is a reading Bond refutes. Beckett 'is said to have shown that however you degrade people an unquenchable spark of humanity remains in them', writes Bond, with 'experience in concentration camps offered as proof'.[28] But the argument, insists Bond, is 'false': not only did those who ruled the camps fail to retain the human 'spark', but even if 'the theory of the spark were true – how would that guide us through the desperately needed reorganization of society, or teach us to express our humanity in the changing world?'[29]

Bond considers *King Lear* to be beset by the same problem. Lear might provide a powerful critique of social injustice but his final acceptance of suffering as the result of an absurd cosmos retards any possibility of concerted political engagement and reform. By rewriting the play, Bond aims to supplant its resigned, metaphysical absurdism with a newly

---

[25] Bertolt Brecht, 'On the Experimental Theatre', trans. Carl Richard Mueller, *Tulane Drama Review*, 6:1 (1961), p. 12.

[26] The year *Lear* was staged (1971) was the same year Brook released his film version of *King Lear*. *Lear* is far closer in its political outlook to *Korol Lir* – the 1971 film version of *King Lear* by Soviet director Grigori Kozintsev. See my 'Crowding out Dover "Cliff" in *Korol Lir*', *Adaptation*, 10:2 (2017), pp. 210–29.

[27] Quoted in Graham Saunders, '"A theatre of ruins": Edward Bond and Samuel Beckett: Theatrical Antagonists', *Studies in Theatre and Performance*, 25:1 (2005), p. 67

[28] Ibid. pp. 68–9.

[29] Ibid. p. 69.

political version of *King Lear* that holds out the possibility that humanity can change its (apparent) 'destiny'.[30] Bond states:

> Shakespeare took the character of Lear and I wished to correct it so that it would become a viable model for us and, I would like to think, for our society. Shakespeare does arrive at an answer [...] and that was the idea of total resignation [...], discovering that a human being can accept an enormous lot and survive it. He can come through the storm. What I want to say is that this model is inadequate now, that it just does not work. Acceptance is not enough. Anybody can accept. You can go quietly into your gas chamber at Auschwitz; you can sit quietly at home and have an H-bomb dropped on you. Shakespeare had time. He must have thought that in time certain changes would be made. But time has speeded up enormously, and for us, time is running out.[31]

Bond explicitly situates his response to *King Lear* in the social world of Auschwitz and post-Auschwitz culture, a milieu that, far from simply confirming the inherent absurdity and cruelty of existence, underscores the need for progressive social and political intervention. Bond contends that the 'moral' of *King Lear* is to 'endure until in time the world be made right' – but it is now 'frivolous to say that a man can survive in Auschwitz and so prove the strength of the human spirit'.[32] Shakespeare is very far from being 'our contemporary': his vision of resignation has become not only redundant but regressive and dangerous in the face of the concentration camps, the Nazi Holocaust and the H-bomb, not 'pertinent' because of a transhistorical insight into a timeless, existential absurdity. *King Lear*, as far as Bond understands it, needs revising if it is to be understood as politically 'relevant' for modern, post-Holocaust audiences – 'for ourselves, for our society, for our time, for our problems'.[33] Bond adopts an ideologically and politically 'corrective' ('Shakespeare took the character of Lear and I wished to correct it') approach to appropriation: for him, the 'holy script' that is Shakespeare serves, in the wake of catastrophe, to promote values that no longer apply.

---

[30] Edward Bond, *Selections from the Notebooks of Edward Bond: Volume 2 1980–1995*, ed. Ian Stuart (London: Methuen, 2000), p. 26.
[31] Quoted in Hay and Roberts, *Edward Bond: A Companion*, p. 18.
[32] Quoted in Spencer, *Dramatic Strategies in the Plays of Edward Bond*, p. 91; Edward Bond, *Selections from the Notebooks of Edward Bond: Volume 1 1959–1980*, ed. Ian Stuart (London: Methuen, 2000), p. 218.
[33] Quoted in Lynne Bradley, *Adapting King Lear for the Stage* (Farnham and Burlington: Ashgate, 2010), p. 124.

Politicising *King Lear*

In his 'Preface' to *Lear*, Bond sets out his conception of the way in which modern society has developed:

> [W]e live in what is more and more becoming a technosphere. We do not fit into it very well and so it activates our biological defences, one of which is aggression [. . .] What ought we to do? Live justly. But what is justice? Justice is allowing people to live in the way for which they evolved [. . .] That is the essential thing I want to say because it means that in fact our society and its morality, which deny this, and its technology which more and more prevents it, all the time whispers in your ear 'You have no right to live.' That is what lies under the splendour of the modern world.[34]

The rhetoric Bond uses is telling – where he refers to 'our society', with '*its* morality', '*its* technology' – as it implies that both rational morality and scientific technology have become independent, divorced from the human(e) ends of 'our society'. Under the conditions of modernity ('the modern world') the forces of history have become reified and, as Lukács and Adorno also contend, autotelic.[35] The processes instigated by human agents in modern times come to appear self-determining and so impervious to intervention and change. This means that the subject is disempowered, appearing to be at the mercy of abstract and impersonal social and political systems, turning the world into an arbitrary – even absurd – place. The autonomous metaprocesses of modernity 'whisper' menacingly, insisting on the unreality, the total contingency, of the individual human being: 'You have no right to live.' Hubert Zapf makes the case that for Bond 'the "subject" of the historical process may not be humanity any more but the social constructions themselves which it has created'.[36] The individual is transformed through the process of reification from an active subject into a mere object of history.

This vision of history is typified in *Lear* by the representation of the Wall. The construction of the Wall is symptomatic of history-turned-autonomous – or reification. Lear believes that he is building the Wall in order to protect and emancipate the people. He states:

> I started this wall when I was young. I stopped my enemies in the field, but there were always more of them. How could we ever be free? So I built this

---

[34] 'Bond, 'Preface', in Bond, *Lear*, p. lxiv.
[35] For more on Lukács, see Chapter 1.
[36] Hubert Zapf, 'Two Concepts of Society in Drama: Bertolt Brecht's The *Good Woman of Setzuan* and Edward Bond's *Lear*', *Modern Drama*, 31:3 (1988), p. 357.

wall to keep our enemies out. My people will live behind this wall when I'm dead. You may be governed by fools but you'll always live in peace. My wall will make you free. (1.1.3–4)

Despite his grandiose claims that the Wall will 'free' his people from suffering, however, Lear – in a moment of obvious irony – begins the play by shooting a hapless worker (1.1.6) for an accident that delays the building works, so that the (impossible) completion of the Wall takes precedence over the very lives it is supposed to protect and enfranchise. Freedom reverts to domination, the subject to an object of a process that has become alarmingly independent of its creators. This is even true of Lear himself, who briefly strays in front of the firing squad, implying that he is equally prey to wider social and political forces and the unintentionally self-destructive consequences of an ideology that so degrades the subject (1.1.4).

The seeming imperviousness of the Wall to human intervention becomes increasingly apparent over the action of the play. Bodice purposes to have the (as she tellingly calls it) 'absurd' (1.1.5) Wall torn down. But after taking power, she fails to enact any control over the Wall, coming to realise that her newfound position, far from freeing her from patriarchal authority, has turned her into a puppet of a grotesquely self-perpetuating, reified process of 'War' and 'Power' (2.5.48). 'I started to pull the Wall down, and had to stop that,' reflects Bodice: 'I am trapped' (2.5.48–9). Cordelia does not even attempt to tear down the Wall, which she sees (in the same vein as Lear) as a means of instituting an improved life for the people of the kingdom: 'The government's creating that new life' (3.3.83). 'Then nothing's changed! A revolution must at least reform!' Lear angrily insists, with Cordelia offering the utterly feeble riposte: 'Everything *else* has changed' (3.3.84).[37] Once again, the Wall appears as an 'impersonal, non-human "meta-subject"', beyond 'change'.[38]

The impersonal quality of the Wall in *Lear* also conditions personal relationships, whereby an invisible 'wall' of cold disinterest grows between human beings, alienating people from reality and from each

---

[37] Bond calls the Cordelia of *King Lear* 'an absolute menace' because – in trying to restore Lear to the throne – her military intervention does nothing to challenge the underlying injustice of the social and political system represented in the play. The same is clearly true of his Cordelia. Quoted in Sonia Massai, 'Stage Over Study: Charles Marowitz, Edward Bond and Recent Materialist Approaches to Shakespeare', *New Theatre Quarterly*, 59 (1999), p. 248.

[38] Zapf, 'Two Concepts of Society', p. 361.

other.³⁹ There is, as Lear begins to realise, 'a Wall everywhere!' (3.2.80) as the edifice fatefully intrudes on every aspect of human life and interaction. This idea of 'a Wall everywhere!' was powerfully realised in the original production of the play, where, in a self-reflexive *coup de théâtre*, the Wall itself was not seen onstage until Act Three, when Lear attempts to dig it up. Up until that critical point, the actors referred to the Wall as if it occupied the same offstage space as the audience. This self-reflexive gesture (which draws on Brecht) worked to break down the distanced, 'aesthetic' space of the stage and the 'social' space of the audience, reinforcing the sense of the Wall being 'everywhere' as an obstacle to more humane personal relations and the underlying cause of social and political violence, for Bond symbolic of a wider cultural malaise.⁴⁰

It is that same cold disinterest – the failure of properly empathetic engagement and the deadening of interpersonal, human relations – which drives the arbitrary and yet also compulsive acts of violence found in *Lear*, most obviously the horrific blinding of Lear in Act Two. This is the act undertaken by a former prisoner turned state official, who uses a (so-called) 'scientific device' on Lear. To quote the dialogue again:

Fourth Prisoner:	(*Produces a tool*): Here's a device I perfected on dogs for removing human eyes.
Lear:	No, no. You mustn't touch my eyes. I must have my eyes!
Fourth Prisoner:	With this device you extract the eye undamaged and then it can be put to good use. It's based on a scouting gadget I had as a boy.
Soldier N:	Get on, it's late.
Fourth Prisoner:	Understand, this isn't an instrument of torture, but a scientific device. See how it clips the lid back to leave it unmarked.
Lear:	No – no!
Fourth Prisoner:	Nice and steady (*He removes one of LEAR'S eyes*) [. . .]
Fourth Prisoner:	Note how the eye passes into the lower chamber and is received in a soothing formulation of formaldehyde

---

³⁹ So alienating is the Wall that Lear even thinks of himself as being 'buried alive': 'I'm buried alive in a Wall!' (3.2.80). The idea of being buried alive alludes to Lear and his 'You do me wrong to take me out o'the grave' (IV.vii.45).

⁴⁰ I am also reminded of Günther Anders and his contention that *Hiroshima ist uberall* – or 'Hiroshima is everywhere'. Anders contends that Auschwitz revealed that all men are exterminable, while Hiroshima shows that mankind as a whole is exterminable. See Holger Nering, 'Remembering War, Forgetting Hiroshima: "Euroshima" and the West German Anti-Nuclear Weapons Movements in the Cold War', in Michael D. Gordin and G. John Ikenberry (eds), *The Age of Hiroshima* (Princeton: Princeton University Press, 2020), pp. 179–200.

crystals. One more, please (*He removes LEAR'S other eye*) [...] Perfect. (2.4.63)

The interaction between Lear and the coolly detached official typifies the petrification of human relationships in *Lear*. The 'device' and cleanly 'perfected' process the official deploys – in which Lear has his eyes automatically 'sucked out' (2.6.63) into a container – represents the way that modern scientific reason, which is supposed to procure freedom, actually reifies the subject and conditions disengaged relationships between people. It is also telling that the eyes, in a display of utilitarian pragmatism, are going to be put 'to use' – perhaps not unlike the industrial uses found for human remains in the Holocaust. Even the actions of the servants who bring 'egg whites' and 'flax' to relieve Gloucester in *King Lear* (III.vii.105) are transformed into the far more perfunctory spraying of a healing '*aerosol*' to encourage the 'formation of scabs' and to 'discourage flies' (2.6.63) – so that cold, scientific processes once again take the place of a more sensuous relationship between concrete, engaged individuals.[41] Jean Améry, reflecting on his own internment at Auschwitz, Buchenwald and Bergen-Belsen, contends that the Nazis used 'scientific' torture to atomise the individual, who is unable to think reflexively beyond his or her own bodily suffering or to enter into any form of engaged dialogic relationship with the other.[42] The same atomisation is apparent in *Lear* – indeed when Bodice and Fontanelle torture the old retainer Warrington, it is to 'shut him up inside himself' (1.4.15): torture makes him unable to think beyond his pain and engage with the world.

Thomas Cartelli contends that Bond purposefully evokes a 'concentration camp atmosphere' in the prison scene by portraying 'a would-be Joseph Mengele'.[43] But the actions, deportment and detached language of the official also recall Adolf Eichmann and the concept of the 'banality of evil', as developed by Arendt.[44] Arendt famously makes the case that the Final Solution was not necessarily undertaken by sociopaths, but by

---

[41] Bond originally planned to have Lear blinded by 'a sword slash' before settling on the far more powerful image of his being blinded by the device operated by the Fourth Prisoner. See Bond, *Selections from the Notebooks of Edward Bond: Volume 1*, p. 97.
[42] See his *At The Mind's Limit: Contemplations by a Survivor on Auschwitz and its Realities* (Bloomington: University of Indiana Press, 1980), pp. 28–40.
[43] Thomas Cartelli, 'Shakespeare in Pain: Edward Bond's *Lear* and the Ghosts of History', *Shakespeare Survey: Volume 55*, ed. Peter Holland (Cambridge: Cambridge University Press, 2002), p. 166.
[44] Hannah Arendt, *Eichmann in Jerusalem: A Report on the Banality of Evil* (London: Penguin, 2006).

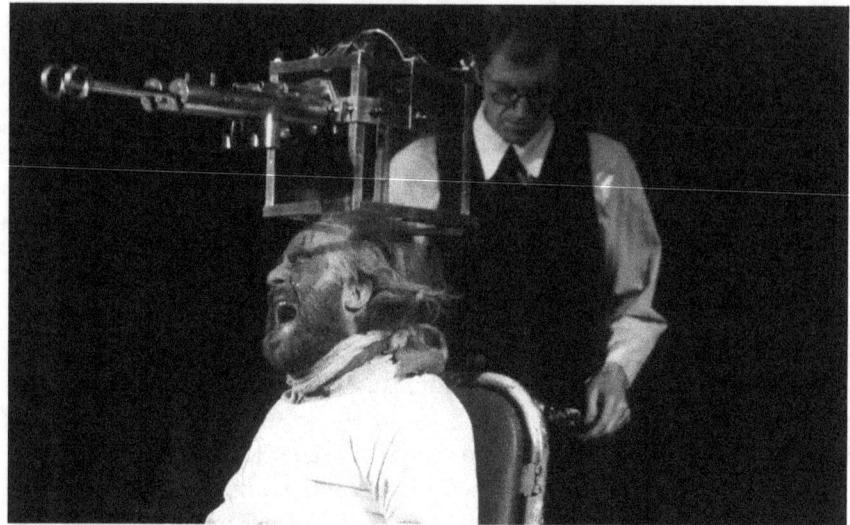

Figure 4.1   Lear (Bob Peck) is blinded by the Fourth Prisoner (David Bradley). (1982: The Other Place, dir. Barry Kyle. Photograph: Donald Cooper. © Donald Cooper/Photostage)

seemingly unremarkable officials who were able to free themselves from personal culpability and interpersonal empathy by complying with the demands of an impersonal, rationalised system of bureaucracy – an irrational psychopathology that, in the words of *King Lear*, 'Allows itself to anything' (III.vii.104). 'He did his *duty*' writes Arendt of Eichmann, 'he not only obeyed *orders*, he also obeyed the *law*' – with Eichmann even quoting Kant to show the individual should necessarily acquiesce to the needs and 'general laws' of the wider community, represented by the state.[45] Eichmann, as understood by Arendt, was motivated more by the (banal) prospect of promotion than by a fervent commitment to Nazi ideology.[46] 'This', as the operator of the 'device' in *Lear* states, 'is a chance to bring myself to notice' (2.6.62). Ironically, even he is at the mercy of a system of administration: before so dispassionately blinding Lear, he admits he is currently 'waiting for [. . .] papers' (2.6.58) that will confirm his identity and possibly allow him to take up a more senior position in the hierarchy (Figure 4.1).[47]

---

[45] I return to Kant in Chapter 6. The lead prosecutor Gideon Hausner quoted *King Lear* to describe Eichmann – though he did so because he believed Eichmann's apparently respectable bourgeois demeanor was an act: 'The prince of darkness is a gentleman' (III.iv.139).

[46] Arendt, *Eichmann in Jerusalem*, p. 63.

[47] For his own part, Bond has spoken about 'the banality of evil' and Eichmann in

While the Wall in *Lear* is most obviously related to the Berlin Wall, the authorial discourse around the play also comprises the Nazi concentration camps and Auschwitz, which occupies a central place in the way Bond conceptualises modernity and his own dramaturgy. Bond, writing in his remarkable piece 'The First Word', reflects on his critical discourse:

> I use Auschwitz as a generic name for the [...] horrors [of the 20th century] because it most clearly used the apparatus of modernity. It had the efficiency and expediency of a Ford production line. The raw materials received at one end were human beings, the finished product at the other end was ash. There is an easy Brueghel image for it – the locations of the human mouth and anus reversed. But the deformity is more extreme than that. Auschwitz used the scientific technology that should emancipate us [...] Auschwitz is not a cancer that destroys, it is not even a disease that poses as a cure – it has infiltrated and taken over the processes of life and made *them* death.[48]

These remarks are indebted to Adorno and his conception of the deathly process of the dialectic of enlightenment, though Bond only ever refers directly to Adorno in relation to his dictum about the barbarity of poetry 'after' Auschwitz: 'Auschwitz used the scientific technology that should emancipate us', but 'it has infiltrated and taken over the processes of life and made them death'.[49] The language Bond uses is akin to his thoughts on the 'technosphere' and his discourse around the Wall in *Lear*: as with the Wall, Auschwitz typifies the process of reification – the transformation of subjects into objects ('products') of history, which seems to be catastrophically unmoored from human influence. Auschwitz, for Bond as for Adorno, becomes a metonym for the reifying legacy of industrial modernity and the various disasters of the twentieth century. But it is a critique that Bond also relates to postmodern (late) capitalist consumer culture – something I touch on again in analysing his concept of Radical Innocence. Bond writes that 'When you enter a supermarket you enter the *logic* of Auschwitz' – by which he means the

---

interviews and also discusses the concept in some of his notebooks. He sometimes endorses the theory, but has also been critical, as when he writes that 'evil is the least banal of things', quoted in Bond, *Edward Bond: The Playwright Speaks*, p. 141.

[48] Edward Bond, 'The First Word', <http://www.edwardbond.org/Comment/comment.html> (accessed 3 May 2018).

[49] Bond writes: 'What Adorno and Auden said about poetry and Auschwitz misses the point. They would have hit it only if Auschwitz had been the summing up of history,' 'Introduction', *The Fool, Plays 3*, p. 79. Bond states elsewhere that 'the Enlightenment failed to make us rational and armed irrationality with the weapons of mass murder – as if science and technology had made a nail so big it could crucify the world', Edward Bond, 'Introduction: The Third Crisis', in Edward Bond, *The Chair Plays* (London: Bloomsbury Methuen, 2012), p. xxviii. This essay differs from the online 'Third Crisis: The State of Future Drama'.

'logic' of mass, rationalised society.⁵⁰ 'Auschwitz was run to be productive,' Bond states, in some of his more provocative remarks: 'You could say it was a factory but I prefer to call it a department store because it incorporated manufacture and commerce under one roof' – or 'behind one barbed wire'.⁵¹

Even while the Wall stands and modern systems seem resistant to change, however, Bond insists that, 'after' Auschwitz, social and political engagement is both possible and necessary. '[W]e made the world' (3.3.84) Lear tells Cordelia – the implication being that the world can be unmade and made over again. The change that Bond makes from a resigned, metaphysical vision of suffering in *King Lear* to an engaged, socially materialist understanding of suffering in *Lear* is epitomised by the action around the autopsy of Fontanelle:

Fourth Prisoner:	You can see how she died. The bullet track goes through [. . .] the lungs.
Lear:	But where is the . . . She was cruel and angry and hard [. . .] So much blood and bits and pieces packed in [. . .] Where is the . . . where . . . ?
Fourth Prisoner:	What is the question?
Lear:	Where is the beast? [. . .] Did I make this – and destroy it? (2.6.59)

The scene obviously alludes to (and literalises) the proposed 'anatomisation' of Regan in *King Lear*. Lear famously wants to undertake an anatomisation of Regan to see if there is any 'cause in nature' which makes 'hard hearts' (III.vi.74–5). Lear is seeking for a metaphysical 'cause' for human hard-heartedness – or coldness – in 'nature'. This means that Lear cannot realise a properly social and political understanding of human suffering. His approach reifies wickedness ('the beast') into a metaphysical absolute that presides above and beyond human agency, rendering life completely absurd. The answer which the autopsy of Fontanelle provides in *Lear*, however, is that evil and suffering do not have a metaphysical 'cause' in 'nature', but are products of materially human social and political agency: 'Did I make this – and destroy it?'⁵² This newfound awareness allows Lear to begin to under-

---

⁵⁰ Bond, 'The First Word'.
⁵¹ Edward Bond, *Edward Bond: Letters Volume 2*, ed. Ian Stuart (Amsterdam: Harwood Academic Publishers, 1995), p. 166.
⁵² I return to the relationship between the metaphysical and material post-Auschwitz in Chapter 7. So committed is Bond to a materialist analysis of society that even the ghost that haunts Lear is subject to material change, as he rots over the action of the play and, eventually, dies: 'O Lear, I am dead!' (3.3.86).

stand that reification can be undone – that human actors can intervene to reshape the world:

> Look! I killed her! Her blood is on my hands! Destroyer! Murderer! And now I must begin again. I must walk in weariness and bitterness, I must become a child [. . .] I must open my eyes and see! (2.6.60)

To 'see' and 'begin' again involves Lear becoming a 'child' – a point I will touch on again below. Lear may have his eyes surgically removed, but his blindness is, as Bond puts it, 'a metaphor for insight'.[53] The play charts the moral and social progress of Lear from an ideologically driven despot in Act One, through to insight (as in *King Lear*, through blindness) in Act Two and finally (and unlike 'King' Lear) to committed political engagement in Act Three. This culminates in his attempt to dig up the Wall, an act of intervention against the 'technosphere' and a reappropriation of alienated human labour that undoes the deadening 'coldness' which deforms life in the reified world: 'Work soon warms you up' (3.4.87):

> **Lear:** A shovel. (*He climbs the wall*). It's built to last. So steep, and my breath's short. (*He reaches the top*). The wind's cold, I must be quick. (*He digs the shovel in.*) Work soon warms you up. [. . .]
> LEAR *digs the shovel into the earth. The* FARMER'S SON *fires.* LEAR *is killed instantly. He falls down the wall* [. . .] *The* WORKERS *go quickly and orderly. One of them looks back* [. . .] *LEAR'S body is left alone on stage.* (3.4.87–8)

Peter Billingham contends that the image of Lear digging up the Wall remains 'one of the most iconic in post-war British theatre and even twentieth-century British drama', offering an image of 'revolutionary intent and potential' in a 'radical humanist re-write of *King Lear*'.[54] It should be observed, however, that from its opening performance the final image has been as apt to cause confusion as it has the type of eulogies proffered by Billingham. The case might be made that the final image of Lear digging 'up' an ever-growing Wall is as Sisyphean a struggle as anything Beckett or Camus might imagine and hardly shaped to inspire the type of moral and political engagement Bond sees as being vital after the Holocaust.

Bond seemed aware of the criticisms that might be made against his play. Writing in his Programme Note for the 1975 revival of *Lear* at the

---

[53] 'Bond, 'Preface', *Lear*, p. lxv. 'I stumbled when I saw', says Gloucester (IV.i.21).
[54] Billingham, *Edward Bond: A Critical Study*, p. 52 and p. 51.

Liverpool Everyman theatre ('Saving Our Necks'), Bond defends his play against the idea that the 'final' stand Lear takes is 'absurd':

> My Lear makes a gesture in which he accepts responsibility for his life and commits himself to action [. . .] [But that] gesture must not be seen as final. That would make the play a part of the theatre of the absurd and that, like perverted science, is a reflection of no-culture. The human condition is not absurd; it is only our society which is absurd. Lear is very old and has to die anyway. He makes his gesture only to those who are learning to live.[55]

To imply that the closing action of *Lear* is in any way complete in itself would be to reduce the play to the Theatre of the Absurd – a decadent 'reflection of no-culture'. Bond insists that Lear makes a 'gesture' purposed with shaping the consciousness of those who witness the act of defiance. This is reflected in the stage direction in which, as Lear digs up the Wall and leaves his shovel stuck *'upright in the earth'* (3.3.88), a worker *'looks back'* (3.3.88) – before being pushed offstage by a foreman to continue building the Wall. This consciousness-raising also comprises the audience itself: the final image is intended to convince the audience of the necessity of engaged moral and political action, as opposed to the apathy of absurdism or the disengagement Bond believes to result from the Brechtian *Verfremdungseffekt*.

This reflects the divergent understandings of tragedy and the subject in Brecht and Bond. As discussed in Chapter 1, tragedy as far as Brecht understands it is too preoccupied with a single tragic 'hero' whose inability to overcome society transforms his/her demise into 'fate'. The sympathy tragedy engenders for the fate of the individual inhibits the type of detached collective consciousness needed to bring about a more critical understanding of society and history.[56] Bond is similarly suspicious of the significance of individual action – as the final and seemingly 'meaningless' death of Lear shows. But he does see tragedy as amenable to a properly dialectical understanding of human history, where defiant action negates the inhumanity of a reified society. Bond demands from the audience a response that is at once sympathetically engaged in the individual, heroic fate of Lear and yet sufficiently detached to allow an objective grasp of the political necessity of collectivity. The final action

---

[55] Quoted in Hay and Roberts, *Edward Bond: A Companion*, p. 154.
[56] For more on Brecht and tragedy, see Chapter 1. Brecht (or rather, his 'Philosopher' figure) states that *King Lear* should be staged so that 'the audience doesn't feel completely identified with this king' – typifying his *Verfremdungseffekt*. See Bertolt Brecht, *The Messingkauf Dialogues*, ed. and trans. John Willett (London: Bloomsbury, 2014), p. 56.

of Lear is intended to address the audience as a collective entity capable of radical change.

There is, however, another criticism that might be made of the play aside from the possible absurdity of its final image of Lear on the Wall: that Bond ultimately fails to challenge the Christian-humanist problematic that informs the pre-Kott understanding of *King Lear* and, as a result, equally fails to challenge the Enlightenment narrative of rational human 'progress' which had been so severely disabused by the war and the Holocaust. *Lear* displays an underlying faith in the forces of historical progress and the eventual control of an enlightened and 'redeemed' humanity over the abstract social and political system that it has itself created and which now destroys it. This, in itself, is not necessarily problematic. What is problematic, however, is the way that narrative overdetermines subjectivity. The result of the rational and humanistic view of historical progress Bond relies on is that *Lear* ultimately reinscribes the subject into an overarching historical process, once again turning the subject into an object as it fulfils the teleological destiny towards a 'rational' and 'just' society. This produces a tragic aesthetic in which the subject is ultimately bound in – and negated by – generic and aesthetic closure, as opposed to a more fragmentary, open-ended form.

Bond, Humanism and the Dialectic of Enlightenment

Bond may have intensified the cruelty and violence of *King Lear*, but *Lear* also recapitulates the redemptive understanding of the play derived from Christian-humanist readings, where the 'growth' of Lear into a form of critical self-knowledge remains the central concern, even if that 'pilgrimage' now comes to signify a 'scientific' and secularised humanist teleology. The overarching three-act structure of *Lear* is indicative of the residual dependence of the play on a humanist understanding of the historical process. Bond writes that, in Act One, Lear is trapped in a world of 'myth' – a false perception of reality. In Act Two, Lear 'progresses' to a correct (objective or scientific) perception of material 'reality' and, in Act Three – which Bond considered integral to his appropriation – Lear engages in rational moral and political action against a world he proves 'real' by tragically 'dying in it'.[57] The whole movement echoes the Enlightenment progression from false belief (myth) into rational

---

[57] Bond, 'Preface', *Lear*, p. lxvi.

knowledge (science) and into agency based on that newfound knowledge – producing an emphatic image of formal closure as Lear attempts to remove the Wall he himself had instigated. The central pattern of the play recalls the 'sin-suffering-redemption' paradigm of pre-absurdist, Christian readings of *King Lear*, in which Lear learns through his suffering the reality of a society that is inimical to human life. Lear, in a critique of his apparent resignation, states that 'If I saw Christ on his cross I would spit at him' (3.2.76); but Lear undergoes his own pilgrimage over the course of the play: 'I'm going on a journey' (3.3.85). During the original production, Lear even fell to his knees in Act Two, a gesture that recalls Gielgud in 1940 and his prayer-like posture in the storm: '*LEAR falls down on to his knees*' (2.7.66).

Undergoing a radical transformation in his perception of himself and the world, Lear engenders a dialectical synthesis between his subjective consciousness and the objectivity of reality – and society. Lear 'See[s] better' (*King Lear*, I.i.159) and, in doing so, acts against the social and political oppression he is witness to. But his revolutionised (or 'enlightened') consciousness has, in the inadvertently telling words of Billingham, '*inescapably* political consequences': the digging up of the Wall.[58] The cycle of history in *Lear* has become nothing other than (tragic) fate. This is conveyed (or perhaps more appropriately, betrayed) by the foreshadowing of the final action of Act Three in Act One. During the opening moments of the play, Lear reports that displaced rural farm workers have been digging up the Wall (1.1.3). Lear, in an act that reveals his cold misperception of reality, wants to have all 'diggers' shot; but, as he grows into a more enlightened social and political consciousness, Lear finally attempts to dig up the Wall himself before he too is shot ('The wheel is come full circle', as Edmund says, 'I am here' (V.iii.172)). This foreshadowing is intended to reveal in a relatively simple way the progression from ignorance to knowledge. But it also betrays the 'inescapable' teleology of a humanist narrative form, as Lear becomes an object as opposed to the subject of historical 'progress', moving inexorably towards the ending intimated (or in the words of *King Lear*, 'promised') from the outset.

Despite setting his 'political' interpretation of *King Lear* in opposition to the resigned 'metaphysical' interpretation of the absurdists, Bond is similarly culpable of turning history into the type of impersonal 'mechanism' imagined by Kott, where the subject is no more than a cog in the wider machine of a historical process that is, finally, beyond his or her direct control. This – as much as the apparent impossibility

---

[58] Billingham, *Edward Bond: A Critical Study*, p. 49 (emphasis added).

of the act itself, digging 'up' a wall – is arguably the underlying reason for the final scene of *Lear* being viewed as a confused and possibly even absurdist image.[59] The deterministic conception of history and progress that underpins the form of *Lear* points to a deep-seated contradiction in Bondian drama. On the one hand, Bond develops a conception of the historical process that is more in keeping with the dialectic of enlightenment than it is with a more conventional (vulgar) Marxist understanding of the progress of humanity. On the other hand, Bond often seems indebted to the very problematic of social and historical progress he brings into question. Bond positions his appropriation of *King Lear* as a response to Auschwitz and the dangers of post-Auschwitz 'resignation'. *Lear*, however, relies both thematically and formally on the idealist-humanist philosophy that – for the Frankfurt theorists – lay behind the dialectic of enlightenment and, in the most radical realisation of its desubjectifying tendencies, the Holocaust.

Bond and *King Lear* 'After' *Lear*: *Bingo* and Beyond

Bond would soon return to Shakespeare and *King Lear* in the form of his 1973 play *Bingo*, in which Bond places Shakespeare 'himself' onstage. The play, which is subtitled *Scenes of Money and Death*, depicts the historical events surrounding the enclosure of common land around Welcombe in 1615 and 1616, a process in which Shakespeare is known to have acquiesced by signing a contract that protected his landholdings, on the condition that he would not interfere with the enclosure or support any form of popular resistance.[60] Not unlike *Lear*, the play evinces a split understanding of Shakespeare: *Bingo* portrays the contradiction between the acute social and political insight Shakespeare seems to evince in his plays – and perhaps most obviously in *King Lear* – and his seeming failure to resist the enclosure, which disenfranchises the very same rural poor whose fate Lear so powerfully laments in the storm scenes of *King Lear*.[61] Writing about Shakespeare, Bond reflects that his actions as 'a property-owner made him closer to Goneril than Lear. He supported and benefited from the Goneril society – with its

---

[59] See also Cartelli, 'Shakespeare in Pain', p. 165.
[60] Bond writes about the enclosure in his 'Introduction', *Bingo*, *Plays 3*, pp. 3–12. For a concise synopsis of the incident, see also Katherine Duncan-Jones, *Shakespeare: An Ungentle Life* (London: Bloomsbury Arden, 2010), pp. 299–302.
[61] In *Lear*, Lear refers to a worker that he has 'taken off his land' (1.1.3) – much in the same vein as Shakespeare in *Bingo*.

workhouses, whipping, starvation, mutilation, pulpit hysteria and all the rest of it.'[62] Lear 'divided up his land at the beginning of the play, when he was arbitrary and unjust' and 'not when he was shouting out his truths on the open common'.[63]

Shakespeare seems initially to be resigned to events he believes he cannot influence, the same worldview which Bond relates to Beckettian absurdism, being utterly 'stupefied' by the scale of human 'suffering' he witnesses in society: 'The shapes huddled in misery that twitch away when you step over them' (2.3.40). William Combe – a private landowner, who pushes for the enclosure – epitomises the self-interest that can be sublimated by absurdist resignation when he pompously states that there will 'always be real suffering, real stupidity and greed and violence': 'I live in the real world and try to make it work' (2.4.50). Shakespeare, however, ultimately has a more self-reflexive response. Once again, it is the storm scenes from *King Lear* that Bond turns to and refigures in *Bingo* – only now it is Shakespeare, who appears as something of a disillusioned and raging Lear in the play, who is cast out onto a cold and snowy (as opposed to rain-lashed) heath, where he undergoes a series of personal and political realisations about his past 'mistakes, mistakes' (2.5.55) and his failure to act against suffering: 'Was anything done?' (2.5.59). 'I could have done so much', reflects Shakespeare, as he considers his inaction and culpability: 'Absurd! Absurd!' (2.6.62).[64]

These self-criticisms ultimately culminate in suicide, with Shakespeare taking poison obtained from his rival, Ben Jonson. It is an act that obviously evokes the suicidal bid Lear makes to dig up the Wall in *Lear* – and has provoked the same type of confusion: does suicide grimly testify to resigned despair over the absurdity of the human condition, or does the action of *Bingo* open out a perspective beyond absurdism for concerted social and political engagement? Billingham relates the final suicide of Shakespeare to the figure of the Beggar Woman – a displaced peasant who turns to prostitution – who is hanged and gibbetted for starting fires in privately owned property. Her hanging – which Shakespeare attends, shamed and ashamed – and decaying body, which

---

[62] Bond, 'Introduction', *Bingo*, *Plays 3*, p. 6.
[63] Ibid.
[64] There are other parallels between *King Lear* and *Bingo*, perhaps most obviously in the deeply troubled relationship between Shakespeare and his children. 'I couldn't cut you out, you were my flesh,' Shakespeare tells Judith (2.5.56), echoing Lear and his 'But yet thou art my flesh, my blood, my daughter / Or rather a disease that's in my flesh, / Which I must needs call mine' (II.ii.410–12). Anne Hathaway – though alluded to throughout the play – is also notably absent from the stage in *Bingo*, akin to the missing mother of *King Lear*.

is reduced to 'Strips of skin' (1.3.39) and little more, emblematises the 'Goneril-society' and the reifying carceral systems it uses; but it also represents a 'harrowing icon of the persecuted victims of history, from Auschwitz to Srebrenica'.[65] Far from being a resigned gesture, over the play Shakespeare displays a 'growing awareness' of suffering and 'chooses suicide as an existentially radical and morally revolutionary act', conducted in sympathy with the victims of history.[66] It is a boldly made point – but it ought to be observed that *Bingo* ends with the same contradiction found in *Lear*: the story of human progress over time, and the action against an inhumane and reifying system that progress entails, ultimately requires the self-negation of the engaged subject.

Both *Lear* and *Bingo* are relatively early Bond plays and can be seen as emblematic of an initial stage of his 'Rational Theatre', which both drew on and developed Brecht.[67] More recently, Bond has become more formally experimental and theoretically multifaceted, particularly since the mid-1990s, in his so-called 'Parisian Pentad' (*The Crime of The Twentieth Century*, *Coffee*, *Born*, *People* and *Innocence*) and in his ongoing collaboration with Big Brum Theatre-in-Education Company, for which he has written some of his most compelling plays for the stage (from the 1995 play *At the Inland Sea* to the 2010 *A Window*). For some critics, the most recent plays are 'consistent' with previous forms – even 'remarkably so' – while others have insisted that the pieces Bond has written since the mid-1990s are so radically distinct from past plays that these have now become impossible to interpret through the dramaturgical theories Bond has developed, with Christopher Innes observing that 'the criteria established by early plays are totally inappropriate to his later work'.[68]

Bond continues to think about – and write through – Shakespeare and *King Lear*, most obviously in his pieces 'Lear War' (1993) and 'William Shakespeare's Last Notebook' (1995) – a poem and a short, a purportedly 'found' work by Shakespeare, made up of aphoristic observations about history and catastrophe. These more recent appropriations of Shakespeare and *King Lear* show that the early and late Bond periods cannot be 'cleanly' separated. The stylistic and theoretical development

---

[65] Billingham, *Edward Bond: A Critical Study*, p. 61.
[66] Ibid.
[67] For more on the 'Rational Theatre', see Hern, 'Commentary', pp. xi–xx.
[68] Bill Roper, 'Imagination and Self in Edward Bond's Work', in Davis, *Edward Bond and the Dramatic Child*, p. 127; Christopher Innes, 'The Political Spectrum of Edward Bond: From Rationalism to Rhapsody', *Modern Drama*, 25:2 (1982), pp. 190–1.

that Bond has undergone cannot be understood in a 'narrowly linear fashion'; it is more the case that Bond has developed in a way that is 'organic and interwoven', as pre-existent ideas and preoccupations are rethought and refashioned in emergent forms.[69] This is perhaps most obvious in his conception of Radical Innocence, which Bond began to develop in the mid- to late 1980s and which continues to inform his understanding of the post-Auschwitz self and drama.[70]

Radical Innocence: 'Lear War' and 'William Shakespeare's Last Notebook'

'[W]e live in the false triumph of the capitalist revolution and the actual catastrophe of Auschwitz'

Edward Bond[71]

The notion of Radical Innocence is, as with much recent Bondian theory, deeply convoluted, but for Bond it ultimately designates a time (or 'site') when the child cannot distinguish between its 'self' and 'the world', or a time 'before' subject and object are split. This radically innocent site, which draws on the theories of Jacques Lacan around pre-individuation, can be situated as a response to postmodernity.[72] Bond relates globalised postmodern capitalism (or as he sometimes calls it, the posthumous society) to the 'Third Crisis' – by which he means the crisis of 'after' Auschwitz and the violence of autotelic rationality, with previous crises being reflected for Bond in the development of Greek and Jacobean drama.[73] Far from a seismic break, postmodern (or late) capitalism is a continuation of the reifying processes of modernity – and brings with it the possibility of future annihilative catastrophe. Bond does not see the fall of the Berlin Wall as the end of history – a new dawn in which

---

[69] Billingham, *Edward Bond: A Critical Study*, p. 23.
[70] For a theoretical statement of Radical Innocence, see Edward Bond, 'Commentary on *The War Plays*', in Edward Bond, *The War Plays* (London: Methuen, 1988), especially pp. 251–8.
[71] Bond, 'The Third Crisis: The State of Future Drama'.
[72] For more on the relationship between Bond and Lacan, see Kate Katafiasz, 'Drama and Desire: Edward Bond and Jacques Lacan', PhD (Reading University, 2011).
[73] Bond contends that Greek drama represents the challenge laid down by the tragic protagonist to divine forces, while the Jacobeans 'colonised the globe, unleashed the power of technology, unveiled the vast incarceration of the universe and in the beginnings of the Enlightenment began to rediscover democracy'. 'What is the transcendent of our age?', asks Bond: 'The market' ('The Third Crisis', *The Chair Plays*, pp. xxxi–xxxii).

the disasters of the past have been finally transcended. On the contrary: Auschwitz is 'the catastrophe that will repeatedly threaten the modern world'.[74] Bond writes that 'the modern market world' is shaped by a wholly rationalised 'consumer-culture' – the Culture Industry – that 'devours everything that is not itself', degrading human imagination and freedom by turning people into little more than ciphers in the system.[75]

Over and against the totalised world of late capitalist culture, Bond identifies the radically innocent state as a moment in which the subject does not conceptually identify – and dominate and consume – the material world in which it finds itself, the same reifying process Adorno and Horkheimer critique in *The Dialectic of Enlightenment*. This creates a space in which the subject engages in a spontaneously creative relationship with material reality, prior to his or her ideological 'indoctrination' by society. This more imaginatively open relationship with the world undoes the reifying (il)logic of instrumental rationality and its dialectical tendency to rebound on the subject, who is ultimately transformed into an object of that very same reason. 'We understand the world better and can manipulate it for our own uses but we always turn it against ourselves.'[76] Bond fuses the idea of Radical Innocence with a dialectical critique of history, where the pre-social capacity for imaginative and creative engagement with the material world is 'corrupted' by society. The mind of a child is radically innocent, but, writes Bond, 'corruption, not innocence, nurtures the child in grown people; if anything of the child survives in adult innocence it is a very old child'.[77] This means that, in the form of its Radical Innocence, the subject can be transcendentally lifted – if only for a moment – out of the corrupted sphere of reified life, rediscovering an inherent childlike propensity for an engagement with the world that is intuitively creative, not reductively dominative.

These ideas around the radically innocent neonatal state are reflected in 'Lear War'. Over the poem, Bond once again reflects on the contradiction between enlightened reason and human suffering, bemoaning that 'War will follow war'.[78] The narratorial voice of the poem – powerfully introduced in the opening, 'As I lie dying on the wooden floor of the station waiting room' – is, it would seem, none other than Lear. Lear, in

---

[74] Ibid. p. xxviii.
[75] Ibid. p. xl.
[76] Ibid. p. xxviii.
[77] Bond, 'Commentary on *The War Plays*', *The War Plays*, p. 256. It is worth noting, as Lynne Bradley has, that Bond persistently likens Lear to a child. See Bradley, *Adapting King Lear for the Stage*, p. 125. This likening of Lear to a child is something that recurs in the work of Barker in his *Seven Lears* (see Chapter 6).
[78] Bond, *The Hidden Plot*, p. 164.

words that resonate with the storm scenes of *King Lear* and the action of *Lear*, states that 'There are rich and poor':

> One is better fed than another
> And one wears rags and his head is haunted by holy tunes
> They search for reasons
> Split matter in cells – raise up gases and search in them for phantoms
> But the map of war is on their streets
> It is the rags – the empty tins held out for coins on the steps of the subway
> The abandoned lot behind hoardings where drunks sleep their faces made foul by spittle
> The leering young – the frightened old
> They do not see it.[79]

Lear critiques a world where ('cold') scientific rationality – the 'reasons' sought in split cells and gases, which alludes to genetics, the splitting of the atom, the development of the atomic bomb and the gas chambers – has not been purposed with remedying social inequality, becoming detached from the human(e) ends it is supposed to serve. This inequality – the 'rags' and the 'holy tunes' obviously recall Poor Tom from *King Lear* – is a state akin to permanent war, as 'there will be no peace till they live justly'.[80] The idea of 'peace' and 'living justly' implies an end to a situation where some are 'rich' and others 'poor' – a more humanely socialistic world. Lear identifies hope for that more 'just' and playfully creative world in the Radical Innocence of the child – only that promise is violently corrupted in modernity. 'Those who make weapons are not fit to have care of children', opines Lear:

> Now the children who came to bury me are old
> Wizened – grey – crouched with heads on knees as still as stones in a desert
> Spiders spin on their faces
> They did not play
> And the lessons they wrote in the dust have been blown away.[81]

This same preoccupation with Radical Innocence informs 'William Shakespeare's Last Notebook', a fragmentary work that has supposedly been pieced together by an anonymous editor, who observes that Shakespeare seems to have bitten and even eaten his final writings – a sort of literary self-ingestion or 'suicide', perhaps akin to the final action of *Bingo*.[82] Shakespeare, in a series of aphoristic observations, condemns the social and political ills he sees around him, which (anachronistically)

---

[79] Ibid. p. 163.
[80] Ibid. p. 164.
[81] Ibid.
[82] Ibid. p. 102.

comprise the Holocaust ('The brutal SS-man said he obeyed the law,' says Shakespeare, echoing Arendt) and other twentieth-century catastrophes, which arise from a culture of administrative rationality and impersonal technocracy: 'Once the machines were weak, now they are so strong they make what were once mistakes, disasters; executions, genocides; religions, holocausts; the agitations of a parish, the wars of continents.'[83] This catastrophic dispensation is not something Shakespeare sees ending with the fall of the Berlin Wall and the supposedly history-ending victory of late global capitalism over totalitarianism. 'The Berlin Wall was not destroyed when it was pulled down. It was carried away in hands and pockets and unfreedom spread', as 'poverty, robbery, violence' only intensifies.[84] Shakespeare states that, in 'Western Consumer Democracy all people are fictions'.[85] This reification of subjectivity is because 'capitalism now owns the Imagination – it is an aesthetics without content. When your Imagination is owned you become fictional, you are not the author of yourself. That is the form enslavement takes in our democracy.'[86] Late capitalist culture, as Shakespeare would have it, degrades human imagination and freedom, making people into little more than enslaved 'fictions' of a deathly system.

These developments pose foundational questions about humanity. 'How to be human?' wonders Shakespeare, 'What do human beings do?'[87] The answer lies – again – with a prelapsarian childhood state: 'The Imagination of the child endows all things with life. The child gives value to a doll, a toy, a piece of wood.'[88] Even 'its rage is creative because it is an attempt to cast a spell that will restore justice to the world'.[89] 'The child', confirms Shakespeare in his final observations, 'is the only author of value' – even if that is ultimately compromised by late capitalist ideology, which violently turns 'the child from freedom to submission'.[90]

Bond would perhaps deny that his notion of Radical Innocence has a determinate *telos* – and it is worth observing that 'William Shakespeare's Last Notebook' ends abruptly, mid-observation, as opposed to achieving any obvious formal closure of the type seen in *Lear*.[91] But as David

---

[83] Ibid. p. 98 and p. 99.
[84] Ibid. p. 99.
[85] Ibid. p. 101.
[86] Ibid. p. 102.
[87] Ibid. p. 100.
[88] Ibid.
[89] Ibid.
[90] Ibid. p. 101.
[91] The piece ends with: 'the Imagination is dissatisfied and technology is impatient

Davis has written, it implies that 'the only hope for humanity lies in each human being bringing back to life the way the mind "naturally" begins to work: immediately able to engage with objective reality and to develop the active, searching, creative, value-laden struggle for a socialised/socialist humanity'.[92] The concept of Radical Innocence is a form of engagement that involves nothing short of 'universalized imperatives emanating from the social nature of human life and self' and encompasses the 'prescription to choose and act in line with those imperatives'.[93]

The problem, however, returns: the subject might be lifted out of society and history, but – if Radical Innocence implies an inherent capacity for (social) justice – it is surely only to find itself in a predetermined Marxist-humanist historical teleology, where 'inner' imagination (subject) and 'outer' reality (object) are dialectically synthesised in the promise of new, more humane social and political relationships. Once again, the engaged subject is reinscribed as the object of historical (and, to quote the 'Preface' to *Lear*, finally even 'biological') necessity.[94] The notion of Radical Innocence involves collapsing the subject back into its supposed 'nature' and – finally – undermining the possibility of human freedom from necessity and determinate forces. It is a similar contradiction that informs *Lear* (and *Bingo*) and that I have been calling the dialectic of engagement. To contest the reification of the subject and the ongoing legacy of Auschwitz, Bond insists on the necessity of engagement – whether that is political action against suffering and/or Radically Innocent acts of creation/destruction. This engagement, however, only takes place within a predetermined (and enlightened) teleology, so that the subject is reified as it necessarily enacts a wider process over which it has little to no obvious freedom. With his staunch criticism of Brecht in mind, the question might be asked: is not Bond the theatre of Auschwitz?

    – and you might as well tell a leaf not to tremble in the wind as tell a human being that the – [The rest of the notebook has been eaten, partly by the author and partly, as teeth marks indicate, by a mouse – Editor]', p. 102. This allusion to a mouse perhaps recalls King Lear and his 'Look, look, a mouse: peace, peace, this piece of toasted cheese will do't' (IV.vi.88–9). It is an intriguing moment of interspecies, empathetic engagement that has been oddly overlooked by critics, despite the repeated injunction to 'look' foreshadowing the end of the play, where Lear insists those about him 'look' to Cordelia.

[92] David Davis, 'Introduction', 'Appended Letters of Edward Bond', in Davis, *Edward Bond and the Dramatic Child*, p. 183.
[93] Roper, 'Imagination and Self', p. 146.
[94] Bond, 'Preface', *Lear*, p. lxiii.

Conclusion

Through his various appropriations of *King Lear*, Bond develops a critique of post-Auschwitz modernity and its destruction of subjectivity; but the notion of engagement which Bond develops through his writing on Shakespeare – and that he proposes as a 'corrective' to reification and political resignation – still ultimately inheres within a humanist conception of the necessary progress of human history towards a more rational and enlightened state, which reifies the subject. This criticism is not to underestimate the importance of Bond and his *Lears*. Perhaps most of all, *Lear* remains among the most well-known theatrical appropriations of Shakespeare and, in many ways, its historical relevance may be becoming more acute in an age of both symbolic and literal 'wall-building'.[95] The play represents a decisive moment in the post-war reception of *King Lear*: other playwrights who use *King Lear* to interrogate the catastrophes of the twentieth century – and beyond – are writing in its wake.

Lear uses his status as an exile in *Lear* to try and evade engagement, before he comes to a fateful understanding of the necessity of revolutionary action. But for David Rudkin, exile is not merely a temporary state which is transcended when the subject fulfils his or her (predetermined) 'responsibility' for engagement. On the contrary: for Rudkin, the state of exile is, in and of itself, socially and politically meaningful. Chapter 5 shows that through his appropriation of Edgar, Rudkin develops an understanding of exile as a form of tragic non-identity, which in an era of totality must be preserved at all costs.

---

[95] I am thinking most obviously of Donald Trump and his bid to erect a wall along the American/Mexican border, though similar attempts have been (and are being) made by European nations in response to the ongoing refugee crisis. I return to *King Lear* and the figure of the modern refugee when I consider Forced Entertainment.

Chapter 5

'Rudkin I nothing am': Edgar, Exile and Self Re-authorship in David Rudkin's *Will's Way*

Introduction

Though he has been described by *The Observer* as perhaps the 'greatest living dramatic poet' and won the 'Most Promising Playwright' *Evening Standard* award for his remarkable 1962 theatre debut *Afore Night Come*, David Rudkin is perhaps the least well-known playwright under study.[1] His profoundly transgressive dramas of exile and self-transformation, from *The Sons of Light* (1976) and *The Triumph of Death* (1981) to *Red Sun* (2003) and his recent *Place Prints* (2015–) series, remain understudied – though in recent times there has been something of a revival of interest in his writing, particularly for film and television.

By concentrating on his appropriations of *King Lear*, I situate Rudkin in a wider constellation of catastrophic playwriting and drama in post-war theatre. Most of all, I want to analyse the figure (or perhaps figures) to which Rudkin has returned throughout his playwriting and drama: Edgar/Poor Tom. To do so, I consider a variety of Rudkin plays, many of which invoke Edgar. I also draw on an interview I conducted with Rudkin and on some of the revealing public statements he has made in regard to his own playwriting craft and process. This analysis culminates in a close reading of the play *Will's Way*, which was originally staged at The Other Place in 1984.[2] Not unlike *Bingo*, the play places Shakespeare 'himself' on stage. This version of Shakespeare delivers a personal – and seemingly extemporised – talk on the recurring themes to be found in

---

[1] Quoted from the David Rudkin website, <http://www.davidrudkin.com/more/commentary.html> (accessed 6 July 2019).
[2] See '*Will's Way*', <https://theatricalia.com/play/h6/wills-way/production/1ys> (accessed 3 February 2018). The play was directed by Alison Sutcliffe, with Nick Woodeson taking the role of Shakespeare.

his plays, his imaginative 'process' and the unique cultural role of the playwright in society.[3] The talk traverses a variety of Shakespeare plays, from the early comedies to the tragedies and the late romances.

Will's Way is not a wholesale rewriting of *King Lear* – in the same vein as *Lear*. *King Lear* is, however, a play that Rudkin has been in dialogue with throughout his writing (and indeed, his personal) life and which has profoundly shaped his own playwriting and dramaturgy.[4] *Will's Way* is an important play in his *oeuvre* as it casts a light on the profound impact that Edgar – and his self-transformations over a desolately exilic landscape – has had on Rudkin.[5]

Through an analysis of *Will's Way* and other plays and writings Rudkin has produced, I want to show that Edgar, with his transformation into Poor Tom, typifies the vital concept of 'self re-authorship', as Rudkin calls it.[6] This names a process whereby the subject continually re-authors him or herself, never fully embodying any final identity, but engaged in the open-ended process of authoring new selves and subjectivities. Rudkin eloquently states:

> It's not granted to each of us to be a hero or a martyr. But in our culture, with its benign appearance of satisfying our primary needs, and its increasingly sophisticated techniques of diverting and exhausting our essential energies, it is more and more a struggle for us, this constant process of *re-authoring* ourselves. If I insist on the vital necessity of this *self re-authoring*, it's because the impulse of political institutions is always reductive: to limit us to identities that can be mechanically satisfied, thereby 'managed' – i.e. controlled; to reduce us to identities that are predictable. I see it as our human duty to resist that reductive pressure; as our existential duty, to subvert it at every turn. I won't describe this as moral. It's a matter of survival, really.[7]

---

[3] David Rudkin, *Will's Way* (Halford: The Celandine Press, 1993), p. 21. All references are to the Celandine edition. I refer to the text throughout by quoting page numbers. The title *Will's Way* has obvious resonances with Sonnet 135, with its punning elaboration on the various meanings of the word 'will'.

[4] Rudkin describes *King Lear* in a 1964 interview for *Encore* as 'the greatest achievement of the human mind' ('An Affliction of Images: An Interview with David Rudkin', *Encore*, 11:4 (1964), p. 15). This is the same interview where Rudkin refers to his early attempt to write a play set in a concentration camp (p. 11).

[5] There are also not inconsiderable parallels between *King Lear* and *The Saxon Shore*, which frequently alludes to *King Lear* and even stages the 'missing' funeral rites from Shakespeare, when the funeral brier of 'Llyr' – 'King of the Britons' – is brought across the stage (David Rudkin, *The Saxon Shore* (London: Eyre Methuen, 1986), p. 22). I concentrate on *Will's Way* because of its remarkable, reflexive engagement with Edgar and his exilic subjectivity.

[6] David Rudkin, 'A Politics of Body and Speech', quoted in David Ian Rabey, *English Drama Since 1940* (Oxford: Routledge, 2014), p. 133.

[7] Ibid.

The notion of self re-authorship is not to say that Rudkin embraces the 'fluidity' of the (so-called) postmodern condition. His conception of self re-authorship should be understood as a response to the reification of the subject in the totalised world of late capitalist culture. Where modern culture ('our culture') forever strives to identify and so 'reduce' the subject, it becomes necessary, if reification is to be contested, for the subject continually to re-author the self.[8]

The urgency of that undertaking is revealed by Auschwitz and its total destruction of subjectivity. Rudkin reveals in a 1964 *Encore* interview that, before he become a professional playwright, he had written an (ultimately abortive) one-act play set inside a Nazi concentration camp. Nearly all of his subsequent plays depict similarly reifying systems of social control, which are based on 'rational' Enlightenment principles. These range from 'the Pit' in *The Sons of Light*, a vast underground system designed to achieve 'total' control over the subjects that make it up by dispelling 'The popular dogma of the Self' – which for 'all its mystique of Dignity, Liberty, is a romantic archaism' – to the G.O.D. (Global Online Distribution) Tower in the 2012 play *Merlin Unchained*, which is purposed with stimulating conformity and productivity by dominating 'all outward life' and 'all inner life'.[9] '[W]e have', states Rudkin, 'a responsibility to endeavour to integrate the Holocaust (and all its freight) into [. . .] our art.'[10] Rudkin does not directly depict the Nazi concentration camps in his plays. But his drama and his idea of self re-authoring are informed by the spectre of Auschwitz and its horrifying destruction of the subject:

> The Holocaust can be characterised in many ways: in one sense, it's the ultimate manifestation of German Romanticism, a cultural self-idealising that repudiates its own 'shadow'; in another, it's an expression of the psychopa-

---

[8] There are overlaps with self re-authorship and the concept of self-fashioning, as described by Stephen Greenblatt in his *Renaissance Self-Fashioning: From More to Shakespeare* (Chicago: University of Chicago Press, 2005). Greenblatt makes the case that the early modern era was marked by a newly emergent awareness 'about the fashioning of human identity as a manipulable, artful process' (p. 2). Far from marking the autonomy of the subject from traditional forms of social authority, however, self-fashioning, as Greenblatt understands it, actually involves 'submission to an absolute power or authority situated at least partially outside the self' (p. 9).

[9] David Rudkin, *The Sons of Light* (London: Eyre Methuen, 1981), p. 26; David Rudkin, *Red Sun and Merlin Unchained* (Bristol: Intellect, 2011), p. 177. 'The Pit' might be seen as an inverse image of the Wall from *Lear*, though the image of a pit also recurs in *Seven Lears*.

[10] David Rudkin, personal interview, 24 August 2016.

thology of capitalism – a denial of human excrementality [...] Worse than the Holocaust is already on its way. We humans are feeble creatures driven by an urge to catastrophe for ourselves and abjection for others, and to an infantile fantasising of the universe: and in the chasm into which that will plunge us, [*King*] *Lear* shall always speak. If any of us survive to hear it.[11]

Rudkin views self re-authorship as a necessary process for the very 'survival' of subjectivity itself – but at a cost. The process of constant self re-authorship involves being expelled from any reified category – and so community – the subject may identify with. This means that self re-authoring necessarily entails a permanent state of exile. This is not a process with a determinate *telos*. On the one hand, the loss of identity which exile involves necessitates self re-authorship, the reinvention of the self. On the other, self re-authorship occasions a continuous exilic condition. This is something Rudkin has called 'catastrophic existentialism'.[12] The idea is that catastrophic self-loss enables new 'existential' possibilities, as the subject is exiled from an inherited social and political identity that is violently disrupted.

Rudkin is averse to applying overdetermined generic categories, but his preoccupation with exile and catastrophe is indicative of a tragic aesthetic idiom. This discourse of tragic exile also relates to Rudkin himself. Despite the relative success of *Afore Night Come*, his next play – *The Sons of Light* – would not be staged until 1976 ('I knew I was going into a lifetime in the wilderness', states Rudkin).[13] Other important plays – including *Sovereignty Under Elizabeth* (1977) and *The Saxon Shore* (1986) – followed, but Rudkin has spent no small part of his writerly career on the margins of the theatrical and cultural establishment – an exile, with professional stagings of his plays a rarity after the 1980s. Being bisexual and half-English, half-Irish, Rudkin has not only spent his professional life on the boundaries, but also his personal life, challenging as he does conventional categories of identity (heterosexual or homosexual, English or Irish – for Rudkin it is 'both-and' as opposed to 'either-or').

Such non-identity has arguably become more and not less vital in totalised society, as reflected by the renewed attention now being paid to Rudkin. There was a (sold-out) BFI Rudkin retrospective in 2016, concentrating on his writing for film and television, while the British Library acquired the Rudkin Archive in 2010. Rudkin is also beginning

---

[11] Ibid.
[12] Ibid.
[13] David Rudkin, '*The Sons of Light*', <http://www.davidrudkin.com/theatre/the-sons-of-light.html> (accessed 3 February 2018).

to find his way back to the stage, after a lengthy period without any professional productions of his plays: *Afore Night Come* was revived at the Young Vic, London, in 2001; *Red Sun* was staged by the AJTC Theatre Company in 2003; New Perspectives Theatre staged *The Lovesong of Alfred J. Hitchcock* in 2013; and in 2017 the 1973 play *Ashes* was revived at the Octagon Theatre in Bolton.

Rudkin understands his conception of exile and self re-authorship as a challenge to the reification of the self in post-Auschwitz culture. There are intriguing parallels with Adorno. Exile represents a deeply formative experience for Adorno and other German intellectuals: Adorno fled Nazi Germany with other Frankfurt School thinkers in 1938, spending time as an exile in England (at Oxford) and the United States (in New York and California) before he returned to Germany permanently in 1953.[14] During his time away from Germany, Adorno wrote both *Dialectic of Enlightenment* (1944) and *Minima Moralia* (1951). The analysis of the exiled Odysseus in *Dialectic of Enlightenment* is often seen as a prelude to the more direct and sustained contemplation of the life of the homeless émigré in *Minima Moralia*, where Adorno often reflects on the 'damaged life' of the intellectual in exile. Both works shed light on exile as an experience of 'permanent change, upheaval and catastrophic loss'.[15] The fractured, aphoristic form of *Minima Moralia* and its failure to achieve any obvious resolution – or 'homecoming' – can even be seen as an imprimatur of an exilic condition.

Exile should not, however, only be seen as an adverse condition – an imposed state to be endured until a time of homecoming. The time Adorno spent abroad as a social and cultural 'outcast' also had a deep impact on his theoretical and political orientation. This relates most obviously to his conception of non-identity. Lisa Yun Lee writes that, for Adorno,

> the painful experiences of anxiety, alienation and estrangement that resulted from emigration coalesced into a form of resistance in both his theoretical and personal life as the inability and refusal to achieve complete integration into a social system characterized by radical self-preservation and instrumental rationality.[16]

---

[14] See Theodor Adorno, 'On the Question: "What is German?"', *New German Critique*, 36, 'Special Issue on Heimat' (1985), pp. 125–6.

[15] Lars Rensmann, 'Returning from Forced Exile: Some Observations on Theodor W. Adorno's and Hannah Arendt's Experience of Postwar Germany and Their Political Theories of Totalitarianism', *Leo Baeck Institute Year Book*, 49 (2004), p. 173.

[16] Lisa Yun Lee, *Dialectics of the Body: Corporeality in the Philosophy of T. W. Adorno* (London: Routledge, 2005), p. 2.

On the one hand, exile imperils the received identity of the displaced subject, whose attachments to the 'home' culture are radically disrupted; on the other, the exile can also never 'fit' completely into the officially sanctioned social practices – and identities – of the new social order: 'He who integrates is lost.'[17] With neither nostalgic attachment to the old nor assimilation to the new viable possibilities, the exiled subject fails to integrate into any customary social and political collectivity – s/he is, as Adorno writes in *Minima Moralia*, 'always astray'.[18] The state of exile involves the 'identity' of not having a fully culturally recognisable identity: it is a form of non-identity, an indeterminate non-coincidence with all identity-categories. It is for that reason Adorno, under the conditions of post-Auschwitz culture, sought to preserve the status of the exile. Using the same word Lear uses to describe Edgar/Poor Tom in *King Lear*, Edward Said writes that Adorno privileges 'unaccommodated, essentially expatriate or diasporic forms of existence'.[19] Even though Adorno would return to Germany, he self-consciously adopted an alienated state of 'permanent exile'.[20] This aligns Adorno with a new form of post-Auschwitz tragic subjectivity.

Exile and Tragedy

Exile is a motif in tragic drama from its beginnings in ancient Greece, where exile is often the price paid by the tragic protagonist for his/her violation of the shared norms and values of the *polis*.[21] Jennifer Wallace writes that 'to be exiled was to be *apolis*, outside the city and, by implication, outside humanity' – a fitting punishment for those who transgress the limits of the political (and so human, as opposed to animal) order.[22] By losing his/her place in the collective, the tragic exile

---

[17] See Theodor Adorno, *Minima Moralia: Reflections on a Damaged Life*, trans. Edmund Jephcott (London: Verso, 2005), pp. 46–7; Theodor Adorno, *The Stars Down to Earth and Other Essays on the Irrational in Culture*, ed. Stephen Crook (New York and London: Routledge, 2004), p. 174.
[18] Adorno, *Minima Moralia*, p. 33.
[19] Edward Said, *Reflections on Exile: And Other Literary and Cultural Essays* (London: Granta Books, 2000), p. xxxiv.
[20] Martin Jay, *Permanent Exiles: Essays on the Intellectual Migration from Germany to America* (New York: Columbia University Press, 1986), p. xii.
[21] See Sara Forsdyke, *Exile, Ostracism, and Democracy: The Politics of Expulsion in Ancient Greece* (Princeton: Princeton University Press, 2005).
[22] Jennifer Wallace, 'Exile and Tragedy', in Sarah Brown and Catherine Silverstone (eds), *Tragedy in Transition* (Oxford: Blackwell, 2007), p. 149.

suffers a devastating loss of self and identity – even humanity. 'To be exiled', writes Wallace, is 'to become nobody', a 'no one, nothing' – an 'O without a figure' (I.iv.183–4).[23]

Precisely by virtue of being expelled, however, 'the order of the city, from which one might be exiled, is questioned'.[24] On the one hand, exile serves to uphold the values of the community, even providing the basis for the original creation of a community through the exclusion of the 'other'; on the other hand, the exile outside the rest of the community brings the social and political identity of the collective into question. By disintegrating the subject from the dictates of the community, exile instantiates a tragic conflict between the autonomy of the subject and the identity of the social and political order. If that order is to be reinstated, the homeward return of the exile – or failing that, his or her death – is required.[25]

Hal Duncan writes that 'the tragic hero is that member of society (that part of us) who becomes distinct from it, ceases to be a part of it and is denied, prohibited, an object of revulsion'.[26] This obviously speaks to the relationship between tragic exile and the abject, as theorised by Julia Kristeva. Kristeva shows that the abject is that which causes disgust and, as a result, must be cast aside from both self and society (Kristeva cites faeces and corpses, among other provocations).[27] This conceptualisation of the abject derives from tragic drama ('the true theatre', as Kristeva calls it) and its representation of exile, where exile involves expelling the *pharmakós* or scapegoat, who is cast out of society in a ritual of public purification.[28]

Where in tragic drama the conflict between subject and society is typically resolved, for Adorno 'no reconciliation or identification is possible for the exile'.[29] This ongoing division between subject and society obviously forecloses the possibility of tragic closure. By turning exile into a permanent condition, Adorno paves the way for a tragic form where the

---

[23] Ibid. pp. 148–9.
[24] Ibid. pp. 150–1.
[25] Ibid. p. 150.
[26] Hal Duncan, *Rhapsody: Notes on Strange Fictions* (Maple Shade, NJ: Lethe Press, 2014), p. 113.
[27] Julia Kristeva, *Powers of Horror: An Essay on Abjection*, trans. Leon S. Roudiez (New York: Columbia University Press, 1982).
[28] Ibid. p. 3. Kristeva makes the case that Oedipus is an abject subject, 'a *pharmakós*, a scapegoat who, having been ejected, allows the city to be freed from defilement' (ibid. p. 84).
[29] Joshua Rayman, 'Dialectics of Exile: Adorno, Mann, and the Culture Industry', *Monatshefte*, 106:3 (2014), p. 421.

exile – the abjection – of the subject is retained. The way Adorno conceives exile, I would contend, potentiates catastrophic theatre, with its unresolved contradiction between subject and society. These reflections have a distinct bearing on Rudkin and his appropriation of Shakespeare and Edgar. I want to begin by showing that Edgar/Poor Tom embodies the condition of exile, abject and scapegoat, as iterations of his tragic non-identity with society.

Edgar and/as Poor Tom

Poor Tom and Non-Identity: Exile, Abject, Scapegoat

The idea that Edgar provides an image of exile and self re-authorship revolves around his transformation into the outcast figure of Poor Tom. Over his speech in Act Two, Scene Two, Edgar, ripped from his inherited social and political identity, responds by authoring and embodying the persona (or perhaps *persona non grata*) of Poor Tom. Edgar is not officially 'banished' from the state in the same way as Kent is (I.ii.174–80). The sentence given to Edgar is more serious: capital punishment, a result of his supposed 'plot' against Gloucester (II.i.56–63). But for Jane Kingsley-Smith, the representation of Edgar, escaping as he does into the wilderness, is indebted to the tropes of Shakespearean exile, where characters, forced from a socially sanctioned role, respond to self-loss in a process of re-authorship.[30] 'I heard myself proclaimed', whispers Edgar, as he evades capture and his death sentence:

> And by the happy hollow of a tree
> Escaped the hunt. No port is free, no place
> That guard and most unusual vigilance
> Does not attend my taking. While I may scape,
> I will preserve myself, and am bethought
> To take the basest and most poorest shape
> That ever penury in contempt of man
> Brought near to beast. My face I'll grime with filth,
> Blanket my loins, elf all my hair in knots,
> And with presented nakedness outface
> The winds and persecutions of the sky.
> The country gives me proof and precedent
> Of Bedlam beggars, who, with roaring voices,
> Strike in their numbed and mortified bare arms
> Pins, wooden pricks, nails, sprigs of rosemary;

---

[30] Jane Kingsley-Smith, *Shakespeare's Drama of Exile* (Basingstoke: Palgrave Macmillan, 2003), pp. 127–30.

> And with this horrible object, from low farms,
> Poor pelting villages, sheepcotes and mills,
> Sometime with lunatic bans, sometime with prayers,
> Enforce their charity. Poor Turlygod, poor Tom,
> That's something yet: Edgar I nothing am. (II.ii.172–92)

There are no more powerful instantiations of the Shakespearean exile who 'must rewrite him- or her-self'.[31] Edgar responds to his outlaw status by radically re-authoring himself: his catastrophic self-loss, paradoxically, opens the way for a new form of (non-)being: Poor Tom. Emerging as he does from the 'hollow' of 'a tree', Edgar even undergoes something akin to a (re)birth.

The speech begins with a burgeoning sense of self-estrangement. 'I heard myself proclaimed' introduces a split between subject ('I') and object ('myself'): Edgar is suddenly able to hold his received social and political identity – Edgar, the son and heir of Gloucester – at a distance, in self-reflexive contemplation. This self-estrangement reaches its crescendo at the end of the speech, with the syntactically contorted declaration 'Edgar I nothing am'. The basic meaning is relatively straightforward: Edgar has lost his official self, his title as the son and heir of Gloucester. This has devolved to his bastard half-brother, Edmund. To be without that officially ratified self – that title – in the social and political totality is to become a 'nothing'. Paradoxically, however, Edgar is able to turn that nothing into a 'something': Poor Tom.

Emily Sun perceptively writes that 'To play the part of Poor Tom is to substantialize the condition of banishment as an identity': it is, however, 'the identity of not having an identity within the kingdom'.[32] Sun does not use the phrase, but the figure of Poor Tom can be understood as a form of non-identity, a type of identity without any ratified place in the social and political totality, from which Edgar is outcast. Poor Tom represents a fundamental non-coincidence with 'any given identity', which ensures 'his radical unknowability to others and himself; his singularity'.[33] By transforming himself into Poor Tom, Edgar comes to exist outside of the normal system of cultural identification, having 'no place' – 'None at all' (I.ii.157) – in socially continuous identitarian categories. Poor Tom is not even a fully personalised identity: it is more of a generic name in the play for exilic life, which is lived outside

---

[31] Jane Kingsley-Smith, 'Banishment in Shakespeare's Plays', PhD (Birmingham: Shakespeare Institute, 1999), p. 3.

[32] Emily Sun, *Succeeding King Lear: Literature, Exposure and the Possibility of Politics* (New York: Fordham University Press, 2010), p. 41.

[33] Ibid.

society and its totalising system of identity (Edgar markedly refers to 'Bedlam beggars' in the plural and not to any specific 'Bedlam beggar' he has chanced across). It is in that sense that Edgar/Poor Tom truly is an embodiment of 'nothing': '*I nothing am*'. Poor Tom embodies the negation of identity. He is an amorphous 'shape' – not so much the identifiable subject of a social and political world as an unidentifiably negative 'deformity' (IV.ii.61) of it.

The figure of Poor Tom might seem weirdly gratuitous. It almost seems as if Edgar discovers a dissonant, darker self in the form of Poor Tom, an unsuspected 'inner' stranger who appears out of nowhere and yet might also have been present from the outset, lurking – 'Lurk, lurk!' (III.vi.112) – somewhere on the peripheries of consciousness and reality. Edgar takes the form – the 'shape' – of Poor Tom, however, precisely because 'Poor Tom' is not a recognisable identity. If he is to continue to evade 'the hunt', Edgar must 'scape' identification, must be fundamentally unidentifiable. This distinguishes Poor Tom from the gruff retainer, 'Caius' – the disguise Kent adopts. Through his new identity, Kent seeks for a place in the society from which he has been exiled, offering to serve 'Authority' (I.iv.30). He also defends the status quo by 'teaching' Oswald to respect hierarchical distinctions (I.iv.88). By contrast, Poor Tom seems to generate only indistinction: he similarly casts himself as a former 'serving-man' (III.iv.83) but at no point seeks for an identifiable 'place' in the social totality.

The exilic condition Edgar embodies involves a spatial shift. Edgar is thrust from the (presumed) civility of the court into a desolate wilderness of 'winds and persecutions' and 'pelting villages', a world where there is 'scarce a bush' (II.ii.492). This wild scenescape is usually described as 'the heath'. It is, however, worth observing that the heath is an editorial intervention on the part of Nicholas Rowe, who introduced it as part of his 1709 edition of Shakespeare.[34] There are, in both the Quarto and Folio versions of *King Lear*, very few determinate signifiers that might serve to more firmly locate the space Edgar (and also Lear and the Fool) occupy from Act Three onwards, aside from that it is 'out o' door' (III.ii.11). The 'heath' gives determinate shape to a space that is far less defined than even that open-ended descriptor would allow. Exile in *King Lear* involves 'a new spatio-temporal dynamics', which takes the form of an 'open place, vague and frontierless, a sort of wasteland' that is 'devoid of [. . .] landmarks' – truly the 'obscured course' (II.ii.166) Kent

---

[34] See James Ogden, 'Lear's Blasted Heath', in James Ogden and Arthur Scouten (eds), *Lear from Study to Stage: Essays in Criticism* (Madison and London: Associated University Presses, 1997), pp. 135–45.

forlornly imagines: 'I know not whither' (II.ii.487).³⁵ This scenescape is a windswept wasteland – an exilic space. But it is also chthonic: in his transformation into Poor Tom, Edgar enacts something of a descent underground, into the primal, pre-evolutionary mud and 'grime'.³⁶

The move into exilic space also entails a radical discursive shift, from the light-hearted and self-satisfied irony of a civilised courtier – 'How now, brother Edmund, what serious contemplation are you in?' (I.ii.138–9) – to a 'roaring' voice of 'lunatic bans' and demented 'prayers'. The word 'bans' is telling: as Edgar uses it, the most obvious meaning is 'curse'; but the etymological root of 'bans'/'ban' also relates to banishment – the 'curse' of exile.³⁷ Exile involves a new 'lunatic' way of speaking, which takes place outside of conventional social discourse – though the allusion to 'prayers' may also adumbrate a more supplicatory form of speech that witnesses a (finally, unrealisable) desire for divine and/or social succour. It is worth recalling that Poor Tom repeats over and over again that he is 'a-cold' (III.iv.81).

If, in his transformation into Poor Tom, Edgar embodies the negative state of exile, he also embodies the abject. Lear touches on the relationship between the abject and exile when banishing Cordelia – who is 'strangered with our oath' (I.i.205) – which he thinks of as a sort of self-excision, or blood-letting, both from his own body and the body politic (I.i.114–17). Gloucester thinks in the same way about Edgar, who is 'outlawed' from his 'blood' (III.iv.162–3). The abject, as with exile, involves the subversion of usual categories; it is that which cannot be made to 'fit' into systems of identity. Being abject means being unidentifiable. Edgar even 'grime[s]' his face with 'filth' – a word which, in early modern usage, connoted various forms of excrement, which is expelled from the 'clean and proper body'.³⁸ Defiling his physical identity, embodied by his face, Edgar quite literally 'outfaces' – dis-guises – himself.

Derek Cohen has written that *King Lear* can be read as 'a secular re-enactment of a sacrifice ritual', where the 'physical removal' – by death or exile – of a subject understood to be the root of 'discord, dissension,

---

³⁵ Pascale Drouet, '"Strangered with our Oath": The Dynamics of Banishment in *King Lear*', in François Laroque, Pierre Iselin and Sophie Alatorre (eds), *And That's True Too: New Essays on King Lear* (Newcastle: Cambridge Scholars Publishing, 2009), pp. 186–7.

³⁶ For more on the relation between Poor Tom and the chthonic, see Ted Hughes, *Shakespeare and the Goddess of Complete Being* (London: Faber and Faber, 1992), p. 275.

³⁷ 'ban, n.', <http://www.oed.com/view/Entry/15092?rskey=WXQg3f&result=1> (accessed 20 November 2017).

³⁸ Kristeva, *Powers of Horror*, p. 71.

and danger' is a necessary precondition of the 're-establishment of the cultural practices and norms that enable the supposedly peaceful continuance of social order'.[39] This subject is known as the scapegoat. Cohen picks out Oswald and Edmund as scapegoats in *King Lear*; but Edgar/Poor Tom also – and perhaps more powerfully – embodies the ritual place of the scapegoat, at one point revealing the way he has been 'whipped from tithing to tithing and stocked, punished and imprisoned' (III.iv.130–1).

Chapter 1 provided an analysis of the deep relationship between the scapegoat (the sacrifice ritual) and tragic subjectivity, making the case that for Adorno the sacrifice at once ensures the survival of the commons but also lays the foundation for the autonomy of the tragic subject – and, indeed, of the aesthetic. Cohen makes the same point: 'Every scapegoating, every cleansing in blood, is fraught with insoluble contradiction.'[40] The scapegoat figure pays witness to the 'insoluble' non-identity of the subject, who challenges the hegemony of the community from which s/he is exiled. This same contradiction is apparent in Poor Tom: his exclusion from the *polis* aligns him with the archetypal scapegoat and the autonomous tragic subject, with his/her negation of the prevailing social and political totality.

So far, I have argued that Poor Tom can be thought of as embodying a form of non-identity. This would align him with negativity and freedom. By defying socially and politically prescribed categories, Edgar (as Poor Tom) enables non-identity and the autonomy of the subject. But is Edgar/Poor Tom free? He is certainly able to escape detection, but whether or not exile represents a state of freedom in *King Lear* is open to question. Does the exile escape identitarian determination? It is possible that the exile is not so much 'outside' of totality as circumscribed 'within' it. To consider these fraught questions around 'bare life', I return to Agamben.

Edgar/Poor Tom and 'bare life'

Lear, in his storm-flung ravings, identifies Poor Tom as 'the thing itself': 'Unaccommodated man is no more but such a poor, bare forked animal as thou art' (III.iv.105–6). From his encounter with Poor Tom, Lear takes away an image of bare life, or of life lived outside the social and political 'accommodations' that imbue human existence with symbolic cultural value and meaning. Such life seems – to Lear – to precede

---

[39] Derek Cohen, 'The Malignant Scapegoats of *King Lear*', *Studies in English Literature 1500–1900*, 49:2 (2009), pp. 385–6.
[40] Ibid. p. 387.

cultural 'legitimation'. What he misses, however, is the way in which new systems of thought and social organisation produce bare life in his world (a process analysed in Chapter 2, with an interpretation of Edmund and his universalisation of 'base life'). Critics are not necessarily wrong to concentrate on the political 'moral' Lear draws when he meets Poor Tom – that a king and a beggar are, after all, fundamentally the same and that the 'superflux' might be shaken in the name of a more equitable society. The problem, however, is that Lear reifies human life as inherently debased, as much as Edmund does in his equalisation of all human life as 'base' (or 'bare'). This is not the 'natural' state of humanity 'outside' of society; it is a condition produced by society. 'That all men are alike', as Adorno warns, 'is exactly what society would like to hear'.[41]

Agamben theorises the state of exile through the Aristotelian *zoē–bios* distinction, where *zoē* connotes the bare 'animal' life of the human being and *bios* a historical form of 'political' life.[42] Agamben famously makes the case that the state of exile, outside the *polis*, constitutes a form of bare life. But he also contends that modern bio-political society is remarkable for the complete integration (the paradoxical 'inclusive exclusion') of biological life into the political state. This reached its nadir at Auschwitz, which Agamben reads as the catastrophic culmination of biopolitics and the total domination of the body and its 'naked life'.[43]

This interpretation of exile does partially speak to *King Lear*. It is worth noting that, in *The True Chronicle History of King Leir*, Leir and the other exiles ultimately find refuge in France – another place outside the rule of Britain. There is, however, no 'other place' in *King Lear*. Shakespeare excises France, so that exclusion – paradoxically – is internal. 'Am I in France?' (IV.vii.76) wonders Lear, as he awakens to see Cordelia in Act Four. The answer is – of course – no: Lear is in his 'own kingdom' (IV.vii.76). So when he uses the legalistic language 'proof and precedent / Of Bedlam beggars', Edgar might be viewed as inadvertently betraying the comprehensive inscription of base life within the compass of the juridical-political totality. Simon Palfrey writes that Poor Tom 'prefigures the Holocaust', as the nadir of Western modernity and its bio-political regime: 'he haunts it, expects it, is unsurprised by it'.[44]

---

[41] Adorno, *Minima Moralia*, pp. 102–3.
[42] Giorgio Agamben, *Homo Sacer: Sovereign Power and Bare Life*, trans. Daniel Heller-Roazen (Stanford: Stanford University Press, 1998), pp. 1–9.
[43] Ibid. pp. 166–80.
[44] Simon Palfrey, *Poor Tom: Living King Lear* (Chicago: Chicago University Press, 2014), p. 113.

There is, however, a potential problem with the idea of the total integration of the supposedly outlawed (legally 'bare') subject into the ambit of the state: it leaves little to no room for resistance or autonomy. Agamben – as a result – pays scant attention to the sort of social and political transgressions that might lead to a subject being exiled from the space of the commons. This understanding of the relationship between subject and society tends to elide tragedy. The idea that bare life is integrated into the social and political totality means that Agamben cannot conceptualise the challenge that the exile represents to the dominance of the *polis*; he cannot conceptualise non-identity.[45]

It is important to recall that Poor Tom is not 'the thing itself' – as a deranged Lear imagines – and so a petrified image of base life. Poor Tom is, as Edgar states, a radically indeterminate '*something*' (II.ii.192). Poor Tom is far more open-ended and undefined than Lear is able to imagine in his reifying conception of de-cultured 'base life' – 'the thing itself'. It is his status as a provisional, indeterminate 'something', as opposed to the idea of 'the thing itself', which implies that 'Poor Tom' will ultimately cede to a host of other identities. Over the course of the play, Edgar engages in a process of continuous self re-authorship, conducting a whole legion of voices and identities in and through his fissiparous 'self', from a country yokel – 'Chi'll not let go, zir, without vurther 'cagion' (IV.vi.231) – to a many-nosed, horned 'fiend' (IV.vi.72) and, in his final triumph over his rival Edmund, a heroic knight: 'Draw thy sword' (V.iii.124). This self-fragmentation is physicalised by Edgar: by sticking 'pins', 'wooden pricks', 'nails' and 'sprigs' in his 'bare and mortified' arms, Edgar enacts something akin to the ritual of *sparagmos* – a form of self-rending that symbolises violent self-dispersal. What unites the various 'selves' that Edgar adopts 'post-Tom' is that they are all unnamed and 'untitled' – and even Poor Tom is more of a generic name than a fully conceived 'personal' identity. These figures can be understood as yet further embodiments – further iterations – of 'nothing'. With no name – and no 'title' – the figures Edgar transforms into over the course of the play can all be said to inhere to his self-negation ('Edgar I nothing am') and his radical subversion of normative social and political identity.

There is some ambiguity about Edgar and his transformation into Poor Tom and other figures, which may bring his apparent non-identity

---

[45] It is precisely that sense of non-identity, of being somewhere else, which is captured in 'The Other Place', where *Will's Way* was originally staged (Shakespeare remarks that he prefers the space of The Other Place to 'the main house', as it is 'Much more me' (9)).

into question. How far does Edgar remain Edgar 'underneath' his disguises? Does the 'disguise' gain autonomy over its overwhelmed originator? These often-asked questions around Edgar/Poor Tom are no doubt important.[46] What is more important, however, is whether or not Edgar is able to enact a return to the social totality, taking up his 'lost' place in the order from which he is outcast.

The indeterminate topology of *King Lear* is, as Michel Goldman has shown, unique in Shakespeare, in that the central characters of the play are all displaced into a vast transitional space without any sense of a final destination – aside, perhaps, from Dover, which itself becomes a shifting and liminal (non-)place in the play, perhaps most obviously in the scene at Dover 'cliff': 'Wherefore to Dover?' (III.vii.51).[47] Without any final and 'fixed place' (I.vi.261) to which the characters can 'fly' (II.i.56) or return, *King Lear* obviates resolution, whereby the 'promised' place – or indeed the Promised Land – is never realised. Edgar may seek to perform a process of self-return, from 'my name is lost' (V.iii.119) to 'My name is Edgar' (V.iii.167). There is, however, no final return to identity by the catastrophic end of the play. *King Lear* – as shown in Chapter 2 – has no obvious restitution of the social and political order, to which the outcasts may return. Even if he is given the final speech, Edgar speaks from the position of 'exclusion, exile and expatriation' – not necessarily as heir.[48] Poor Tom is perhaps not as far away as he might appear in the final moments of the play: Edgar remains in a state of exile, revealing the ongoing non-identity of subject and society.

Rudkin shares the idea that Edgar cannot enact a process of self-return or social restitution, making the case that Shakespeare 'recognizes that at the ending of a play whose cosmos is so faulted and flawed, and whose pessimism is so deep, a formal promise of a "healer" will not sit well' (Shakespeare left that sort of formal closure, quips Rudkin, 'to the Nahum Tates of the world').[49] I want now to consider more deeply the influence which Edgar, and his transformation into Poor Tom, has had on Rudkin, identifying the way in which Edgar informs the representation of dramatic character in Rudkin, before showing that Edgar

---

[46] For competing views see Ewan Fernie, *The Demonic: Literature and Experience* (London: Routledge, 2013), p. 224, and Stephen Greenblatt, *Shakespearean Negotiations: The Circulation of Social Energy in Renaissance England* (Berkeley and Los Angeles: University of California Press, 1988), pp. 94–128.

[47] Michael Goldman, '*King Lear*: Acting and Feeling', in Laurence Danson (ed.), *On King Lear* (Princeton: Princeton University Press, 1981), pp. 43–4.

[48] Drouet, '"Strangered with our Oath"', p. 180.

[49] Rudkin, personal interview, 24 August 2016.

also informs the way Rudkin conceptualises his own self-transformative authorial 'process'.

Rudkin and Edgar

Rudkin has acknowledged the way in which his conception of dramatic characterisation and his ideas around self re-authorship and exile are indebted to *King Lear* and Edgar. Rudkin remarks that *King Lear* sends its characters 'flying out from the centre to the extremes, where they are rendered conventionally meaningless, and become self-performing existential figures in a void'.[50] 'Particularly formative', reveals Rudkin, is 'the transformation speech'.[51] 'Edgar invents and tries on a role in the "Edgar I nothing am" speech': 'The series of performances that thereafter constitute his journey remains influential.'[52] Rudkin typically depicts protagonists who undergo an Edgar-like process of self re-authorship, abandoning an official social self for a non-official self which does not fit into the regulatory identity-systems of the social totality (is 'conventionally meaningless'). This can be a response to exile – and the catastrophic loss of self it involves – or can equally occasion exile, as the subject is forced from the community as a whole because of his/her contravention of culturally ratified identities. This process entails a radical physical and linguistic shift. Rudkin depicts characters that physically 'transform' themselves on stage, often through self-abasement. This is paralleled by a linguistic shift towards a type of lunatic 'bans' Edgar takes up.[53]

Many of the characters Rudkin has created in his plays – including Merlin ('Now nothing am'), Hitchcock ('Hitchcock Eye; nothing am'), Amadu ('What I Amadu am?') and even Shakespeare himself ('Shakespeare I nothing am' (14)) – directly echo Edgar, typically in moments of catastrophic personal and social upheaval that challenge the presumed identity of the self.[54] The same influence can be traced in those Rudkin characters who are 'determined to play the role of a filthy "thing" pelted out onto the very margins of society and history' – the 'filthy "thing"' Rudkin refers to obviously recalling Poor Tom as 'the

---

[50] Quoted in David Ian Rabey, *David Rudkin: Sacred Disobedience – An Expository Study of His Drama 1959–1996* (Oxford: Routledge, 1997), p. 95.
[51] Ibid. p. 96.
[52] Ibid. p. 95.
[53] See also, 'Burning Alone in the Dark: David Rudkin Talks to David Ian Rabey', *Planet*, 114 (1995–6), pp. 93–4.
[54] *Merlin Unchained*, p. 81; David Rudkin, *The Lovesong of Alfred J. Hitchcock* (London: Oberon Books, 2014), p. 43; *Red Sun*, p. 40.

thing itself', while the word 'pelt' similarly alludes to those who – like Edgar – 'abide' the 'pelting of the pitiless storm' in *King Lear*.[55] These range from the 'uncertain person' of Child Manatond in *The Sons of Light* to Athdark in *The Saxon Shore* and Gil/Giles in *The Triumph of Death*, all of whom wrestle with the negative *persona* of a 'Nobody' and a 'Not': 'This is not Not'.[56]

Rudkin states that Edgar underpins his thinking about the dramatic character 'alone on stage' (something echoed in his notion of 'self-performing' figures 'in a void').[57] Whether or not Edgar is truly 'alone' on stage during his transformation is something of a moot point. The transformation scene (as Rudkin calls it) occurs after Kent is put in the stocks – his 'shameful lodging' (II.ii.170) – and, in the Quarto version at least, falls asleep. Neither version has a scene-break – though both editors and directors have traditionally introduced a break after Kent drifts into sleep, turning the transformation scene into a soliloquy. Rudkin obviously visualises the scene in an individualised way. This stress on existential isolation – on being 'alone' – reflects the way in which Rudkin conceives of exile and self re-authorship: as processes that individuate the subject from society. The idea of the 'void' is similarly telling: Rudkin draws on the indeterminate topology of exile in *King Lear*, where the subject is left 'alone on an empty blasted earth, beneath a polluting sky'.[58] This conception of spatiality owes something to Brook and his 1962 production. Only where the empty space of the Brook production signified an absurd, godless wasteland where subjects were left forever paralysed, Rudkin understands the desolate spaces of *King Lear* through Edgar: as exilic spaces that allow the subject to cast off inherited identities and radically re-author the self.[59]

Rudkin draws an intriguing distinction between 'theatre' and 'drama'. Where theatre names the physical and public space where plays take place – the institution of theatre, which Rudkin was forbad by his

---

[55] Quoted in Rabey, *Sacred Disobedience*, p. 96.
[56] Rudkin, *The Sons of Light*, p. 9 and p. 70.
[57] Quoted in Rabey, *Sacred Disobedience*, p. 96.
[58] David Rudkin, 'Being an Artaudian Dramatist', collected as part of the conference papers of *Past Masters: Antonin Artaud Conference, 8–10 November 1996* (Aberystwyth: Centre for Performance Research, 1996), p. 11. Rabey adapts the title for his own 'Being a Shakespearean Dramatist'; see Introduction.
[59] It is worth recalling that *Afore Night Come* emerged from the radical revolution of Shakespearean staging in 1962. See Colin Chambers, *Inside the Royal Shakespeare Company: Creativity and the Institution* (London: Routledge, 2004), p. 21.

strict religious upbringing – 'drama' names something quite distinct: the deep 'impression' which plays 'stamp' on the individual, most obviously through the act of reading. This distinction is revealing: drama seems to be an 'internal' process, which is produced by overpowering (Rudkin says 'nightmarish') images in the plays, while theatre is 'external' – involving the practicalities of staging.[60] This distinction speaks to a wider scope of engagement between Rudkin and *King Lear*. The figure of Edgar, his self-loss and re-authoring, manifestly preoccupies Rudkin and has found a unique place in his theatrical understanding. But for Rudkin, Edgar is also related to the dramatic, authorial process itself: playwriting involves a continuous process of crisis and self-transformation, 'not on the space, but for the *author* to do', so that self re-authorship – even its 'indistinguished space' (IV.vi.266) – is psychically 'internal', a form of inner exile.[61]

Rudkin, writing in his 1996 talk 'Being an Artaudian Dramatist', offers a particularly revealing exposition of his process of self re-authorship. Rudkin provides a brief reading of his works and makes the case that 'being' an Artaudian dramatist – as opposed to simply writing Artaudian plays – means shedding old selves 'like a skin', so that 'a new self emerges': 'Again and again, one re-invents oneself.'[62] Yet while the talk putatively relates that process to Artaud, the figure that (once again) emerges, and informs the reading of Artaudian dramaturgy Rudkin develops, is Edgar. Rudkin concludes his address by alluding to Edgar, insisting that self re-authorship ('forever re-midwifing oneself') parallels Edgar and his transformation into 'the Bedlam beggar'.[63] Rudkin also underscores the exilic state that self re-authorship necessarily involves, stating that by 'the same act, again and again, one re-exiles oneself', as Edgar similarly 'puts himself out beyond the boundaries'.[64] Through his constant self-transformations, Rudkin makes himself – as he puts it – 'indigestible' within any community, so preventing his inclusion within any 'constituency' that may reduce him to a static identity.[65]

To understand the way in which Rudkin writes his own authorial subjectivity through Shakespeare and Edgar, I turn now to analyse his conceptualisation of the act of appropriation, which in his drama tends to be 'biographical' – the appropriation of past artists. I consider some

---

[60] Rudkin, personal interview, 24 August 2016.
[61] Rudkin, 'Being an Artaudian Dramatist', p. 5.
[62] Ibid. p. 1 and p. 14.
[63] Ibid. p. 14.
[64] Ibid.
[65] Ibid. pp. 12–13.

of his other appropriations of 'Shakespeare', before I analyse the way *Will's Way* thematises ideas around exile and self-authorship through its appropriation of Edgar.

Rudkin, Shakespeare and Appropriation

In his remarkable 1995 interview 'Burning Alone in the Dark' – a notably exilic title – Rudkin sets out his approach to biographical writing and appropriation, which in various media has included Gustav Mahler, Dmitri Shostakovich, Antonin Artaud and Alfred Hitchcock – all figures that can be situated in the modernist and late modernist tradition and who have inspired and continue to haunt Rudkin.[66] Rudkin states that his appropriations do not develop 'a dramatic deconstruction' – a sceptical 'writing back' to a past artist from the perspective of a prescribed identity politics.[67] He recalls his disillusionment with the Gay Liberation movement of the 1970s, where he 'encountered institutionalized bigotries and prescriptivism' as 'narrow, closeted and self-stereotyped' as anything he found in the wider 'administered world'.[68] 'I would not wish to be categorized in any way which is limiting or prescriptive', states Rudkin: 'I believe that also an essential part of liberation is to confront that exile and experience of being excommunicated by one's own brethren.'[69] Rudkin reveals that, far from politically interrogatory or historically 'factual' representations, writing about the lives and work of other artists is a means of self-authorship, whereby he finds that the works of past masters 'yield questions' he discovers to be 'pertinent' to his 'own existence' and 'relevant' to his own 'inner journeys'.[70] The lives and the artistry of the figures Rudkin appropriates become, he contends, 'metaphors' for, and 'aspects' of, his 'own biography' and creative processes.[71] This is not to say that Rudkin completely 'colonises' his predecessors, reducing these figures to a mere inflection of his own biography or dramaturgy. This would be tantamount to a form of identity-thinking – a reduction of the other to the same. Rudkin is writing through, as opposed to over, the figures he appropriates.

Shakespeare has made appearances in several Rudkin plays, where

---

[66] Rudkin, 'Burning Alone in the Dark', pp. 91–9.
[67] Ibid. p. 99.
[68] Ibid.
[69] Ibid.
[70] Ibid. p. 97.
[71] Ibid.

his presence tends to thematise ideas around exile, fragmentation and self-authorship. These interwoven ideas can be traced back to *Afore Night Come*. The play depicts a gang of fruit-pickers who ritually decapitate an Irish vagrant called Roche, who is dubbed 'Shakespeare' by his 'fellow' workers.[72] The situation in *Afore Night Come* resurfaces in the 2012 play *Merlin Unchained*, in which the spatially and temporally displaced Merlin is misidentified as Irish and, intriguingly, as Shakespeare.[73] Rudkin also began a Shakespeare monologue in 1974, which he left unfinished. This short solo play occurs at the end of a personal diary – much of which is comprised of early drafts of *The Triumph of Death* – which I discovered in the British Library Rudkin Archive. Shakespeare, entering the stage alone, is burdened by a raft of papers and a calculator. It transpires he is completing his tax return. This imposition on his writing time causes Shakespeare to reflect on the contradiction between economic and artistic production. Where economic production simply treats art as a means to an end – profit – artistic production, as Shakespeare understands it, responds to existential necessity: the need to author and re-author the self. This process turns the playwright into an inherently 'ungovernable' outsider, who provides a 'token of our freedom' in a 'corporate Age'.[74]

These appropriations of Shakespeare can all be understood in relation to *Will's Way*. The play is distinct, however, in its self-reflexive engagement with the figure of Edgar. In his address, Shakespeare dedicates

---

[72] David Rudkin, *Afore Night Come* (London: Oberon Books, 2001). Recalling the German premiere of the play, Rudkin states that the play was:

> iinterrupted by disturbances in the auditorium that 'froze' the performance for some half-hour; the older generation in the audience were shouting protests, 'We don't want this filth in our theatre!' and the younger generation were countering with 'No, you want it in the camps!' (See David Rudkin, '*Afore Night Come*', <http://www.davidrudkin.com/theatre/afore-night-come/afore night-comep2. html> (accessed 6 July 2019))

Roche is sacrificed so that the land may remain fertile – echoing with the blood and soil ideology of the Nazis. I return to conceptions of food in Chapter 8.

[73] David Rudkin, *Merlin Unchained*, p. 164. 'Alas, I live before his time', responds Merlin, alluding to the Fool in *King Lear* (p. 161): 'This prophecy shall Merlin make, for I live before his time' (III.ii.95–6).

[74] Rudkin Archive, handwritten diary, dep. 10624, folder 3 (1974). This play cannot necessarily be considered a 'draft' for *Will's Way*, seeing the play pre-dates *Will's Way* by around ten years, with no indication Rudkin returned to the script. But there are some uncanny parallels which indicate the consistency of his thinking around Shakespeare and exile. This play also includes an abrupt exit on the part of Shakespeare ('He simply walks away').

substantial time to discoursing on his unique relationship with one of his more ambiguous creations. In creating Edgar, reflects Shakespeare – 'finding out how to inhabit that character on that journey', which is 'a journey, / out into the wilds' – 'I fell back on myself as an author' (24, 37). Shakespeare reveals that authorship is – for him – a process of self-authorship and re-authorship. Through his playwriting and the various characters he creates, Shakespeare is able to author and re-author his self. 'As a playwright you blindly touch that unhatched self / or selves, / into life', remarks Shakespeare, so that the plays are 'myself, all broken up' into various characters, which find vicarious literary and dramatic 'life' on stage, a continuous form of self-'splitting', with the 'fragments growing' (26, 9, 33). Over the course of his address, Shakespeare refers to a variety of other characters drawn from the canon, from Othello to Cymbeline. But it is Edgar who embodies the authorial process as a whole, the way in which Shakespeare is 'always on the change', authoring and re-authoring his self through his playwriting (32).[75] Like his creation, Shakespeare exhibits a powerful 'negative force' (21): the ability to negate his officially sanctioned social self and embrace exilic, self-transformative change: 'Shakespeare I nothing am' (14).

Rudkin appropriates Shakespeare to reflect on his own authorship, turning Shakespeare into a sort of dramatic surrogate.[76] Shakespeare, as Robert Wilcher has contended, ought to be seen as 'a symbolic embodiment' of Rudkin, epitomising the idea that 'the dramatist goes through a self-transforming process in the course of writing a play'.[77] This idea of a 'process' is critical to *Will's Way* and its portrayal of Edgar, where the authorial process is one of constant self re-authorship that produces a fragmentary, exilic aesthetic form.

Will's Way

The Process Play

Through his appropriation of Shakespeare and Edgar, Rudkin defines the type of playwriting he practises as 'the process play', in which

---

[75] It is precisely for his unruly transformations from one identity into another that Rabey promotes Edgar to the station of 'tragic hero' in his 'Wye' plays – though by the end of the play it is Echternacht who most powerfully bodies transmutations that outrun 'the will's control' (5.2.72): 'I Nothing am' (5.2.70).

[76] See also Palfrey, *Poor Tom*, pp. 10–11, and Fernie, *The Demonic*, p. 228, for Edgar as a theatrical surrogate of Shakespeare.

[77] Robert Wilcher, 'Only a Bard: The Theatre of David Rudkin' in Rudkin, *Red Sun and Merlin Unchained*, p. 248.

he undergoes a process of continual self-transformation. Like his avatar Edgar, Shakespeare continuously authors and embodies new subjectivities – new 'selves' (39). Shakespeare, in his thoughts on his ongoing 'process', observes:

> There comes a point while you're thinking all this
> when you start to say Hang on,
> the story is important
> but the story isn't the be-all and end-all of the play.
> I think a play is a,
> it has to put you through a process,
> so that at the end of it
> [. . .] you're at a new beginning. (20–1)

The process Shakespeare undergoes in his playwriting never truly ends: every (ostensible) 'end' opens up a 'new beginning', so that the process starts over again. This obviously has implications for aesthetic form and, most obviously, for narrative (or as Shakespeare calls it, the 'story'). By drawing a subtle distinction between 'the play' and 'the story', Shakespeare reveals the play and its 'process' cannot be contained by, and tends to violate, narrative, which – in an allusion to *Macbeth* and 'Might be the be-all, and the end-all' (I.vii.5) – can never be the 'be-all and end-all'. Narrative closure (the end of the story) cannot not put an end ('end all') to the process Shakespeare undergoes through his plays or encompass his own constantly shifting being ('be all') – a point I touch on again when I come to analyse the catastrophic non-ending of the play. It is, as Shakespeare declares, not 'the story' but 'the play that matters' (38).

Rudkin created his appropriation of Shakespeare by extemporising – and voice-recording – the talk that would become *Will's Way*.[78] This compositional technique throws light on the way Rudkin turns biographical appropriation into a form of vicarious self-authorship. But it also goes some way to clarifying the discontinuous and fragmentary style of the play, which is meant to resemble 'an unscripted personal address' (7). Shakespeare never settles into a progressive 'story', but moves unpredictably between various ideas and motifs, in a far more irregular and discontinuous way. The 'uneven' form of the address is perhaps most obvious in the constant delays – usually taking the form of parentheses or self-reflective 'mms' – deviations and digressions that punctuate the talk, arresting narrative progress and adumbrating other possible but untaken avenues of exposition (22). Shakespeare even self-reflexively remarks on his own violation of narrative progress – 'How did

---

[78] Rudkin, personal interview, 24 August 2016.

I get onto all that?' – and that various other 'directions' were possible, with 'a thousand paths' which the talk might have instead taken: 'This is the path it took' (36, 40). This violation of narrative progress through disruptions and digressions has obvious parallels with the unsettled physical and psychic 'wandering' of *King Lear* – its errant movement through an indeterminate topology. The deformation of narrative linearity in *Will's Way* testifies to an exilic form of subjectivity, where the subject takes a more 'unpredictable' route.

Shakespeare intuits that his process – his continuous self re-authorship – inevitably makes him an outsider, an exile. He observes that his process means he can never 'fit' into society or its prescribed forms of identity. Shakespeare describes himself as a 'non-belonger' – he does not 'really belong' (11). He is partially a victim of the politics of, as he calls it, 'including' and 'excluding', his status as a 'non-belonger' meaning that he is forever barred from 'being brought / Home', and being allowed 'Within, and not a stranger' (15, 11). The plaintive cry of Poor Tom – that he is 'a-cold' – might also be heard: Shakespeare is also permanently stranded out of doors, exposed to the 'persecutions of the sky'. But at the same time, his experience of non-belonging – his non-identity – also 'equips' (24) him. Shakespeare remarks that his 'outlaw' (20) status, his unaccommodated form of subjectivity, is deeply formative: it allows him to avoid being 'underlined by everybody else' (10), even to exist as 'the opposite of everything' (12) – a powerful form of 'negative mischief' (33). Shakespeare embraces negation, over and above the reifying demands of social belonging.

Once again relating his self and artistry to the figure of the exiled Edgar, Shakespeare pursues the idea that the playwright ought to be 'thrust out / onto the very edges of the universe':

> And the author does in a sense live outside.
> A stranger in his own world, he has to be that,
> in order to see that world.
> And he has to be in contact with the mud at the bottom of the well.
> I mean, for all our sakes,
> it's the dramatist above all who has to have bad dreams.
> Edgar goes physically down into all of that. (24–5)

Not unlike Edgar, who subsists 'on the very edges of the universe', Shakespeare appears in *Will's Way* as an exile, a 'stranger', living 'as an alien' and occupying an exilic space 'outside' (24) society as whole. This marginalisation is, at the same time, a form of chthonic 'descent' – a going 'down' into 'the mud', so as to make 'contact' with 'the darkest reaches' (24). The spatial dynamic owes itself to *King Lear*: the conceptualisation of being 'thrust' outside – 'thrust him out at gates' (III. vii.92) – obviously draws on the exilic topology of *King Lear*, while the chthonic descent Shakespeare describes, a degeneration into 'elemental excrement' (34), reflects the way Edgar 'goes down' into the primordial 'grime' and 'filth' ('the mud at the bottom of the well'). Shakespeare is an abject figure, found in the 'pigsties and the ashes' (20). He becomes, as Edgar does, 'utterly distorted and unrecognized' (24) in his world.

This is a necessary condition ('he has to be that') for the playwright: his outsider status provides the space for a critical perspective on the social totality ('to see that world') and allows him to bring the identity of the community – its norms and values – into question: Shakespeare compares his seemingly 'warped perspective' with 'the eyes of a foreigner' (35). This means the playwright takes an exilic position akin to that of the tragic hero, whose ritual expulsion from society at once serves to solidify the community, but can also entail freedom from a repressive social and political order. Shakespeare even appears as something of a Christ-like, sacrificial martyr, who takes it upon himself to suffer at the hands of, but also paradoxically for, the wider community. His painful experience of marginality is represented as formative, allowing him to provide a negative critique of that order on behalf of others: 'for all our sakes'. Through his appropriation of Shakespeare and Edgar, Rudkin imagines a dramatist whose value – even universal value, reflected in 'all' – to the world flows from a position outside society, as a determinate negation of totality. This serves to put the tragic figure of the playwright at the social and cultural 'centre', as Shakespeare calls it, where a playwright 'should be' (24). Precisely by virtue of his exile to the margins, Shakespeare is able to both 'see' and address himself to the 'centre', from which he is outcast. 'The edge', as an unpublished Rudkin play has it, 'is where the centre is.'[79]

When he remarks that Edgar goes 'physically down' into the 'darkest reaches', the implication is that Shakespeare – as an author – is also going through a psychic process, a dichotomy that arguably speaks to the distinction Rudkin draws between 'theatre' and 'drama'. The 'well', along with the Hamlet-like 'bad dreams' – 'a king of infinite space, were it not that I had bad dreams' (II.ii.257–8) – the playwright suffers from, may indicate a chthonic descent into the subconscious, a 'well' where other possible but normally repressed selves are buried. This would serve to turn the process of self re-authorship into a psychoanalytic process, an engagement with the dark 'shadow' self – those aspects of the self the

---

[79] Quoted in Sukhdev Sandu (ed.), *The Edge is Where the Centre Is: David Rudkin and Penda's Fen, An Archaeology* (Brooklyn: Keegan and Cooke, 2015), p. 47.

ego would disavow, but which can be brought to consciousness as part of a wider process of self-transformation. Rudkin has an ongoing interest in Freudian and Jungian theory – and often refers to his time with the Reichian Robert Ollendorf, to whom *The Sons of Light* is dedicated.[80]

This would mean 'theatre' serves to embody the inner physic 'drama' of the playwright, as an externalisation of 'inner life' (10).[81] Shakespeare even goes as far as to say that the continuous process of self re-authorship has a vicarious, therapeutic value for the playwright:

> I think that's the only play worth writing,
> from the author's point of view.
> The process play.
> It's the only kind of play that the writing
> is going to do him any good. (21)

Rudkin concedes that his concentration on self re-authorship and its related exilic processes might appear 'solipsistic' and that the 'constant re-emergence of new selves' might be viewed as being at risk of 'disappearing up its own arsehole'.[82] 'What is its *meaning* for the audience? For the community? Society? The world?'[83] But for Rudkin, self re-authorship and the exile it involves are profoundly political – even a means, to quote Palfrey in his analysis of Poor Tom, of '*living political*'.[84] The act of 'refusing to be, or remain, *defined*' is for Rudkin an existentially and politically 'subversive' act in the increasingly reified and administered world of post-Auschwitz culture.[85] His appropriation of Edgar-Tom should be situated as a deeply political response to that reified, post-Holocaust world and its petrified forms of identity.

'The temper of the time'

While it is valuable from the 'point of view' of the author, self re-authorship also has a public (even universal) political meaning. Shakespeare remarks that the 'conjunction / between the inward, and the public, / is vital for a dramatist to make / if his drama is to have meaning':

> If all I did as a playwright
> was stand up on stage and beat my breast

---

[80] See Rudkin, 'Burning Alone in the Dark', p. 98.
[81] Shakespeare remarks that the 'creative energy' which comes from inner 'pain' must be 'transmuted, / into a world onstage' (28).
[82] Rudkin, 'Being an Artaudian Dramatist', p. 10.
[83] Ibid.
[84] Palfrey, *Poor Tom*, p. 5.
[85] Rudkin, 'Being an Artaudian Dramatist', p. 10.

how frightened I am, how miserable I am,
how confused I am, oh how I suffer:
no one quite rightly would want to know. (28)

Shakespeare disclaims declamatory, Lear-like apostrophes to a hostile universe. He states that, while his 'creative energy' springs from personal pain and his own personal 'struggle', his process of self re-authorship has 'public' implications far beyond the life of the playwright (27–8). Shakespeare may be able to engage creatively in the act of writing; but he is also conscious of nascent socio-historical shifts that may narrow the possibilities for self-authorship and re-authorship. Shakespeare voices concerns about the dehumanising impact of 'new social principles', paying witness to a violent epochal transition to a new dispensation:

I think there are new social principles coming in
which do not seem to have the same room
for the wholeness of human nature;
a much more mechanistic and mercenary approach to a man. (27)

This reductively 'mechanistic' and 'mercenary' approach to humanity portends the beginnings of capitalist modernity, which Shakespeare denounces as 'a whirlwind utterly without humane values, / charged with a terrible unprinciple. / A new breed of people are given license to ravage' (32). The 'new breed of people' Shakespeare rails against – recalling the language of figures from John F. Danby to Arnold Kettle – is principally represented by Goneril, Regan and Edmund, whose amoral intrigues epitomise the 'terrible unprinciple' that underpins capitalistic self-interest: 'a whole new generation / motivated by greed, for power, wealth, land' (22). These figures 'are muggers basically. Grab grab grab, and to hell with ethics' (22). This compulsion to 'grab' captures the fusion of Enlightenment instrumentality with capitalistic consumption, where the drive to dispel myth and make the world fully knowable and graspable – to bring every 'thing' within the sphere of consciousness and utility – is formally commensurable with capitalist interchangeability, in which potentially everything is 'up for grabs' by virtue of being speciously equalised by market forces.

By depicting a Shakespeare who condemns the cost of capitalist modernity, Rudkin posits a dialectical historical continuum between the beginnings of the bourgeois 'revolution' and his own post-Auschwitz critique of a society in which the subject is at risk of being completely absorbed into the social totality. The critique Shakespeare provides of the 'temper of the time', as he calls it, is obviously as much a critique of late capitalist culture as it is of the beginnings of early modern capitalism. The 'temper of the time' relates to the contemporaneous Thatcher revolution and its 'reductionist and inhumane political ethos', as Rudkin calls it.[86] This critique has less to do with the loss of communal social and political values than it does with the totalisation of society under the capitalist principle, which in contradiction to the late globalised ideology of the 'free' individual, mechanically liquidates the subject.

Rudkin understands capitalist modernity as an inherently catastrophic dispensation, which has 'proved a colossal failure on a historic scale'.[87] But 'for all that capitalistic progress is a terribly convincing lie, it is comfortingly anti-paradoxical in its profession to have defined, colonized and expunged all contradictions'.[88] This idea of the 'contradiction' that capitalist reification has failed to completely 'colonize' and 'expunge' relates to the subject – and most obviously, to the exilic subject of tragedy. Rudkin writes that exile testifies to the 'limits of self-control' and reminds the 'citizens of the *polis* just how shapeless, (self-)destructive and unregenerate an individual can be in official terms'.[89] This, as Rudkin sees it, has 'universal political significance': where globalised late capitalism turns reification into a worldwide phenomenon, non-identity takes on meanings far beyond the exiled individual.[90]

Kingsley-Smith has made the case that the way Edgar transforms into Poor Tom is as significant for its 'impact on others' as it is for 'its impact on Edgar'.[91] By transforming into Poor Tom, Edgar catalyses new insights and understanding in those around him – not least Lear, who is acutely sensitive to the 'unaccommodated' state of Poor Tom and its wider social and political implications ('Consider him well'). Not too dissimilarly, the Shakespeare of *Will's Way* – and, by implication, Rudkin himself – aspires to rouse both self and others into an awareness of a common crisis through a creative and political practice of self re-authorship.

Exile, Self Re-Authorship and the Audience

Rudkin has recently set out his 'intention' for his art:

> Certainly my wish for it – my intention and purpose for it – is to address itself to, to awaken [. . .] the *unsuspected* within the listener, viewer, auditor;

---

[86] Ibid. p. 11.
[87] Rudkin, 'Burning Alone in the Dark', p. 96.
[88] Quoted in David Ian Rabey, 'Broken Magic? A Director's Perspective on Merlin Unchained', in Rudkin, *Red Sun and Merlin Unchained*, p. 242.
[89] Ibid.
[90] Rudkin, 'Burning Alone in the Dark', p. 97.
[91] Kingsley-Smith, *Shakespeare's Drama of Exile*, p. 130.

to *individuate* that person. Where I feel *betrayed* – yes, I will say that – by much, much of what calls itself cinema and television and art now, is that it somehow addresses me as a member of a *homogeneous* public, which I don't think I am. So I think that art's function is to individuate and, by that same token, inevitably, to subvert [. . .] I mean, this is not a popular view, in context, but the flight *into* forms of collective faith seems to be queuing up to have your hands chopped off [. . .] Its [sic] opting into a form of slavery [. . ."]We leave these questions for the apparatus to answer! Just tell us what we have to think; just tell us what we have to do."[92]

Rudkin understands aesthetic response in terms of exile. Whereas the Culture Industry – with its pretensions to authentic 'art' – catalyses a 'flight' into collectivity, Rudkin wants to inspire a 'flight' out of collectivity, to distantiate the subject from society. Rudkin intends for his art to displace the subject, for it to produce a state of exile from a homogenised 'public'.[93] This exilic withdrawal from the collective, is, as Rudkin sees it, a politically 'subversive' process: by exiling – or 'individuating' – the subject from all collectives, Rudkin intends to produce forms of non-identity that serve to bring the status quo into question. Rudkin wants to catalyse the self-reflexivity of the subject, which the Culture Industry inhibits by homogenising audience response ('We leave these questions for the apparatus to answer!'). To simply adopt the dictates of collective faith is, as Rudkin sees it, a form of self-mutilation ('queuing up to have your hands chopped off') – or, as Adorno and Horkheimer call it, the introversion of sacrifice. So when he states that he intends for his art to arouse the *'unsuspected'* in his audience, he means the unsuspected 'inner' exile lurking, as Poor Tom does with Edgar, within the subject – or the 'stranger from within', as Kristeva famously calls it.[94] This shuddering 'awakening' of the unrealised is the same type of affect Adorno analyses.

Rudkin, as with the other playwrights under study (and indeed Adorno) does not necessarily substantiate his claims about aesthetic response and the processes it is supposed to catalyse. With the relatively infrequent stagings of his plays in mind, it should also be observed that Rudkin has, all too often, not even had an audience to 'address'. His conception of aesthetic response is, as a result, more reliant on a theoretical understanding of form. Rudkin – in the same vein as Adorno – tends to think about the affective (and, relatedly, the political) dimension of art in terms

---

[92] Sandu, *The Edge is Where the Centre Is*, p. 48.
[93] In our interview, Barker similarly talks of audience response as a process of 'dislocated thought' (Howard Barker, personal interview, 26 August 2016).
[94] Julia Kristeva, *Strangers to Ourselves*, trans. Leon S. Roudiez (New York: Columbia University Press, 1991), p. 1.

of aesthetic form, as opposed to content (or as Rudkin calls it, 'the formal necessities of the material itself').[95] He states in our 2016 interview that he does not go 'all the way' with Adorno and his belief that Auschwitz renders all 'symphonic' (harmonious) art not only obsolete, but indefensible. But his preferred aesthetic has some undeniable overlaps with Adorno and his understanding of fragmented post-Auschwitz art. Most obviously, Rudkin violates aesthetic closure in his plays.

I have observed that the autonomous tragic subject, by refusing final resolution, instantiates a type of open-ended aesthetic form.[96] This process is obviously at work in the (non-)ending of *Will's Way*. Even at the end of his address, Shakespeare remains inscrutable, ultimately refusing to give a cumulative, closing statement on himself or his artistry. Shakespeare is only too keen to abort the talk – 'I think perhaps I should not say any more. / I should stop there' – calling for questions ('Are there any questions?') that remain unanswered as he suddenly disappears from the space, as the play ends with the stage directions calling for an abrupt '*Cut to black*' (40). Shakespeare does not fulfil any 'formal promise' of resolution. He transgresses the aesthetic limits that may constrain his subjectivity, preserving his restless, exilic refusal of a 'fixed' identity, which may end his self-transformations.

The (non-)ending of *Will's Way* also provides a compelling image of catastrophic performance. The abrupt 'turn' Shakespeare performs away from the audience recalls the etymology of the word catastrophe as 'a sudden turn'.[97] The oldest of the Three Fates in Greek mythology is Atropos, whose name signifies 'without turn'.[98] Atropos implies the impossibility of turning away from fate, the end which is allotted to the tragic hero in Greek tragedy. But a subject who has the capacity to turn reveals a form of tragedy where the subject can resist the 'inevitable' end and preserve his or her bid for freedom – precisely as Shakespeare does. By abruptly turning away from the audience and disappearing from the stage, Shakespeare epitomises the type of sudden 'turn' to be found in catastrophic drama, as his *volte-face* subverts both narrative and aesthetic closure. Much the same might be said of Rudkin as his avatar. At the end of a workshop for aspiring playwrights at the

---

[95] Quoted in Karoline Gritzner, *Adorno and Modern Theatre: The Drama of the Damaged Self in Bond, Rudkin, Barker and Kane* (Basingstoke: Palgrave Macmillan, 2015), p. 104.
[96] See Chapter 1.
[97] See Chapters 1 and 2 for more on the etymology of catastrophe.
[98] Quoted in Knut Ove Eliassen, 'Catastrophic Turns – From the Literary History of the Catastrophic', in Carsten Meiner and Kristin Veel (eds), *The Cultural Life of Catastrophes and Crises* (Berlin and Boston: de Gruyter, 2012), p. 40.

1984 Birmingham Theatre Festival – the same year as *Will's Way* was written and performed – Rudkin gave a talk on his playwriting process and its wider cultural ramifications, recorded in the film *Interrogations*. Rudkin, at the end of his talk, abruptly left the stage, without taking (or answering) any questions, in precisely the same way as Shakespeare does at the end of *Will's Way*.[99]

If the deformation of closure preserves the autonomy of the tragic subject, however, it is also crucially intended to shape the type of aesthetic response Rudkin intends for his drama. By calling for – but then refusing to answer – questions, Shakespeare returns the responsibility for interpretation to the individual subject, a process Rudkin has aligned with the rabbinic tradition.[100] Where questions answered by the author may serve to unify audience response, as if there were a singular 'authoritative' interpretation to be had, Shakespeare/Rudkin intend to individuate the subject, to force the spectator to consider the play and the questions it raises for him or herself, without recourse to forms of 'collective faith' – the 'apparatus' that may otherwise answer 'for' the subject and so prescribe his or her understanding. Rudkin wants to fragment audience response. The idea – once again – is to separate the subject from a homogeneous public, to sever him or her from forms of collectivity and awaken the 'unsuspected' exile within. Shakespeare even goes as far as to undermine the textual and interpretive authority over the plays his position as author should grant him – 'Now don't quote me on any of this. / I'm not sure that any of what I say can be found in the text' – and acknowledges that there can finally be no authoritative reading or interpretation of his work (12–3). By having Shakespeare deny his interpretive authority over the plays, Rudkin implicitly denies his interpretive authority over Shakespeare. It is finally left up to the individual to interpret the meaning of the play and 'Shakespeare'.

Conclusion

With his transformation into Poor Tom, Edgar provides a paradigmatic image of a self re-authoring subject, profoundly influencing the way Rudkin conceptualises the tragic protagonist and his understanding of his own authorial selfhood and process. This self re-authoring – and the

---

[99] David Rudkin, *Interrogations*, dir. Stephen Garrett (Central Independent Television Video, 1985).
[100] For more on Rudkin and Jewish history/culture, see Rabey, *Sacred Disobedience*, pp. 39–44.

exile it necessarily involves – is conceived by Rudkin as a response to the reified identities of post-Auschwitz culture – though for Rudkin reification also relates to contemporary identity politics and the dehumanising system of capitalist exchange, as it is totalised by a late capitalist social system. By subverting aesthetic closure, Rudkin instantiates a catastrophic aesthetic that, in the same vein as *King Lear*, retains the non-identity of subject and society. This violation of formal resolution plays a vital role in the way Rudkin understands aesthetic response: by subverting closure, Rudkin intends to fragment his audience, to individuate – or exile – the subject from collectivity and collective action.

Not unlike David Rudkin, Howard Barker has described himself as an 'exile *par excellence*' and fundamentally 'incomprehensible' to those around him, with his plays representing 'a challenge to the whole principle of enlightenment' and the ideology of 'liberal humanism'.[101] This position of non-identity, as discussed in the next chapter, is for Barker profoundly bound up with questions of ethics and morality, the idea of the 'good life'.

---

[101] Howard Barker/Eduardo Houth, *A Style and Its Origins* (London: Oberon Books, 2007), p. 25.

Chapter 6

'WHAT IS THIS GOOD?':
The Ethics and Aesthetics of the 'Good Life' in Howard Barker's *Seven Lears*

'[T]he Theatre of Catastrophe is more painful than tragedy, since tragedy consoles with restoration, the reassertion of existing moral values'
Howard Barker[1]

'[The] belief that the norms of the good are directly anchored and guaranteed in the life of an existing community, can no longer be assumed'
Theodor Adorno[2]

Introduction

Howard Barker is a playwright whose drama interrogates the moral and ethical *aporias* of a period of history devastated by unparalleled catastrophes and mass violence, with Lara Kipp observing that his plays contend with the 'European memory of the Holocaust' and 'systematic dehumanisation and humiliation'.[3] Barker understands Auschwitz as 'the symbol of [. . .] historical rupture', which requires a profound questioning of liberal humanist, Enlightenment ideals of progress and culture.[4] To confront that 'rupture', Barker turns to *King Lear*.

---

[1] Howard Barker, *Arguments for a Theatre*, 3rd edn (Manchester and New York: Manchester University Press, 1997), p. 70. All subsequent references to this title are to the third edition unless otherwise noted.
[2] Theodor Adorno, *Problems of Moral Philosophy*, ed. Thomas Schröder, trans. Rodney Livingstone (Cambridge: Polity, 2001), p. 12.
[3] Lara Kipp, 'Between Excess and Subtraction: Scenographic Violence in Howard Barker's *Found in the Ground*', *Sillages Critiques*, <https://journals.openedition.org/sillagescritiques/4830?lang=en> (accessed 13 November 2019).
[4] Elisabeth Angel-Perez, 'Facing Defacement: Barker and Levinas', in Karoline Gritzner and David Ian Rabey (eds), *Theatre of Catastrophe: New Essays on Howard Barker* (London: Oberon Books, 2006), p. 136.

This chapter will analyse the Barker play *Seven Lears*.[5] The play was originally staged at the Leicester Haymarket Theatre in 1989 and was among the first plays produced by The Wrestling School, a company solely dedicated to staging Barker plays, with Kenny Ireland taking the role of director.[6] The play is a prodigiously imaginative 'prequel' to *King Lear* that (ostensibly) portrays the 'Seven Ages' of Lear in a series of *tableaux*-like scenes, which depict Lear as he progresses from boyhood to old age – some time before the action of *King Lear* begins. The play also presents the famously 'missing' wife/mother from *King Lear*, whom Barker gives the name Clarissa.[7] Over the action of the play and its series of scenes – entitled First Lear, Second Lear and so on, with an 'Interlude' between Fourth and Fifth Lears that alludes to the 'interlude!' (V.iii.90) of *King Lear* – Clarissa tries to make Lear 'See better' (I.i.159) and to make him fit 'the hand of intelligence into the glove of government' (4.26). Lear, however, engages in a series of disastrous misadventures that imperil 'the tender of a wholesome weal' (I.iv.201). Sixth Lear ends with the murder of Clarissa – in which the whole Lear family participates – while Seventh Lear ends with the total destruction of the commons, represented in the play by a Chorus, which is finally hanged.

Through his appropriation of *King Lear*, Barker is primarily concerned with the question of morality and ethics – the possibility of the 'good life' (*Seven Lears* is subtitled *The Pursuit of the Good*). Barker appropriates *King Lear* to enact a radical interrogation of conventional philosophical and ethical understandings of the good life and the idea, which has its roots in antiquity, of the 'common good' – the notion that the common good of society takes priority over the individual and should ethically orientate his or her actions. The revised understanding of morality and ethics Barker develops through his appropriation of *King Lear* insists that the good life rests, not as thinkers from Aristotle to Kant would have it, in conformity with the common good of life in the

---

[5] Howard Barker, *Seven Lears and Golgo* (London: Calder, 1990). All references to *Seven Lears* are from the John Calder edition, except where otherwise indicated. I refer to the text using scene and page numbers. Some of the text is in bold, which usually indicates where a character suddenly realises something new or original, a forcefully articulated idea, or anger. I have retained the bold of the original text because it is an important part of the way the text generates characterisation and meaning.

[6] See Andy Smith, '"I am not what I was": Adaptation and Transformation in the Theatre of Catastrophe and the Wrestling School', in Gritzner and Rabey, *Theatre of Catastrophe*, pp. 40–2.

[7] While Lear mentions his father in the play, his mother is – ironically – notable for her absence.

community, but in autonomy, in a state of non-identical deviance from that community and its ostensible 'good'. This is a conception of the good life that should be situated against the catastrophe of Auschwitz. John K. Roth reminds us that, while the Holocaust and inherited ideas of the common good of society may seem entirely antithetical, 'Nazi Germany did not lack a vision of the common good':

> To the contrary, its conception of the common good did much to unleash the Holocaust, for Nazi ideology held with a vengeance that the common good [. . .] entailed a world where Jews and other allegedly inferior people would not exist.[8]

Adorno similarly confronts the ethical and moral dilemmas posed by the camps. Adorno is not always consistent in his usage, but he does draw a distinction between 'ethics' and 'morality'.[9] This division broadly inheres to the Hegelian distinction between ethical life (*Sittlichkeit*) – the 'customs' (*Sitten*) and rules that make up the life, the ethos, of the community – and moral will (*Moralität*) – which connotes the moral self-reflexivity of the individual subject. Where ethics is made up of the customary 'rules' of the community, which interpret actions and people based on prescribed standards, such as 'right' or 'wrong', morality denotes autonomous moral reflection, the ability to consider and critique the ethical norms and values that obtain in the life of the community. The split between morality and ethics – between individual moral agency and a collective ethos – is the split between the subject and society as a whole. This is the 'central problem of moral philosophy'.[10]

The problem with post-Auschwitz culture is that it is so ethically integrated that the subject has been robbed of the capacity self-reflexively to motivate and direct practical and moral orientation about the ends of society as a whole. The particular (subject, morality) has been completely drowned by the universal (society, ethics). This process can, in its most dangerous form, be seen to have created the conditions under which Auschwitz was made possible. Adorno contends that the Holocaust typifies the way in which individual subjects failed morally to interrogate the prevailing ethos of society – which in the case of Nazi Germany meant the total destruction of so-called inferior races for the

---

[8] John K. Roth, *Ethics During and After the Holocaust: In the Shadow of Birkenau* (Basingstoke: Palgrave Macmillan, 2005), p. 174.
[9] See also Judith Butler, *Giving an Account of Oneself* (New York: Fordham University Press, 2005), pp. 3–9.
[10] Adorno, *Problems of Moral Philosophy*, p. 18.

'good' of the Aryan community. Auschwitz represents a totalised system in which subjects were completely incapacitated; but it also reveals the morally complacent and compliant response from subjects who failed to reflect on the 'ethical' ends of the community. If the atrocities of the Nazi concentration camps require a newly configured understanding of ethics and morality, it is the imperative of abandoning communitive appeals to ethical life and resuscitating a morally diminished subject otherwise undergoing 'the last surrender of his will' (*King Lear*, I.i.306). There is an 'element of compulsion' to be found in customary ethical life, states Adorno: 'it is that violence and evil which brings these customs [*Sitten*] into conflict with morality [*Moralität*]'.[11]

It is the ongoing 'quest' for moral reflection that constitutes the 'good life' in post-Auschwitz culture – and indeed holds out the hope that Auschwitz will not happen again. The word that Adorno uses to signify such critical self-reflection is *Mündigkeit*. He writes that 'the single genuine power standing against the principle of Auschwitz is *Mündigkeit*', which he defines as the 'power of reflection, of self-determination, of not co-operating'.[12] *Mündigkeit* means engaging in proper moral enquiry and critique, in a way that places inherited ethical norms and values into question without prescribing positive 'rules' that must be obeyed. It signifies a capacity to take a critical stand, but a stand which is also vigilantly conscious of its own fallibility (and revised by continuous self-criticism) as opposed to propagating compulsory 'laws'. Bound up with the operation of critique, morality involves:

> self-conscious non-cooperation with institutionalized forms of social unfreedom and with prevailing norms and values. Adorno maintains that practical resistance to the bad is possible even in the absence of any positive or 'normative' conception of the good.[13]

This notion of the non-co-operator, of the non-corporate subject, aligns the morally reflexive subject with a figure that Aristotle calls the *azux* – the 'apolitical' being who does not contribute to the common good of the community.[14] This non-corporate subject is, for Aristotle,

---

[11] Ibid. p. 17.
[12] Theodor Adorno, 'Education After Auschwitz', in Theodor Adorno, *Can One Live After Auschwitz?*, ed. Rolf Tiedemann, trans. Rodney Livingstone et al. (Stanford: Stanford University Press, 2003), p. 23.
[13] James Finlayson, 'Adorno on the Ethical and the Ineffable', *European Journal of Philosophy*, 10:1 (2002), p. 6.
[14] For more on the *azux*, see Jacques Rancière, *On the Shores of Politics*, trans. Liz Heron (London and New York: Verso, 1995), p. 27.

'like an isolated piece in a game of draughts'.[15] But for Adorno, the non-co-operator is the properly moral post-Auschwitz subject and even provides a new image of the good life, for 'the very possibility of the good life in the forms in which the community exists, which confront the subject in pre-existing form, has been radically eroded'.[16] Adorno is principally concerned with the categorical imperative of Kantian ethics, the notion that the subject '*act only in accordance with that maxim through which you can at the same time will that it become a universal law*'.[17] The problem with the categorical imperative is that it presupposes the actions of a rational subject can be transformed into a universally binding law. This means that the categorical imperative ultimately slides into the demand that the subject act in conformity with values that have already been established and that proceed from outside the self – most obviously from the state. This can lead to unthinking norm conformity, as was the case with Eichmann.[18] The new categorical imperative Adorno calls for 'after' Auschwitz – that it will never happen again – necessitates a more morally autonomous subject who interrogates the ethical values of society.[19]

Barker has described Adorno as his 'philosophical master' and self-consciously echoes Adorno when he observes 'the death of enlightenment in the ashes of Auschwitz' (he even once observed that *Minima Moralia* was for a long time his 'bedtime reading').[20] When critiquing the 'intellectual impotence' fostered by post-war absurdist theatre, a form

---

[15] Aristotle, *The Politics*, trans. T. A. Sinclair (London: Penguin, 1992), p. 60.
[16] Adorno, *Problems of Moral Philosophy*, p. 10.
[17] Immanuel Kant, *Groundwork of the Metaphysics of Morals*, trans. Mary Gregor (Cambridge: Cambridge University Press, 1997), p. 31.
[18] Eichmann invoked the Kantian idea of obeying universal laws in his trial (see Chapter 4).
[19] Horkheimer writes in 'The Jews and Europe' that Kant 'embraces the theory "that whoever is in possession of the supreme ruling and legislating power over a people, must be obeyed [. . .] to doubt it, in order to resist it in case of some failing, is itself punishable; that it is a categorical imperative: Obey authority that has power over you (in everything which does not contradict the inwardly moral)"'. But 'the scholar of Kant knows: the inwardly moral can never protest against an onerous task ordered by the respective authority', Max Horkheimer, 'The Jews and Europe', in Stephen Eric Bronner and Douglas Kellner (eds), *Critical Theory and Society: A Reader* (London: Routledge, 1989), p. 85.
[20] Howard Barker/Eduardo Houth, *A Style and Its Origins* (London: Oberon Books, 2007), p. 116; quoted in David Ian Rabey, *Howard Barker: Ecstasy and Death – An Expository Study of His Drama, Theory and Production, 1988–2008* (Basingstoke: Palgrave Macmillan, 2009), p. 71; quoted in Dan Rebellato, '"And I Will Reach Out My Hand With A Kind of Infinite Slowness And Say The Perfect Thing": The Utopian Theatre of Suspect Culture', *Contemporary Theatre Review*,

that he believes grows out of a frustrated or disappointed rationalist humanist ethos, Barker observes:

> The whole Enlightenment project has collapsed [...] Everything that happened since 1789 more or less led to the camps [...] [R]ationalism could not deal with [the Holocaust]. Only if you were an irrationalist would you be able to answer some of that – or not answer but respond to it.[21]

My analysis of *Seven Lears* will show that Barker, in producing his profoundly divergent conception of the good life, is influenced by Adorno and his questioning of ethical life 'after' Auschwitz.

The interpretation I develop will concentrate on the way Barker revisions Lear, whom Barker has called 'perhaps the greatest tragic figure of the modern world'.[22] Barker sets out to upend a humanist reading of *King Lear* that he takes to have become routine. He does so by subverting the conventional image of Lear as an initially hubristic but finally humbled and all-too-human figure, who – through his own sufferings – comes to recognise the suffering of others, reconciles with those he has wronged and even begins to provide a powerful critique of his failure to attend to the common good of his kingdom. Barker produces a Lear who fails to 'repeal and reconcile' (III.vi.110) with others, challenging the reconciliatory figure that has often been read out of *King Lear* by portraying a Lear far closer to the non-cooperative subject Aristotle and, after him, Adorno, imagines. This subversive appropriation of *King Lear* principally involves a newly configured understanding of the storm scenes, where Lear laments his failure to provide for the common good of society and prays for the impoverished 'naked wretches' (III.iv.28) on the heath. 'When Shakespeare made Lear rage did he not love him more than when, humiliated and broken by events, he brings him to the brink of an apology?'[23] For his epigraph to *Seven Lears*, Barker chooses a quote from Goneril about Lear: 'The best and soundest of his time hath been but rash', adumbrating that 'rashness' may (as Barker sees it) be truly the 'best' and 'soundest' aspect of Lear.[24]

This analysis will involve a close reading of *Seven Lears* and *King Lear*. It will also involve some performance analysis of the original 1989 staging, which forms part of the Exeter Digital Archives. The recording does not comprise the whole of the play and the film is of relatively poor

---

13:1 (2003), p. 63. Barker also states: 'Adorno began as a passion for me and ended as a puzzle' (ibid. p. 64).
[21] Howard Barker, personal interview, 26 August 2016.
[22] Barker, *Arguments for a Theatre*, p. 154.
[23] Ibid. p. 157.
[24] Barker, *Seven Lears*, p. viii.

quality, but the recording does shed some light on the way Nicholas Le Provost (who played Lear) embodied sudden, unpredictable 'turns' in both body and voice. I also draw on and analyse some of the critical writings Barker has produced in relation to his conception of the Theatre of Catastrophe. I will refer particularly to his *Arguments for a Theatre*, which was originally published in 1989 – the same year that *Seven Lears* was written and staged. By analysing a range of critical as well as theatrical works, I want to demonstrate the vital role *Seven Lears* – and indeed *King Lear* – plays in the development of Catastrophist form. I will also draw on an interview I conducted with Barker about his play.

Howard Barker and the Theatre of Catastrophe

Barker, who was born in South London in 1946 to a working-class family, began his playwriting career as an avowedly political writer, part (if always a distinctive part) of the wider wave of post-1968 British playwriting, which produced provocative socialist drama clearly influenced by the Marxist Epic theatre of Brecht and the post-war interest in social realism.[25] Over the 1970s, Barker produced a range of startling 'State of the Nation' plays, from his landmark *Claw* (1975) to *That Good Between Us* (1977) and *The Hang of the Gaol* (1978).[26] These darkly satirical plays portray the many 'squandered opportunities of the British Left' while also critiquing 'the demagogic and atavistic tendencies of the extreme Right'.[27]

Early in the 1980s, however, Barker began to question his political outlook – or at least the notion that theatre might provide a useful vehicle for political and ethical analysis and agitation. He remarked in 1981 on a personal and artistic 'sense of overcoming' and the 'stirrings of some change in form'.[28] This formal and thematic shift would be

---

[25] The first professional play Barker wrote was *One Afternoon on the 63rd Level of the North Face of the Pyramid of Cheops the Great* (1970) for BBC Radio. See David Ian Rabey, *Howard Barker: Politics and Desire – An Expository Study of His Drama and Poetry, 1969–87* (Basingstoke: Palgrave Macmillan, 2009), pp. 10–11.

[26] *That Good Between Us* finds an echo in *Seven Lears* and its *The Pursuit of the Good*. So too does *The Hang of the Gaol*, given the Chorus in *Seven Lears* is made up of a gaol of maltreated prisoners, which is finally hanged.

[27] Chris Megson, '"England brings you down at last": Politics and Passion in Barker's "State of England" Drama', in Gritzner and Rabey, *Theatre of Catastrophe*, p. 127.

[28] Mark Brown (ed.), *Howard Barker Interviews 1980–2010: Conversations in Catastrophe* (Bristol: Intellect Books, 2011), p. 35.

reflected in a new preoccupation with tragedy. Over the course of the 1980s, Barker became increasingly drawn to the dramatic idiom of tragedy. Writing in a 1986 article for *The Guardian*, 'Forty-Nine Asides for a Tragic Theatre', Barker sets out a series of aphorisms in which he (elliptically) advances his conception of a new tragic form and, crucially, its relevance to a new cultural and historical moment. Barker writes that 'Tragedy resists the trivialization of experience'; that tragedy 'restores pain to the individual'; and that 'Tragedy is not about reconciliation.'[29] Barker would increasingly identify his new tragic form as 'The Theatre of Catastrophe' over the mid- to late 1980s, with *The Bite of the Night* (written 1986, staged in 1988) and a series of other plays – *The Possibilities* and *The Last Supper* (1988) and *Seven Lears* and *Golgo* (1989) – all representative of the shift towards a Catastrophist form of tragedy.[30]

Of the playwrights under study, none has theorised the role that tragedy and the autonomous tragic subject might play in the totalised milieu of contemporary, post-Auschwitz society as powerfully as Barker, most obviously in his *Arguments for a Theatre* and his other critical works, *Death, the One and the Art of Theatre* (2004) and *A Style and Its Origins* (2007). Barker, in the same vein as Adorno before him, believes that progressive humanist ideals, derived from the Enlightenment, have produced 'a culture of moral totality'.[31] Most of all, Barker is suspicious of liberal humanist democracy in a period of late capitalist globalisation. This, as Barker understands it, represents a new consensus around which the political left and right have homogenised, a theme that Barker returns to time and again in his critical writings of the mid- to late 1980s.[32] Barker contends that late capitalist society is dominated by shared liberal values that leave little room for proper moral interrogation – a collectively approved ethos that dominates the social and ethical 'ecology' of global capitalist life. This ethical consensus involves a 'by-passing of moral will' and 'moral suicide'.[33]

---

[29] Barker, *Arguments for a Theatre*, pp. 17–19.

[30] Barker began to use the phrase 'catastrophe' and 'The Theatre of Catastrophe' regularly in the late 1980s, as reflected by his 1988 pieces 'The Consolations of Catastrophe' and 'Beauty and Terror in The Theatre of Catastrophe'. See Barker, *Arguments for a Theatre*, pp. 51–4 and pp. 55–60.

[31] Howard Barker, 'The Sunless Garden of the Unconsoled: Some Destinations Beyond Catastrophe', in David Ian Rabey and Sarah Goldingay (eds), *Howard Barker's Art of Theatre: Essays on His Plays, Poetry and Production Work* (Manchester: Manchester University Press, 2013), p. 208.

[32] See Barker, *Arguments for a Theatre*, p. 20, p. 49 and p. 53.

[33] Ibid. p. 169 and p. 168.

Barker understands the contemporary cultural moment as 'authoritarian and totalitarian in its propagation of false humanistic ideals'.[34] This totalising ethical consensus also comprises culture and theatre. Barker, once again evincing the influence of Adorno, makes the case that late capitalist society has produced a totalising world of administered 'mass' consumption – a Culture Industry, which propagates anodyne liberal humanist values for the public and its 'good'.[35] This even comprises politically oppositional art and theatre, with Barker identifying the prevailing orthodoxy of political art as 'liberal-humanist, left-leaning, socially progressive'.[36] Such theatre is – for Barker – guilty of promulgating already established ethical values that do little to inspire the moral freedom of the subject; it tends to emit 'normative calls to be "good subjects", "good citizens"'.[37] Barker writes: 'All mechanical art, all ideological art (the entertaining, the informative) intensifies the pain but simultaneously heightens the unarticulated desire for the restitution of moral speculation':[38]

> it is precisely in the hinge between the independence of moral will, claimed and performed [by the tragic protagonist] and the crushing imperatives of public order and its necessary pieties, that a drama of moral speculation discovers its resources, and fractures the repression of experience that characterizes a culture industry [...] bent on [...] seamless narratives.[39]

It is the totalisation of ethical and political life that underpins the turn to tragedy and the tragic subject in the Theatre of Catastrophe. 'Tragedy is the art form of resistance in an age like this', writes Barker in *Arguments for a Theatre*; 'it resists incorporation by its very *form*'.[40] Barker views tragedy and the tragic as the properly critical, morally negative aesthetic form in a time of ethical totality precisely because it stages the clash between the moral will of the tragic hero and the dominant ethical norms and values of the community. This move causes Liz Tomlin to critique Barker. By virtue of privileging the idea of tragic

---

[34] Karoline Gritzner, *Adorno and Modern Theatre: The Drama of the Damaged Self in Bond, Rudkin, Barker and Kane* (Basingstoke: Palgrave Macmillan, 2015), p. 114.
[35] Barker uses the phrase 'culture industry' on several occasions in *Arguments for a Theatre* (p. 99, p. 148), and also 'leisure industry' (p. 145, p. 146).
[36] Ibid. p. 79.
[37] Mary Karen Dahl, 'The Body in Extremis: Exercises in Self Creation and Citizenship', in Gritzner and Rabey, *Theatre of Catastrophe*, p. 95.
[38] Barker, *Arguments for a Theatre*, p. 69.
[39] Ibid. p. 99.
[40] Ibid. p. 142 and p. 145.

autonomy over the period of the 1980s, Barker prioritises 'the individual over and above the demands or needs of a social collective'.[41] This aligns Barker with the Thatcherite, capitalist ideology of the 'individual', whose self-actualisation takes priority over progressive humanist ideals of a personal and ethical obligation towards others or the collective improvement of society ('there is no society').[42] But for Barker, late capitalism is a totalising system that, far from freeing the individual from society, diminishes opportunities for subjectivity. This totalisation of the capitalist system only became more apparent in 1989 and the fall of the Berlin Wall – an event that Barker understood to challenge the precepts of previous, radically leftist theatre and that called for a newly conceived genre of tragic drama.

As already shown in Chapter 1, Hegel takes up an Aristotelian reading of tragic form when he contends that tragedy depicts the clash between subject and society, individual and collective. He also takes up the conflict between the tragic hero and the Chorus to elaborate his distinction between *Moralität* – the moral will of the individual subject – and *Sittlichkeit*, or the customs that make up the prevailing ethos of the polity. Hegel contends that in tragic drama the subject pursues a moral claim that is overly partial – overly individual – and imperils the universal system of rights embodied in and by the community, represented by the Chorus. Either the tragic hero realises the partiality of his or her claim – or dies. The individual must be absorbed by the universal: morality must be sublated by ethics.[43] Only where conventional (Aristotelian/Hegelian) tragedy usually punishes moral transgression – 'Aristotle and tragedy – nothing too great that it cannot be annexed in the interests of the social order', quips Barker – in the Theatre of Catastrophe the clash between morality and ethics is never resolved.[44] Quite the contrary: Barker insists on the continued non-identity of the tragic subject, who resists the ethos of the community and remains morally irreconcilable with others. The Catastrophist subject typifies the idea of *Mündigkeit* – or not co-operating. There is, as Barker provocatively contends, no

---

[41] Liz Tomlin, 'The Politics of Catastrophe: Confrontation or Confirmation in Howard Barker's Theatre', *Modern Drama*, 43.1 (2000), p. 67.

[42] Ibid.

[43] See also Robert R. Williams, *Tragedy, Recognition, and the Death of God: Studies in Hegel and Nietzsche* (Oxford: Oxford University Press, 2012), pp. 120–42.

[44] Howard Barker, *Death, The One and the Art of Theatre* (London: Routledge, 2005), p. 68.

'possibility of the Solution': for even 'an idea as seemingly innocuous as Harmony hides within it the shadow of the torture chamber'.[45]

This critique of ethics also comprises a critique of conventional narrative form ('seamless narratives'). '[N]arrative is itself the first element in the construction of moral meaning,' writes Barker: 'What occurs in the form of consecutive scenes, or in real time played on the stage, inevitably implies a moral perspective.'[46] Barker contends that narrative, by portraying consecutive scenes that end with resolution, conveys simplistic 'meanings' for the audience – or 'the moral of the story'. This underpins the fractured, non-narrative aesthetic that Barker adopts as part of the Theatre of Catastrophe. Barker tends to present, in place of any simple overarching story, a series of constellatory scenes – or individuated 'minima moralia' that speculate on various themes and ideas, often of an ethical and/or moral quality, but without arriving at any obvious overarching conclusion (or as he also calls it when writing of the perils of 'Harmony', 'the Solution'). With the totalisation of ethical life in late capitalist society, Barker turns to the fragmentary, non-narrative style of late modernist aesthetics to produce a more open-ended form of moral speculation.

The way in which Barker conceptualises moral autonomy owes an obvious debt to Adorno. The word 'moral' appears on forty-six occasions in the most recent (2016) edition of *Arguments for a Theatre*, as does the word 'morality'.[47] The way Barker uses these terms shifts. On the one hand, 'moral' often signifies for Barker in the same way that ethics signifies for Adorno – as the constraining precepts of the commons. On the other hand, 'moral' and 'morality' can also signify a situation in which the suspension of obligatory ethical values invites autonomous moral reflection and action. 'I am a moralist, but not a puritan', states Barker: 'By moralist I mean one who is tough with morality, who exposes it to risk, even to oblivion.'[48] Elisabeth Angel-Perez writes that Barker is 'a moral activist who paradoxically discards all set morals'.[49] This abandonment of ethics, in the service of moral freedom, is something that the atrocity of 'Auschwitz has horrendously compelled us to realise and which is confirmed by the genocidal episodes of recent history'.[50]

---

[45] Barker, *Arguments for a Theatre*, p. 121.
[46] Ibid.
[47] Howard Barker, *Arguments for a Theatre*, 4th edn (London: Oberon Books, 2016).
[48] Barker, *Arguments for a Theatre*, p. 76.
[49] Angel-Perez, 'Facing Defacement', p. 137.
[50] Ibid.

Part of the challenge that Barker has mounted against collectivist ethics are his profoundly disorientating appropriations of plays (and other works) that have been integrated into the modern liberal humanist canon, which are typically reduced to a state of catastrophic aesthetic fragmentation. Such plays have been identified as promoting universally valid ethical values, which Barker sets out to subvert, opening the space for autonomous moral interrogation. These have included appropriations of Thomas Middleton (*Women Beware Women* – 1986), Thomas More (*Brutopia* – 1990), Gotthold Lessing (*Minna* – 1994) and, perhaps most notoriously, Anton Chekhov (*(Uncle) Vanya* – 1992).[51] The place that Shakespeare occupies in the Theatre of Catastrophe is, however, more fraught. Barker considers Shakespeare to be the figure that stands atop the modern liberal humanist canon and, at the same time, represents a powerful antecedent for his own Catastrophist aesthetic form.

The Theatre of Catastrophe and Shakespeare: The 'monstrous assault' as an 'act of reverence'

Barker is deeply ambivalent about Shakespeare. On the one hand, Shakespeare is the playwright Barker has returned to and appropriated most frequently – in his 1971 satirical radio play *Henry V in Two Parts*, in *Seven Lears* and in his landmark 2002 appropriation of *Hamlet*, *Gertrude – The Cry*. Barker has also identified Shakespeare as the only playwright who is a conscious influence on his writing, lamenting the 'tragedy' that Shakespeare is now a 'negligible influence on the tone of contemporary writing in Britain'.[52] On the other hand, Barker has dismissed outright the idea – routinely peddled by critics and dramatists alike – of a debt or an artistic resemblance to Shakespeare as 'sheer ignorance'. 'The critical class knows nothing about creativity', states Barker, and so is only able to make 'facile 'identification[s]'.[53]

Whenever critiquing Shakespeare, Barker seems torn between the disruptive potential that he acknowledges in the works of his early modern predecessor and the embodiment of canonical literary and ethical value that Shakespeare has come to represent. Barker states that 'Shakespeare was the last English writer who was not a moralist' and praises the catastrophic situations in which he unleashes his protagonists, stating that the distinctive feature of Shakespearean drama is a situation of

---

[51] For his thoughts on Chekhov, see Barker, *Arguments for a Theatre*, pp. 168–70.
[52] Ibid. p. 153.
[53] Brown, *Conversations in Catastrophe*, p. 166.

'crisis' – or catastrophe.[54] Barker is, however, also deeply suspicious of Shakespeare. While praising Shakespearean tragedy for its refusal to propagate prescribed ethical ideas – 'meaningless pain is the thing that drives Shakespeare into his highest ecstasies', writes Barker – he also contends that Shakespeare has come to embody the literary and theatrical canon, his plays turned into symbols of the presiding ethos of liberal humanist Western culture and its ideals about self and society.[55]

King Lear has been interpreted through various matrices in the post-war era. But for Barker, it is the Christian-humanist interpretive schema, which is derived from the storm scenes and the way Lear identifies with the poor, that has come to dominate conceptions of *King Lear* in the popular imaginary, even becoming the culturally dominant understanding of the play and its 'meaning'. Barker, in our interview, states that *King Lear* has been 'contaminated' with a culturally 'fixed Christian, humanist view' and 'absurd' liberal platitudes.[56]

Barker questions the prevailing humanist conception of *King Lear*. He sees *King Lear* as an irruptive play that violates both aesthetic closure and conventional ethical 'meanings'. This aspect of the play is typified by the violent, catastrophic deaths of Lear and Cordelia. Barker observes that it would be 'whimsical' to try and make the case that 'the humiliation and death of Cordelia was a sacrifice to the eventual civilizing of King Lear'.[57] It is, however, precisely the 'civilizing' of Lear that has come to dominate common understandings of the play. *King Lear* has been turned from a 'savage play' into a '*placid* [...] story'.[58] This shift from 'play' to 'story' is telling: Barker makes the case that *King Lear* has been transformed from a challenging play into a placid and ethically recognisable story, a *Bildung* narrative which depicts the enlightenment of Lear, from a wildly tyrannical despot to a compassionate humanitarian.

Barker, in his appropriation of *King Lear*, is less concerned to challenge the play 'itself' than to question the social and political uses it has been conscripted to serve: 'The depth of social and political investment in classic texts, ironically enhanced by apparently daring modernizations can only be properly shifted by an equivalent bravery made by a new

---

[54] Quoted in Vanasay Khamphommala: '"Watch Out for Two-handed Swords': Double-Edged Poetics in Howard Barker's *Henry V in Two Parts* (1971)', *Shakespeare Survey: Volume 63*, ed. Peter Holland, (Cambridge: Cambridge University Press, 2010), p. 169; Brown, *Conversations in Catastrophe*, p. 166.
[55] Brown, *Conversations in Catastrophe*, p. 88.
[56] Barker, personal interview, 26 August 2016.
[57] Barker, 'The Sunless Garden of the Unconsoled', p. 209.
[58] Barker, *Arguments for a Theatre*, p. 155.

interrogation.'⁵⁹ He writes that to 'deface a monument, to smear a public property, is an act of reverence more profound, because of the investment of will, than any common genuflection of the uncritical believer'.⁶⁰ The act of appropriation is – for Barker – an act of desecrating violence, a 'monstrous assault'; but it is also 'an act of reverence'.⁶¹ Barker undertakes a violent onslaught against *King Lear*, but, both 'more and less reverential' in his approach to the play, he does so in order to 'open up' its 'moral fissures', to show the play for the 'frail and naked exposition of feeling, tender and afraid, that it once was'.⁶² This is a critical point: the violation of *King Lear* is, at the same time, an act of fidelity – even recovery. Barker is appropriating (or reappropriating) a play which, despite being used to serve liberal humanist ideology, is genealogically Catastrophist in its transgression of ethics and aesthetics.⁶³

This is a reading which allows for a timely reconsideration of the place *Seven Lears* occupies in the Barker *oeuvre*, while also revealing the critical role played by *King Lear* and appropriation in the development of a Catastrophist aesthetic that challenges the standardisation of post-Auschwitz culture and subjectivity. The appropriations of Shakespeare that Barker has undertaken all take place at critical moments in his development as a playwright. His very early 1971 appropriation *Henry V in Two Parts* is a satirical radio play that critiques the 'war criminal' Henry from a socialist perspective, while Barker has identified the 2002 play *Gertrude – The Cry* as a formative moment in the development of the 'Art of Theatre', with its fascination for the sacred and death.⁶⁴ While it has drawn some attention from critics, however, *Seven Lears* has often been overlooked in Barker studies in favour of *Gertrude – The Cry*, which is usually taken to be the more 'significant' Shakespeare appropriation, a valuation endorsed by Barker himself, who describes *Gertrude – The Cry* as his 'greatest play'.⁶⁵ But while *Gertrude – The Cry* has usually been considered the key Shakespeare appropriation,

---

⁵⁹ Ibid. p. 157.
⁶⁰ Ibid. p. 153.
⁶¹ Ibid. p. 28.
⁶² Ibid. p. 154, p. 156 and p. 157.
⁶³ See also Elisabeth Angel-Perez and Vanasay Khamphommala, 'Les 7 *Lears* de Barker: pour une Généalogie de la Catastrophe', *Shakespeare en Devenir*, 1 (2007), <http://shakespeare.edel.univ-poitiers.fr/index.php?id=65> (accessed 8 November 2019).
⁶⁴ For the Art of Theatre and the sacred, see Peter Groves, 'Sacred Tragedy: An Exploration into the Spiritual Dimension of the Theatre of Howard Barker', PhD (Warwick University, 2014).
⁶⁵ Barker/Houth, *A Style and Its Origins*, p. 19.

Seven Lears represents a formative moment in Catastrophism and the way Barker conceptualises aesthetics and morality.

The most obvious intervention that Barker makes against the Christian-humanist interpretation of *King Lear* is his transformation of Lear himself, who fails to fit into a narrative of redemptive enlightenment. Barker purposefully sets up the prospect of a politically motivated feminist interrogation of *King Lear* (and Lear) in *Seven Lears* which is radically subverted, as his play revolves around Lear and his morally transgressive bid for autonomy.

Seven Lears

'I am not what I was': 'De-humanizing' *King Lear*

In the Programme Note for the original 1989 production of *Seven Lears*, Barker gives a short introductory statement on *King Lear* and its 'missing mother', which, though it appears in the 1990 John Calder edition, is missing from the 2005 Oberon *Barker: Plays Five* edition:

> *King Lear* is a family tragedy with a significant absence.
> The Mother is denied existence in *King Lear*.
> She is barely quoted even in the depths of rage or pity.
> She was therefore expunged from memory.
> This extinction can only be interpreted as repression.
> She was therefore the subject of an unjust hatred.
> This hatred was shared by Lear and all his daughters.
> This hatred, while unjust, may have been necessary.[66]

This short introduction is typical of Catastrophist form and its subversion of expectations. Everything about the Introduction to *Seven Lears* indicates a politically interrogatory feminist interpretation of *King Lear*: the idea that the play is 'a family tragedy'; that the 'absence' of the wife/mother – and the apparent failure to 'quote' her – is symptomatic of 'repression'; and that she was the victim of an 'unjust hatred'. It would seem Barker is intending to write the missing mother back 'in' to *King Lear* in order to interrogate the play and its privileging of male subjectivities, as in other feminist appropriations of Shakespeare and *King Lear*.

The final remarks in the introduction, however, subvert the idea of an ideologically feminist hermeneutics: for while the 'hatred' is deemed 'unjust', it 'may have been necessary'. The idea of a 'hatred' which is

---

[66] Barker, 'Introduction', in Barker, *Seven Lears*, p. vi.

unjustified but still 'necessary' complicates the idea of socially unjust familial and patriarchal 'repression'. Barker writes that his appropriation of *King Lear* is not undertaken with a prescribed identity politics in mind, or 'prompted by a spasm of feminist sensibility'.[67] Such a concept of political identity would be part of a socially progressive form of theatre that aims at achieving some form of public 'good'. Despite its professed prioritisation of the mother figure, *Seven Lears* concentrates on the character of Lear, for whom Barker has an 'unhealthy curiosity'– a reversal that has drawn criticism from some feminist critics.[68] Barker is drawn to the missing mother because the silence around her is a 'dark space' that betrays a profound moral transgression, a transgression that complicates normative understandings about the nature of 'goodness' and 'necessity'.

By writing a prequel and calling it *Seven Lears* – which recalls Jacques from *As You Like It* and his famous 'Seven Ages of Man' speech, though it may also echo the 'seven stars' (I.v.34) of the Fool in *King Lear* – Barker implies that his Lear-play will portray something akin to a *Bildungsroman*, a coming-of-age that represents the ethical and spiritual development of the hero. Barker, however, offers something far less predictable – and a far less predictable Lear. The play, far from providing the progression of conventional narrative form, is made up of a series of individuated scenes, from the First iteration of the Lear figure to the final Seventh iteration of Lear. These fragmentary *tableaux* all depict Lear as he violates his personal and political obligations for the good life of the kingdom, his subjects and – indeed – his family. The violations range from initiating a disastrous war without any obvious purpose in Third Lear – 'disaster was not the failure – but the purpose of the War!' (3.16–17); to inventing a flying machine that requires an immense and catastrophic diversion of resources, which are desperately required elsewhere, in Fourth Lear: 'For this a hundred children starved' (4.28); to attempting to drown the infant Cordelia in a barrel of gin, only to 'rescue' her from death at the final moment in Sixth Lear: 'Oh, was that a good thing, hey?' (6.46). From the inordinately sensitive 'child' Lear in First Lear to the ageing and senile Lear in Fifth, Sixth and Seventh Lears, the Seven Lears presented in the play might represent Lear as he 'progresses' from boyhood to old age, but that hardly covers the volatility Lear embodies.[69]

---

[67] Barker, *Arguments for a Theatre*, p. 154.
[68] Ibid. See in particular Susan Bennett, *Performing Nostalgia: Shifting Shakespeare and the Contemporary Past* (London: Routledge, 1996), pp. 50–1.
[69] In the original production of the play at the Leicester Haymarket in 1989, the

Barker is most concerned to contest the image of Lear derived from the storm scenes. These scenes famously depict a raving Lear who, deprived of the usual sophisticated accommodations that attend on his position, is reduced to the same state as the impoverished 'wretches' that make up his kingdom. Based on his discovery of his own common, suffering humanity and the empathy for the less fortunate that his pain ultimately engenders, Lear begins to regret his past 'blindness' and even begins to develop a more humane conception of the social and political community he rules over, for which he suddenly realises he has taken all 'too little care' (III.iv.33). These scenes, as I demonstrated previously, have been critical in various Christian, liberal humanist and also Marxist readings of *King Lear*. Once thrust out into the storm, Lear discovers that he is not 'everything' (IV.vi.104) and begins to understand that he has blindly abnegated his responsibility for the kingdom. This leads him to a new political vision of the basis of the common good of the community.

It is not necessarily wrong to read *King Lear* as a humanist play. But as David Lowenthal shows, such a reading of *King Lear* ultimately invokes a classically Aristotelian interpretation of the nature of the good life, in which Lear engages with the fundamental questions of 'good political order and life in a community and the principles and activities that make that life good'.[70] Lear sets out the foundational principles of the good life of the community – the way in which the *polis* may be (re)organised so that the political question of the good life, or of the good society, may be addressed and resolved. Even in politically radical readings of *King Lear* that underscore the apparent *Bildung* of Lear, critics are – as Lowenthal shows – recycling conceptions of the common good that stretch all the way back to classical antiquity.

Barker engages with the Aristotelian precepts that underpin the Christian-humanist interpretation of *King Lear* by turning the 'poor naked wretches' Lear imagines in the storm into a Chorus – a figure more familiar from classical Greek than Shakespearean tragedy. The Chorus – notably described in the stage directions as a '*Chorus of the poor*' (5.37) – appears in the form of a gaol of neglected and ill-treated prisoners, who continually intervene in the action of the play to remind Lear of his pressing ethical responsibilities and of the social injustice to

---

'child' Lear and the 'aged' Lear were both played by Nicholas Le Provost, without any attempt to alter his apparent age, undermining any sense of maturation/progression.

[70] David Lowenthal, *Shakespeare and the Good Life: Ethics and Politics in Dramatic Form* (Lanham, MD: Rowman & Littlefield, 1997), p. xi.

be found in the kingdom: '**Injustice yes / That is the word for it**' (2.7). This Choric 'voice' is, as Jens Peters also shows, the voice of the community and ethical consensus, which repeatedly harangues Lear for his various perceived failures and misunderstandings: '**For every child that dies we fly a kite / Lear / Are you not blind with kites?**' (5.36).[71]

The clash between Lear and the Chorus is established from the outset of the play – First Lear – in which Lear and his brothers originally 'discover' the gaol and its suffering prisoners. In the opening moments of the play, Lear and his brothers Arthur and Lud – both named, in the same vein as Lear himself, after mythic pre-modern English kings – stumble across a (Rudkin-like) '*Pit*' in which the 'enemies' of the kingdom are gaoled – '**The dead who aren't dead yet**' (1.1). Arthur and Lud complacently identify the prisoners as 'bad' – even abject, 'filthy' – confirming themselves as 'good' (and, indeed, 'clean'): 'We are clean children and our mother loves us' (1.1). But while Arthur and Lud make superficial distinctions (good/bad, clean/dirty, pure/smelly, light/dark) based on the ethical norms of the kingdom, Lear has a more reflexive response. Lear intuits that 'something bad is *happening*' (as opposed to merely contained) in the Pit and even echoes *Hamlet* in his conviction that the kingdom – for Hamlet famously nothing but a 'prison' (II.ii.246) – is founded on 'Something rotten' (1.1): 'Something is rotten in the state of Denmark' (I.iv.67). The allusion to *Hamlet* adumbrates a dawning socio-political consciousness on the part of Lear: the 'badness' of the prisoners becomes the 'badness' ('rottenness') of the socio-political system as a whole, manifest in its failure to inculcate 'goodness' in 'ordinary people' (1.2).

The discovery of the gaol in the opening moments of the play restages the equally revelatory discovery Lear makes of the destitute and wretched masses that go to make up his own kingdom – with its unequal distribution of wealth and power – in *King Lear*. The language that First Lear uses in his response to the gaol alludes to and re-envisions the language used in the storm scenes. The 'poor naked wretches' who 'abide' the 'pelting' of the storm are reimagined as the 'poor, wet things' (1.2) of the gaol. The prisoners have 'no sheets' (1.1) and so suffer the same 'looped and windowed raggedness' (III.iv.31) that Lear bewails, while the rattling '*keys*' (1.1) the princes use to open the gaol similarly revises the words of the Fool: 'Fortune, that arrant whore, / Ne'er turns the key to the poor' (II.ii.242–3). 'I never knew', reflects Lear on

---

[71] Jens Peters, 'Crowd or Chorus? Howard Barker's *mise-en-scène* and the Tradition of the Chorus in the European Theatre of the Twentieth Century', *Studies in Theatre and Performance*, 32:2 (2012), pp. 305–16.

discovering the gaol, 'the ground was so full of bodies' (1.2). Like his Shakespearean antecedent, First Lear comes to a realisation of the suffering of others – '**Lear is thinking of our pain tonight**' (4.25) – and the (ostensible) obligation to put an end to that suffering: 'I shan't be king, because I am not the eldest but . . . if I were king . . . for one thing . . . I'd stop this!' (1.2). The storm scenes are even recalled in the way that Lear 'unbutton[s]' (III.vi.107) in *Seven Lears* by '*taking off his shirt*' (1.2) and removes the 'lendings' that furnish otherwise 'Unaccommodated man' (III.vi.105–6) – though as his shirt is taken off to provide a '**Penalty spot**' (1.2) for the game of football Arthur and Lud insist on, the gesture represents less of a spontaneous identification with the 'poor' so much as it wittily parallels a speech on the 'proper approach' for the 'correct punishment' of 'bad actions' (1.2).

On the basis of his discovery of the gaol and his empathy with its seemingly unwarranted suffering – '**Whatever it did / Whatever it was / How could it justify this?**' (1.1) – Lear begins to formulate a philosophical response to the question of the way 'government' might be used to promote the 'good life' of the community. 'The function of all government must be –', Lear reflects, as he tries to talk to his unresponsive siblings, 'the definition of, and subsequent encouragement, of goodness, surely?' 'You would', Lear goes on:

> define goodness in such a way that ordinary people – who at the moment are so horribly attracted to bad things and immoral actions – would find it simple to appreciate and consequently act upon – (1.2)

In First Lear, Lear has the insight that 'government' should work to make people 'good' (or, at the very least, 'better') so that the type of punishment meted out in the gaol would no longer be 'necessary' (1.2): 'No criticism of our father, but I wonder is it necessary that –' (1.2). It is – as far as Barker perceives it – the same role that modern humanist theatre has allocated itself, which, as Barker puts it in *Arguments for a Theatre*, is driven by the ostensibly selfless desire to 'make people better' – something that Barker sees as being offensively paternalistic.[72] Lear begins *Seven Lears* as a rationalistic and 'enlightened' – 'They have no light . . .!' (1.1) – liberal-humanist reformer: his belief that the state might be used to 'improve' people articulates a vision of the common good in which a simple and shared understanding of morality – of 'goodness' – prevails in the ethical life of the community.

The problem with the humanistic plan that Lear begins to formulate is that, by 'defining goodness' in a 'simple' way that 'ordinary people'

---

[72] Barker, *Arguments for a Theatre*, p. 72.

can 'understand' and 'consequently act upon', the autonomous practice of moral reflection on the part of the very same subjects putatively made 'good' is necessarily inhibited. This, as Adorno writes in *Negative Dialectics*, is the 'supreme *injuria* of the law-making subject': the universalisation of ethical norms that, far from providing subjective autonomy, come to dominate the subject as a form of heteronomy, so that subjects are unable to self-reflexively motivate moral reflection and action.[73] Without the struggle – the 'pursuit' – of goodness, there would be nothing to motivate the will, as the subject simply comes to conform to ethical dictates that proceed from the social totality. The way in which Lear formulates 'goodness' – in other words – denies and diminishes the subject: the rational programme of ethical enlightenment that Lear proposes in First Lear partakes of the dialectic of enlightenment, becoming a form of domination that incapacitates the subject. It is, as I show above, such a situation that Adorno sees as being so acutely dangerous 'after' Auschwitz: as Lear devises it, 'goodness' would simply produce unthinking norm-conformity and a homogenised subject.

Lear, however, quickly abandons his burgeoning humanist ideals. In a flash of *'inspiration'* – typical of his mercurial changeability – Lear ditches his plan to find a way of instituting a shared vision of the good life of the community, coming to an understanding of the good that requires the autonomy of the subject, as opposed to diminishing it. He declares:

> (*He stops. He is inspired.*) No! No! That's wrong! The opposite is the case! That's it! You make goodness difficult, if anything. You make it apparently impossible to achieve. It then becomes compelling, it becomes a victory, rather as acts of badness seem a triumph now! (1.2)

Lear refuses any communal understanding of the good life that would allow 'ordinary people' simply to comprehend and obey prescribed rules. By making goodness not 'simple' but virtually 'impossible to achieve', Lear prioritises the moral autonomy and agency of the subject. Lear intertextually recalls the language of some of the Barker plays that precede *Seven Lears*: *Victory* (1983) and *The Castle: A Triumph* (1985). The 'victory' and 'triumph' of the subject in *Seven Lears* involves nothing less than resisting the unifying forces of ethics in pursuit of autonomous morality. Lear instantly forsakes his **'civic sense'** (4.31) and denies **'responsibility for all'** (3.23). He identifies the good with the

---

[73] Theodor Adorno, *Negative Dialectics*, trans. E. B. Ashton (London and New York: Continuum, 2007), p. 250.

moral empowerment – the 'substantiation' (3.24) – of the subject, even where that imperils the well-being of the commons.

This irreconcilable contradiction between Lear and the Chorus, between morality and ethics, complicates received ideas around the nature of good and evil and, indeed, the nature of the human animal itself: *Seven Lears* is a play that challenges the very idea of human commonality.

Good, Evil and the Human in *Seven Lears*

Lear is not slow to recognise that his 'pursuit' of goodness and the good is ethically ambiguous – to say the least. 'The nature of beauty, as of goodness, rests in its power to substantiate the self,' reflects Lear in Third Lear, 'Which is not goodness at all, is it?' (3.23–4). By prioritising the subject over and above the common good of life in the community as a whole, Lear allows the kingdom to crumble, and partakes in acts that range from attempted infanticide to various war crimes: 'Burn the villages!' and 'all the infants, massacre!' (3.13). **'I think I am evil!'**, howls Lear in Third Lear: 'Evil because . . . / Evil accommodates every idea' (3.23).

The way Barker appropriates the word 'accommodates' is typical of the way he transforms *King Lear*. Lear uses the word in his identification with the 'unaccommodated' poor, damning the accommodations – the 'Robes and furred gowns' (IV.vi.161) – which obfuscate the identity of a king with a beggar and which forestall a conception of the common needs and interests that all of suffering humanity shares. But turning 'the word itself against the word' (*Richard II*, V.iii.120), Barker uses the word 'accommodation' to adumbrate the non-coincidence between Lear and the good life of the *polis*, as Lear accommodates 'every idea' no matter its 'consequences' (4.28) for others. 'Think of the people, the people will deduce –': 'I decline, I decline, and all deductions, pox!' (2.10).

Lear recognises that his understanding of the good is paradoxically close to the conventional understanding of 'evil': if the good life reckons the common interest, evil – as the opposite of the good – conventionally means abrogating the common good, or stressing the priority of the subject over and above the needs of the commons. The distinction between good and evil becomes hard to disentangle – as apparent in First Lear, when Lear states that treating the good as a 'triumph' of the will makes acts of goodness akin to 'acts of badness' (1.2). Lear collapses the usual ethical distinction between good and evil, where the 'evil' of a subject free of the obligations of the *polis* becomes – paradoxically – a form of 'good'. This fraying of the boundaries between good and evil is something that also troubles Aristotle in his definition of life 'outside' the communal authority of the *polis*, which would require a subject 'either too bad or too good, either subhuman or superhuman'.[74] The *azux* – the non-co-operator – cannot for Aristotle be said to be entirely 'human'. If humanity is, as Aristotle famously contends, the political 'animal', the non-co-operator – by virtue of not partaking in the human community of the *polis* – wants some basic quality of the human condition.[75]

These questions about the nature of the human pertain to *Seven Lears*. Lear not only denies inclusive notions of the common good, but even the whole notion of human(e) commonality itself, which should form the basis of the good life of the *polis*. In Fourth Lear, Barker once again rewrites the action of the storm and its humanist vision of communal ethics. This time, however, Lear comes face to face with a Poor Tom-esque beggar, whom Lear completely repudiates. 'I do think it's funny, that you and I have nothing in common,' Lear tells the beggar, 'Less even than a cow and a crow. Or a worm and a horse. Less than them, even' (4.26). This catalogue of non-human animal life, which recalls *King Lear*, as Lear cradles the corpse of Cordelia – 'Why should a dog, a rat, a horse have life / And thou no breath at all?' (V.iii.305–6) – is produced to deny that Lear and the beggar even belong to the same underlying kind, the same species. The beggar responds by paraphrasing the Renaissance essayist Michel de Montaigne ('Kings and philosophers shit: and so do ladies') and insists that both he and Lear 'shit' and 'piss' – though Lear denies the supposed 'obviousness' of a shared mortality and its related elimination of the inhuman and the 'uncommon' (3.14).[76] 'Perhaps', Lear plaintively tells the beggar, 'you are immortal?' (4.27).

Where in Shakespeare Lear identifies with Poor Tom – 'thou art the thing itself. Unaccommodated man' (III.vi.104–5) – in *Seven Lears* Lear disclaims any sense of basic human commonality and, with it, any notion of the common good, of shaking the 'superflux' to the less fortunate. Lear may arbitrarily promote the beggar to the aristocratic rank of Gloucester, but it is not with the selfless intention of making sure 'each man has enough' (IV.i.74): Lear – tellingly – ignores the mute beggar the newly risen Gloucester tramps with (who, in his mutilated and dependent state, ironically recalls the blinded Gloucester from *King Lear*) and tells him that 'This is a journey you must make alone' (4.27) – a haunting echo of Kent: 'I have a journey, sir, shortly to go' (V.iii.320). The

---

[74] Aristotle, *The Politics*, p. 59.
[75] Ibid. p. 60.
[76] Michel de Montaigne, *The Complete Essays*, trans. M. A. Screech (London: Penguin, 2003), p. 1231.

scene reverses the action of *King Lear*: by denying any 'shared' (4.27) identity with the beggar, Lear disallows any notion of a common ethos or an inclusive understanding of the good life – and even questions the hidden motivation for his supposed acts of 'charity', which in a distinctly Nietzschean reversal is a form of '*cruel*[*ty*]' (4.27). 'I can't stick this!', the beggar wails when faced with the unrelenting 'generosity' of Lear, who keeps providing him with more and more money. 'What is this?', asks the beggar, 'Torture?' (4.27). Lear quite literally 'enforce[s]' his 'charity' (II.ii.191); it is an image of 'distribution' that inverts humanist and Marxist interpretations of *King Lear*.

While he denies ideas about the commonality of the human, in his radical pursuit of the 'good' Lear is nevertheless admired and abetted by others. These include the Bishop, who provides Lear with some of his anti-ethical (anti-*Bildung*) 'education' (1.2) and insight, and Prudentia, the mother of Clarissa, who has a sexual relationship with Lear that pre-dates his marriage to her daughter. Both tend to facilitate Lear, while other characters – most notably Horbling, Kent and, most powerfully, Clarissa – echo the Chorus.[77] These figures all variously castigate Lear for failing to govern – 'Come out and govern the world!' (5.36) – and strive to 'correct' Lear of his unruly waywardness and his ethically baffling contrariness: 'Why don't you give [the people] bread? I don't understand it. There is bread enough' (5.34). The notion of the common good is, however, frequently shown to be problematic – most obviously when the 'good' characters engage in, or directly and/or indirectly support, acts of bloody murder designed to promote and enable the good life. Ostensibly meritorious ideas about the so-called common good of society are often used to sanction the destruction of individual subjects, while also sublimating deeply personal motivations.

Speaking 'for' the Commons

Before he disappears inexplicably from the play, the Fool of Shakespeare criticises Lear for his chaotic misrule: 'Thou shouldst not have been old till thou hadst been wise' (I.v.41–2). He even provides a wider social critique in his riddling (Folio-only) 'prophecy' (III.ii.80) of Act Three, Scene Two: 'Then shall the realm of Albion / Come to great confusion' (III.ii.91–2). Not unlike the Fool in *King Lear*, the Fool in *Seven Lears*

---

[77] Until the penultimate Sixth Lear – in which Clarissa discovers the gaol and asks Lear to 'Free them' (6.47) – only Lear and the Bishop interact with the Chorus, sharpening the sense of a clash between particular and universal, subject and society.

often admonishes Lear for his apparent failures. Barker, in a witty play on his conservatism, transforms the Fool into Horbling – a reforming government minister whom Lear arbitrarily 'promotes' (2.10) to the station of court Fool. Horbling, as part of his enlightened politics of liberal ethical values, has a series of Soviet-style 'five' and 'ten' year plans for the improvement of the kingdom, which go unheeded, leaving him to reflect that 'Humour is the grating of impertinence upon catastrophe' (3.13). But while he does make half-hearted attempts at humour – '**I so hate comedy it makes men cruel!**' (4.29) – more often than not Horbling tries to encourage others to assassinate Lear so that his plans for the 'improvement' of the kingdom might be finally enacted: 'Stab him now! I have the policies. I have the plans' (3.15). Horbling keeps his unused plans under his Foolscap – though by the end of the play these plans have disintegrated into *'tatters'*, resembling the way in which the map of the kingdom is often torn apart in productions of *King Lear*: '*He drags off his cap and takes out the now decaying papers*' (6.46). Obsessed with instituting his plans, Horbling calls for the murder of Lear, all in the name of the common good: 'There he sits! Eliminate the bloody oppressor of widows and orphans!' (5.34). The idea that such murder might 'perchance do good' (V.iii.199) is deeply problematic: it involves the destruction of the individual subject in the name of society as a whole. Through the figure of Horbling, Barker critiques the potentially totalitarian nature of collectivist appeals to ethics by drawing parallels between an enlightened, liberal politics and Stalinism, indicating (not unlike Bond) that the fall of the Berlin Wall does not necessarily usher in a new, postmodern era of history (the end of history) after the horrors of modernity.

Where Horbling only calls for the assassination of Lear – never doing the 'required' deed himself – Kent and Clarissa both murder those who abet Lear: the Bishop and Prudentia. In the 'Interlude' between Fourth and Fifth Lears, Kent confronts and kills the Bishop, whom Kent accuses of 'legitimiz[ing]' (33) every thought that Lear pursues: 'They say you spoiled the king' (32). Kent rationalises his murderous intent by recycling conventional notions of the common good. By killing the Bishop, Kent aims to remove a wholly negative influence on Lear and so encourage his sovereign to act in conformity with the material and ethical well-being of his subjects as a whole: '**We must protect the weak against the cunning**' (33). The twisted 'logic' (33) of Kent is, however, mercilessly ridiculed by the Bishop, who pours scorn on the notion that Kent acts selflessly, all in the interests of the community. 'Who are you doing this for?', wonders the Bishop: 'Everybody? I do love that! You are smothering your personal dislike of violence in the interests of the community!' (32). The notion that Kent abrogates his own will in murdering the Bishop is impossible to countenance: by the end of the scene, in which the bloated corpse of the Bishop returns posthumously to harangue his murderer, Kent confesses to the Bishop that he would 'walk over the mouths of the world's poor to grab you by the –' (34) and admits that his bloodied victim is his 'superior in perception' (34). The notion of the common good is – for Kent – a pretext, a means by which he may enact his own usually smothered desires and satisfy his hatred.

In Fifth Lear, Barker restages the action of the Interlude, as Clarissa confronts and – ultimately – sanctions the murder of her mother, Prudentia. Once again, the murder is undertaken with the putative rationale of reversing the decline of the kingdom by 'removing' a negative influence on Lear: 'out there is all starvation and mismanagement and you encourage him!' (5.38). 'I so hate lies', remarks Clarissa, 'But, look, the poor!': 'I so hate subterfuge. But, look, the destitute!' (5.37). In the same vein as Kent, however, Clarissa struggles to disentangle her own personal motivations from her apparently disinterested desire to improve the lives of the poorest in the kingdom, confronting her mother with knowledge of the affair she has conducted with Lear: '**I think you lie in bed with my husband and –** / No! / No! / Do what you wish, I am not censorious' (5.38). Her outburst and sudden about-turn are indicative of the way a reified conception of the common good in *Seven Lears* sublimates deep-seated personal motivations – motivations which may ultimately have little to do with the well-being of the *polis*, or for which the good life acts as a pretext.

The gaol negates the divided motives driving Clarissa, in its most telling intrusion into the action:

Oh, good!
She is evil, if the word has meaning
Oh, good!
We do hate punishment but some it must be said
Deserve
Oh, good!
In such a case human dignity cries out for
One of those rare occasions when everybody must
Agree
Collectively we must respond. (5.39–40)

With its repeated cry of 'good', the designation of Prudentia as 'evil' and its allusion to 'human dignity', the gaol reinforces conventional ethical dictates on the notion of the good life – but does so in the name of murder. The repressive heteronomy of the Chorus is only too clearly indicated by its insistence that the goodness of the murder is something on which 'everybody must' (not can) agree and that the 'collective' requires (or once again, 'must' have) a common 'response', subsuming the particular (subject) under the universal (society). But while Clarissa may agree that the murder of Prudentia is an ethical necessity, she also subverts the notion of the same 'absolute morality' for which she kills. When she appears in the Interlude to remove a young Goneril from the lethal fight between Kent and the Bishop, Clarissa remarks that 'I never thought I would give thanks for murder, but I must not hide behind the fiction that all life is good. How simple that would be. How simple and intransigent. Such absolute moralities are frequently the refuge of misanthropy' (33). The murder of the Bishop ironically prompts Clarissa to abandon the (supposedly) 'absolute moralities' for which the murders of both the Bishop and Prudentia are conducted: the idea of the common good.

By virtue of her desire to '**correct**' (6.48) and 'improve' Lear, Clarissa (whom Barker describes as 'an intolerably, unbearably moralistic person') is an intertextual analogue for the famously truth-telling Cordelia.[78] In Second Lear, Clarissa recycles the language and action of the love-test, telling Lear that it would be wrong 'if I praised things merely to please you': 'So I will say – as best I can – only the truth' (2.11). Clarissa obviously echoes Cordelia in her conviction of the possibility of 'truth without contradiction' (3.25) – a possibility that, in *Seven Lears*, Lear disclaims – and of the ethical righteousness of truth over falsehood: 'She does not put on lipstick, Clarissa. Or any false thing' (6.46). But the name Clarissa is also an intertextual echo of the 1748 novel *Clarissa, or, The History of a Young Lady* – by Samuel Richardson.[79] The novel is typical of the type of conventional *Bildung* narrative of personal and ethical development that Barker believes *King Lear* has been reduced to, in which the hero or heroine achieves a form of ethical knowledge and self-identity (in the novel, Clarissa remains utterly virtuous, against all the odds of her situation).

Clarissa is counterpointed to Lear throughout the play: where Lear engages in a series of transgressive self re-authorisations – 'But that was another Lear' (3.15) – Clarissa insists on a principle of ethical self-identity: 'I like to be myself' (2.12); where Lear engages in rhetorical 'bollockry' (3.18), Clarissa speaks only the 'truth' and refuses 'gesture and false movements' (3.18); and where Lear ignores the needs of the kingdom – 'What, brothers, no clinic? No warm house? No hot dinners?' (4.26) – Clarissa insists on the need to pity '**the poor**' (5.38)

---

[78] Barker, personal interview, 26 August 2016.
[79] Samuel Richardson, *Clarissa, or, The History of a Young Lady* (London: Penguin, 1985).

and on the absolute necessity of following her 'conscience' (5.38) in reprimanding the waywardness of Lear: 'You should not do that because in governors extremes of emotion are not liked!' (2.9). It would not be stretching the point to say that Barker purposefully alludes to *Clarissa* in his appropriation of *King Lear* to instantiate a conflict between the narrative of ethical self-development that typifies the novel form and the far less predictable, non-narrative subjectivity that typifies his own morally speculative Catastrophist form.

The clash between *Clarissa* and *Lear* is perhaps most apparent in Third Lear, in which Lear undertakes an utterly disastrous war with a rival state before retreating under the protection of Clarissa and her Second Army (the way Cordelia leads the French troops into Britain to save Lear in *King Lear* is an obvious parallel). Clarissa upbraids Lear for his disastrous leadership – but Lear refuses the idea that there is an ethical 'lesson' to be taken from his apparent failure: 'It is not the circumstance, it is the exposure, it is not the subject but the experience which –' (3.16). Clarissa, however, repeatedly interrupts Lear to insist on the idea that the failure of the war offers an opportunity for ethical education and reformation:

> You must be sensible, and hear advice. You must regard the judgement of others as equal to your own. I think if this is to be a happy kingdom you must study good, which is not difficult, and do it. I will help you. I will criticise you, and I will say when you are childish or petulant, and you must try to overcome the flaws in what is otherwise, I am sure, a decent character! (3.17)

'You are often amusing, which is surely a sign of goodness!' (3.17), Clarissa concludes, in an incurably optimistic reading of the 'decent character' of Lear. Such 'advice' about the inculcation of 'goodness' and the good life – 'the happiness of the kingdom' – has its precedent in First Lear, in which Lear also ponders the possibility that goodness might be 'defined' and 'taught', so that those now 'horribly attracted' to acts of 'badness' would find goodness 'simple to appreciate and consequently act upon'. Yet as Adorno contends, 'To impute that one ever knows, without doubt and unproblematically, what the good is is itself, one might say, already the beginning of evil'.[80] It is in such a way that Clarissa might – in Adornian terms – be thought of as evil: she insists on universally binding ethical principles, which she overconfidently proclaims are 'not difficult', in a way that dominates and deprives the subject.

Clarissa persists in her desire to support Lear in overcoming his tragic

---

[80] Quoted in Andrew Bowie, *Adorno and the Ends of Philosophy* (Cambridge: Polity, 2013), p. 118.

'flaws', but Lear produces a response that Clarissa (and, indeed, Lear himself) is finally unable to provide an answer for:

> Clarissa: What was good in me, through seeing, is now more good. What was less good, there is less of.
> Lear: WHAT IS THIS GOOD? (3.17)

This is the most decisive moment in the play: the question '**WHAT IS THIS GOOD?**' typifies the foundational critique of ethics that Lear enables in *Seven Lears*. His transgressive actions are a catalyst for a properly moral enquiry into normative ethical mores and beliefs – into the 'first principles' of ethics – which may otherwise be precluded by prevailing hegemonic understandings of the good life that stretch from antiquity to the modern day.[81] Like various characters during the action of *King Lear*, Clarissa encourages Lear to try and improve both himself and his society; yet ultimately it is Clarissa who has a superficial understanding of morality, constrained as she is by received ethical norms which she fails at any time to question.

The case might be made that *Seven Lears* dramatises the 'slow moral decline of Lear', who fails in his responsibilities as ruler and comes to realise that Clarissa would have made the more capable – and more ethical – monarch: 'no, she is exemplary, and I should commit suicide': 'She should govern' (3.18).[82] But the ethical disintegration of Lear is the point: the play does not allow for a determinate ethical frame through which to condemn Lear for his morally transgressive actions, even if he lapses into self-doubt. It is also to overlook the finale of the play, in which the rest of the Lear family conspire in the murder, not of Lear, but of the ethically '*pristine*' (2.11) Clarissa, forestalling any sense of narrative or ethical closure.

The murder of Clarissa is driven principally by Cordelia. 'I have', Cordelia tells her mother, 'a deep and until today, an unstirred hatred for you' (6.48). The language that Cordelia uses alludes to the Introduction ('She was the subject of an unjust hatred / This hatred was shared by Lear and all of his daughters'). Clarissa is all too conscious of the apparent injustice of her assassination – 'Someone must do good. And of all people I've done least to –' (6.48) – but the vital word in the prologue is 'necessary', or the way in which the need is reasoned, to paraphrase *King Lear*. Where the murders of Prudentia and the Bishop

---

[81] Barker, *Arguments for a Theatre*, p. 54.
[82] Graham Saunders, '"Missing Mothers and Absent Fathers": Howard Barker's *Seven Lears* and Elaine Feinstein's *Lear's Daughters*', *Modern Drama*, 42:3 (1999), p. 404.

are understood to be 'necessary' to facilitate the common good of the commons, the murder of Clarissa – the personal motivation for which is stated quite openly – would seem to derive from a completely distinct sense of 'necessity': that of obviating absolutist appeals to ethics that are unfeasible and which serve to endanger the properly moral autonomy of the subject.

Even in the final Seventh Lear, Lear remains implacably resistant to the common good of the *polis*: in a reversal of the usual action of classical tragedy, it is the Chorus, as opposed to the transgressive tragic 'hero', that ends up dead: '**How could we be allowed to live?**' (7.49). With the figures of the Chorus dead about him, Lear is discovered – in the same vein as Ferdinand and Miranda at the end of *The Tempest* – playing a game of chess with Kent, in which both participants have been openly cheating. The image provides a profound inversion of the usual early modern understanding of chess as a symbol for astute statecraft.[83] There is no resolution – no synthesis – of the contradiction between individual and collective, morality and ethics at the end of *Seven Lears*. It is not for Lear to institute the common good and finally 'pluck the common bosom on his side' (V.iii.50).

Throughout his performance in 1989, Nicholas Le Provost, who played Lear, relied on constant shifts – constant 'turns' – in both voice and action: 'Time to unlock the gaol! Or maybe not!' (3.16). When Lear originally discovered the gaol in First Lear, Le Provost paced from left to right, his head often in his hands, while he contemplated the way in which government might be harnessed to make people 'good'. But when he is '*inspired*' to take another view – when his 'wits begin to turn' (III.ii.67) – Le Provost physicalised the shift with a violently sudden turn, as he threw his hands down and changed direction in an abrupt *volte-face*. This turn, which also saw Le Provost shift into a more antagonistic vocal range, subverted linear, narrative progress and the movement towards a 'conclusion' of the ethical ideas Lear was in the process of developing, creating both a physical and intellectual space for a more open-ended form of moral self-reflexivity.[84] It was a performance style that contrasted strongly with the Chorus, which both moved and

---

[83] See Bryan Loughrey and Neil Taylor, 'Ferdinand and Miranda at Chess', in Catherine Alexander (ed.), *The Cambridge Shakespeare Library, Volume II: Shakespeare Criticism* (Cambridge: Cambridge University Press, 2003), pp. 30–5.

[84] In our interview, Barker states that 'when I sense the appearance of a cliché, I'll do anything to evade it. I'll take a sharp turn away. Nothing that happens is really predictable.' He also describes his writing, and his non-linear 'development' as a playwright, in terms of 'sharp' catastrophic turns that deny more 'predictable' routes (Barker, personal interview, 26 August 2016).

spoke in a shared, rhythmic fashion. This gave the interventions and indictments of the Chorus a strong collective force; but at the same time, the presentation of the Chorus – who were all dressed in draped grey costumes, which obscured the features of the various actors involved – indicated a homogenised 'mass' where the individual was obscured. The production created a striking visual and aural disparity between Lear and the Chorus and contradictory conceptions of the moral basis of the 'good life'.

This contradiction between subject and society reflects a radically reconfigured understanding of the role of theatre (and tragedy) in an age of cultural and ethical totality – to free spectators into autonomous moral reflection, as opposed to prescribing shared ethical meanings. Barker writes that his theatre aims to 'return the responsibility for moral argument to the audience itself' – or perhaps more precisely, to the 'audience in its individual, atomized form'.[85] This most obviously relates to the suspension of closure in Catastrophist theatre. By refusing to align with the commons – by remaining morally non-cooperate, with his constant turns away from more predictable forms of thinking and action – Lear forestalls the final confirmation of shared ethical values for the common good. This transgressive violation of ethical values means that the audience becomes as fragmented as the play, forced morally to 'wrestle' with the 'meaning' of the play alone, without the crutch of normative collective values and ideas: 'in tragedy, the audience is disunited. It sits alone. It suffers alone. In the endless drizzle of false collectivity, it restores pain to the individual.'[86] Barker states in our interview that, with the catastrophic death of Cordelia in *King Lear*, 'something is released in the audience': 'an innate sense of chaos', something that he thinks 'theatre can liberate all the time' but which 'conscience-driven' theatre 'continually represses and tries to replace by enlightenment'.[87] This individuating 'liberation' from the 'dominant pattern of thought of our time' is the same affect Barker wants to catalyse in his *Seven Lears*, a shuddering distantiation from collective ethical ideas and values.[88]

Seven Lears is, without doubt, an ethically problematic play. Lear resists calls for the common good in his radical bid for moral autonomy and, as a result, the commons is finally destroyed. But for Barker as for Adorno, artworks should pose moral problems, not ethical solutions. *Seven Lears* instantiates a contradiction between moral autonomy and

---

[85] Barker, *Arguments for a Theatre*, p. 52 and p. 111.
[86] Ibid. p. 19.
[87] Barker, personal interview, 26 August 2016.
[88] Ibid.

ethical collectivity. It is a contradiction sorely absent during some of the worst catastrophes of the twentieth century.

Conclusion

This chapter has analysed the appropriation of *King Lear* in *Seven Lears* and shown that, through his appropriation of Shakespeare and his subversion of the conventional humanist image of a 'humbled' Lear, Barker produces a foundational critique of normative understandings of the ethics of the good life, which after the catastrophe of the Holocaust must be radically rethought. Barker views *King Lear* as at once a regressively humanist play and, at the same time, an important precursor to his own morally and aesthetically Catastrophist form. This serves to situate *King Lear* as a vital intertext in Catastrophism and the way Barker challenges the ethical totality of life in late (post-Auschwitz) capitalist culture.

Sarah Kane often cited Barker and his Catastrophist form as an influence on her own playwriting. In the next chapter I turn to Kane, who – like both Rudkin and Barker – creates spaces of non-identity through her appropriation of *King Lear*. These spaces are understood as transcendent of a totalised material reality, creating a metaphysical rift in society.

Chapter 7

'Thought you were dead': Dover Cliff, Death and 'Ephemeral Life' in Sarah Kane's *Blasted*

Introduction

After its debut at the Royal Court Upstairs in 1995, *Blasted* was met with notoriously histrionic reviews that condemned its portrayal of violence.[1] The play, which is set in a hotel room in Leeds, depicts the relationship between Ian – a terminally ill alcoholic, who writes salacious articles for the tabloid press – and Cate, his far younger former girlfriend, who suffers from intermittent fits.[2] The action is split into five scenes: in between Scenes One and Two, Ian rapes Cate, before Cate plaintively – and without warning – declares that there is 'a war on' (2.33) in the city. Shortly after that declaration, an anonymous Soldier makes his way into the hotel room, before the room is hit by a mortar blast and reduced to rubble. The Soldier goes on to rape and blind Ian in Scene Three, before he kills himself. Ian also tries to commit suicide in Scene Four, only for Cate to intervene. In Scene Five, Cate leaves the room, while Ian is seen in various states of physical and mental degradation. Ian finally buries himself under the floorboards of the room, with only his head visible, before 'dying'. Ian, however, suddenly returns to 'life', before Cate finally returns to offer him some sustenance.

---

[1] For an astute analysis of the rather prurient critical 'controversy' around *Blasted*, see Elaine Aston 'Reviewing the Fabric of *Blasted*', in Laurens de Vos and Graham Saunders (eds), *Sarah Kane: In Context* (Manchester: Manchester University Press, 2010), pp. 13–27. Jack Tinker of the *Daily Mail* condemned *Blasted* as 'This Disgusting Feast of Filth', quoted in Hillary Chute, 'Victim. Perpetrator. Bystander. Critical Distance in Sarah Kane's Theatre of Cruelty', in de Vos and Saunders, *Sarah Kane: In Context*, p. 163.

[2] Sarah Kane, *Blasted*, *Complete Plays* (London: Methuen, 2001). p. 2. All references to the play are to the Methuen edition. I give references to the scene and page numbers.

Some of the original reviewers of the play intuited a relationship between *Blasted* and *King Lear* – though often that relationship was alluded to with the sole intention of showing that Shakespeare uses violence for a dramatic purpose, taken to be missing in Kane.[3] This chapter will show that Kane, in the same vein as Bond, Rudkin and Barker, uses *King Lear* to dramatise and interrogate the crisis of the post-Auschwitz subject, who is trapped in a totalised system that destroys the possibility of autonomy. Kane does not tend to depict radically self-authoring figures in her plays, however.[4] Her drama testifies more readily to a 'fading of the subject', as Karoline Gritzner eloquently calls it, a 'fading' that is only intensified in the plays *Crave* (1998) and *4.48 Psychosis* (1999).[5] Kane dramatises a world where any hope there might be for transcendence – of a world 'beyond' – is hanging by a thread. Kane understands the crisis of the post-Auschwitz subject as a metaphysical crisis, as the waning of anything beyond the seemingly endless horizon of late capitalist modernity.

The appropriation of *King Lear* in *Blasted* may not be instantly obvious. Kane herself revealed that she only became aware of the kinship between the plays towards the end of the drafting process, slowly coming to the realisation that she was – in part – motivated by 'a subconscious drive' to 'rewrite' *King Lear*.[6] 'When I was writing *Blasted*', Kane revealed in a 1998 interview, 'there was some point at which I realized that there was a connection with *King Lear*.'[7] This intertextual 'connection' can be seen in the various palimpsestic traces of *King Lear* perceptible in *Blasted* – not least the depiction of Ian and his combined embodiment of the physical (Gloucester) and mental

---

[3] Charles Spencer recalls that he compared *Blasted* not to *King Lear*, but to *Titus Andronicus*, but concluded Kane 'could not write as well'. See his belated 2001 reconsideration in 'Admirably repulsive: Charles Spencer reviews *Blasted* at the Royal Court', <https://www.telegraph.co.uk/culture/4722664/Admirably-repulsive.html> (accessed 7 January 2020).

[4] The possible exception to the rule is Hippolytus in *Phaedra's Love* (1996), who self-consciously transgresses conventional social and moral norms in a suicidal bid for experiential 'authenticity'.

[5] Karoline Gritzner, 'The Fading of the Subject in Sarah Kane's Later Work', in Daniel Meyer-Dinkgräfe (ed.), *Consciousness, Theatre, Literature and the Arts* (Newcastle-upon-Tyne: Cambridge Scholars, 2006), p. 249.

[6] Sarah Kane, interview with Graham Saunders, quoted in Graham Saunders, '"Out Vile Jelly": Sarah Kane's *Blasted* & Shakespeare's *King Lear*', *New Theatre Quarterly*, 20:1 (2004), p. 76.

[7] Sarah Kane, interview with Dan Rebellato, 'Brief Encounter: An Interview with Sarah Kane', <http://www.danrebellato.co.uk/sarah-kane-interview/> (accessed 18 June 2020).

(Lear) blindness of *King Lear*; the putrefying 'stink' (1.8) caused by his terminal illness, which means he 'smells of mortality' (IV.vi.129); the operation he alludes to where his lung was removed – a 'rotting lump of pork' (1.11) – which literalises the proposed anatomisation (III.vi.73) of Regan; and his constant 'love-testing', where Cate refuses to 'heave' (I.i.91) her heart into her mouth and tell Ian she loves him simply because he (repeatedly and belligerently) asks her to (1.6). Even the title of *Blasted* can be interpreted as an allusion to *King Lear*. Kane chose '*Blasted*' because of the representation of drunkenness in the play; it was only after the event that she came to realise it also alludes to the 'blasted heath' depicted in the storm scenes of *King Lear*, the scenes that so preoccupy Bond and which have been radically challenged by Barker.[8]

These are only some of the points of contact between the plays that might be proposed by an intertextual reading. To trace the way in which her appropriation of Shakespeare enables Kane to interrogate post-Auschwitz subjectivity, however, I concentrate squarely on the penultimate and final scenes of *Blasted* – Scene Four and Scene Five.

I begin by analysing the way Kane appropriates the Dover 'cliff' scene from *King Lear* in Scene Four of *Blasted* to interrogate the prevailing immanence of totalised society, which by trapping the subject, seems to disallow any possibility of transcendence, of anything 'other' than the world 'as it is'. This interrogation involves the deconstruction of both metaphysical and material worldviews – propounded by Cate (metaphysical) and Ian (material) in the scene. Both are shown to be flawed and unable to challenge the dominance of the social totality. I go on to analyse Scene Five of the play and the puzzling moment where Ian 'dies', only to simply go on 'living'. This has been taken, by several Kane critics, to dramatise his continued entrapment within a prevailing immanence; however, I contend that by deconstructing both conventional materialist and metaphysical understandings of the world in Scene Four, Kane

---

[8] See Saunders, '"Out Vile Jelly"', p. 76. Of course, the heath is, as shown in Chapter 5, an editorial intervention: the 'blasted heath' Kane refers to in her interview with Saunders is a direct quote from *Macbeth*: 'Say from whence / You owe this strange intelligence, or why / Upon this *blasted heath* you stop our way / With such prophetic greeting?' (I.iii.73-76; emphasis added). *King Lear* undeniably provides the principal Shakespearean intertext for *Blasted*, but the play also contains not insignificant allusions to *Macbeth*. *Macbeth* is also echoed in the way Ian talks about his ex-wife, Stella, whom Ian calls a 'witch' (1.19) due to her starting a relationship with another woman. Stella has – as far as Ian is concerned – become part of a 'coven' (1.18). It is a homophobic designation that recalls *Macbeth* and its own 'coven' of witches, who similarly represent a threatening and shadowy all-female presence on the periphery of the play.

forms a space for transcendence in Scene Five. Both alive and dead, Ian is at once bound 'in' the material world and yet also thrown metaphysically 'beyond' it. He is also both 'in' and catastrophically 'out' of tragic closure. This paradoxical 'in-out' subjective condition appropriates the liminal, even ecstatic, states 'between' life and death that Shakespeare dramatises time and again in the action of *King Lear*.

To read the final scene of *Blasted*, I utilise the notion of 'ephemeral life', proposed by Adorno.[9] Ephemeral life names a form of 'immanent transcendence' – or a fleeting moment of transcendence that happens from within a totalised immanence. It reflects the way in which Adorno, in a move similar to Kane, challenges the usual philosophical distinction between the material and the metaphysical, which in the wake of Auschwitz must be re-evaluated.

Adorno contends in *Negative Dialectics* and its famous 'Meditations on Metaphysics' that the irredeemable horror of the camps invalidates the basic premise of metaphysical thought: the idea that there is a world 'beyond' material reality, which imparts meaning to immanence and where the 'true' and 'right' life is possible.[10] This can only be an insult to the suffering of the victims of the Holocaust. Even more ominously, however, the camp can also be said to realise the immutable and unchanging realm beyond the normal world posited by traditional metaphysics. Adorno argues the camps instituted a closed world apparently outside the unstable exigencies of fallen historical time, a world that transformed (material) particularity to (metaphysical) universality. This has become the organising principle of modern society as a whole, which by violently colonising every form of otherness, admits of nothing beyond its own borders and begins to take on the guise of a metaphysical absolute.[11]

Adorno makes the case that contemporary philosophy – most particularly the 'logical' positivism of his contemporary Ludwig Wittgenstein – has set out to completely overturn metaphysics.[12] His analysis of

---

[9] Theodor Adorno, *Negative Dialectics*, trans. E. B. Ashton (London and New York: Continuum, 2007), p. 156; see also Alistair Morgan, 'Mere Life, Damaged Life and Ephemeral Life: Adorno and the Concept of Life', *Angelaki: Journal of the Theoretical Humanities*, 19:1 (2014), pp. 113–27. I will cite and analyse the work of Morgan again below.

[10] Adorno, *Negative Dialectics*, pp. 361–408. See also his *Metaphysics: Concepts and Problems*, ed. Rolf Tiedemann, trans. Edmund Jephcott (Cambridge: Polity, 2000).

[11] See also Espen Hammer, 'Metaphysics', in Deborah Cook (ed.), *Adorno: Key Concepts* (Oxford: Routledge, 2004), p. 66.

[12] Adorno, *Negative Dialectics*, p. 403.

the metaphysical tradition, however, undertakes to revivify metaphysics precisely by abandoning its most fundamental presuppositions. Adorno understands his own idiosyncratic conception of metaphysics as arising from the transformation – even the 'decay' – of the fundamental concept of traditional metaphysical thinking: that of a numinous world beyond material reality. He states that his own conception of metaphysics has 'its basis in the total suspension of metaphysics'.[13] This conception is in 'solidarity' with metaphysics 'at the time of its fall', however: it will allow a new metaphysics to develop that, by breaking with the idea of a 'pure' realm beyond material reality, can merge with materialism.[14] 'The course of history forces materialism upon metaphysics,' writes Adorno, 'traditionally the direct antithesis of materialism.'[15]

For transcendence to be possible in the face of the totalised world of Auschwitz, metaphysics must be stripped of its traditional conceptual ties to the *mundus intelligibilis* notions of the ideal, the absolute and the universal. Adorno makes the case that in post-Auschwitz society transcendence should be sought, not in the order of the immutable *à la* classical metaphysics, but in those fleeting moments that betray the false totality of modern social life and adumbrate something 'beyond' the interminable horizon of modern culture, where 'nothing appears as being outside any more'.[16] This is 'ephemeral life' – a moment where the subject is at once bound in the world and yet also thrown, however partially, however precariously, beyond or outside of it. Adorno rehabilitates metaphysics within a critical materialist theory of society, where the metaphysical consists in the possibility of some form of otherness.

It should be recognised that ephemeral life is not an idea that is fully developed or rigorously applied by Adorno (he states enigmatically in *Negative Dialectics* that 'there is no origin save ephemeral life').[17] This is perhaps because Adorno came to metaphysics towards the end of his life, without having the chance to develop his reinterpretation of the metaphysical tradition. The notion of ephemeral life has, however, been fleshed out in the work of Alistair Morgan, who provides an astute analysis of the various forms of 'life' conceptualised by Adorno. He states that Adorno understands 'mere life' as 'self-preservation in

---

[13] Adorno, *Metaphysics: Concepts and Problems*, p. 110.
[14] Adorno, *Negative Dialectics*, p. 408; see also Adorno, *Metaphysics: Concepts and Problems*, pp. 112–19.
[15] Adorno, *Negative Dialectics*, p. 365.
[16] Ibid. p. 357.
[17] Ibid. p. 156.

nature'; 'damaged life' denotes the reified life of late capitalist society; and 'ephemeral life' means the fleeting moment of transcendence that happens within damaged life.[18] He writes:

> the term ephemeral life refers to a [...] bid [...] to give an interpretation of the possibility of metaphysical experience, a metaphysical experience that contrary to the tradition of metaphysics will lie in the particular, the transitory and the non-conceptual [...] It is these material elements within thought that become speculative or transcendent when trying to think about the possibility of life [...] [and that can] decipher within the negative life the possibility of something different.[19]

Ephemerality is critical: without moments of ephemeral life it would not be possible to confront and resist the radical societal 'evil' the totalised world of Auschwitz both embodied and, ultimately, exposed. Within a totalised world that itself takes on the semblance of the absolute, metaphysics remains, as Espen Hammer states, 'relevant for ethical orientation and political struggle'.[20] The idea of a new type of 'metaphysical experience is Janus-faced: while tracing a moment of transcendence, it also makes us aware of the negativity of immanence'.[21]

I want to develop the notion of ephemeral life by using the concept in a reading of *Blasted*. Kane is similarly concerned with the metaphysical totalisation of post-Auschwitz culture and the need for new forms of transcendence. This is reflected in the way she understands the act of literary/theatrical appropriation and its political consequences. Kane is less concerned with identity politics – and the contestatory approach to the canon it has informed – than with a crisis of the subject as such, which is precipitated by modern, totalised society.

'Last in a long line of literary kleptomaniacs': Kane, Appropriation and Identity Politics

While she was initially branded (and derided) in the British press as the *enfant terrible* of a radical new form of theatrical practice – variously designated as the 'New Brutalism', 'Smack and Sodomy Theatre' and 'The Theatre of Urban Ennui' – that broke radically with past forms, Kane always positioned herself as a product and appropriator of the European canonical tradition, acknowledging her debt to Shakespeare,

---

[18] Morgan, 'Mere Life, Damaged Life and Ephemeral Life', pp. 116–17.
[19] Ibid. p. 115, p. 120 and p. 125.
[20] Hammer, 'Metaphysics', p. 75.
[21] Ibid. p. 73.

Ford, Büchner, Ibsen, Eliot, Camus, Artaud, Huxley, Beckett, Bond, Barker and Crimp.[22] The speaker in the 1999 Kane play *4.48 Psychosis* memorably refers to her/himself as the 'Last in a long line of literary kleptomaniacs', where 'Theft is the holy act / On a twisted path to expression'.[23] While the theatrical voice of the play cannot be wholly identified with Kane herself, it is hard to avoid the implication of *4.48 Psychosis* that Kane is similarly engaged in various acts of literary 'theft'.

The idea of literary 'theft' recalls the Latin root of appropriation in *propruis* – 'belonging to', the 'property of' – with the 'a'-prefix denoting 'an approach towards'. Theft would indicate that appropriation is the seizure of 'property' that belongs to another. But her 'approach' towards literary theft indicates that Kane is not only engaged in acts of violent proprietorial seizure; for her, appropriation is also a 'holy' act imbued with sacred reverence – almost as if Kane were a bowed penitent approaching a religious icon that she is, paradoxically, planning to steal. From the words of *4.48 Psychosis*, it would seem that there is something sacred about the (more often than not, canonical) works Kane appropriates and about the act of appropriation itself, which Kane imagines in *4.48 Psychosis* 'a time honoured tradition'.[24] There are obvious parallels with Barker and his paradoxical conception of appropriation as violation/reverence.

Her indebtedness to the canon and its appropriation caused Kane to remark that her plays 'certainly exist within a theatrical tradition', even if that is at the 'extreme end of the theatrical tradition'.[25] This obviously relates to the idea of being 'last in a long line' of other appropriators; but it also speaks to her particular indebtedness to the more *avant-garde* end of the modernist tradition, which places Kane as a late modernist.[26] Kane was careful to state, however, that, while she appropriated past works, her plays are not about interrogating other works or the

---

[22] See also Antje Diedrich, '"Last in a Long Line of Literary Kleptomaniacs": Intertextuality in Sarah Kane's *4.48 Psychosis*', *Modern Drama*, 56:3 (2013), pp. 374–98. For more on 'The New Brutalism', see Graham Saunders, *'Love Me or Kill Me': Sarah Kane and the Theatre of Extremes* (Manchester: Manchester University Press, 2001), pp. 4–8. The most lasting descriptor has been 'in-yer-face' theatre, as described by Aleks Sierz. See his *In-Yer-Face Theatre: British Drama Today* (London: Faber and Faber, 2001).

[23] Sarah Kane, *4.48 Psychosis*, in Kane, *Complete Plays*, p. 213.

[24] Ibid.

[25] Quoted in Saunders, *'Love Me or Kill Me'*, p. 26.

[26] *Blasted* also shares its title with the short-lived Vorticist journal *BLAST!*, edited by Wyndham Lewis, which had two editions in 1914. See Paul Edwards and Jane Beckett, *Blast: Vorticism, 1914–1918* (London: Ashgate, 2000).

cultural politics of 'representation', whether that is based on feminist, postcolonial or queer politics.[27] Kane viewed appropriation as a way of aligning herself with the canon and enabling the development of her distinct but canonically informed 'vision'.[28]

This approach to the canon and its appropriation is part of a more pervasive refutation of modern-day identity politics. Kane did not set out to represent the cause of marginalised identities in her playwriting and was suspicious of the way identity-categories are produced. 'Class, race and gender divisions are symptomatic of societies based on violence or the threat of violence, not the cause.'[29] The divisions which contemporary identity politics seeks to address and redress are not, Kane insists, the cause of violence, but are the result of societies based on violence. Underlying the divisions of class, race and gender is, for Kane, a more systematic violence, through which divisions are produced: identity-thinking.

In *Blasted*, Ian typifies the prescriptive and intrinsically violent nature of identity-thinking. Ian spends much of the play pinning others to predetermined, categorised identities, epitomised by the classist – 'scum' (1.19) – racist – 'wog' (1.3;6) – sexist – 'witch' (1.19) – homophobic – 'lesbos' (1.18); 'cocksucker' (1.19) – and ableist – 'spaz' (1.5) – ascriptions he directs against Cate and the unseen 'characters' both he and Cate refer to in the play. So pervasive is the violent and abusive language Ian uses to identify others that it finally disarms a reading that would seek to advance a particular identity politics and adumbrates the presence of a deeper 'rationale' underlying his unrepentant racism, sexism, ableism and various other 'isms' – the rationale of identity-thinking. Ian is, however, not only a racist, a sexist and a homophobe – though he does undeniably embody all of those bigotries and more – but also the representative of an 'enlightened' and avowedly 'scientific' (4.56) worldview, which has little truck with the more 'mythic' worldview espoused by the religiously inclined Cate. These ostensibly divergent characteristics are not incidental: the racism, sexism and ableism represented in *Blasted* is tied to a character who stands for modern scientific reason. The violent language Ian uses to identify others is symptomatic of the dialectic of enlightenment: Ian typifies the way in which the discursive categories that enlightenment rationality uses to produce knowledge about the

[27] See Natasha Stephenson and Heidi Longridge (eds), *Rage and Reason: Women Playwrights on Playwriting* (London: Methuen, 1997), pp. 134–5.
[28] For a less canonical intertext for *Blasted*, see my 'Sarah Kane and *Blasted*: The Arcade Game?', *Contemporary Theatre Review*, 28:3 (2018), pp. 431–3.
[29] Quoted in Stephenson and Longridge, *Rage and Reason*, p. 134.

world (and people) invariably result in domination and even a 'mythic' and irrational fear of the presence of the 'other'.

It is not the case that Ian goes unchallenged in the play. During the various dialogic 'battles' that inform the opening scene of *Blasted*, Cate often confronts Ian over his language use, uncomfortable with the universally hostile way in which he categorises others. The way Cate challenges Ian, however, betrays the potential inadequacy of identity politics. The more sensitive language Cate uses, which is intended to minimise prejudice and discrimination, fails to challenge the underlying rationale of identity-thinking by ultimately failing to challenge the 'category' to which Ian and Cate are – in the end – both referring. In the opening moments of the play, Ian tells Cate that he now hates Leeds, which 'stinks' because of the 'Wogs and Pakis' that are 'taking over' (1.4). Not untypically, Cate challenges Ian; but she only contests the words he uses, not the underlying principle of categorisation itself:

Cate: You shouldn't call them that.
Ian: Why not?
Cate: It's not very nice. (1.5)

The use of the word 'shouldn't' implies a linguistic consensus to which Ian should adhere; but revealingly, the 'them' Cate uses in the dispute indicates that she is still talking about the same 'others' referred to by Ian, even if she is trying to advocate for a more 'politically correct' language-game. The referent 'them', grammatically speaking, is still the 'Wogs and Pakis' Ian identifies, so that Cate is saying that 'Wogs and Pakis' should not be called 'Wogs and Pakis' any longer, as society now deems it is 'not very nice'. What the dialogue reveals is that a preoccupation with language use – however well-intentioned – does not necessarily challenge and is even complicit with the oppression it aims to mitigate, as it fails to interrogate the underlying categories that are used to discriminate between and divide human beings.

The suspicion that identity politics serves to pin subjects to prescribed identities is something that Kane publicly addressed, particularly insofar as identity might constrain her own authorial intentions. Kane bristled at the critical presumption that, as a 'female playwright', it was her duty to represent contemporary sexual and gender politics, insisting that she had 'no responsibility as a woman writer', with its attendant obligation to write about 'sexual politics'.[30] Not unlike Rudkin, Kane refused to become a 'representative' of 'any social group to which I

---

[30] Ibid.

happen to be a member', repudiating the prescriptive designation of 'a woman writer'.[31] Kane addressed questions that – as she put it – concerned 'human beings', and even 'all human beings'.[32]

This shift from identity politics to questions relating to human existence in its widest possible sense might seem at best politically retrogressive and at worst hopelessly naïve, implying that there are 'universal' problems faced by 'all human beings' regardless of the culturally determined distinctions of class, race, gender or sexuality.[33] This, however, would be to underestimate the political vision that informs *Blasted*. Not necessarily content to represent the 'cause' of women or any other identifiable subjectivity in society, in *Blasted* Kane puts into question nothing short of the immanent and homogenised totality of contemporary society itself, which by violently erasing any conception of something beyond its borders – and by pinning subjects to homogenised forms of identity – confines and deforms 'human beings'.

Dan Rebellato contends that, in an era of late capitalist globalisation and 'the end of history', Kane was deeply suspicious of 'the totalizing ideological forces whose power over reality had never seemed more complete', precipitating a move away from 'the categories of political identity and action that had been developed in the 1970s and 1980s' towards an interrogation of the (apparent) totality of social and political reality itself.[34] This is typified in *Blasted* by the culturally homogenised space of the hotel room, where the action of the play takes place. The stage directions famously begin with an unmistakable sense of spatial specificity – '*a hotel room in Leeds*' – but go on to completely erase that specificity by stating that the room is of the kind '*so expensive it could be anywhere in the world*' (1.3). Kane begins *Blasted* by presenting a culture that has, to use the term preferred by Adorno, become totalised – the culture of global capital. So firmly pinioned is the subject within the social totality in *Blasted* that no other reality seems remotely possible and there is 'Nowhere to go' (4.53).

This situation is not in any way simply 'equivalent' to the concentration

---

[31] Ibid. pp. 134–5.
[32] Ibid. p. 133.
[33] This is perhaps even more the case in light of recent developments around the Black Lives Matter movement, which has been met with the disingenuous riposte 'All Lives Matter'. I would stress that Kane is not trying to efface distinctions under a false humanistic universalism; the point is to critique totalised structures of social and political control. As *Blasted* demonstrates, Kane is more than alive to racial and other forms of social and economic injustice.
[34] Dan Rebellato, 'Sarah Kane Before *Blasted*: The Monologues', in de Vos and Saunders, *Sarah Kane: In Context*, p. 42.

camp. *Blasted* is, however, a play that has the Holocaust – and its relationship with contemporary totalised society – on its 'mind', most obviously as the concentration camp was brought back into popular and artistic consciousness by the horror of the Bosnian War and the death camps at Srebrenica and Omarska. It was a TV report on the ethnic cleansing which took place during the Bosnian conflict that inspired Kane to include the anonymous Soldier and mortar fire in *Blasted*.[35] These events brought the Holocaust back into the cultural imaginary, as the modern world was 'humiliated, shocked, and haunted by the return of genocide to Europe'.[36]

Ian raises the spectre of the Holocaust when he tells Cate in the opening scene that Hitler was 'wrong about the Jews' and that it is the 'queers' and 'wogs' he should have 'gone after' (1.19) – proclaiming the benefits of a new industrial-military genocide: 'Send a bomber over' (1.19).[37] Kane remarks that to write '"Auschwitz 1944"' would be 'reductive', but that her drama sets out to critique social and political forms that produce 'a loss of self'.[38] Through the uncanny irruption of the Soldier into the 'expensive', culturally recognisable space of the hotel room, Kane brings the apparent distinction between late global capital and the total world of the camp into question, demonstrating the disavowed continuities between various forms of violence while also critiquing any sense of moral complacency about the progress of modern, liberal Western society. 'I think the wall between so-called civilization and what happened in central Europe is very thin', Kane remarks, in language that reverses the action of *Lear*, 'and it can get torn down at any time'.[39] Little wonder Bond saw in *Blasted* reminders of 'Hiroshima, Nagasaki, Auschwitz, Dresden, Babi Yar'.[40]

This shift from identity politics to a political vision that interrogates contemporary totality is reflected – and enabled – by the way Kane appropriates *King Lear*. Far from pursuing a politically or ideologically corrective approach to the appropriation of *King Lear*, Kane uses the

---

[35] See Saunders, '*Love Me Or Kill Me*', pp. 38–9.
[36] Eric Markusen, 'Ethnic Cleansing and Genocide, Bosnia and Croatia', in Paul R. Bartrop (ed.), *Bosnian Genocide: The Essential Reference Guide* (Santa Barbara: ABC-CLIO, 2016), p. 62.
[37] The speaker of *4.48 Psychosis* similarly confesses to a litany of genocidal crimes: 'I gassed the Jews, I killed the Kurds, I bombed the Arabs' (p. 227).
[38] Quoted in Saunders, '*Love me or Kill Me*', p. 93.
[39] Quoted in Saunders, '"Out Vile Jelly"', p. 71.
[40] Edward Bond, 'A blast at our smug theatre', <https://www.theguardian.com/stage/2015/jan/12/edward-bond-sarah-kane-blasted> (accessed 19 July 2019).

play to confront the immanence of totalised, post-Auschwitz society and its damaged subject.

'Rewriting' the Dover Cliff Scene: Problematising the Material and the Metaphysical

While it contains various allusions to and palimpsestic traces of *King Lear*, perhaps the most consistently realised and sustained appropriation of Shakespeare in *Blasted* is its reimagining of the Dover cliff scene in Scene Four, where Ian – reprising Gloucester – tries to kill himself, only to have Cate – reprising Edgar – intervene to stop the suicide, afterward claiming that divine forces have miraculously 'stepped in' to save Ian from committing a grave sin. When asked about the scene, Kane called it 'a blatant rewrite of Shakespeare': 'As straightforward as that'.[41]

Kane is drawn to the scene at Dover cliff due to its existential and metaphysical questions pertaining to human suffering, suicide, the possibility of divine 'intervention' and of a world beyond the material world – reflecting her desire to interrogate a homogeneous present. In the scene from *King Lear*, Edgar extemporises a wholly imaginary 'chalky bourn' (IV.vi.57) for Gloucester to pitch himself from, in a bid to rekindle some of his faith in the benevolent intervention of God (or in the pagan world of *King Lear*, 'the gods') in human life and in a world 'beyond'. 'Why I do trifle thus with his despair', claims Edgar, 'Is done to cure it' (IV.vi.33–4) – though it is hard to avoid the suspicion that a vengeful Edgar is punishing Gloucester by making him 'suffer' more life, as Ian alleges against Cate: 'I know you want to punish me, trying to make me live' (4.55). Of course, the audience is 'in' on the trick Edgar is pulling – at least by the time Gloucester has taken his grotesque 'fall' onto the stage. But while Gloucester does accept the version of events Edgar narrates, the way in which the scene is scripted constantly undermines the narrative of divine intervention and salvation Edgar proposes.

Once he has dispassionately watched his father fall flat on his face, Edgar – dropping the persona of Poor Tom in favour of an anonymous passer-by – tells his prostrate father that his life is 'a miracle' (IV.vi.55) and, with troubling cynicism, ascribes his survival of his deathward fall to the 'gods' (IV.vi.73) who have interceded to save him. Gloucester is initially distraught to find that the gods are even cruel enough to deny him death:

---

[41] Quoted in Saunders, '"Out Vile Jelly!"', p. 77.

> Is wretchedness deprived that benefit
> To end itself by death? 'Twas yet some comfort
> When misery could beguile the tyrant's rage
> And frustrate his proud will. (IV.vi.61–4)

His prolonged existence is for Gloucester less the miracle Edgar says it is than a curse: Gloucester imagines immanence as a 'tyrannical' (Adorno would say totalised) regime, where even death falls outside the 'will' of the individual and any hope that 'things may change, or cease' (III.i.7) has been crushed. But while the language Edgar uses is patently at risk of giving the game away by implying that faith is simply a form of wishful thinking – 'Think that' (IV.vi.73) – Gloucester ultimately takes the moral/theological lesson on board, resolving to 'bear / Affliction till it do cry out itself / "Enough, enough" and die' (IV.vi.75–7).[42]

There is, however, an obvious ambiguity in the wording. On the one hand, Gloucester seems to be saying that he will bear suffering until affliction 'itself' dies. On the other hand, there is nothing to indicate that Gloucester imagines himself surviving beyond the 'death' of his affliction: it may be that Gloucester imagines affliction ending when he dies – as he ultimately does when, as Edgar relates to Kent, his heart bursts 'smilingly' (V.iii.198) on finding that his 'legitimate' (but once 'no dearer' (I.i.19) for that) son is still alive. It is not necessarily the case that 'all sorrows' are 'redeemed' (V.iii.264) by the promise of future happiness – in life or in the afterlife. It might only be the human lot to stoically endure 'going hence' as 'coming hither' (V.ii.10) – without the promise of transcendence.

While his conceit of the cliff-face is intended to impart a 'miraculous' experience and prove to Gloucester that there is another world beyond that inhabited by a suffering humanity, the metatheatrical trick Edgar pulls only goes to show that the universe is as 'dark and comfortless' (III.vii.84) as Gloucester fears, that there is neither a metaphysical beyond nor a benevolently intervening divinity that shapes human ends. This collapse of any metaphysical beyond, as shown in Chapter 3, prompted Jan Kott to contend that *King Lear* should be read as a prototypical piece of absurdist theatre, an *Endgame* of the early modern era that foreshows the godless universe dramatised in the plays of Beckett. Kott makes the case that Dover cliff depicts a fundamentally absurd impasse, where any kind of metaphysical beyond that might provide human

---

[42] In his analysis of the scene, the 'Shakespeare' of *Will's Way* states that Gloucester learns to accept 'the rightness of living on' (25). This more 'positive' reading of the scene on the part of Rudkin may reflect his own desire to embrace 'life' in all its struggles and vicissitudes as a means of 'self re-authorship' and rebirth.

life (and suffering) with meaning has collapsed, God (or the gods) are shown not to exist and faith relies on artifice.[43] Gloucester calls upon the gods to witness his 'tragic' leap into the abyss – 'O you mighty gods / This world I do renounce in your sights' (IV.vi.34–5) – but Edgar (and the audience) is the final and indeed only witness as a duped Gloucester absurdly slumps onto 'even' (IV.vi.3) ground. Quite simply, the gods (God) do not exist: the immanent world is all there is.

By showing the 'cozened and beguiled' (V.iii.152) Gloucester taking his pratfall, Shakespeare dramatises, in the words of Kott, 'a parable of universal human fate': the scene at Dover cliff is a 'total situation' in a cosmos where God has died or gone unanswerably missing, so that there is 'nothing' (IV.vi.9) beyond the world which might suffuse life and the suffering it engenders with meaning.[44] The upshot is an interminable imprisonment within immanence, which Kott takes to be metaphorically rendered through the (apparent) impossibility of death in the play. Kott makes the case that, in the Dover cliff scene, Shakespeare portrays a situation where it is not only impossible to 'die bravely' (IV.vi.194) – or tragically – any longer, but even to die at all.[45] Kott believes that the impossibility of death in Beckett and *King Lear* witnesses the impossibility of tragedy: where tragedy relies on a metaphysical plane and the possibility of transcendence, even if that possibility is thwarted, absurdism allows no way out of a situation because there is no metaphysical beyond to which protagonists can truly 'call' or aspire.[46] This world is, it seems, all that really exists – an all-encompassing 'immanent barrel' from which even the 'out' of death has been cruelly banished.[47]

This reading of *King Lear* has some intriguing parallels with Adorno and his own conception of death in Beckett. Beckett portrays for Adorno the impossibility of transcendence in Auschwitz and post-Auschwitz culture – an imprisonment in immanence. 'Not even the experience of death', writes Adorno, 'suffices as the ultimate and undoubted, as a metaphysics.'[48] Adorno contends that, in the totalised world of Auschwitz, a sort of purgatorial non-existence was created, 'inhabited by living skeletons and putrefying bodies' – perhaps not unlike the 'stinking' and 'rotting' (1.11) body of the terminally ill Ian, who might

---

[43] Jan Kott, *Shakespeare Our Contemporary* (New York: Norton, 1974), pp. 127–68. See especially pp. 142–52.
[44] Ibid. p. 148.
[45] 'Break heart, I prithee break' (V.iii.311) begs Kent, ostensibly urging Lear to finally die but perhaps also willing his own – ultimately deferred – death.
[46] Kott, *Shakespeare Our Contemporary*, pp. 147–52.
[47] Ibid. p. 141.
[48] Adorno, *Negative Dialectics*, p. 368.

be said to resemble a sort of *Muselmann*, or walking corpse.[49] Only where Kott seems to accept that 'there is no escape', for Adorno such a stance 'renders absolute the entrapment of human beings by the totality, and so sees no other possibility than to submit'.[50] It is for precisely that reason Adorno seeks to provide a critical space for transcendence.

Few if any dramatists influenced Kane as profoundly as Beckett, so it should hardly be surprising to find that her appropriation of the Dover cliff scene has parallels with the absurdist reading of *King Lear* famously proposed by Kott. Graham Saunders makes the case that the legacy of Beckett is 'all-pervasive' in the plays of Kane, stating that 'from *Blasted* onwards the plays utilise a variety of dramatic techniques that evoke a Beckettian atmosphere', manifested through 'direct or indirect quotation, the use of pseudo-couples, the recycling of familiar Beckettian imagery and dramatic motifs and the integration of linguistic and rhythmic echoes'.[51] Beckett casts his shadow over *Blasted* and its appropriation of the Dover cliff scene: Saunders notes that, in a reinterpretation of *Endgame* and its famous response to the vexing prospect that God does not exist – 'The bastard!', Hamm famously blasphemes (2.119) – the appropriation of the Dover cliff scene ends with Ian calling the God he does not believe exists a 'cunt' (4.57).[52] Kane – herself a lapsed evangelical Christian – deploys a re-versioned take on the Dover cliff scene in *Blasted* to depict a world where any notion of a pure metaphysical beyond has become untenable. This is not to say, however, that Kane is 'rewriting' the Dover cliff scene solely in order to portray an absurdist Beckettian impasse, where there is no metaphysical beyond and death has been rendered impossible by the uninterrupted reign of immanence. Kane appropriates the Dover cliff scene in *Blasted* to set up a philosophically inflected dispute between material (Ian) and metaphysical (Cate) worldviews. She does so to produce a space for the transcendent, tragic freedom that Kott takes to be dispelled in the closed worlds of absurdism.

---

[49] Theodor Adorno, 'Notes on Kafka', in Theodor Adorno, *Can One Live After Auschwitz? A Philosophical Reader*, ed. Rolf Tiedemann, trans. Rodney Livingstone et al. (Stanford: Stanford University Press, 2003), p. 227. For more on the figure of the *Muselmann* (or Muslim) and related ideas around bare life, see Giorgio Agamben, *Remnants of Auschwitz: The Witness and the Archive*, trans. Daniel Heller-Roazen (New York: Zone Books, 2002), pp. 41–86.
[50] Kott, *Shakespeare Our Contemporary*, p. 133; Adorno, *Metaphysics: Concepts and Problems*, p. 112.
[51] Graham Saunders and Laurens de Vos, 'Introduction', in Saunders and de Vos, *Sarah Kane: In Context*, p. 3.
[52] See Saunders, '*Love Me or Kill Me*', pp. 59–60.

'A blatant rewrite': The 'Cliff' in *Blasted*

In her 'rewrite', Kane puts a Chekhovian spin on the Dover cliff scene, replacing the cliff with a misfiring pistol.[53] Shortly after his rape and blinding at the hands of the Soldier, Ian asks a reluctant Cate to find his gun so that he can shoot himself, which Ian thinks of as simply 'speeding up' (4.56) his terminal illness. Cate, however, removes the bullets from the gun (4.54) before passing it to Ian, afterward imputing his 'miraculous' survival to divine intervention:

Ian:	End it.
	Got to, Cate, I'm ill.
	Just speeding it up a bit.
Cate:	(*Thinks hard.*)
Ian:	Please.
Cate:	(*Gives him the gun.*)
Ian:	(*Takes the gun and puts it in his mouth.*
	He takes it out again.)
	Don't stand behind me.
	He puts the gun back in his mouth
	He pulls the trigger. The gun clicks, empty.
	He shoots again. And again and again and again.
	He takes the gun out of his mouth.
Ian:	Fuck.
Cate:	Fate, see. You're not meant to do it. God –
Ian:	The cunt. (4.56–7)

This ostensibly 'fateful' turn of events is contrived to prove to Ian that 'It's wrong to kill yourself' (4.54) because, as Cate warningly puts it, suicide is a sin and 'God wouldn't like it' (4.55). Ian, however, remains as staunchly atheistic as he was before his 'cliff' moment, telling Cate that it is pointless to pray for the baby she brings to the room in the hope that it does not go to 'bad places' because it is 'dead' (4.58) – and so going nowhere. Despite his lingering hope that Cate will pray for him (4.58) – which perhaps says more about his desire to be remembered by Cate after his death than it does about a nascent religiosity, typical of his growing neediness in the play – Ian does not progress through his brush with death beyond his previous scepticism, where he treats the notion of God with characteristically derisory scorn:

Ian:	There isn't one.
Cate:	How do you know?

---

[53] I touch on the significance of the pistol again below.

Ian: No God. No Father Christmas. No fairies. No Narnia. No fucking nothing.
Cate: Got to be something.
Ian: Why?
Cate: Doesn't make sense otherwise.
Ian: Don't be fucking stupid, doesn't make sense anyway. No reason for there to be a God just because it would be better if there was. (4.55)

What the intervening Cate syllogistically proposes to Ian is a theodicy: there has to be 'something' to 'make sense' of the fallen world and of evil – represented, most urgently, by death – otherwise life is meaningless and irredeemable. Unlike his Shakespearean prototype Gloucester, however, Ian remains stubbornly unconvinced, producing a nihilistic 'nothing' in the face of the 'something' propounded by Cate – a dichotomy that, of course, surfaces time and again in *King Lear*: 'Can you make no use of nothing, Nuncle?' (I.iv.128–9). Ian, not without due cause, declaims that it is 'stupid' to believe in a metaphysical world beyond simply because it would be 'better if there was' to redeem life and the world in the present. God is, as far as Ian sees it, no more than a story told to children, keeping the same ontological company as 'fairies' ('Fairies and gods / Prosper it with thee' (IV.vi.29–30) says Gloucester, making the same mystical analogy) and 'Narnia'.

Ian is convinced that there is no beyond, and that to try and wring some meaning from existence by appealing to 'something' other than the world as it is, is at best misguided and at worst downright idiotic. It is a view he shares, in part, with Adorno: in words that echo the 'cliff' scenes dramatised in both *King Lear* and *Blasted*, Adorno writes in *Negative Dialectics* that

> When a desperate man who wants to kill himself asks one who tries to talk him out of it about the point of living, the helpless helper will be at a loss to name one. His every attempt can be refuted as the echo of a general consensus, the core of which appeared in the old adage that the emperor needs soldiers.[54]

The fallacious dictums used to try and vindicate life inevitably 'make a mockery of the construction of immanence as endowed with a meaning radiated by an affirmatively posited transcendence'.[55] The type of metaphysical beyond that Cate posits has patently become untenable, relying

---

[54] Adorno, *Negative Dialectics*, pp. 376–7.
[55] Ibid. p. 361. This reflects perhaps the most dire charge Adorno lays against metaphysics: that it is 'essentially affirmative', serving to excuse rather than uncover and oppose societal evil (Hammer, 'Metaphysics', p. 65).

on the completely specious reasoning – 'No reason' – that there has to be 'something' other than the fallen world because otherwise life would be unlivable, condemning her faith to the 'mockery' of Ian. It also relies on a deliberate sham: it is, after all, Cate herself who removes all the bullets from the pistol, not God.

But at the same time, the strictly materialist stance represented by Ian is equally problematic. 'Everything', Ian confidently pronounces, has 'a scientific explanation' (4.56) – though there is an obvious contradiction between his conviction that 'everything' is scientifically explainable and that the world simply does not 'make sense'. Even more problematically, by dismissing without hesitation anything outside or beyond the existent material world as 'nothing', Ian inevitably ends up turning the material world into nothing less than 'everything'.[56] Ian, in a paradox that is clearly lost on him, transforms the world as it is into a metaphysical 'absolute' – the type of permanent, unchangeable and 'final' realm imagined by the metaphysically inclined thinking he ostensibly sets himself against. The embodiment of a homogenised rationality, Ian cannot conceptualise otherness: his unreflective commitment to the dictates of identity-thinking means that anything which falls outside of the categories posited by rationalised enlightened thought cannot truly be said to 'exist'.

But while an otherwise desperate Ian articulates his position with undimmed rhetorical force, he ends up (unknowingly) undermining himself. By inadvertently using the double-negative of 'No [. . .] nothing' in his debate with Cate, Ian produces a weakened affirmative, implying there might be something (or at least, not 'nothing') beyond the world as it is – and perhaps even beyond death – after all. The 'no-nothing' inadvertently posited by Ian is clearly not the positively affirmed 'something' propounded by Cate, but it upends his stated conviction that the world he and Cate occupy is 'everything'. It is a negation of a totalised world which appears as 'everything' that also refuses to posit 'something' beyond in the way Cate does – perhaps trying to fortify Ian against suicide, or perhaps cruelly denying him the release which should (but of course, does not) come with death. What may lie beyond the world as it is remains in *Blasted* completely open-ended, arising only through the inadvertent – but nonetheless telling – negation of the 'known world'. Adorno writes that metaphysics rests in the conception of 'something

---

[56] Lear conceives the loss of the all-encompassing metaphysical authority which should be founded in 'the King himself' (IV.vi.83–4) in a not too dissimilar way, damning the flatterers who told him he was 'everything' (IV.vi.104).

which is not' – and 'yet it is not a pure nonbeing', or something which is not only 'not'.[57]

By reworking the constant allusions to 'something', 'nothing' and 'everything' found in *King Lear,* Kane undermines the material and metaphysical worldviews that are voiced by Ian and Cate. She also echoes the philosophical invocation of 'not-nothing' found in Shakespeare. Howard Caygill contends that, in his plays, Shakespeare interrupts the conventional philosophical distinction between being and nothing, so that the question 'To be, or not to be' (*Hamlet,* III.i.58) offers only a limited conception of the way in which Shakespeare thinks about ontology. Caygill notes that Shakespeare often refuses to 'move from the negation of nothing to the affirmation of being'.[58] Shakespeare typically makes 'nothing' substantive, speaking of it as if it had its own peculiar 'being' ('Edgar I nothing am' (II.ii.192) – the contorted, negatively exilic ontology that so preoccupies Rudkin – is a prime evocation of that principle in *King Lear*) and plays (not unlike Kane) with double-negations that leave both something and nothing 'suspended'.[59] It is, contends Caygill, not right for Lear to declare that 'nothing will come of nothing' (I.i.90); however, in *King Lear* the 'negation of the negation has no definite result', so that the 'monster of nothing' is a type of 'not-nothing', the impossible and perhaps even unthinkable state of a nothing that is something.[60]

Despite his perspicacious reading, Caygill – perplexingly – does not refer to Adorno, choosing to bring Shakespeare into a philosophical dialogue with Hegel and Heidegger. But his analysis of the something-nothing of Shakespearean drama might indicate a deep homology between the performative evocation of not-nothing in Shakespeare and the negative dialectics proposed by Adorno, which does not imagine a positive 'something' arising from the 'negation of the negation', but retains a sense of openness – or non-identity, as Adorno calls it. The type of negative dialectical philosophy Adorno proposes does not terminate in a positively affirmed and identifiable 'something'; instead, it results in precisely the same species of indefinite 'not-nothing' that Caygill sees Shakespeare creating in *King Lear.*

By evoking the 'not-nothing' of *King Lear,* Ian raises the open-ended prospect of something other than the world as it stands, adumbrating

---

[57] Adorno, *Negative Dialectics,* p. 393.
[58] Howard Caygill, 'Shakespeare's Monster of Nothing', in John Joughin (ed.), *Philosophical Shakespeares* (London: Routledge, 2000), p. 107.
[59] Ibid. p. 110.
[60] Ibid. p. 107.

the possibility that reality itself is not as enveloping as it might seem – and can even be transcended. Far from settling on a final perspective, the appropriation of Dover cliff in *Blasted* leaves both metaphysical and materialist worldviews destabilised. This lays the ground for the transformed understanding of the metaphysical and material – and the possibility of ephemeral life – in Scene Five of the play.

Death in *Blasted* and *King Lear*

The tension between metaphysics (Cate) and materialism (Ian) in *Blasted* largely revolves around the question of whether or not there is 'life' after death. This is a question that runs throughout the whole action of the play and may even be considered its most enduring theme. From the outset, Ian is in no doubt as to the irresolvable negativity of death, which in his Hamlet-like belief that the fundamental ontological 'question' is 'To be, or not to be', he calls 'not being': 'Death. Not being' (1.10). Ian, in words that will come back to haunt him, tells Cate that it is not possible to 'die and come back. That's not dying, it's fainting. When you die, it's the end' (4.56). Ian reiterates his belief (or rather, his unbelief) in the face of opposition, telling Cate he has 'seen dead people': 'They're not somewhere else, they're dead' (4.55).

Ian is in little doubt that corpses are no more than 'dead meat' (1.7) – or as Lear puts it, 'dead and rotten' (V.iii.283). Cate, however, resists his scepticism, making the case for God – 'I believe in God' (4.56) – and for another life in the beyond. 'People who've died and come back say they've seen tunnels and lights' (4.56). Cate also likens her fits – which, as I will contend below, resemble the 'undead' state of Ian – to the experience of death and 'waking up' in the afterlife: 'You fall asleep and then you wake up' (1.10). She does have moments of doubt – as when she prays for the dead baby 'in case' (5.58) and tells Ian it is pointless to pray for him (5.58) – but, for the most part, she is convinced that death is a transition to 'better places' (1.3) beyond the 'bad places' (5.58) of the fallen world.

Once again, however, the play complicates both positions. At the end of *Blasted*, Ian is depicted in a series of *tableaux*-like moments, as, fleetingly illuminated by flashes of light that interrupt a prevailing darkness, he is seen masturbating, defecating, sleeping and suffering from a nightmare, trying (once again) to commit suicide, hugging the corpse of the dead Soldier for warmth and comfort and, finally, cannibalising the infant brought into the remnants of the hotel by Cate – perhaps not unlike the 'barbarous Scythian' of *King Lear*, who 'makes his generation

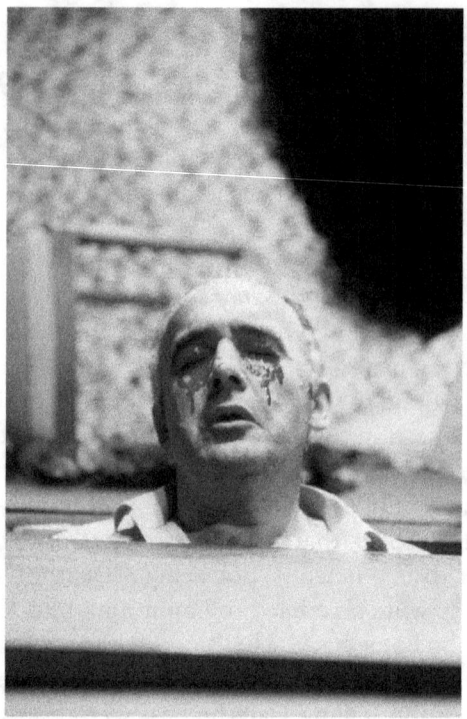

Figure 7.1　Ian (Pip Donaghy), dead and alive. (1995: Royal Court Upstairs, dir. James McDonald. Photograph: Donald Cooper. © Donald Cooper/Photostage)

messes / To gorge his appetite' (I.i.117–19). This series ends with the final death of Ian; however, while he does not ascend to a pure and immutable Christian beyond, death is also far from the unqualified 'end' Ian imagined. Ian dies at the end of *Blasted*, but the demise of his material body is not the wholly negative state it should be:

> *A beat, then he climbs in after it* [the baby] *and lies down, his head poking out of the floor.*
> *He dies with relief.*
> *It starts to rain on him, coming through the roof.*
> *Eventually*
> **Ian:**　Shit. (5.60)

The audience might be forgiven for saying, as Ian does to Cate: 'Thought you were dead' (1.10) (Figure 7.1).[61]

This strange moment – and the scenes of degradation that precede it,

---

[61] In *Crave*, 'C' remarks: 'Someone has died who is not dead' (Sarah Kane, *Crave*, in Kane, *Complete Plays*, p. 157) – clearly an echo of *Blasted*.

where Ian is depicted in various states of physical 'wretchedness' (*King Lear*, IV.vi.61) – has attracted sustained attention. Criticism has tended to fall into distinct camps: humanist interpretations and absurdist interpretations. Both tend to read *Blasted* intertextually by reading its final scene through the work of other playwrights – most notably Shakespeare and Beckett. David Greig writes that Kane depicts a 'Shakespearean anatomy' of 'a reduced man', akin to 'Lear on the heath and Timon in his cave'.[62] Ian is able to rediscover his otherwise 'lost' humanity through his suffering, becoming for Greig 'a human being, weeping, shitting, lonely, broken, dying and, in the final moments of the play, comforted'.[63] The idea that Ian undergoes a Lear-like progression from ignorance to insight caused Bond to remark that he was 'moved' by the 'humanity' of *Blasted* – a reading with parallels to his *Lear*.[64]

Other critics have generally (and understandably) read the final image of the undead Ian through the prism of Beckettian absurdism – most obviously the image of Winnie in *Happy Days*, who is buried up to her neck, and Nag and Nell in *Endgame*, whose heads pop intermittently out of the barrels (the Kottian immanent 'barrel') the pair are interred in. Sean Carney contends that *Blasted* 'resemble[s] the tragedy of the absurd', as by failing to die – 'Away, and let me die' (*King Lear*, IV.vi.48) – Ian embodies the impossibility of metaphysical transcendence.[65] The same point is made by Sara Soncini, who refers to the 'unmistakable visual quotation' of the (quite literally) earth-bound Winnie in *Happy Days*, and Gritzner, who contends that *Blasted* ends in 'a Beckettian domain'.[66] David Ian Rabey similarly states that the final image of the undead Ian is a 'mockery of desecrated absolutes' and 'a *tour de force*' of the 'tragedy of the grotesque' with its total denial of metaphysical transcendence.[67]

These interpretations rely on conceptual categories which the play itself is challenging and deconstructing: humanist readings ignore the way the dead-alive Ian challenges the material limits of the human, while the absurdist take on the play relies on a philosophical distinction

---

[62] David Greig, 'Introduction', in Kane, *Complete Plays*, p. x.
[63] Ibid.
[64] Bond, 'A blast at our smug theatre'.
[65] Sean Carney, 'The Tragedy of History in Sarah Kane's *Blasted*', *Theatre Survey*, 46:2 (2005), p. 287.
[66] Sara Soncini, '"A horror so deep only ritual can contain it": The Art of Dying in the Theatre of Sarah Kane', *Other Modernities*, 4:10 (2010), p. 123; Karoline Gritzner, '(Post)Modern Subjectivity and the New Expressionism: Howard Barker, Sarah Kane, and Forced Entertainment', *Contemporary Theatre Review*, 18.3 (2008), p. 335.
[67] David Ian Rabey, *English Drama Since 1940* (Oxford: Routledge, 2014), p. 205.

between the material and the metaphysical to insist that Ian remains interred within a totalised immanence. Both miss that Kane provides a philosophical 'frame' through which to interpret the image of the undead Ian in her appropriation of Dover cliff, which destabilises the distinction between the metaphysical and material. Through its final image of the 'undead' Ian, *Blasted* precludes the possibility of forming a simple dichotomy between the material and the metaphysical, the 'here-and-now' and the beyond. Ian is at once dead and alive, 'in' the material world, and yet also 'out' of it, a position that is both experiential and transcendent. The material and the metaphysical is not an either/or in *Blasted*, but a both/and. Ian attains a type of transcendence that, at the same time, reflects the totalised immanence of the material world. His sudden return to life and presence in negation is a powerful moment of ephemeral life.[68]

I would contend that there is another way to read *Blasted* through *King Lear*. The strange moment in which Ian dies but also simply continues living has parallels with the 'now dead, now alive' pattern – as Stephen Booth calls it – found throughout the Shakespeare play.[69] For some critics, *King Lear* is a play that dramatises the 'futility' of 'escape from being' through death, where the apparent inability of characters to 'Fall, and cease' (V.iii.262) is symptomatic of the impossibility of transcending a prevailing immanence.[70] Sean Lawrence states that Shakespeare portrays a world where death is horribly (and even possibly permanently) deferred: *King Lear* depicts the 'horrifying tragedy of inescapable being' – a reading that aligns the play more closely with absurdism than with 'tragedy'.[71] It is a (somewhat nihilistic) reading shared by Joseph Wittreich and also Frank Kermode, who makes the case that *King Lear* depicts nothing short of the 'tragedy of sempiternity', where 'everything

---

[68] It would be hard to overstate the status of the image of the undead Ian to *Blasted*. The image, as Carney has also shown, has even come to metonymically 'stand' for *Blasted* itself, often being used to identify or promote the play: it is the front cover of the original Methuen edition of the play; it appears in the 'defence' mounted by James McDonald in *The Independent*; it is on the front cover of the *Blasted* edition of the Modern Theatre Guide; it is printed (along with other images) with the play in *Theater*; and it featured in promotional material for the 2001 Royal Court staging. It is an image that might be said to embody the unique 'rationale' at work in the play, which in the suspension of conventional notions of a metaphysical beyond, pushes towards the conception of a material/immanent transcendence. See Carney, 'The Tragedy of History in Sarah Kane's *Blasted*', p. 277.

[69] Stephen Booth, *King Lear, Macbeth, Indefinition and Tragedy* (New Haven: Yale University Press, 1983), p. 34.

[70] Sean Lawrence, 'The Difficulty of Dying in *King Lear*', *English Studies in Canada*, 31:4 (2005), p. 37.

[71] Ibid. p. 41.

tends toward a conclusion that does not occur': even 'personal death is terribly delayed'.[72]

Such readings can broadly be said to conform to the Kottian reading of *King Lear*, where the impossibility of death speaks to the impossibility of transcending immanence, of going beyond the world as it is. Yet the ostensible impossibility of death in *King Lear* can be – and has been – overstated. It is not that death has become impossible. What the play dramatises is the apparent impossibility of determining the distinction between death and life, being and not being. This is apparent in the 'resurrection' of Gloucester after his 'fall' from Dover cliff; the flickering uncertainty about the final state of Lear; and, perhaps most pressingly, the ambiguity surrounding the untimely 'death' (or otherwise) of Cordelia at the end of the play.

Gloucester 'revives' (IV.vi.47) after (apparently) plummeting from the top of Dover cliff; yet there is some question as to whether Gloucester really might have died in his 'fall'. 'Alive or dead?' (IV.vi.44–5) wonders Edgar with shocking impassiveness, as he looks down on his father, concerned that his 'conceit' (IV.vi.42) of the cliff-face may have been so convincing that it might have robbed the 'treasury of life' (IV.vi.43). 'Gone, sir; farewell' (IV.vi.41) remarks Edgar after Gloucester falls, seemingly moving 'off' (IV.vi.30) as his father demands but perhaps also anticipating that Gloucester may 'pass indeed' (IV.vi.47). The word 'indeed' is both an intensifier and a metatheatrical pun ('in-deed'): on the one hand, it indicates that Gloucester really may have died; on the other hand, it indicates that death in the theatre is and can only ever be in-deed – that is, a performance.

The same ambiguity occurs in the final moment of the play, where Lear finally dies. Or does he? 'O he is gone indeed' (V.iii.314) laments Edgar, repeating the same pun on 'indeed' and insinuating doubt about the death: 'Vex not his ghost' (V.iii.312). Edgar even believes that Lear only 'faints' (V.iii.310) – aligning his death to the fit-induced 'fainting' (1.9) that afflicts Cate in *Blasted*, a state that she compares to death. Kent tells Edgar to let Lear 'pass' (V.iii.312) but, by using the present tense, Kent only throws more doubt on the death of Lear: has Lear passed, or is he still passing? What is the distinction? In the Folio, the stage direction '*He dies*' occurs after Lear insists that those few survivors gathered around him 'look' to Cordelia; yet in the Quarto, no stage

---

[72] Joseph Wittreich, *'Image of that horror': History, Prophecy, and Apocalypse in King Lear* (San Marino: Huntington Library, 1984), p. 101; Frank Kermode, *The Sense of an Ending: Studies in the Theory of Fiction* (Oxford: Oxford University Press, 2000), p. 82.

direction occurs, leaving the question of precisely when (if?) Lear dies potentially open to question (the 'O, o, o, o' (V.iii.309) of the Quarto is, as Foakes writes, traditionally understood to be a dying groan, though it does not have to be).[73]

The most intense ontological scrutiny falls on Cordelia, who seems – at least to Lear – to float precariously between the states of life and death, even putting into question whether these ostensibly distinct states can ever be finally and absolutely distinguished. 'I know when one is dead and when one lives. / She's dead as earth' (V.iii.258–9) howls (V.iii.270) Lear in the crushing finale to the play; and yet, Lear instantly undermines his own certainty with the hope that Cordelia still 'lives': 'Lend me a looking-glass; / If that her breath will mist or stain the stone, / Why then she lives' (V.iii.259–61). The ontological uncertainty surrounding Cordelia is a famed aspect of *King Lear*; yet the apparent unknowability – at least to Lear – of her final state is a single moment among many where the question of whether a character is dead or alive remains disconcertingly open to interpretation.

This 'now dead, now alive' pattern is literalised at the end of *Blasted*. To produce an image of ephemerality, Kane draws on the uncanny states somewhere between dead and alive in *King Lear*, where a dead character seemingly 'returns' to life or does not quite finally and fully 'die', hovering between the world and the beyond in the (often rapturous) moment of 'passing'. This ideational kinship between *King Lear* and the final image of Ian in his contradicted dead-alive state is also evidenced by the visual parallels between *Blasted* and the 1993 Max Stafford-Clark production of *King Lear* at the Royal Court. This production, as various critics noted at the time, visually echoed the Bosnian War, with its *Blasted*-like images of gun-toting soldiers brutalising the 'poor naked wretches' Lear prays to.[74] The production also included a character buried up to his neck – Kent, when he is put in the stocks by the 'fiery' (II.ii.281) Duke of Cornwall and Regan (Figure 7.2). The image has obvious resonances with the end of *Blasted*. It is a speculative point, but it is almost as if Kane amalgamates the image of the partially buried Kent with the recurrent images of dead-and-alive characters in *King Lear* at the end of *Blasted*, to develop a vision of ephemerality.

By denying the finality of death, both Shakespeare and Kane resist positing a final 'status', allowing the dialectic between discrete states (dead

---

[73] R. A. Foakes, 'The Reshaping of *King Lear*', in Jeffrey Kahan (ed.), *King Lear: New Critical Essays* (New York and Oxford: Routledge, 2008), p. 114.

[74] See Jonathan Croall, *Performing King Lear: Gielgud to Russell Beale* (London: Bloomsbury, 2015), pp. 178–80.

Figure 7.2 Kent (Philip Jackson) in the stocks. (1993: Royal Court, dir. Max Stafford-Clark. Photograph: Donald Cooper. © Donald Cooper/Photostage)

and/or alive) to remain open-ended – in other words, a negative dialectic. The ostensible 'death' of Ian is inherently ambiguous and refuses definitive interpretive closure; but it also, I want to contend, refuses conventional generic and aesthetic closure. If in the final moments of *Blasted* Kane produces a 'negative' dialectic, her open-ended theatrical aesthetic can be thought of as structurally homologous with the Theatre of Catastrophe as it has been theorised and practised by Barker.

Death and the Theatre of Catastrophe

Ken Urban notes that, not unlike Barker, Kane does not provide any sense of formal 'resolution' in her plays. By dramatising 'moments where comfortable designations break down' and 'everything must be rethought' – as in the strange 'death' of Ian, which seems to suspend the 'comfortable designations' of life and death – Kane 'literally recasts dramatic form', obliterating the usual generic criterion by which a play may be interpreted.[75] Kane was deeply indebted to Beckett, but she also cites Barker as having a profound influence on her conception of form,

---

[75] Ken Urban, 'An Ethics of Catastrophe: The Theatre of Sarah Kane', *PAJ: A Journal of Performance and Art*, 23:3 (2001), p. 46 and p. 40.

and even drew parallels between Shakespeare and Barker, whom she called 'the Shakespeare of our age' (Kane also played Bradshaw in a student production of the 1983 Barker play *Victory*, while studying at Bristol University).[76] *Blasted* shares with Catastrophist form the violation of tragic closure, aligning the play with both Barker and *King Lear*.

One of the ways in which *King Lear* suspends aesthetic closure is by suspending the finality of death, which is never quite as definitive – never quite as decisive – as it appears to be. The same is obviously true of *Blasted*: Kane appropriates the irresolvable tension about 'when one is dead'/'when one lives' to push beyond the containment of generic closure, where tragedy typically ends in death.[77] Ian, in his contradictory state, is both in and out of the totality; but he is also both in and out of conventional tragic aesthetics. This liminal position testifies to the way in which Ian, however marginally, preserves a form of (tragic) autonomy – freedom. Ian is not finally bounded by the social totality. Neither is he finally bounded by the (deathly) closure of aesthetic form.

Chapters 5 and 6 have analysed the way that sudden, performative 'turns' serve to violate both narrative progression and formal closure, opening the space for subjective autonomy. Ian, however, is immobilised in a makeshift grave, so that an actor is not necessarily able to embody the type of abrupt turn seen in Rudkin and Barker (which leads some critics to align Kane with the incapacitated subjectivities of absurdism). Nevertheless, I would make the case that his sudden return (re-turn) to life still inheres to the idea of the catastrophic 'turn'. It is an abrupt turn in events that violates narrative development, where from the outset Ian is terminally ill and so 'dying', and the possibility of aesthetic closure.

The indeterminacy is only amplified in performance. Unlike the playscript, which provides the stage direction '*He dies*', without some change in the *mise-en-scène* it is not necessarily the case that a theatre audience will comprehend that Ian has died. What precisely has happened to Ian is inherently ambiguous in performance. Writing about the 2001 revival of *Blasted* at the Royal Court, Urban remarks that the actor playing Ian let out a final Lear-esque ('O, o, o, o') groan, 'as if he was finally

---

[76] Quoted in David Ian Rabey, 'Raising Hell: An Introduction to Howard Barker's Theatre of Catastrophe', in Karoline Gritzner and David Ian Rabey (eds), *Theatre of Catastrophe: New Essays on Howard Barker* (London: Oberon Books, 2006), p. 23. Kane described playing in Barker as 'an unusually brilliant experience': 'I think I loved him all the more because none of the teaching staff seemed to share my enthusiasm', quoted in Sierz, *In-Yer-Face Theatre*, p. 91.

[77] The preternatural 'survival' of the Bishop in *Seven Lears* is another point of comparison.

passing on, but nothing in the physical reality of the space – the lighting, sound or set – connoted a transition from one world to another'.[78] The performance provided no obvious illustrative shift through which to interpret the apparent 'death' of Ian. What had happened to him remained completely open-ended.

Part of the way in which *Blasted* achieves its formal ambiguity and openness is by constantly undermining its own theatrical illusion, opening up the dialectical tension between sign and substance, showing and being, illusion and reality that shapes theatrical space. By having Ian preternaturally 'survive' his own end, *Blasted* suspends its own verisimilar play-world, undermining the representation of a 'realistic' theatrical death. Kane is drawing attention to the way in which death in the theatre can only ever be, as Edgar says in *King Lear*, 'an image of that horror' (V.iii.262). The same has been said of *King Lear* and its interrupted deaths, which self-reflexively dramatise the 'foundational impossibility' of death in theatre.[79] This ties the death and resurrection of Ian to the catastrophic bomb blast that shatters the realistic setting of *Blasted*, which begins in the recognisable and realistic theatrical space of a hotel room, but ends up fragmenting beyond recognition. The choice of a pistol in *Blasted* is also revealing. Shakespeare critics have been drawn to the Dover cliff scene because of the way it problematises early modern conventions of stage space and representation. By verbalising the scene from a clifftop, Edgar is providing a piece of rhetorical 'scene-painting' in order to elaborate the unadorned, flat space of the early modern stage into a realistic narrative illusion.[80] This space is shown to be a chimera. But, for Kott,

> In the naturalistic theatre one can perform a murder scene, or a scene of terror. The shot may be fired from a revolver or a toy pistol. But in mime there is no difference between a revolver and a toy pistol: in fact neither exists. Like death, the shot is only a performance, a parable, a symbol.[81]

By having Ian repeatedly fire his ammunition-less pistol, Kane subtly draws attention to the purely symbolic nature of stage space, in the same fashion as Shakespeare with his 'cliff-face'.

Perhaps most critically, the final image of the undead Ian also has

---

[78] Quoted in Soncini, '"A horror so deep"', p. 124.
[79] Simon Palfrey, *Poor Tom: Living King Lear* (Chicago: Chicago University Press, 2014), p. 238.
[80] See also Jonathan Goldberg, 'Perspectives: Dover Cliff and the Conditions of Representation', in Kiernan Ryan, *King Lear: Contemporary Critical Essays* (Basingstoke: Macmillan, 1993), pp. 145–57.
[81] Kott, *Shakespeare Our Contemporary*, p. 146.

parallels with the fits from which Cate intermittently suffers – fits she memorably likens to death. The fits that disturb Cate throughout the opening scenes of the play also suspend 'normal' material reality, showing the world that Cate (and Ian) usually inhabit to be provisional and contingent, not absolute. Such fits mirror the way an audience experiences *Blasted*, which by constantly undermining its own representation of a 'realistic' dramatic world brings the ostensible integrity of reality itself into question. I want finally to show that, by disrupting its own artistic semblance of reality, *Blasted* precipitates the (fit-like) aesthetic affect Adorno calls the shudder.

Fits and Shudders

The way in which Ian dies before being (inexplicably) resurrected finds a parallel in the deathly fits that Cate suffers from whenever she is put under duress. These fits represent a transcendent experience that is at once material and metaphysical, in time and space but also beyond it: 'Don't know much about it, I just go. Feels like I am away for minutes or months sometimes, then I come back just where I was' (1.10). Cate likens her fits to the experience of dying and resurrection in the afterlife – though she, like Ian, does not ascend to the gates of heaven but ends up 'just where I was': 'You fall asleep and then you wake up' (1.10).[82]

Cate also draws a parallel between her fit-induced state and the deathly self-loss precipitated by ecstatic *jouissance* – which is in sharp relief to the shallow and unfulfilling 'enjoyment' the terminally ill Ian claims he finds in gin and cigarettes, an enjoyment which is spatially and temporally constricted to the 'here-and-now' ('Enjoy myself', states Ian, 'while I'm *here*' (1.12; emphasis added)). When Ian tells Cate that she takes him to 'another place', Cate – uninterested in his advances – responds: 'It's like that when I have a fit' (1.22) and when she 'touches' herself: 'Just before I'm wondering what it'll be like, and just after I'm thinking about the next one, but just as it happens it's lovely, I don't think of nothing else' (1.23).[83]

Her fits and *jouissance* endow Cate with a kind of negative existence somewhere between being and not being: 'I am not, I am not' (1.9). Cate is fighting back against Ian and his belittling insults about her

---

[82] These fits resemble the 'tranced' (V.iii.217) state in which Edgar says he leaves Kent, where 'the strings of life / Began to crack' (V.iii.215–16).

[83] By contrast, the 'Scouse tart' whom Ian condemns for 'spread[ing] her legs' is 'not worth the space' (1.13).

being 'stupid' (1.8); but the contradictory declaration of being ('I am') and not being ('not') might also reflect her conflicted ontological status – the same status Ian occupies when he is both alive ('I am') and dead ('I am not'): 'I am, I am not' (1.8). In her most expansive insight on her fits, Cate reproduces the same contradiction between 'being' and 'not being', telling Ian that the world appears 'the same', but that it is also negated:

> The world don't exist, not like this.
> Looks the same but –
> Time slows down
> A dream I get stuck in, can't do nothing about it. (1.22)

The world 'is' but also 'is not': the fits that Cate suffers from happen in the world but also take her out of it, so while the world 'looks the same' it is also radically (if temporarily) negated: 'The world don't exist / not like this'. Through the deathly fits that afflict her throughout the play, Cate undergoes a transcendent experience that, by transitorily taking her beyond everyday quotidian reality, suddenly brings that reality into question: 'That was real?' (1.9).

Kane observes that in art 'the form is the meaning' and, with the bomb blast that rips through the hotel room, *Blasted* formally 'collapses' into a Cate-like 'fit', where normal reality is violently negated and 'don't exist, not like this'.[84] This negation of conventional stage space serves to self-reflexively deconstruct the 'reality' of the *mise-en-scène*, which is broken (or indeed blasted) into so many fractures and fragments. *Blasted* was largely denounced after its debut, as critics condemned its aesthetics of violence and degradation. But the case can be made that Kane draws on a late modernist aesthetics of damage to disrupt scenic 'reality' and precipitate something akin to the type of transcendent, metaphysical experience that Adorno relates to ephemerality – a shuddering response to the non-categorisable 'other'. By breaking its presentation of the material world apart, *Blasted* forms an aesthetic space for transcendence – for ephemerality – as affect: a seemingly recognisable reality is torn asunder and shown to be contingent, not absolute, adumbrating that there might be something other than the the 'closed' world of immanence and 'pure identity'.[85] Kane strives to empower a post-Auschwitz subject dimly imprisoned in the socially sanctioned intuition that the world is all there is, to conceive of the idea of something more than the

---

[84] Quoted in Saunders, '*Love Me or Kill Me*', p. 45 and p. 48.
[85] Adorno, *Negative Dialectics*, p. 403.

existent, beyond the totalised 'immediacy of the reality principle'.[86] She does so by appropriating *King Lear* and its cliff.

Conclusion

Kane appropriates the infamous Dover 'cliff' scene from *King Lear* in *Blasted* to interrogate the unbroken immanence of late capitalist society, which has become so pervasive that it has taken on the guise of a metaphysical absolute. This appropriation evinces a concern with the crisis of the subject at the so-called end of history, where the individual is pinioned within the totality of post-Auschwitz culture in a way that compromises freedom. To confront totality, Kane forges a space for transcendence and a new form of catastrophic, tragic autonomy.

Blasted was partly written in response to the Bosnian War and the return of concentration camps to Europe, evoking the memory of the Holocaust. The final stages of that conflict would also see Forced Entertainment turn to *King Lear* to write the disaster. Before moving on to Dennis Kelly, I provide a short postscript on the *King Lears* of Forced Entertainment.

Postscript: Writing and Performing from the Rubble: Forced Entertainment, *Five Day Lear* and *Table Top Shakespeare: The Complete Works*

Introduction

Five Day Lear was performed for the first (and last) time in early 1999 at the Lantern Theatre, Sheffield, the work of perhaps the best-known experimental performance company in the UK – Forced Entertainment, founded in Sheffield in 1984 by Tim Etchells, Robin Arthur, Huw Chadbourn, Cathy Naden and Susie Williams (Etchells is now artistic director, with Robin Arthur, Richard Lowdon, Claire Marshall, Cathy Naden and Terry O'Connor the core performers).[87] *Five Day Lear*

---

[86] Ibid. p. 397.
[87] For the early history of Forced Entertainment, see Patricia Benecke, 'The Making of ... From the Beginnings to *Hidden J*', in Judith Hemler and Florian Malzacher (eds), *Not Even a Game Anymore: The Theatre of Forced Entertainment* (Berlin: Alexander Verlag, 2012), pp. 27–50. My analysis is indebted to Robert Shaughnessy and his *The Shakespeare Effect: A History of Twentieth Century*

involved a week-long workshop on the play, which culminated in a forty-minute video called *Mark Does Lear* – where Etchells filmed his (clearly, fairly drunk) brother Mark as he provided a retelling of the plot of *King Lear* after a single reading – and the performance of *King Lear* itself. This took the form of a staged reading where fragments from the play were enacted, interrupted and played over again in various discontinuous ways, interspersed with video cuts from *Mark Does Lear* and audio recordings from the abridged, 1962 BBC radio version of *King Lear* from the 'Living Shakespeare' series, where Donald Wolfit performed Lear.[88] The aim of the workshops – and the final performance – was, as Etchells remarks, to reduce *King Lear* 'to rubble', to pound the play into a state of ruination and see if anything 'new and strange and beautiful' emerged from the 'devastation'.[89]

Forced Entertainment have often been viewed as pioneers of a non-text-based, postdramatic theatre form, which eschews a singular or original play-script for a more open-ended and intertextual approach to writing and performance, where various found materials intertwine with allusions to canonical plays and fragments from a constantly shifting mass consumer and media culture.[90] This has produced a series of pieces that tend to share dark comedy, a collage of arresting images and an anarchic performance style. It is an aesthetic which has often been aligned with postmodern appropriation and bricolage, where there is nothing to be found in a performance that is not 'a quotation of something else'.[91] This suspicion of a supposedly 'original' and 'singular' play-script is part of a wider poststructuralist philosophical approach to textuality, which brings traditional conceptions of the unified self, author and artwork radically into question. Etchells states in *Certain Fragments* that

> For us, in the work and out of it, this notion of self has often seemed after all to be simply a collection of texts, quotations, strategic and accidental speakings – not a coherent thing, much less the single-minded author of some text. What I am, in this text (now) at least, is no more (and no less) than the meeting-point of the language that flows into and flows out of me (these past

Performance (Basingstoke: Palgrave Macmillan, 2002), pp. 182–93. Shaughnessy was present at the only performance of the play.

[88] For the 'Living Shakespeare' broadcast, visit <https://www.youtube.com/watch?v=zNtbCKm5qn8> (accessed 14 October 2019). Forced Entertainment are particularly interested in Wolfit and his interpretation of *King Lear*.

[89] Quoted in Shaughnessy, *The Shakespeare Effect*, p. 188.

[90] This – at least – is the interpretation often provided in the wake of Hans-Thies Lehmann and his *Postdramatic Theatre*, trans. Karen Jürs-Munby (Oxford: Routledge, 2006). See especially Karen Jürs-Munby, 'Introduction', pp. 1–14.

[91] Quoted in Shaughnessy, *The Shakespeare Effect*, p. 183.

years, months, days) – a switching station, a filtering and thieving machine, a space in which collisions take place.[92]

This may seem to distinguish Forced Entertainment from the other playwrights and dramatists under consideration, where a formally catastrophic, tragic aesthetic underwrites a discourse of the subject and his/her autonomy from totalising ideologies. But the deconstructed Forced Entertainment aesthetic also evinces another cultural concern: throughout its history, Forced Entertainment has interrogated the conditions of crisis and catastrophe.

This preoccupation with catastrophe and its detritus reflects the genesis of Forced Entertainment in the desolate, wasted landscapes of post-industrial Sheffield, with its 'disused factories and fields of rubble', while Etchells also (and movingly) recalls the rubbish dump where he played as a child, a space on the margins of late capitalist consumer culture that provided a never-ending 'supply of discarded materials with which to work' and where 'new combinations of existing things were possible', an echo of Rudkin and his appropriation of Edgar/Poor Tom: 'They were interested in the margins of life, never the centre.'[93] But it also reflects a wider engagement with the catastrophes of the twentieth century and beyond, where Forced Entertainment replay and interrogate 'the tapes of the twentieth century' to see where modern society and culture have gone so disastrously wrong.[94]

Peggy Phelan has made the case that Etchells might be considered the 'able heir' to Beckett and that Forced Entertainment can be placed along a spectrum that begins with the post-apocalyptic worlds of *Waiting for Godot* and *Endgame*.[95] Phelan contends that, while Beckett was writing during the initial moments of a newly collapsed world and the destruction wrought by the Second World War, the Holocaust and Hiroshima, Forced Entertainment have continued to work through the cultural conditions of catastrophic upheaval and enduring crisis.[96] The detritus and leftovers

---

[92] Tim Etchells, *Certain Fragments: Contemporary Performance and the Theatre of Forced Entertainment* (London: Routledge, 1999), pp. 101–2.
[93] Etchells, *Certain Fragments*, p. 34; Tim Etchells, 'Valuable Spaces: New Performance in the 1990s', in Nicky Childs and Jeni Walwin (eds), *A Split Second of Paradise: Live Art, Installation and Performance* (London and New York: Rivers Oram Press, 1998), p. 40; Etchells, *Certain Fragments*, p. 32.
[94] Etchells, *Certain Fragments*, p. 84.
[95] Quoted in Sarah Jane Bailes, *Performance Theatre and the Poetics of Failure: Forced Entertainment, Goat Island, Elevator Repair Service* (London: Routledge, 2011), p. 66.
[96] Ibid.

that make up (or indeed unmake) the Forced Entertainment aesthetic often have less to do with ironic, postmodern pastiche and parody ('irony doesn't seem like a solution anymore', observes Terry O'Connor) and more to do with 'the fragmentation that follows an explosive event', with Ben Slater contending that Forced Entertainment often present audiences with disorientating 'survivors after a catastrophe' scenarios.[97] These disasters bring instrumental rationality and its fictions of progress into question, profoundly challenging ideologically positivist 'Enlightenment values of reason and order' in contemporary, totalised culture.[98] Forced Entertainment 'continually present us with the catastrophic', states Adrien Heathfield, 'under the shadow of late capitalism'.[99]

While Forced Entertainment and Etchells are influenced by the post-structuralist critique of the idea of the 'self', a concern with disaster and the ongoing impact of a century marked by catastrophe also informs the way in which Forced Entertainment conceptualise the human subject. Far from uncomplicatedly embracing the complete, postmodern repudiation of the self as a fiction of discourse, Forced Entertainment often stage performers who author and re-author themselves through the fragments left in the wake of catastrophe, insisting on the way people have the power 'to change themselves', 'to re-see themselves and the rest of the [. . .] world' by taking from the disintegrated 'scrap-heap of culture that they're born into and to use it' (perhaps also creating something 'new and beautiful and strange').[100] This runs contrary to a cultural system that otherwise reduces subjects to mere 'objects on a production line' and the dangerous ideological fantasy of 'human interchangeability'.[101] Though often critiqued for producing overly pessimistic and even 'apolitical' theatre, Forced Entertainment 'invest in the notion of change and self-authorship', using theatre as a way of staging 'acts of resistance against the hegemonic ideal'.[102]

---

[97] Etchells, *Certain Fragments*, p 45; Matthew Ghoulish, 'Peculiar Detonation: The Incomplete History and Impermanent Manifesto of the Institute of Failure', in Hemler and Malzacher, *Not Even a Game Anymore*, p. 258; quoted in Sarah Gorman, 'Forced Entertainment's Middle to Early Years: Montage and Quotation', in Graham Saunders (ed.), *British Theatre Companies 1980–1994* (London: Bloomsbury, 2015), p. 199.

[98] Gorman, 'Forced Entertainment's Middle to Early Years', p. 204.

[99] Adrien Heathfield, 'End Time Now', in Adrien Heathfield (ed.), *Small Acts: Performance, The Millennium and the Marking of Time* (London: Black Dog Publishing, 2000), p. 107.

[100] Etchells, *Certain Fragments*, p. 44.

[101] Ibid. p. 79

[102] Gorman, 'Forced Entertainment's Middle to Early Years', p. 210.

The collaborative performance style of Forced Entertainment does not necessarily allow for the type of individualised, tragic protagonist I have analysed previously – though it should be said some Forced Entertainment pieces have placed marked stress on the heroic endeavours of a single character to create meaning for him or herself in moments of crisis and disruption.[103] Where Forced Entertainment does consistently seek for a more self-reflexive, autonomous subject, however, is in its relation to the audience. The very name 'Forced Entertainment' obviously alludes to the modern, late capitalist Culture (or, for Arendt, 'Entertainment') Industry and a system of consumption in which the spectator is, as Adorno trenchantly states, 'forced to have fun', so integrating the individual into the cultural collective and its false veneer of 'pleasure' and 'happiness'.[104] Etchells contends that Forced Entertainment want to catalyse, not the passive consumers of the Culture Industry, but witnesses – or an imaginatively and morally engaged individual spectator who actively traces a path through the fragments, making his or her own individual 'connections, reasons, speculations'.[105] No small part of the rationale behind the catastrophic Forced Entertainment aesthetic is to fragment the audience and to empower the individual subject to respond in his or her own way to disastrous events that challenge the limits of comprehension and understanding. There is no obvious collective response to be had for Forced Entertainment; it remains up to the individual spectator to bear moral witness to sites of catastrophic disintegration. Writing and performing in the wake of 'the violently repetitive genocides of the twentieth century', Forced Entertainment seek to confront the audience 'with the challenge of witnessing traumas' that are 'psychically and politically unbearable'.[106]

Five Day Lear

Perhaps unsurprisingly, *King Lear* haunts a variety of Forced Entertainment performances, with snatches of dialogue and action making appearances in the 1988 piece *200% & Bloody Thirsty* ('Howl! Howl! Wake it up poor dead person for we are upset and grieving

---

[103] I am thinking particularly of Helen X in the 1993 piece *Club of No Regrets*, a director who desperately tries to wring some personal and communal meaning from a botched theatre/film piece.
[104] Theodor Adorno, *The Stars Down to Earth and Other Essays on the Irrational in Culture*, ed. Stephen Crook (New York and London: Routledge, 2004), p. 102.
[105] Etchells, *Certain Fragments*, p. 77.
[106] Peggy Phelan, 'Foreword', in Etchells, *Certain Fragments*, p. 10.

angels'), the 1992 piece *Emmanuel Enchanted* ('We did not weep though we had full cause of weeping' – the piece also alludes to 'A MAD OLD KING') and the 1994 piece *Speak Bitterness*, with its remarkable collection of confessions ('We dropped atom bombs on Nagasaki, Coventry, Seattle, Belize, Belsize Park and Hiroshima', 'We hated Jews', 'We were at Tet and May Lai') paraphrasing the proposed anatomisation of Regan: 'We cut open our own bodies to try and find the evil in them, we found nothing'.[107] Shakespeare is also present in the 1998 piece *Dirty Work*, which presents various 'Great Scenes' from the canon, from 'The Old Monarch Lear in his Madness on the Heath' to the 'Beautiful Juliet Drinking Poison in the Tomb'.[108] Etchells also retains an ongoing interest in the 1980 Ronald Harwood play *The Dresser* and its staging of *King Lear*, particularly the storm scenes and the way the Wolfit-like Mr Sir (as Lear) demands 'More storm!' from his stagehands, a moment that, as with many Forced Entertainment pieces, self-reflexively reveals the 'work' that takes place in producing theatre.[109] 'Go too far, go too far,' Etchells stresses: 'More storm. More storm. More storm.'[110]

Five Day Lear is unusual for Forced Entertainment, however, in that it represents the first time that the company attempted a sustained engagement with (and appropriation of) a single 'play' – a practice that Forced Entertainment have generally eschewed. Though Forced Entertainment cite a variety of influences – from postmodern American formalism (Robert Wilson and The Wooster Group) to contemporary European performance art (Marina Abramović and Uwe Laysiepen) – the fragmented aesthetic of *Five Day Lear*, along with a wider discourse around devastation and rubble, has obvious overlaps with late modernism and a post-Auschwitz aesthetic of catastrophe, where *King Lear* is shattered for the purposes of a theatre of the ruins. Sarah Gorman contends that the Forced Entertainment aesthetic emanates from modernism and its disintegration of conventional 'dramatic form' (or naturalist theatre) and that the company 'critique, rather than celebrate, postmodern aesthetics'.[111]

---

[107] Etchells, *Certain Fragments*, p. 31, p. 155, p. 183 and p. 185.
[108] Quoted in Jan Suk, 'Glocal Spin-Offs: Ghostings of Shakespeare in the Works of Forced Entertainment', <https://www.academia.edu/21331643/Glocal_Spin-Offs_Ghosting_of_Shakespeare_in_the_Works_of_Forced_Entertainment> (accessed 2 October 2019).
[109] Etchells, *Certain Fragments*, p. 85.
[110] Ibid. p. 69.
[111] Sarah Gorman, 'Chronicles of the Indeterminate: Ordering Chaos in the Retrospectives of Forced Entertainment', *Performance Research: A Journal of the Performing Arts*, 10:1 (2014), p. 85; Sarah Gorman, 'Theatre for a Media-Saturated Age', in Nadine Holdsworth and Mary Luckhurst (eds), *Concise*

This aligns *Five Day Lear* with other post-Auschwitz appropriations of the play. The idea of reducing *King Lear* to a state of ruination so that something 'new' may emerge has particularly distinct resonances with the intertextual poetics of Barker, who similarly sets out to 'desecrate' the play – though he does so as a paradoxical act of 'reverence'. Most of all, however, *Five Day Lear* shares its catastrophic aesthetic form and its historical concerns with Kane and *Blasted*. Robert Shaughnessy makes the case that the relationship between *King Lear* and *Five Day Lear* should be seen 'in terms of bombing and being bombed'.[112] The piece, which had its single performance on 9 April 1999, took place at the end of a fortnight of NATO bombing in the former Yugoslavia, in a conflict that involved the horrific ethnic cleansing of Albanian Kosovans.[113] Forced Entertainment had turned to *King Lear* at a time when Europe had (once again) lurched into a genocidal ethnic war, the violent shudders of the same conflict that had inspired Kane to appropriate *King Lear*. These were not events that Forced Entertainment held at a safe remove from liberal Western society, even while the conflict was often treated as an atavistic outbreak of premodern religious and tribal violence.[114] Etchells remarks that, when Mark retold the narrative of *King Lear* for *Mark Does Lear*, he turned the fate of Lear into a 'mad bad luck story that happened to some bloke he met somewhere' – 'perhaps in Bosnia, maybe in Ghana or a pub in rural Derbyshire', an observation that enacts the same spatial collapse seen in *Blasted*, where apparently remote events (Bosnia, Ghana) are uncannily charted onto a more recognisable world ('a pub in rural Derbyshire').[115]

The staged reading of *King Lear* began with the performers taking up seats at a row of tables at the back of the space. On the tables were piles of typewritten scripts – *King Lear* set out on A4 – and handwritten placecards denominating characters (LEAR, KENT, CORDELIA). Various scenes from the play were attempted, abandoned, attempted again and abandoned again, before the performers moved on to another

---

Companion to Contemporary British and Irish Drama (Oxford: Blackwell, 2013), p. 268.

[112] Shaughnessy, *The Shakespeare Effect*, p. 188.

[113] See Judith Armatta, *Twilight of Impunity: The War Crimes Trial of Slobodan Milosevic* (Durham, NC and London: Duke University Press, 2010).

[114] For a collection dealing with the media response to the crisis, see Philip Hammond and Edward S. Herman (eds), *Degraded Capability: The Media and the Kosovo Crisis* (London: Pluto Press, 2000). This collection includes a foreword by Harold Pinter (pp. vii–x).

[115] Tim Etchells, personal communication.

scene from the play, shuffling noisily through the scripts. Perhaps the most startling aspect of the discontinuous, fragmented form of *Five Day Lear* was the way it allowed the performers to punctuate the action and draw parallels between the violence of *King Lear* – particularly the blinding of Gloucester, a scene played many times over, while helicopters were heard buzzing overhead – with acts of contemporary mass violence and total warfare. At the start of the reading, the performer acting/reading the Lear part peremptorily announced that he would not be giving 'any details' of the airstrikes of the 'previous evening' or 'the specifics of Serbian collateral damage', as Lear was transformed into a NATO general or perhaps a modern-day European politician.[116] These allusions to the conflict and the crisis it provoked culminated at the end of the performance, where a halting 'update' was given on the catastrophic plight of refugees:

> Forty thousand refugees have gone missing. Thirteen thousand of them are reported to ... be ... fine. Ten thousand of them are still ... it is still unknown ... of their whereabouts ... The United States will take – [117]

Forced Entertainment transformed the destitute wretches of *King Lear* into Kosovan and Albanian refugees – the people who, outcast from society and denied any form of political or legal rights, could be genocidally rendered 'missing'. The pause which followed 'The United States will take –' obviously worked to critique the apparent reluctance of Western powers to 'accommodate' the many 'houseless heads' (III.iv.30) produced by the conflict, while the banal statement that other refugees 'are reported' to be 'fine' was deeply and bitterly ironic.

The performance ended with the final speech from *King Lear* with its reflections on the contradictions of witnessing ('never see so much') while, in the background, the video shifted to a bloodied Gloucester, silently mouthing the words. Finally – 'from beneath the rubble of the play' – the sound of a crying baby was heard.[118] It was an ambiguous *dénouement* that at once signified suffering innocence and the faint possibility of hope. *Five Day Lear* was left precariously somewhere between nihilistic despair – 'We came crying hither' (IV.vi.174) – and a more Christian-humanist interpretation of *King Lear* that insists on the redemptive possibility of new life. This indefinite ending obviously forestalled the type of resolution that may provide the basis for a collective response to the performance: it was left to the witnesses to respond

---

[116] Quoted in Shaughnessy, *The Shakespeare Effect*, p. 189.
[117] Ibid. p. 193.
[118] Ibid.

Figure 7.3 Performer Richard Lowdon uses various objects to narrate *Much Ado About Nothing*. *Table Top Shakespeare: The Complete Works, Much Ado About Nothing.* (2015: Barbican Theatre. Photograph: Hugo Glendinning. © Hugo Glendinning. All Rights Reserved, DACS/Artimage 2020)

to acts of cataclysmic violence and upheaval, to piece together a way through the wreckage.

Table Top Shakespeare: The Complete Works

Etchells has observed that it was *Five Day Lear* (and particularly *Mark Does Lear*) which inspired the popular 2016 *Table Top Shakespeare: The Complete Works* series, in which individual performers from Forced Entertainment use everyday objects to narrate the plots (but not the original language) from Shakespeare, with the objects representing various characters (Figures 7.3 and 7.4).[119] It is a process that Etchells has described as forming a new 'Shakespearean schematic' – by which he means a new way of charting the spatial and temporal movements his plots involve.[120]

---

[119] Tim Etchells, 'Interview with Dan Rebellato, Richard Ashby and Jessica Chiba: *Table Top Shakespeare: The Complete Works*', <https://www.youtube.com/watch?v=nu8C5eJc0pc> (accessed 5 September 2019).

[120] For more on the project, see the Forced Entertainment website: <https://www.forced

Figure 7.4 The objects used for the *Table Top Shakespeare: Complete Works* series are typically in a state of disuse, even ruination. *Table Top Shakespeare: The Complete Works, Much Ado About Nothing*. (2015: Barbican Theatre. Photograph: Hugo Glendenning. © Hugo Glendinning. All Rights Reserved, DACS/Artimage 2020)

These performances have been interpreted through the prism provided by developments in contemporary philosophy and theory, where movements in materialist thought from Actor-Network Theory (Bruno Latour) to Object-Orientated Ontology (Graham Harman) have witnessed a recent 'turn to the object'.[121] These theories have sought to show that subjects are enmeshed in and constituted by a world of objects, as opposed to dominating the object world through rational agency and conceptual language. This has parallels with Adorno and his own decentring of the humanist subject, while New Materialism also tends to impute disaster (particularly climate change and the collapse of the biosphere) to the legacy of Enlightenment rationality and

entertainment.com/projects/complete-works-table-top-shakespeare/> (accessed 6 September 2019).

[121] See in particular Nick Kaye, 'On Objects', *Performance Research*, 23:4–5 (2018), pp. 277–8. For an introduction to Actor Network Theory, see Bruno Latour, *Reassembling the Social: An Introduction to Actor-Network-Theory* (Oxford: Oxford University Press, 2005); for Object-Orientated Ontology, see Graham Harman, *Object-Oriented Ontology: A New Theory of Everything* (London: Penguin, 2018).

the domination of nature, opening out political and ethical perspectives beyond anthropocentric thought.[122] Where the New Materialism departs from critical theory, however, is in the way it elides the qualitative distinction between subject and object. New Materialism tends to ascribe 'lively' agency to objects, so that

> Agency cannot be viewed in terms of human meaning and intentionality, but as effects of actions between objects. Interactions between nonhuman/nonanimal objects are of just as much significance as interactions involving human/animal objects, and there is no difference in kind between interactions/relations involving humans and those not involving humans.[123]

The subject – as far as most New Materialist thought is concerned – is only really another object, inscribed in a mutually informing, ever-shifting network of various other objects, not a privileged (or indeed immanently transcendent, *à la* Kane) locus of autonomy or conceptuality. This philosophical position entails 'a full-blown re-description of the nature of all agency that involves a suspension of the central defining features of subjectivity; namely conscious experience, meaning, intentionality and reflection', though it can be said that there is a philosophical parasitism involved in emergent materialist thought that 'borrows the language of autonomous [. . .] agency and ascribes it plurally to all objects, but then critiques it whenever the concept of the subject raises its head'.[124]

There can be little doubt that *Table Top Shakespeare* has some resonances with New Materialist philosophy around things and the 'entanglement' of the subject in a world of objects, not least by turning characters from Shakespeare into (usually, blasted) objects.[125] But the series clearly retains something of a privileged position for the subject as performer/author, as s/he intentionally acts on objects through movement and language to tell a story – perhaps something of a shift from *Five Day Lear* and its more collective approach to performance. The status of the objects Forced Entertainment use in *Table Top Shakespeare* is also of interpretive import, where New Materialism – somewhat paradoxically – tends to obscure the specific form of individual objects by refusing to think about the way certain objects conceptually signify in human discourse. For the most part, the objects Forced Entertainment deploy are clearly (or were previously) in a state of prolonged disuse

---

[122] See again the work of Alistair Morgan, 'A Preponderance of Objects: Critical Theory and the Turn to the Object', *Adorno Studies*, 1:1 (2017), pp. 14–30.
[123] Ibid. p. 16.
[124] Ibid. p. 21.
[125] Kaye, 'On Objects', p. 278.

or even ruination – half-empty plastic bottles, rusted metal tins, dented pots and so on. This evinces a cultural concern with reusing and recycling in an era of environmental degradation and climate change – and indeed the strictures of modern, post-2008 financial austerity. But it also continues a visual discourse around catastrophe and apocalypse present throughout the Forced Entertainment aesthetic where, as Etchells states:

> There's always a point when we're making our shows, even now, when you say 'These are the only people left in the world, all they've got are these ten bits of paper, and this great pile of crap and they've somehow got to sort it out'.[126]

The objects which the performers use in *Table Top Shakespeare* might almost be the remnants from some cataclysmic, apocalyptic event – the detritus of human culture, through which 'the survivors' have to pick in order to tell meaningful stories about the world. Not unlike previous performances, *Table Top Shakespeare* reveals an ongoing concern with the way in which subjects recreate themselves and the world in situations of catastrophic upheaval, investing in the possibility (and necessity) of human agency in the midst of disaster. With its genesis in *Five Day Lear*, the *Table Top Shakespeare* series shows the way that *King Lear* continues to inform a writing/performance of the ruins in the Forced Entertainment aesthetic and its emphasis on the subject as a site of meaning – even freedom.

The emergent forms of New Materialist thought – Actor-Network Theory, Object-Orientated Ontology – through which Forced Entertainment Shakespeare has been analysed are largely a response to the humanly caused climate catastrophe, where any conception of a voluntaristic subject shaping the world as s/he wishes is completely displaced in favour of analysing the object. There is, however, a certain irony in denying human agency at the very moment when anthropogenic climate change threatens to completely destroy the ecosphere – and indeed when only humans can intervene to stop a total worldwide catastrophe. The possibility of human freedom in a post-Auschwitz world of precipitous environmental collapse and worldwide economic catastrophe leads us to *The Gods Weep*, the remarkable 2010 *King Lear* play by Dennis Kelly, and the final case study under consideration.

---

[126] Quoted in Gorman, 'Forced Entertainment's Middle to Early Years', pp. 199–200.

Chapter 8

'And I was struck still . . .': Nature, the Sublime and Subjectivity in Dennis Kelly's *The Gods Weep*

Introduction

Dennis Kelly has been described as the most 'thrillingly inventive' playwright to 'emerge in the last decade' and as 'a distinctive new voice in British playwriting', providing 'the answer to anyone who longs for the return of metaphor, imagination, formal invention, and savage humour on our stages'.[1] From his 2003 debut *Debris* to *Osama the Hero* (2004), *After the End* (2005), *Love and Money* (2006), *Orphans* (2009), *The Gods Weep* (2010), *The Ritual Slaughter of Gorge Mastromas* (2013) and *Girls and Boys* (2018), Kelly has produced a variety of formally innovative new plays confronting global capital and the credit crunch, post-9/11 terrorism and cultures of surveillance, mass immigration and racism, patriarchal violence, nuclear war and environmental collapse. Kelly is, in the words of Dan Rebellato, 'the writer who perhaps has most convincingly shown us how to write plays not just in this new century, but about this new century' – a century that has, so far, been marked by crisis and catastrophe.[2]

Not unlike other contemporary writers, Kelly writes in a variety of media, co-writing the BBC sitcom *Pulling* (2006–9) while also adapting *Matilda* into a (hugely successful) musical in 2010. But as Vicky Angelaki has contended, while Kelly tends to write in a more comic vein in other media, his original stage plays are generally tragic (sometimes even dystopian) in theme and form, with Kelly writing 'human tragedies'

---

[1] Aleks Sierz, 'Introduction', in Dennis Kelly, *Dennis Kelly: Plays Two* (London: Oberon Books, 2013), p. xiv; Dan Rebellato, 'New Writing: Dennis Kelly', 'Backpages', *Contemporary Theatre Review*, 17.4 (2007), p. 607.
[2] Rebellato, 'New Writing: Dennis Kelly', p. 607.

in an era when untrammelled 'capitalist dependencies can lead to the abuse and even sacrifice of human life'.³

Aleks Sierz has described *The Gods Weep* as perhaps 'the most extraordinary play in an extraordinary career'.⁴ The play was staged in 2010 at the Hampstead Theatre, London, and was conceived by Kelly as a sequel to his 2006 play *Love and Money*, in which a couple (David and Jess) struggle with the damaging impact of debt, culminating in the suicide (or, possibly, murder) of Jess, which David purposefully fails to intervene in.⁵ Where the 2006 play had portrayed a concentrated view of the profound intertwining of personal and financial relationships through the struggles of a single couple, *The Gods Weep* sought to provide a more comprehensive, totalised view of the capitalist process and its damaging impact on people – a view obviously inspired by the worldwide economic crash of 2008, which profoundly challenged the post-1989 liberal democratic consensus that capitalist relations provide continuous economic growth and social progress over time.⁶ This aligns *The Gods Weep* with a series of other dramas that emerged in response to the crunch – or 'post-crash' plays – including *Faces in the Crowd* (Leo Butler, 2008), *The Power of Yes* (David Hare, 2009), *Precious Little Talent* (Ella Hickson, 2009) and, perhaps most famously, *Enron* (Lucy Prebble, 2009).

The play itself is a wholesale rewrite of *King Lear* which takes place over three acts.⁷ Lear is transformed into Colm (played originally by Jeremy Irons) – the founder and CEO of a vast international company with interests across the globe. At the start of the play, Colm reveals his decision to step down as CEO – but to keep the title of 'Chairman', splitting the power and duties of the CEO between his mutually antagonistic subordinates, Richard and Catherine. Colm also states his intention to take control of Belize, where the company is involved in 'Food security' (1.35) – which entails buying up fertile land in poor regions of the world in order to lease it out to richer nations. The plan is scuppered by Jimmy – the 'weak' son of Colm, previously responsible for Belize – who forces a lawyer (Beth) to provide insurance for inspectors to travel

---

³ Vicky Angelaki, *Social and Political Theatre in 21st Century Britain: Staging Crisis* (London: Methuen, 2017), p. 82.
⁴ Sierz, 'Introduction', *The Gods Weep*, p. xi.
⁵ Dennis Kelly, *Plays One* (London: Oberon Books, 2008), pp. 216–17. I will return to *Love and Money* (and the Holocaust) below, where I cite the play using scene and page numbers.
⁶ Dennis Kelly, 'Dennis Kelly talks about *The Gods Weep*', <https://www.youtube.com/watch?v=vnpdWqsV5CI> (accessed 4 February 2018).
⁷ This form obviously has resonances with *Lear*.

to the country.⁸ These inspectors are kidnapped by rebels, plunging the company into the 'disaster' of a precipitous crash where millions are wiped off its share price (1.81). Colm is also undermined by both Richard and Catherine who, disgusted to find that he intends to use his control of Belize to sell produce back to the local population at a reduced rate in a bid for some form of personal redemption, plan to seize control of the country (Richard suspects Colm of reading *Das Kapital*). The united front presented by Richard and Catherine does not last, however, with the Astrologer Richard employs to predict the futures market and other events prophesying that the company is 'going to war' (1.37).

This prophesy of corporate infighting comes literally – and bloodily – to pass at the start of Act Two, as the battle between Richard and Catherine degenerates, without warning, into a civil war fought over an indeterminate territory, with Nazi-type war crimes committed by both camps (Richard even intends to have fifteen per cent of his poorest performing soldiers executed – a punishment which ironises the perverse, commodifying approach to human beings taken in mass corporate layoffs).⁹ While the rival factions destroy each other, an increasingly demented Colm finds refuge living in anti-pastoral isolation with Barbara, the daughter of a man he once ruthlessly destroyed. Over the course of Act Three, Colm and Barbara scrape a meagre subsidence life, while Colm holds out hope that his suffering – and the forgiveness of Barbara, whom he starts to call his daughter – might deliver 'absolution', even while he struggles with the idea that there is not 'a solitary reason' why 'I should be absolved' (3.172). At the end of the play, Barbara is suddenly shot, as Jimmy – who seems to have prevailed in the war – comes to find and 'rescue' the surviving Colm. Jimmy tries to address himself to Colm and enact a reconciliation, but Colm seems to have been left totally 'broken' by the death of Barbara: 'We should put him out of his misery' (3.180).

While it has gained some praise from critics, for the most part *The Gods Weep* met with underwhelming – and often downright hostile – reviews, while Kelly himself stated that part of his aim was to produce an 'epic' that was 'big, unwieldy, flawed and messy'.¹⁰ What seemed to

---

⁸ Colm brutally describes Jimmy 'as a kind of tumour' (1.31) – echoing Lear when he tells Goneril that she is a 'disease' in his 'flesh' which 'I must needs call mine' (II.ii.411–12).

⁹ I will return to the layoffs below, when I discuss the idea of the vitality curve.

¹⁰ 'Dennis Kelly talks about *The Gods Weep*'. See also Charles Spencer, '*The Gods Weep*, RSC', <http://www.telegraph.co.uk/culture/theatre/london-shows/

most perplex critics was the sudden transformation of a drama seemingly about the world of corporate capitalism into scenes of a mass conflagration with parallels to the atrocities of the Second World War, which contravenes the usual naturalistic conventions of progressive action. No few reviewers complained of the 'explosive disorientation' that took place at the start of Act Two, which abruptly calls for *'Soldiers, Militia, Noise'* (2.83) as the action descends into 'shelling', 'firebomb[ing]', 'debris, rubble' and 'piles of dead' (2.110–11).[11]

Charles Spencer confesses to finding Act One 'moderately entertaining' for 'an anti-capitalist soap opera'; but the 'fantastic shift' in Act Two – where 'the suits are discovered in battle fatigues, and a brutal guerrilla war has broken out among the executives, with interminable scenes of shooting, torture and atrocity' – seemed unmotivated, a conclusion also drawn by Michael Billington, who opined that 'Kelly never makes it clear why corporate rivalry leads to armed conflict.'[12] Paul Taylor, who seems to have intuited the resonances between the imagery of the play and the concentration camps, instructed all playwrights who want to 'deal with atrocity responsibly and illuminatingly' – something Kelly had obviously failed to do by suddenly turning the 'promising' opening act into scenes of 'human degradation' – to read the Anthony Hecht poem 'More Light! More Light!' before starting rehearsal.[13] This poem is about a real-life event on the outskirts of a concentration camp, where a Polish prisoner who initially refuses to dig a grave for Jews is himself buried – 'The thick dirt mounted toward the quivering chin. / When only the head was exposed the order came / To dig him out again and to get back in' – before being shot.[14] These grievances about the formal disintegration and grotesquely violent action of *The Gods Weep* also relate to its failure to provide the redemptive 'closure' and 'compensation' of *King Lear* – an indictment that

---

7472953/The-Gods-Weep-RSC-Hampstead-Theatre-review.html> (accessed 4 February 2018).

[11] Paul Taylor, '*The Gods Weep*', <http://www.independent.co.uk/arts-entertainment/theatre-dance/reviews/the-gods-weep-hampstead-theatre-london-1925376.html> (accessed 5 February 2018).

[12] Spencer, '*The Gods Weep*, RSC'; Michael Billington, '*The Gods Weep*', <https://www.theguardian.com/stage/2010/mar/18/the-gods-weep-review> (accessed 5 February 2018).

[13] Taylor, '*The Gods Weep*'.

[14] See Anthony Hecht, 'More Light. More Light!', in *Selected Poems*, ed. James McClatchy (New York: Alfred Knopf, 2011), pp. 62–3. It is a powerfully Lear-like image that has intriguing resonances with the final moments of *Blasted*, where Ian is buried up to his neck.

reveals a relatively conventional, Christian-humanist interpretation of Shakespeare and the ending of his play, which would see Lear 'learn' through his suffering.[15]

Spencer is in little doubt as to who is to blame for the apparent formlessness of *The Gods Weep*:

> This is a piece strongly influenced by the grim, preachy dramas of horror and catastrophe that were dished up for so long by Edward Bond and Howard Barker. I thought we had more or less banished their baleful influence from our stages, but now up pops Kelly like some unstoppable, living-dead monster in a horror movie intent on wreaking further havoc.[16]

It would seem Spencer has not seen much Bond recently – and possibly any Barker at all, who could never be described as 'preachy'. He is, however, not necessarily wrong to point out the parallels between *The Gods Weep* and catastrophic (anti-)form. Perhaps most of all, the sudden shift from a claustrophobic boardroom to a full-scale war has obvious resonances with *Blasted*, its own abrupt war and the mortar blast that reduces the hotel room to ruins. Like its Lear-influenced antecedent, the play suddenly collapses the formal and spatial perimeters between a reifying late capitalist culture and fascistic violence. This sudden turn obviously perplexed many critics – but the formal fragmentation of *The Gods Weep* can be placed in a wider genealogy of catastrophic appropriations of *King Lear* 'after' Auschwitz. This, more than the so-called 'crash' plays, is the lineage in which *The Gods Weep* should be placed.

Kelly has remarked that he was more influenced by the remarkable 1985 Akira Kurosawa film *Ran* – a Samurai adaptation of *King Lear* – than the 'original' Shakespeare play, with its vast set-piece battles and violent scenes of mass destruction.[17] My own take on the play, however, is that it represents a deep engagement with *King Lear*, while the relationship with *Ran* is generally limited to reusing some of its plot changes and some dialogue – a more cosmetic relation.[18] Kelly appropriates *King Lear* to provide a powerful critique of late globalised capitalism and its tendency towards disruption and disaster, as evidenced by the

---

[15] Billington, '*The Gods Weep*'.
[16] Spencer, '*The Gods Weep*, RSC'.
[17] Akira Kurosawa, *Ran* (London: WHV DVD, 2004).
[18] Kurosawa changes the daughters of *King Lear* to sons – Taro, Jiro and Saburo. Kelly also transforms the daughters into a single son – Jimmy. Cordelia is adapted in *Ran* to Lady Sue – the daughter of a rival whom the Lear-figure, Hidetora, previously destroyed. Barbara in *The Gods Weep* is also the daughter of a former rival, as opposed to the daughter of Colm.

worldwide economic crash of 2008 – the fallout of which is still impacting culture and society, not least through the ongoing rise of right-wing ethno-nationalist populism.[19]

By dramatising a deeply brutal war as it emerges from a transnational corporation, Kelly seeks to demonstrate the potential outcomes of the violence inherent in the late capitalist system, showing that its reification of human beings may have dire consequences. Not unlike the other playwrights I have analysed, Kelly does not necessarily engage with the politics of identity, refuting the idea that his working-class roots mean that he should necessarily write plays about 'life on council estates'.[20] His dramatic and political vision is more concerned with the degraded status of the subject in post-Auschwitz culture. Kelly, as Chris Megson has contended, posits a world where capitalism has 'colonized' the subject, as 'economic competition and physical brutality have become indivisible'.[21] This is signalled through images that purposefully draw on the mass destruction of human beings that took place in the Holocaust, as Kelly draws controversial parallels between late capitalist culture and Auschwitz.

Kelly is, however, also concerned to interrogate the relationship between the reification of human beings and the reification of the natural world. His critique of post-Auschwitz culture and the catastrophes of modernity also comprises anthropogenic climate change and the degradation of the environment. This is something Kelly achieves by appropriating the anti-pastoral imagery of *King Lear* and – perhaps most startlingly – its concern with a blasted world of hunger and food scarcity. Both plays depict a situation where the collapse of the environment means that people have become disturbingly 'belly-pinched' (III.i.13).

Over and against the reification of people and nature, Kelly proposes a distinct conception of the subject and his/her transcendent freedom from totality. Other playwrights I have studied have tended to present

---

[19] There have been a variety of studies on the rise of 'populism' on both the left and right in the wake of the crash; but for a cogent, empirically adduced analysis of the way in which far-right parties have recently (and historically) benefited from financial crises, see Manuel Funke, Moritz Schularick and Christoph Trebesch, 'Going to Extremes: Politics after Financial Crises, 1870–2014', *European Economic Review*, 88 (2016), pp. 227–60.

[20] Dennis Kelly, 'Identity Crisis', <https://www.theguardian.com/stage/2008/feb/28/theatre.television> (accessed 29 September 2019).

[21] Chris Megson, '"And I was struck still by time": Contemporary British Theatre and the Metaphysical Imagination', in Vicky Angelaki (ed.), *Contemporary British Theatre: Breaking New Ground* (Basingstoke: Palgrave Macmillan, 2013), p. 48.

self-fashioning, transgressive tragic protagonists, particularly Bond, Rudkin and Barker. Kelly, however, presents a tragic subject who confronts the overwhelming, incomprehensible temporal and spatial plenitude of the natural world – and is struck still by it. What is found in *The Gods Weep* is something akin to the sublime, which displaces the awed subject outside of the totalised world of concepts by challenging the limits of perception. I want to make the case that a modern, tragic conception of the sublime can underpin the autonomy of the subject and, vitally in an age of environmental degradation, the radically 'alien' otherness of the non-human natural world.[22]

Writing in his 'Analytic of the Sublime' in *Critique of Judgement*, Kant famously contends that the sublime is to be found in nature – in threatening rocks, thunderclouds, volcanoes, hurricanes, boundless oceans and mighty rivers and so on.[23] But for Kant, the mind overcomes the power of nature by producing ideas of reason – the concepts of infinity, limitlessness and totality – so that 'true sublimity' must be sought only in the mind of the subject.[24] Adorno, however, tends to foreground the negative moment of the sublime in his refiguring of Kantian aesthetics, a move that is developed by Lyotard and Derrida.[25] Adorno stresses the moment at which the perceptual 'control' of nature is at risk – the precarious points where the overwhelming spatial and temporal presence of nature cannot be rationally captured through the use of delimiting (human) concepts. Adorno writes in *Aesthetic Theory*:

> Rather than that, as Kant thought, spirit in the face of nature becomes aware of its own superiority, it becomes aware of its own natural essence. This is the moment when the subject, vis-à-vis the sublime, is moved to tears.

[22] For climate change as itself a sort of 'sublime', beyond conceptual limitation or understanding, see Maggie Kainulainen, 'Saying Climate Change: Ethics of the Sublime and the Problem of Representation', *symploke*, 21:1–2 (2014), pp. 109–23.

[23] Immanuel Kant, *Critique of Judgment*, trans. James Creed Meredith (Oxford: Oxford University Press, 2007), p. 91 and p. 93.

[24] Ibid. p. 86. Kant also contends that the sublime is 'an object (of nature) *the representation of which determines the mind to regard the elevation of nature beyond our reach as equivalent to a presentation of ideas*' (ibid. p. 98).

[25] See also Karoline Gritzner, 'Adorno and the Sublime in Live Performance', *The European Legacy*, 21:7 (2016), pp. 633–43. Lyotard provides a scrupulous close reading of Kant in his *Lessons on the Analytic of the Sublime: Kant's Critique of Judgment*, trans. Elizabeth Rottenberg (Stanford: Stanford University Press, 1991) and formulates his conception of the sublime in *The Inhuman: Reflections on Time*, trans. Geoffrey Bennington and Rachel Bowdy (Stanford: Stanford University Press, 1988), while Derrida analyses the sublime in his *Truth in Painting* (Chicago: University of Chicago Press, 1987).

Recollection of nature breaks the arrogance of his self-positing: 'My tears well up; earth, I am returning to you'.[26]

Adorno aligns the sublime with the non-identity of nature – its resistance to conceptual human control. This is all-important in an era where human mastery over nature seems to have become all but complete, as modern capital establishes a 'racket' in nature that has precipitated the deterioration of the environment through the depletion of resources, the destruction of ecosystems and habitats, the extinction of wildlife and continuous pollution.[27]

Adorno writes in *Negative Dialectics* of 'a universal feeling, a universal fear that our progress in controlling nature may increasingly help to weave the very catastrophe it was supposed to protect us from'.[28] The uninterrupted reign of instrumental reason not only dominates non-human nature (object) but also leads to the domination of human nature (subject) – in the sense that humans too are a part of nature. Adorno and Horkheimer (citing Freud and his *Civilization and Its Discontents*) contend that in modernity subjects are required to renounce instinctual 'natural' needs (say supposedly deviant forms of sexual pleasure) for the sake of civilisational adaptation and that subjects are themselves transformed into objects of social and political exploitation, in the same way as the natural world.[29]

This take on the domination of both non-human and human nature through enlightened reason is particularly important because it establishes a genealogical relationship between the human misuse of nature, the degradation of the earth and the Holocaust. Deborah Cooke writes

---

[26] Theodor Adorno, *Aesthetic Theory*, trans. Robert Hullot-Kentor (London: Continuum, 2004), p. 356. I return to the idea of the subject 'becoming nature' when I analyse *The Gods Weep*.

[27] Ibid. p. 27. The use of the word 'racket' is important: Adorno, not unlike Brecht in his 1941 *The Resistible Rise of Arturo Ui*, sometimes refers to fascism as a 'racket' – alluding to both the violent practices of fascism and its tendency to amass capital and people. See Stephen Crook, 'Introduction', in Theodor Adorno, *The Stars Down to Earth and Other Essays on the Irrational in Culture* (New York and London: Routledge, 2004), p. 22. For more on Adorno, Frankfurt School theory and modern environmental studies, see Andrew Biro (ed.), *Critical Ecologies: The Frankfurt School and Contemporary Environmental Crises* (Toronto: University of Toronto Press, 2011).

[28] Theodor Adorno, *Negative Dialectics*, trans. E. B. Ashton (London and New York: Continuum, 2007), p. 67.

[29] The idea of natural and artificial needs is a fraught one in Adorno and includes a complex engagement with the intertwining of nature and history. See his recently translated 'Theses on Need', trans. Martin Shuster and Iain Macdonald, *Adorno Studies*, 1:1 (2017), pp. 101–4.

that for Adorno, 'reification and the annihilation of nature are of a piece'.[30] 'Even as nature has been turned into an object, human beings themselves began to be treated as objects of manipulation and control', as most harrowingly revealed by the concentration camps of the Second World War.[31] Cooke contends that in *Negative Dialectics* the

> new categorical imperative – that nothing like Auschwitz should happen again – is a response to a situation in which human and non-human nature have been reduced to so many commensurable units of value, to lifeless, reified objects, and are either literally destroyed or damaged to the point where it can plausibly be said that they no longer live because they are prevented from developing freely.[32]

On the one hand, the Holocaust bears witness to the rational domination of nature in enlightened modernity, while on the other, the instrumentalisation of nature in post-war society also offers a glimpse of the continuing possibility of another lapse into genocidal barbarity: the corruption of nature and the collapse of the ecosphere are marked by the traces of Auschwitz.[33] Through his appropriation of *King Lear*, Kelly draws similar parallels between the reification of human beings and the destruction of the environment in late capitalist culture.

The Vitality Curve: Kelly, Late Capitalism and Auschwitz

The Gods Weep is an undeniably violent play, where the conflict that rages over Act Two rips people into 'fragments of, exploding, disintegrating, into plumes of pain, agony, screaming frivolous devastation with cuts and cuts and cuts' (2.96). The imagery draws on *King Lear*, not least the moment when Albany threatens to 'dislocate and tear' the 'flesh and bones' (IV.ii.66–7) of Goneril – though Kelly also draws on other artworks that represent atrocity, most obviously Francisco Goya and his 'A Heroic Feat! With Dead Men!' from *The Disasters of War* series:

---

[30] Deborah Cook, *Adorno on Nature* (London: Routledge, 2014), p. 102.
[31] Ibid. p. 21.
[32] Ibid. p. 127.
[33] Critics are increasingly drawing connections between climate change denial and right-wing populism, while at the same time keeping the historical ideological relationship between some forms of right-wing discourse and environmentalism in sight (sometimes described as eco-fascism – though that term is now being liberally applied to supposedly repressive elements in the left environmentalist movement). See in particular Bernhard Forchtner (ed.), *The Far Right and the Environment: Politics, Discourse and Communication* (Oxford: Routledge, 2020).

They took them into the woods. Hacked them to pieces. With mattocks, rakes, implements, farm implements, they cut them into chunks of meat, they decorated a tree with their guts. (2.97)

The violent disfiguration of aesthetic form in *The Gods Weep* is paralleled by the violent disfiguration of the human body, which is transformed into so many lifeless fragments, revealing the reification of the subject (and its disintegrated 'parts') in the capitalist process.[34]

The pressing irony, however, is that Colm begins the play by trying to foster a more compassionate global capitalism, or *'global capitalism with a human face'*, as Slavoj Žižek calls it.[35] This names 'an attempt to minimize the human costs of the global capitalist machinery', though crucially its 'functioning is left undisturbed' (Žižek cites charity, philanthropism, recycling policies and other practices that bid to 'incorporate' an ideological critique of capital into its very production process).[36] Colm – arrested by the thought that 'growth has its limits' (1.28) – takes control of Belize so as to sell twenty-five per cent of the produce grown there 'locally at below market value' (1.46) in a proposal that is described as a 'Humanitarian provision' (1.46). Colm contests the idea that under capitalist relations 'Humanity must perforce prey on itself, / Like monsters of the deep' (IV.ii.50-51) and that he and his partners are mere 'monsters' who 'make things that can only destroy, ravenous engines of wealth that can only move in one direction' (1.29). Using the language around the 'love-test' that begins *King Lear*, Colm grandiloquently proclaims that his new, compassionate vision for global capital – which Richard and Catherine dismiss as mere 'legacy stuff' and 'Gandhi peace prize shit' (1.46) – is 'a test': 'For all of us. For everything. For everything in the world' (1.30).

Not unlike Lear, Colm intends to 'shake the superflux' (III.iv.35) of global capital to the poor and destitute, imagining a new world where 'distribution should undo excess' (IV.i.73). But as Kiernan Ryan has persuasively shown, while Lear may imagine a more equitable world in his prayer to the 'naked wretches' in the storm, his idea of beneficently sharing riches with the less fortunate does not challenge the underlying principle of hierarchy *per se*; his 'prayer on the threshold of the

---

[34] Siegfried Kracauer famously analyses the way capital (and particularly the industrial process) reduces human body parts to reified objects in his treatment of the dancing of the 'Tiller Girls'. See his *The Mass Ornament: Weimar Essays*, trans. Thomas Y. Levin (Cambridge, MA: Harvard University Press, 1995), pp. 75–86.
[35] Slavoj Žižek, *The Fragile Absolute: Or, Why is the Christian Legacy Worth Fighting For?* (London: Verso, 2000), p. 63.
[36] Ibid.

hovel presupposes the same stratified society, in which "pomp" would persist, but would treat those at its mercy with greater sympathy and generosity'.[37] The same is true of Colm and *The Gods Weep*: while it is met with vociferous opposition from Catherine and Richard, inspiring the corporate takeover that will descend into bloodshed, the plan for Belize retains the inequitable, hierarchical balance of global capital and leaves its reifying systems largely intact – an underlying continuity between systems revealed by the way Colm wants to retain the title of 'Chairman' (1.30) at the start of the play, even while enacting his plan for redistributive justice.

The violent reification of people under capital is most powerfully disclosed in *The Gods Weep* through its allusions to the idea of the 'vitality curve'. Vitality refers to a practice pioneered in the 1980s by Jack Welch – former CEO of the American corporation General Electric – in which workers are ranked in a so-called '20-70-10 system': the 'top' twenty per cent of the workforce is most productive, another seventy per cent (the 'vital 70') work adequately, while the remaining ten per cent are non-producers, parasitic on the corporation as a whole, and should be fired on a rolling yearly basis – gaining vitality the less euphemistic name of 'rank and yank'.[38] Practitioners of vitality have ranged from General Electric to IBM, Amazon to Enron and, perhaps most revealingly in age of supposedly compassionate global capital, Microsoft.[39] Colm, when berating Jimmy for his imagined 'weakness' – 'I had to fight back the desire to swing you by your feet and dash your brains out on the wall' (1.32) Colm states, echoing Lady Macbeth – tells his son that his most vital 'innovation' was 'to fire the bottom eight percent' 'every year' (1.32).[40] It is a process that transforms vital, living subjects into devitalised, dead objects, to be cruelly disposed of as Colm deems fit.

---

[37] Kiernan Ryan, 'Introduction', in William Shakespeare, *King Lear* (London: Penguin, 2015), p. xxvi.

[38] See Jack Welch, *Jack: Straight from the Gut* (London: Headline, 2001), pp. 58–62.

[39] Reed Abelson, 'Companies Turn to Grades, and Employees Go to Court', <https://www.nytimes.com/2001/03/19/business/companies-turn-to-grades-and-employees-go-to-court.html> (accessed 14 February 2018).

[40] When he seems to blanch at the idea of assassinating Duncan, Lady Macbeth tells her husband that

> I have given suck, and know
> How tender 'tis to love the babe that milks me:
> I would, while it was smiling in my face,
> Have plucked the nipple from his boneless gums
> And dashed the brains out, had I so sworn
> As you have done to this. (I.vii.54–9)

The violence inherent in that reifying practice is literalised over the action of the play. From the eight per cent fired by Colm, Richard proposes to have the bottom-performing fifteen per cent of his army not sacked, but summarily destroyed: 'I have decided that anyone who doesn't fight well enough will be executed after the battle. The bottom fifteen percent. The bottom fifteen percent will be executed' (2.106). After finding out that Richard has duped her, Beth kills him, declaring (in another echo of *Macbeth*) that the 'tyrant' is 'gone': 'Now is a new, now is our, now is a new time, our time. We shall remake the world in our image' (2.128); but, not unlike the Cordelia of *Lear*, the revolution Beth proposes only repeats and even intensifies the violence of the previous regime (as indicated by her convoluted, strangely repetitive discourse).[41] Her order is not only to kill 'all prisoners' (2.128) but also to rank the survivors of the conflict 'by value' (2.128): 'Assess the people by usefulness and value. Cull the bottom twenty-five percent' (2.129). Kelly inverts the process Shakespeare depicts in *King Lear*: where in that play a rationalistic, instrumental approach to human life leads Goneril and Regan to whittle the train of knights Lear demands from fifty to twenty-five and eventually down to zero, in *The Gods Weep* quantities tend to tick inexorably up, from eight to fifteen to twenty-five. Use-value in *The Gods Weep* is being completely colonised by exchange-value: Colm, Richard and Beth all reduce human life to its 'usefulness' and 'value', disregarding the possibility that it has any inherent worth beyond ideologically utilitarian considerations, while the standards required to meet the vital threshold (or 'curve') of productivity and value become more and more stringent.

The idea that only those people who are 'valuable' or 'useful' in society should be allowed to live, while anybody that fails to prove themselves able to contribute, or who parasitically lives off the work and struggle of other people, has to be removed, reverberates with the ideology around the Holocaust, which similarly sought to purge any socially unproductive and undesirable people from the Nazi body politic. Kelly alludes to the Holocaust in Act Three of *The Gods Weep*, when it 'suddenly' (and unseasonably) begins to 'snow':

> It is perhaps the most violent articulation of the individualist credo that 'For mine own good / All causes shall give way' (III.iv.134–5) – a worldview that chimes with the capitalist world of *The Gods Weep*.
>
> [41] For more on Kelly and the traumatic lack around which discourse revolves in his plays, see Julien Alliot, '"I Know How that Sounds and I Do Not Mean that as an, but I Mean Christ": The Disturbance in the Symbolic Order in Dennis Kelly's Theatre', *E-rea*, 12:1 (2014), <http://journals.openedition.org/erea/3990> (accessed 5 September 2019).

>   *Suddenly it starts to snow. They look up.*
> Barbara: What?
>   *They hold their hands out.*
> Colm: Snow? It's not cold.
>   *She rubs some in her hand.*
> Barbara: Ash.
> Colm: Ash? Falling out of the sky? Someone must be burning something. It's not from near here. What do you think they're burning?
>   *They stand for a moment. They suddenly run into the shelter, away from the ash. They brush it off them, desperate to get it away from their bodies. They stare at each other. They watch the ash fall.* (3.155)

The implication is all too obvious: the ash – so dense it is initially mistaken for snow – comes from burnt human bodies, occasioning the disgusted response from both Colm and Barbara, as both try to remove the ash by brushing it away.[42] The scene is reminiscent of the storm scenes from *King Lear* and its 'scorching' downpour, and perhaps also picks up on the moment where Albany tells Goneril she is 'not worth the dust which the rude wind / Blows in your face' (IV.ii.31–2).[43] But the ash is also a visual allusion to the 1993 Stephen Spielberg Holocaust film *Schindler's List*, which contains an iconic shot in which snow (or something resembling snow) is seen cascading from the sky and falling onto passers-by, as children play in a park.[44] Otto Schindler (played by Liam Neeson) collects some of the ash in his hands, before rubbing it away, precisely as Barbara does. The action cuts to the site of the Plaszow and Krakow Ghetto massacres as concentration camp inmates are forced to disinter the remains of thousands of Jews slaughtered by the Nazis, with the corpses piled into a bonfire and incinerated. The snow seen falling in the previous scene is revealed to be ash from the mass burning of human remains – a process that took place throughout the Nazi concentration camp system.[45] Precisely where the ash comes from in *The Gods Weep* is never fully established, but Kelly is obviously using the imagery from *Schindler's List* to show the depth of the atrocities that are taking place

---

[42] The snow may also recall *Bingo*, while the revelation that it is ash falling from the sky also has resonances with the events of 9/11 and the vast amounts of dust produced by the falling of the Twin Towers.

[43] 'Spit fire, spout rain!' (III.ii.14) Lear yells in the storm and thunder.

[44] Over the period of the 1990s, the film was increasingly used in British schools to teach younger people about the Holocaust, meaning its themes and images were often the first 'contact' students had with the Holocaust. See Andy Pearce, 'The Development of Holocaust Consciousness in Contemporary Britain, 1979–2001', *Holocaust Studies*, 14:2 (2008), pp. 71–94, especially p. 83.

[45] Steven Spielberg, *Schindler's List* (London: DVD Universal Pictures UK, 2019).

Figure 8.1 Colm (Jeremy Irons) and Barbara (Joanna Horton) retreat from the falling ash. Note also the striped pyjamas Colm wears. (2010: The Hampstead Theatre, dir. Maria Aberg. Photograph: Keith Pattison. © RSC)

in the conflict and to indict capitalist social and political relations, which transform concrete individuals into abstract financial entities – into so much (c)ash (Figure 8.1).

This same, no doubt controversial equation between late, post-industrial finance capital and the Holocaust occurs in *Love and Money* – the play *The Gods Weep* provides a sequel to. Over Scene Four of that play, a fragmentary discourse (Rebellato calls the scene 'a Kanean play of voices', akin to *Crave* and *4.48 Psychosis*) takes place in which telesales representatives, who offer credit to 'anyone', but at 'incredibly high rates of interest', reflect that the financial 'figures' involved are not simply abstract quantities, but 'people' (4.243):[46]

> and you might find yourself thinking that what one person does to another is a real thing. Like a real thing. And that systems and numbers and the way we do those things are in some way not real, even though everything we have

[46] Rebellato, 'New Writing: Dennis Kelly', p. 607.

ever learnt has taught us to believe that they are real, you might now come to believe that in actual fact they aren't, and the only thing that is real is the thing that you have done to another human being. And strangely you begin to feel alone. Separate. And you might begin to think – and this is silly – but you might begin to think of something you saw on a documentary, a card written in German that was part of a filing system – and this is really not the same at all, it's ridiculous – but you might think of the person who put those terrible figures on that card, and that they must've thought of them as figures and figures only and you might wonder how they managed to live with, and though this is silly and this is ridiculous and though you know you're being stupid and that this really is not the same at all you know that in some way it might be, in the mechanics of how you do something, and you can't get the image of the fucking card out of your fucking head. (4.247–8)

Though the event itself is never named, remaining something of an unspeakable absence in discourse and thought, the writing in German, the filing system and the card all allude to the Holocaust and the systematic, administrative de-realisation of people into abstract 'figures'. *Love and Money* interrogates the same ethics of comparison I analysed in Chapter 1 – whether the Holocaust reflects wider developments (and disaster) in modernity, or whether it represents a unique event that cannot be understood through conventional comparative discourse.

On the one hand, the speaker(s) attempt to deny the intuited commonality between the concentration camp and the capitalist world of credit and sales, repeating the (by no means unfounded) conviction that these phenomena are not simply 'the same' and that the comparison is 'silly', 'stupid' and 'ridiculous'. On the other hand, it becomes impossible for the speaker(s) to deny that the underlying processes – the practical, disenchanted 'mechanics' of abstract 'systems' and 'figures' – share a kinship, whereby both turn (living) subjects into (dead) objects. There are parallels with the thought of Elias Canetti, who contends that there is a relationship between the hyperinflation that occurred in Weimar Germany and the Nazi Holocaust: in times of inflation, money increases numerically but decreases in value, becoming worthless. This same 'inflationary' increase/decrease clears the way for genocide and a state of mind in which larger numbers become all but meaningless.[47] Later in the play, Jess critiques the alienating ('you begin to feel alone. Separate') culture of late capitalism as inherently deathly by stating that money is 'dead', insisting on 'choosing a world that is more than numbers and quantities and saving and choosing a world that is flesh and bone and / love or, / more than just [. . .] money' (7.284). Over and

---

[47] Elias Canetti, *Crowds and Power* (Harmondsworth: Penguin, 1974), p. 220.

against the reification of the subject, Jess insists on the living, material reality of human beings and the social and moral responsibilities that a common embodiedness requires, where 'the only thing that is real is the thing you have done to another human being'.

The Gods Weep also presents a realist, materialist critique of late capitalist culture and its amoral system of abstraction, which renders 'Life dead' (2.87) and destroys human relationships by turning the subject into 'a living corpse in the arms of another living corpse' (2.102). When (like Lear) Colm loses the aura of authority and the 'respect' and 'fear' his position as CEO previously granted him, he is (for Richard) transformed into nothing more than a 'sack of shit and bones' (1.81). Yet that lowly status – the brute, sensuous reality of the suffering human body – also occasions a more empathetic response, most obviously from Barbara. After a confused Colm finds his way into her small and makeshift flat, Barbara tells Castille (Kent) that Colm has simple but pressing bodily needs that she feels she is morally obliged to try and meet: 'I mean he needs, stuff. Food and . . .', 'you have to feed, sustenance, he needs . . .' (2.92). The language around basic 'needs' recalls *King Lear* and its invocation of the 'art of necessities' (III.ii.70) – the 'raiment, bed, and food' (II.ii.345) Lear sarcastically 'begs' his daughters on bended knee to provide, before he is denied all such comforts.

Terry Eagleton has contended that Shakespeare develops a 'materialist morality' in *King Lear*, whereby Lear is 'forced up against the brute recalcitrance of Nature', which reminds him 'that he has a body': 'Nature terrorizes him into embracing his own finitude.'[48] This same (re)discovery of the needs that are attendant on the 'natural' human body also appears in *The Gods Weep*. There is a transvaluation of values around human (and indeed non-human) 'nature' in the play, as the dictates of late capitalist ideology are challenged by the suffering it causes. Not unlike *Seven Lears*, the play repeatedly poses the question: 'Is that good?' (1.55): 'Is that good, a good thing?' (1.35). 'Is that good?', wonders Colm, when he asks about the 'respect' that his ruthless dedication to his own life has brought him, 'because I am not sure if that is good anymore?' (1.55). This displacement of abstract capitalist ambitions for a materialist morality that attends to the needs of the human body is perhaps most powerfully dramatised in *The Gods Weep* during the scene where Barbara – providing her Cordelia-like 'kind nursery' (I.i.124) to other people – carefully feeds a starving Colm porridge, using only her fingers (2.100). 'There is tenderness only in the coarsest

---

[48] Terry Eagleton, *After Theory* (London: Penguin, 2004), p. 182.

demand', as Adorno unforgettably observes in *Minima Moralia*, 'that no-one shall go hungry any more'.[49]

Not unlike Bond, Kelly portrays an 'ice cold' (2.102) world, though some vestiges of human warmth – 'still warm' (1.81) – do emerge. This is not, however, a vision that Richard subscribes to any point in the play. His use of the Astrologer typifies his alienation from human life and his belief in a coolly impassive universe. Richard keeps the Astrologer in his employ to try and predict future movements in the corporation and the market, something that ironises the preoccupation with 'Futures and Hedge Funds' (2.112) – where investors 'bet' on the future performance of a company – in contemporary finance capitalism.[50] Richard intends to keep in mystical contact with 'the powers that control the universe' (2.106) and, in an obvious parallel with Gloucester in *King Lear*, sets prognostic store in unusual planetary events, whether Saturn, Uranus, Pluto and Jupiter are forming 'The Cardinal Cross' (1.38) or a sudden 'meteor shower' (2.105) supposedly reveals an opportune moment to strike at his various enemies. When he and Catherine are trying to determine which is going to seize control of Belize from Colm, Richard insists on simply (if irrationally) tossing a coin, stating that the decision should be 'in the hands of the gods. Let fate decide' (1.51). 'It is the stars', declares Kent in *King Lear*, 'The stars above us govern our conditions' (IV.iii.33–4).

Where the superstitious Richard subscribes to the idea that the planets and gods determine human fate – bolstering his 'dark view of human nature' (2.102) that rivalrous competition is a natural 'fact' of life, written in the stars – Colm begins to realise that ultimately humanity itself is responsible for its present degraded condition. He tells Barbara in Act Two:

> I used to believe that the universe was cruel, that gods made things this way so that cruelty was the only way of existence. But now I see the truth. That they watch us and what we make and what we do with our lives and to each other and they weep. They watch us and weep. (2.122)

'We make our own hells' (2.113) states the Old Soldier: it is not the case that the malign deities supposed to determine fate thrown down 'agony into our lives to keep themselves amused' (2.118).

---

[49] Theodor Adorno, *Minima Moralia: Reflections on a Damaged Life*, trans. Edmund Jephcott (London: Verso, 2005), p. 156.

[50] The idea of 'financial astrology', as it has been called, has become (perhaps not unexpectedly) popular: there are any number of astrologers who claim to be able to predict movements in the market.

This speech quotes the powerful ending of *Ran*: after the (Fool-like figure) Kyoami indicts Buddha and the gods for being 'mischievous and cruel' – 'Are you so bored up there you must crush us like ants? Is it such fun to see men weep?' – the (Kent-like figure) Tango angrily upbraids him, telling him that: 'It is the gods who weep. They see us killing each other over and over since time began. They cannot save us from ourselves.'[51] But the speech also has parallels with *Lear* and its critique of the absurdist interpretation of Shakespeare, which deems that 'cruelty' is apparently the 'only way of existence' – or a 'natural law'. Kelly, in an interview with Sierz, states that he had not read *Lear* before writing *The Gods Weep*, but his play similarly displaces an absurdist ('cruel') interpretation of *King Lear* with a socially materialist, humanistic understanding of the play, which shows that violence is a result of human agency, not an unchanging, metaphysical absolute that obtains through time. This insight opens the way for humanity to change the reified social system it has created.

Kelly, however, does not posit a narrative or political teleology in the way Bond does in *Lear*, as his conception of freedom and indeed his play is more open-ended. His figuration of the subject ultimately has to do with a transcendent experience of natural plenitude, in circumstances where the very existence of nature as a non-identical force is imperilled. It is that experience which – however fleetingly – distantiates the subject from 'naturalised' social conditions.

Food and Scarcity, Nature and Sublimity

By revealing that the 'snow' which falls in Act Three is really ashes from burnt corpses, Kelly relates the mass destruction of human beings to disturbing climatic changes and environmental degradation, creating a visual and conceptual relation between the Holocaust and the present-day climate emergency, the destructive reification of human beings and the destructive reification of nature. Once it had fallen in the 2010 production, the ash remained onstage throughout the rest of the play, so that the earth came to resemble a post-apocalyptic wasteland, creating an image of environmental deprivation comparable to that of the 2006 Cormac McCarthy novel *The Road*, in which a climatic, nuclear winter creates a world covered in scorched dust, compromising all animal and plant life as humans resort to cannibalism to survive.[52]

---

[51] Kurosawa, *Ran*.
[52] Cormac McCarthy, *The Road* (London: Picador, 2010).

This concern with climate shifts and the endangered natural world was also signed by the presence of a blackened tree throughout the entirety of the production – similar to the blasted tree that appeared in the 2016 RSC production of *King Lear*.[53] This hung over the internecine boardroom disputes of the opening act and, as the play progressed, was also used by Colm, when he makes a (largely futile) attempt to shelter himself from the onset of adverse weather in Act Three of the play.

These images obviously draw on *King Lear*, from the 'dreadful pudder' (III.ii.50) of the scorching storm that rages in the 'wild night' (II.ii.498) of Act Three, to the heath with its infertile 'Blasts and fogs' (I.iv.291), to the unseasonable (and unreasonable) natural and astronomic events that Gloucester worries over in Act Two when he observes sunless 'late eclipses' (I.ii.103). *King Lear*, as Stephen Mentz has observed, is 'obsessed with nature': the very word appears over thirty times in the play.[54] Yet the nature the play depicts is very far from the idealised, Romantic conception of nature as a utopian or Edenic place of harmony and equilibrium; it presents an ecosphere that has become 'an opaque world of catastrophe and crisis'.[55] The play has evident (if also disconcerting) resonances for a world 'disnatured' (I.vi.275) by climate change and environmental degradation.

Jayne Elisabeth Archer, Richard Marggraf Turley and Howard Thomas have made the case that, in its presentation of a disordered, catastrophic natural world, *King Lear* is primarily concerned with (as Gloucester calls it) 'dearth' (I.ii.145) – or with the prospect of harvest failure, food scarcity, hunger and starvation.[56] Throughout the play, 'sustaining corn' (IV.iv.6) has been displaced by the type of 'idle weeds' (IV.iv.5) that Lear wears for a crown after he loses his sanity – 'rank fumitor and furrow-weeds', 'burdocks, hemlock, nettles, cuckoo-flowers' (IV.iv.3–4) – where he becomes a sort of anti-pastoral king of material scarcity. Wheat goes unharvested and is overgrown with weeds – it as, as Poor Tom states, 'wild' and 'mildew[ed]' (III.iv.115) and fit only for burning. There is 'no food' for 'Hoppedance', who 'cries' in the belly of Poor Tom for

---

[53] See Chapter 3 for ecocritical productions of *King Lear*. I am thankful to director Maria Aberg for confirming the presence of the tree throughout the production, and for her confirming that the ash that falls in Act Two also remained on stage for the rest of the production (Aberg, personal communication).

[54] Steven Mentz, '"Strange Weather" in *King Lear*', *Shakespeare*, 6:2 (2010), p. 143.

[55] Ibid. p. 146.

[56] Jayne Elisabeth Archer, Richard Marggraf Turley and Howard Thomas, 'The Autumn King: Remembering the Land in *King Lear*', *Shakespeare Quarterly*, 63:4 (2012), pp. 518–43.

some 'white herring' (III.vi.30–1); the Captain cannot 'eat dried oats' (V.iii.39); and Albany challenges Edmund to fight 'Ere I taste bread' (V.iii.95) – so delaying the moment of eating. Poor Tom, perhaps out of his apparent insanity, but also perhaps out of sheer necessity, reveals to Lear that he 'swallows the old rat and the ditch-dog' and even 'drinks the green mantle of the standing pool' (III.iv.128–9).

This scarcity is captured in the word 'blast', which in early modern usage connotes an infectious disease of arable crops, so that the 'blast[ed]' (III.vi.43) world of *King Lear* is, by implication, also a world of hunger: 'I have no food for thee' (III.vi.31–2). These images of dearth partly reflect the emergence of agrarian capitalism in the early modern era, which reconfigured relations with the land through the process of enclosure, whereby once common land was privatised, causing hunger for displaced farming peasants who were transformed into Poor Tom-like itinerants.[57] This cultural and economic shift – ironically – created a new form of production which systematically generates scarcity and insecurity. Land in *King Lear*, as Stuart Eldon has shown, is not common property; the rise of capitalist relations means that it has become something that is 'controlled, fought over [. . .] and bought and sold'.[58] Much the same can be said of *The Gods Weep* and its representation of the battle over Belize.

One of the more distinctive features of *The Gods Weep* is the way it picks up on the thematic of food and scarcity found in *King Lear* in its portrayal of the environment, presenting as it does an image of 'the end of days' (2.113) where the 'the food is running out' (2.97) – though hunger is also (if less consistently) present in *Seven Lears* and *Blasted*.[59] The war that rages in Act Two is partly a war over resources – a genocidal war of starvation, where Catherine has monopolised the 'land' and 'food' in a way that deprives Richard and his camp (2.90). It is a bio-political process that Richard, in his increasingly demented state, wholeheartedly embraces, telling an underling before the climactic battle with Catherine to adopt something of a scorched-earth policy, only against his own men: 'Destroy all rations. Let them know that Catherine has surplus, let them know they win or starve' (2.106). The conflict has some disturbing parallels with the rationale for the Nazi invasion of the

---

[57] Ibid. For more on *King Lear* and enclosure, see Chapter 4 and the analysis of *Bingo*.

[58] Stuart Eldon, 'The Geopolitics of *King Lear*: Territory, Land, Earth', *Law & Literature*, 25:2 (2013), p. 161.

[59] In *Seven Lears*, Lear purposefully (and perversely) denies food to the people, while Horbling creates various agricultural plans; in *Blasted*, Ian goes hungry after Cate leaves him in the hotel room – though, like Barbara in *The Gods Weep*, she does eventually feed Ian.

East, which – for Hitler and others – was largely derived from a pseudo-Darwinian, racialised conception of 'natural' competition over access to food and land, or living space (*Lebensraum*) – a critical part of the wider ideological struggle between Nazism and Bolshevism.[60]

Most of Act Three is spent with Barbara and Colm, both of whom are in a state of hunger, trying to figure out a way of producing and/or finding food, from scavenging leftover tins to creating various forms of animal trap (3.163). Yet the 'irony' (3.150) is that Barbara and Colm occupy a space on the edge of a farm, used and surveilled by Richard. The problem is not only to do with the ability of the earth to produce food, but also with the social and political conditions as to who can access food. Barbara and Colm recognise that any attempt to take resources from the farm will result in death: food is dominated by the powerful and remains unavailable to others. The same dynamic underpins transnational 'food security' (1.34) – the multi-billion-pound 'growth industry' (1.35) and 'the crucible of all our hopes' (1.35) introduced at the outset of the play and the driving motive of its plot and action.

Food security has become a pressing concern as anthropogenic climate change continues to worsen, while Jürgen Zimmerer and Mark Levene and Daniele Conversi have also contented that climate change is liable to increase the chances of mass violence and genocide, as competing powers and peoples struggle over who controls dwindling reserves of space and food – precisely the type of conflict Kelly dramatises in Act Three of *The Gods Weep*.[61] It is also worth recalling that the crash of 2008 caused a global food price crisis which precipitated urgent questions about security and, as Olivier de Schutter calls it, 'the right to

---

[60] For more on the relationship between food and Nazi racial ideologies, see Timothy Snyder, *Black Earth: The Holocaust as History and Warning* (London: Penguin, 2015), particularly pp. 194–5. Snyder writes that for Hitler, in nature, 'conflict was over food, and the weaker races were to starve' (p. 194).

[61] Jürgen Zimmerer, 'Climate Change, Environmental Violence and Genocide', *Climate Change and Genocide: Environmental Violence*, ed. Jürgen Zimmerer (London: Routledge, 2015), pp. 3–18; Mark Levene and Daniele Conversi, 'Subsistence Societies, Globalisation, Climate Change and Genocide: Discourses of Vulnerability and Resilience', *The International Journal of Human Rights*, 18:3 (2014), pp. 281–97. Others have contended that the destabilising impact of climate change has led to the increased popularity of the far right because, in a time when people begin to feel threatened by forces from 'the outside', it offers the reactionary illusion of national 'safety' – or 'tightness'. See Joshua Conrad Jackson and Michele Gelfand, 'Could Climate Change Fuel The Rise of Right-Wing Nationalism?', <https://theconversation.com/could-climate-change-fuel-the-rise-of-right-wing-nationalism-123503> (accessed 1 October 2019).

food'.[62] Through the theme of food security, Kelly represents a world where global capital is producing climatic and environmental problems that have impaired the ability of the human race to perpetuate itself and that underpin a lurch towards mass (and even genocidal) violence. This takes on a particularly post- (or indeed neo-)colonial cast, positing relations between a dispossessed global south (Belize) and a more dominant global north (Britain) – a situation where non-Western 'others' are treated less as subjects than as disposable objects, as the West produces the conditions necessary for its prosperity and survival ('our hopes').[63]

The relationship to both human (subject) and non-human (object) nature in *The Gods Weep* is largely one of rational, instrumental domination and rapacious economic corruption, creating a world where subjects are routinely destroyed and in which the environment suffers the devastating impacts of industrial and post-industrial global capitalist production. Yet amid the devastation of the play, other approaches to nature do begin to emerge. This is particularly true of Act Three, where Barbara and Colm are forced into a subsistence life. Colm admits to Barbara that, after his time in the wilderness, he is becoming oddly 'animistic' (3.171). Colm states that he has 'imbued' everything around him 'with a kind of spirit', something that 'feels so real' even though he finds it 'hard to believe in' (3.171).

This animism – as Adorno and Horkheimer contend in *Dialectic of Enlightenment* – is the type of mythic thinking about nature that the Enlightenment displaces, fostering as it does a retrograde belief in fate and divine powers that shape human life. But as J. M. Bernstein has argued, animism is not an entirely regressive force. This relates to the 'non-projective core' of animism, as Bernstein calls it: for him, Adorno relates 'the excess beyond phenomenal appearing' to that which 'has *powers* of resistance to the subject and its own ends, possesses a "life" of its own'.[64] This means that animism creates the conditions under which the fallacy of constitutive subjectivity may be undone and the non-identity of nature – its existence 'beyond' conceptual control and economic exploitation – can emerge. Where that non-identity challenges a reifying system of concepts, it can also catalyse the freedom

---

[62] Olivier de Schutter, 'The Role of Global Governance in Supporting Human Rights: The Global Food Price Crisis and the Right to Food', in Aoife Nolan (ed.), *Economic and Social Rights after the Global Financial Crisis* (Cambridge: Cambridge University Press, 2014), pp. 90–118.

[63] Snyder, once again, is instructive on the colonial aspect of Nazi racial and food policy. See *Black Earth*, p. 194.

[64] J. M. Bernstein, *Disenchantment and Ethics* (Cambridge: Cambridge University Press, 2001), p. 192 and p. 193.

of the subject, who is displaced outside of a spatially and temporally homogenised world of domination and forced into a posture of critical self-reflection. This is a process that occurs towards the end of *The Gods Weep*. When he returns to Barbara after searching (typically) for food, Colm reflects on an experience he had while contemplating seashells on top of a mountain:

> I began to realise that this tip, this piece of rock being pushed up through the hillside had once been the bottom of an ocean.
> And I was struck still by time.
> I was struck still by time.
> And I suddenly saw my infinitesimal place in it and it was . . . Infinitesimal.
> And I felt such a peace, such a weightlessness, that I had never known since I was a boy. (3.162)

The sheer spatial and temporal plenitude of nature occasions something akin to experience of the sublime – an overwhelming experience of the otherness of nature, which cannot be reduced to fallible, finite systems of human concepts and control. Nature challenges the conditions of human meaning-making, appearing as profoundly non-identical with anthropocentric ends. This creates a transcendent 'moment' (3.175) – or a sort of metaphysical spatial and temporal rift that challenges the reified time of late capitalist production and consumption, with its unreflective, linearly prescribed and supposedly rational forward march. This conception of time is epitomised by Gavin when he tells Jimmy to 'not reject the realities of the time as it is the logical conclusion of previous times and I strongly advise you to understand that. Now' (2.85). Through his astonished experience of overwhelming natural plenitude, Colm is displaced outside the spatial and temporal exigencies of the social totality – 'the realities of the time' – in a moment of transcendent freedom.

This singular, non-instrumental experience of non-human matter is short-lived: Colm will discard the seashells he brings back with him when Barbara perfunctorily declares that they (and Colm) are 'useless' (3.161) and will not serve any obvious human purpose. Nevertheless, it opens out a moment of freedom and even reconciliation ('peace') between humanity and nature, which is allowed to appear in its fundamental non-identity from determinant human aims and ambitions. This 'rebirth' is symbolically marked by the apparent 'death' of Colm in Act Three – and his return to life. Colm, in the same vein as Ian and the image of ephemeral life in *Blasted*, seems to pass away – as Barbara checks his pulse (3.159) and, not finding any, pulls a blanket over his body (3.160) – only to return to life: '*Suddenly COLM sits up with a start, bolt upright*' (3.160). Echoing Lear when he is roused from his 'restorative' sleep – 'Where am I?' (IV.vii.52) – Colm wonders 'Is this the afterlife?' (3.160) and, when Barbara apologises for going to bury him, states: 'Maybe I was dead' (3.164).[65]

Through its image of nature, *The Gods Weep* can be situated in a lineage of Romantic criticism of *King Lear* which, as shown in Chapter 2, tended to align the play with the notion of the sublime and the awesome power of nature, which outstrips the limits of human comprehension and control – or the 'little world of man' (III.i.10), something Romantic writers related to the raging storm. The idea that Colm is 'struck still' means that he does not perform the sort of spontaneous, catastrophic 'turn' I have identified as vital to the figuration and performance of tragic subjectivity – and the disfiguration of aesthetic form – in other plays (particularly by Rudkin, Barker and Kane). Yet the idea of being 'struck still' and rendered 'infinitesimal' does involve a moment of freedom from reification and has some important parallels with the notion of the shudder, where 'Natural beauty is suspended history, a moment of becoming at a standstill'.[66] Adorno writes in *Aesthetic Theory* that

> Shudder, radically opposed to the conventional idea of experience [*Erlebnis*], provides no particular satisfaction for the I; it bears no similarity to desire. Rather, it is a memento of the liquidation of the I, which, shaken, perceives its own limitedness and finitude. This experience [*Erfahrung*] is contrary to the weakening of the I that the culture industry manipulates [. . .] For a few moments the I becomes aware [. . .] of letting self-preservation fall away [. . .] [T]his transforms art into what it is in-itself, the historical void of repressed nature, ultimately critical of the principle of the I, that internal agent of repression. This subjective experience [*Erfahrung*] directed against the I is an element of the objective truth of art.[67]

Adorno contends that the shudder is a response to the aesthetic that, at the same time, represents a 'trace' of a more 'primordial' confrontation with the overwhelming presence of nature ('the historical void of repressed nature').[68] The subject (and the concepts s/he uses for the purposes of identity) are shown to be finite and fallible, not all-encompassing. This 'limitedness and finitude', however, is not

---

[65] After Barbara is shot, Colm states: 'I know when someone is alive and when they are dead and she is dead' (3.179); his own resurrection parallels that of the cat he runs over in Act Two – perhaps another allusion to the nonsense of Poor Tom: 'Purr, the cat is grey' (III.vi.45) There is another allusion to *Blasted* in Act Two, when Beth repeatedly fires an ammunition-less pistol (2.88).
[66] Adorno, *Aesthetic Theory*, p. 93.
[67] Ibid. pp. 319–20.
[68] Ibid. p. 106.

necessarily 'a weakening' of the subject, but a moment of emancipation from totality – a 'liquidation' of the 'I' as the 'constitutive subject' and a revelation of the 'preponderance of the object', or the non-identical. By showing the finiteness and limitation of the subject, the 'shudder' makes subjectivity 'conscious of itself *as nature*', or as dependent on natural processes of both spatiality and temporality that cannot be controlled.[69] The process of becoming-nature implies a new experience of space and time and a new relation to the non-human, the inorganic material 'other' represented by nature.

This means that Colm, in his confrontation with natural plenitude, undergoes an experience that has parallels with the way in which Adorno understands the aesthetic. Colm, to quote Adorno, represents 'a subjectivity turned to stone' ('struck still'); he is 'astonished' – a word that stems from the obsolete word 'astone', to 'stun, stupefy', from *estoner*, based on Latin *ex-* 'out' and *tonare* 'to thunder' (perhaps recalling the thunderous storm of *King Lear*).[70] This challenges the destructive human reification of nature as a mere means to an end and indeed the destructive reification of humans in modern society. The experience of natural plenitude – 'all the more compelling for its ephemeralness', as Adorno puts it – adumbrates a radically new approach to both nature and people than that fostered by the demands of modernity.[71] Colm tells Barbara that, despite being left destitute, he feels 'happier now' (3.168) than when he was successful and feared – typifying the *promesse du bonheur* ('promise of happiness') that Adorno sees secreted in the artwork and its (partial) 'redemption' of nature.[72]

The Gods Weep opens a perspective on nature and the subject that runs contrary to the demands of identity-thinking – but it is only fleeting. Despite finding 'happiness' in his isolated life with Barbara, at the end of the play she is suddenly shot from a point offstage – as Saburo is shot from somewhere off-screen in *Ran* – leaving Colm alive, but psychologically 'broken'. This incursion represents the return of a more utilitarian approach to both human and non-human nature – 'What use is he to us?' (3.180) wonders a soldier as he coldly considers Colm – which is poised against a non-dominative view of nature and the subject:

---

[69] Theodor Adorno, 'Late Style in Beethoven', in Theodor Adorno, *Essays on Music*, ed. Richard Leppert, trans. Susan H. Gillespie (Berkeley and Los Angeles: University of California Press, 2002), p. 567.

[70] 'astonishment, n.', <https://www-oed-com.ezproxy01.rhul.ac.uk/view/Entry/12178> (accessed 30 September 2019).

[71] Adorno, *Aesthetic Theory*, p. 93.

[72] Ibid. p. 14.

I had this dream. This awful terrible dream, a dream raped, I dreamt that I would regain myself, that I would live, that I would breath, that I would [. . .] come to an understanding of beauty so that this moment could be snatched away from me while I watched. (3.178)

Kelly keeps *The Gods Weep* precariously suspended between the utopian 'dream' of Colm, which has a viable space for natural and human 'beauty', and the crushing realities of utilitarian ideologies, which can only view the world and the people in it through the prism of 'reason'. There is, as Kelly states, the 'possibility of redemption' – but it is not necessarily realised.[73] If it were, the play would give a false image of reconciliation in an unreconciled world.

Not unlike the other *King Lear* plays under study, *The Gods Weep* catastrophically violates formal closure – or the promised end. Angelaki has recently made the case that, where his plays override the limits of formal containment, Kelly aims for an aesthetic where the 'unfathomable may be represented' in its 'open-endedness'.[74] This speaks to an aesthetic of the sublime. When he wrote *The Gods Weep*, Kelly was intentionally aiming for a 'big', 'epic' play that did not cohere into a fully resolved whole, but that remained 'unwieldy, flawed and messy'. The discourse Kelly draws on to describe his play adumbrates a sublime aesthetic ('big', 'epic') that does not resolve its fragments or aporias ('flawed, unwieldy, messy') but seeks to preserve the non-identical – or, as Colm calls it, 'beauty'. This represents a challenge to the audience. By pushing beyond and denying order or finality, Kelly retains the negative moment of the sublime, confronting the spectator with an overwhelming experience that cannot be conceptually bound or limited. This confrontation with the 'unfathomable' in its overpowering 'open-endedness' obviously has resonances with Colm and his own transcendent 'moment' in *The Gods Weep*, when he is suddenly 'struck still'.

Whether or not the play is successful, however, is an open question. *The Gods Weep* certainly provoked disorientation and incomprehension, as the almost universally negative reviews show – but whether that was occasioned by anything resembling the awed shudder Adorno relates to the sublime or simple derision at its mangling of *King Lear* is a moot point. Nonetheless, a newly imagined, post-Auschwitz sublime is perhaps even more urgent now than when *The Gods Weep*

---

[73] Dennis Kelly and Maria Aberg, interview with Aleks Sierz, <http://www.theatrevoice.com/audio-tags/aleks-sierz/> (accessed 23 August 2019). This is the same interview where Kelly reveals that he had not read Bond before embarking on his own appropriation of *King Lear*.

[74] Angelaki, *Social and Political Theatre in 21st Century Britain*, p. 106.

was originally staged. Nearly all of the original reviewers questioned the violence of the play, which did not seem to establish a causal relationship between the crises of late capitalist culture (Act One) and genocidal fascistic atrocities (Act Two). Since the crash of 2008, however, the far right has only gained in global influence and political power. This newly dominant right, as Andreas Malm has shown, not only reduces subjects (typically 'others' who do not belong to the nation state, most obviously in the form of immigrants, Muslims and Jews) to mere objects, but also tends to deny climate change and environmental collapse – embodying precisely the relationship between the domination of people and the domination of nature Adorno posits.[75] From that perspective, *The Gods Weep* appears prescient: the vision it offers of nature and people free from domination has become all the more relevant – and fragile – as the far right returns, seemingly from the grave, to a position of influence and power. Through his vision of the subject and nature, Kelly ensures that *King Lear* continues to speak to damaged, post-Auschwitz culture.

Conclusion

Despite the negative reviews it has received, *The Gods Weep* represents a deep engagement with *King Lear*, where Kelly appropriates the play to critique the crises of late capitalist culture and the reification of both nature and the subject. His tragic, sublime aesthetic strives to emancipate both non-human and human nature from the domination of capital, in a way that aligns his play with the other, post-Holocaust appropriations of *King Lear* under study. What sets his play apart, however, is its presiding concern with the relationship between the reification of the natural world and the destruction of human beings in the Holocaust. His play places particular stress on the relationship between nature and genocide through the theme of food and food security, drawing on the images of desolation and dearth found in *King Lear*. *The Gods Weep* is the most recent appropriation of *King Lear* by a significant British playwright and obviously responds to both the credit crunch of 2008 and climate change; but the conversation around *King Lear* and catastrophe continues.

---

[75] Andreas Malm, *The Progress of This Storm: Nature and Society in a Warming World* (London: Verso, 2018), pp. 137–40.

Conclusion: 'Storm Still'

'The current amazement that the things we are experiencing are "still" possible in the twentieth century is *not* philosophical. This amazement is not the beginning of knowledge — unless it is the knowledge that the view of history which gives rise to it is untenable'

Walter Benjamin[1]

It is in the nature of any study of the distant or recent past that it forms a constellation with the present in which it is rememorialised. The research and writing for *King Lear 'After' Auschwitz* has taken place against the backdrop of an increasingly catastrophic age, from climate change and the destruction of the natural environment to refugee crises caused by conflicts on a scale not seen since the Second World War. Perhaps most concerning is a resurgent far right, which has taken hold not only in Europe and America, but also other parts of the world. Since the economic dislocation of 2008 and the so-called credit crunch, late global capitalism has taken an alarmingly fascistic turn of the type Kelly so presciently predicted in *The Gods Weep* – cueing the type of unphilosophical amazement that 'such things are "still" possible', not only in the twentieth century, but also the twenty-first.[2] Even the recent outbreak of the coronavirus pandemic, still in its early stages at the time of writing, seems to have exacerbated nationalistic and xenophobic rhetoric in some quarters.

Jean-Luc Nancy, taking up Adorno and his conception of an 'after'

---

[1] Walter Benjamin, 'Theses on the Philosophy of History', in Walter Benjamin, *Illuminations*, ed. Hannah Arendt, trans. Harry Zorn (London: Pimlico, 1999), p. 249.

[2] For an analysis of the recent 'post-truth' phenomenon and right-wing politics, see my '"Retailed to All Posterity": "Post-Truth", Oral History and the Popular Voice in *Richard III*', *Cahiers Élisabéthains* <https://journals.sagepub.com/doi/full/10.1177/0184767820936688> (accessed 2 September 2020).

Auschwitz, contends in his 2015 *After Fukushima: The Equivalence of Catastrophes*, that 'the general equivalence' rendered by the commodity-form has now absorbed 'all the spheres of the existence of humans, and along with them all things that exist'.[3] The Fukushima disaster – which is a geological, biological, social, economic, and political disaster – reveals that 'the interdependent totality of our technologized world' is a world of human creation and at the same time 'a world to which virtually all beings are entirely subjected'.[4] Andrew Bowie similarly contends that 'the idea that modern capitalism makes the world into a totality, in which systematic factors deeply affect aspects of everyday life all over the globe, has become hard to ignore', as culture is 'more and more dominated by universalizing forms'.[5] The totalisation of late capitalist society has seen the reification of ever more inclusive areas of human life. It is that reifying approach to people and the world which has conditioned the catastrophic rise of new forms of fascist ideology and power in a supposedly postmodern world.

King Lear has come to occupy a vital place in post-Auschwitz theatres of catastrophe, from Bond and Rudkin to Forced Entertainment and Kelly. The play has been used time and again to respond to the catastrophe of the Holocaust and the total destruction of human beings in the concentration camps. This tie between *King Lear* and catastrophe continues today, most obviously in the Edward St Aubyn and Preti Taneja 2017 novels *Dunbar* and *We That Are Young*.[6] Perhaps evincing the influence of Kelly, both novels set the action of *King Lear* in vast, transnational corporations and indict the reification of both people and nature in an era of right-wing populist politics and climate catastrophe (Taneja also cites Bond as an influence).[7]

This study has analysed *King Lear* over the period 1939–2010. But it is also a timely intervention in our own contemporary moment. The unnerving lurch to far-right politics in Europe and across the world have made *King Lear* and catastrophic ideas around disaster and the

---

[3] Jean-Luc Nancy, *After Fukushima: The Equivalence of Catastrophes* (New York: Fordham University Press, 2015), p. 5.
[4] Ibid. p. 31.
[5] Andrew Bowie, *Adorno and the Ends of Philosophy* (Cambridge: Polity, 2013), pp. vii–viii.
[6] Edward St Aubyn, *Dunbar* (London: Hogarth Press, 2017); Preti Taneja, *We That Are Young* (Norwich: Galley Beggar Press, 2017).
[7] Urvashi Bahuguna,'"I wrote in a fury against gender violence, right wing nationalism, toxic masculinity": Preti Taneja', <https://scroll.in/article/858290/i-wrote-in-a-fury-against-gender-violence-right-wing-nationalism-toxic-masculinity-preti-taneja> (accessed 8 January 2020).

possibility of autonomy all the more urgent. 'The fundamental feature of contemporary society', writes Slavoj Žižek, 'is the irreconcilable antagonism between Totality and the individual'.[8] Ours is an age in which people are more and more being treated as 'things' – where subjects are reduced to objects – and where nationalist movements are sweeping up ever increasing sections of the population. Under such conditions, the necessity of autonomy – of freedom from reifying institutions and oppressive systems of thought – may perhaps be more critical than at any time since the early twentieth century. Robert Hullot-Kentor writes:

> the interregnum of the post-war years is over. We are experiencing a return of the great fear, as if it never ended—and perhaps it never did. We are, without a doubt, the occupants of the most catastrophic moment in the whole of human history, in all of natural history, and we cannot get our wits about ourselves. What is being decided right now for all surviving generations including our own, is the exact sum total of the irreversible remainder, the unalterable 'How it might have been'.[9]

This is a study that, not unlike catastrophic drama, does not 'end', but opens out into an uncertain future.

---

[8] Slavoj Žižek, *The Parallax View* (London: MIT Press, 2006), p. 26.
[9] Robert Hullot-Kentor, 'What Barbarism Is?', in Fabio Akcelrud Durão (ed.), *Culture Industry Today* (Newcastle: Cambridge Scholars Publishing, 2010), p. 24.

Bibliography

Abelson, Reed, 'Companies Turn to Grades, and Employees Go to Court', *New York Times*, <https://www.nytimes.com/2001/03/19/business/companies-turn-to-grades-and-employees-go-to-court.html> (accessed 14 February 2018).

Adelman, Janet, *Suffocating Mothers: Fantasies of Maternal Origin in Shakespeare's Plays,* Hamlet *to* The Tempest (London: Routledge, 1992).

Adorno, Theodor, *Aesthetic Theory*, trans. Robert Hullot-Kentor (London: Continuum, 2012).

Adorno, Theodor, *Beethoven: The Philosophy of Music: Fragments and Texts*, ed. Rolf Tiedemann, trans. Edmund Jephcott (Cambridge: Polity, 1998).

Adorno, Theodor, *Can One Live After Auschwitz? A Philosophical Reader*, ed. Rolf Tiedemann, trans. Rodney Livingstone et al. (Stanford: Stanford University Press, 2003).

Adorno, Theodor, *Critical Models: Interventions and Catchwords*, trans. Henry W. Pickford (New York: Colombia University Press, 2005).

Adorno, Theodor, *Essays on Music*, ed. Richard Leppert, trans. Susan H. Gillespie (Berkeley and Los Angeles: University of California Press, 2002).

Adorno, Theodor, *History and Freedom: Lectures, 1964–1965*, ed. Rolf Tiedemann, trans. Rodney Livingstone (Cambridge: Polity, 2008).

Adorno, Theodor, *Metaphysics: Concepts and Problems*, ed. Rolf Tiedemann, trans. Edmund Jephcott (Cambridge: Polity, 2000).

Adorno, Theodor, *Minima Moralia: Reflections on a Damaged Life*, trans. Edmund Jephcott (London: Verso, 2005).

Adorno, Theodor, *Negative Dialectics*, trans. E. B. Ashton (London and New York: Continuum, 2007).

Adorno, Theodor, *Notes to Literature, Volume Two*, ed. Rolf Tiedemann, trans. Sherry Weber Nicholson (New York: Columbia University Press, 1992).

Adorno, Theodor, 'On the Question: "What is German?"', *New German Critique*, 36, 'Special Issue on Heimat' (1985).

Adorno, Theodor, *Problems of Moral Philosophy*, ed. Thomas Schröder, trans. Rodney Livingstone (Cambridge: Polity, 2001).

Adorno, Theodor, 'The Actuality of Philosophy', *Telos*, 31 (1977).

Adorno, Theodor, *The Culture Industry*, ed. J. M. Bernstein (London: Routledge, 2001).

Adorno, Theodor, *The Jargon of Authenticity* (London: Routledge, 2003).

Adorno, Theodor, *The Stars Down to Earth and Other Essays on the Irrational in Culture*, ed. Stephen Crook (New York and London: Routledge, 2004).
Adorno, Theodor, 'Theses on Need', trans. Martin Shuster and Iain Macdonald, *Adorno Studies*, 1:1 (2017).
Adorno, Theodor, *Quasi Una Fantasia: Essays on Modern Music*, trans. Rodney Livingstone (London: Verso, 2002).
Adorno, Theodor and Max Horkheimer, *Dialectic of Enlightenment*, trans. John Cumming (London: Verso, 2010).
Agamben, Giorgio, *Homo Sacer: Sovereign Power and Bare Life*, trans. Daniel Heller-Roazen (Stanford: Stanford University Press, 1998).
Agamben, Giorgio, *Remnants of Auschwitz: The Witness and the Archive*, trans. Daniel Heller-Roazen (New York: Zone Books, 2002).
Albritton, Robert, Robert Jessop and Richard Westra (eds), *Political Economy and Global Capitalism: The 21st Century, Present and Future* (London: Anthem Press, 2007).
Alexander, Catherine (ed.), *The Cambridge Shakespeare Library, Volume II: Shakespeare Criticism* (Cambridge: Cambridge University Press, 2003).
Alexander, Edward, *The Holocaust: History and the War of Ideas* (New Brunswick, NJ and London: Transaction Publishers, 1994).
Alfaro, María Jesús Martínez, 'Intertextuality: Origins and Development of the Concept', *Atlantis*, 18:1/2 (1996).
Alliot, Julien, '"I Know How that Sounds and I Do Not Mean that as an, but I Mean Christ": The Disturbance in the Symbolic Order in Dennis Kelly's Theatre', *E-rea*, 12:1 (2014), <http://journals.openedition.org/erea/3990> (accessed 5 September 2019).
Alvarez, Alex, *Unstable Ground: Climate Change, Conflict, and Genocide* (London: Rowman and Littlefield, 2017).
Anderson, Perry, *The Origins of Postmodernity* (London: Verso, 1998).
Angel-Perez, Elisabeth and Vanasay Khamphommala, 'Les *7 Lears* de Barker, pour une Généalogie de la Catastrophe', *Shakespeare en Devenir*, 1 (2007), <http://shakespeare.edel.univ-poitiers.fr/index.php?id=65> (accessed 8 November 2019).
Angel-Perez, Elisabeth and Alexandra Poulain (eds), *Hunger on the Stage* (Newcastle: Cambridge Scholars Publishing, 2008).
Angelaki, Vicky (ed.), *Contemporary British Theatre: Breaking New Ground* (Basingstoke: Palgrave Macmillan, 2013).
Angelaki, Vicky, *Social and Political Theatre in 21st Century Britain: Staging Crisis* (London: Methuen, 2017).
Angermann, Asaf, 'The Ghosts of Normativity: Temporality and Recurrence in Adorno's Ethics of Dissonance', *The Germanic Review*, 90:4 (2015).
Anonymous, 'Documenting Numbers of Victims of the Holocaust and Nazi Persecution', *United States Holocaust Memorial Museum*, <https://encyclopedia.ushmm.org/content/en/article/documenting-numbers-of-victims-of-the-holocaust-and-nazi-persecution> (accessed 18 June 2020).
Anonymous, *King Leir*, ed. Tiffany Stern (London: Nick Hern Books, 2002).
Anonymous, 'Will's Way', *Theatricalia*, <https://theatricalia.com/play/h6/wills-way/production/1ys> (accessed 3 February 2018).
Archer, Jayne Elisabeth, Richard Marggraf Turley and Howard Thomas, 'The

Autumn King: Remembering the Land in *King Lear*', *Shakespeare Quarterly*, 63:4 (2012).

Arendt, Hannah, *Eichmann in Jerusalem: A Report on the Banality of Evil* (London: Penguin, 2006).

Arendt, Hannah, *The Origins of Totalitarianism* (London: Penguin, 2017).

Aristotle, *Nicomachean Ethics*, trans. J. A. K. Thomson (London: Penguin, 2004).

Aristotle, *Poetics*, trans. Gerald Franck Else (Ann Arbor: University of Michigan Press, 1967).

Aristotle, *Politics*, trans. T. A. Sinclair (London: Penguin, 1992).

Armatta, Judith, *Twilight of Impunity: The War Crimes Trial of Slobodan Milosevic* (Durham, NC and London: Duke University Press, 2010).

Artaud, Antonin, *The Theatre and Its Double*, trans. Victor Corti (London: OneWorld Classics, 2010).

Ashby, Richard, 'Crowding out Dover "Cliff" in *Korol Lir*', *Adaptation*, 10:2 (2017).

Ashby, Richard, 'Face-Off: Defacement, Ethics and the "Neighbour" in *The Comedy of Errors*', *Textual Practice*, 32:8 (2018).

Ashby, Richard, '"Multidirectional" Shakespeare: Heiner Müller, *Anatomy Titus, Fall of Rome, a Shakespeare Commentary*, Postcolonialism and the Holocaust', *Comparative Drama* (forthcoming).

Ashby, Richard, 'Pierced to the Soul: The Politics of the Gaze in *Richard II*', *Shakespeare*, 11:2 (2015).

Ashby, Richard, '"Retailed to All Posterity": "Post-Truth", Oral History and the Popular Voice in *Richard III*', *Cahiers Élisabéthains*, <https://journals.sagepub.com/doi/full/10.1177/0184767820936688> (accessed 2 September 2020).

Ashby, Richard, 'Sarah Kane and *Blasted*: The Arcade Game?', 'Backpages', *Contemporary Theatre Review*, 28:3 (2018).

Bahuguna, Urvashi, ,'"I wrote in a fury against gender violence, right wing nationalism, toxic masculinity": Preti Taneja', *Scroll.I*, <https://scroll.in/article/858290/i-wrote-in-a-fury-against-gender-violence-right-wing-nationalism-toxic-masculinity-preti-taneja> (accessed 8 January 2020).

Bailes, Sarah Jane, *Performance Theatre and the Poetics of Failure: Forced Entertainment, Goat Island, Elevator Repair Service* (London: Routledge, 2011).

Baldwin, T. W., *Shakespeare's Five-Act Structure: Shakespeare's Early Plays on the Background of Renaissance Theories of Five-Act Structure from 1470* (Urbana: University of Illinois Press, 1947).

Barker, Francis, *The Culture of Violence: Essays on Tragedy and History* (Manchester: Manchester University Press, 1993).

Barker, Howard, *Arguments for a Theatre*, 2nd edn (Manchester and New York: Manchester University Press, 1993).

Barker, Howard, *Arguments for a Theatre*, 3rd edn (Manchester and New York: Manchester University Press, 1997).

Barker, Howard, *Arguments for a Theatre*, 4th edn (London: Oberon Books, 2016).

Barker, Howard, *Collected Plays: Volume 2* (London: Calder, 1993).

Barker, Howard, *Collected Plays: Volume 3* (London: Calder, 1986).

Barker, Howard, *Collected Plays: Volume 5* (London: Calder, 2001).

Barker, Howard, *Howard Barker Interviews, 1980–2010: Conversations in Catastrophe*, ed. Mark Brown (Bristol: Intellect, 2011).
Barker, Howard, *Plays Five* (London: Oberon Books, 2009).
Barker, Howard, *Plays Eight* (London: Oberon Books, 2014).
Barker, Howard, *Seven Lears and Golgo* (London: Calder, 1990).
Barker, Howard, *Women Beware Women and Pity in History* (London: Calder, 1986).
Barker, Howard/Eduardo Houth, *A Style and its Origins* (London: Oberon Books, 2003).
Barthes, Roland, *Image Music Text*, trans. Stephen Heath (London: Fontana Press, 1977).
Bartrop, Paul R., (ed.), *Bosnian Genocide: The Essential Reference Guide* (Santa Barbara: ABC-CLIO, 2016).
Bashevkin, Sylvia, *Women on the Defensive: Living through Conservative Times* (London and Chicago: University of Chicago Press, 1998).
Bate, Jonathan, *Shakespearean Constitutions: Politics, Theatre, Criticism 1730–1830* (Oxford: Clarendon Press, 1989).
Baudrillard, Jean, *Jean Baudrillard: Selected Writings*, ed. Mark Poster, trans. various (Stanford: Stanford University Press, 2001).
Bauman, Zygmunt, *Modernity and the Holocaust* (Cambridge: Polity, 1989).
Beckett, Samuel, *The Complete Works of Samuel Beckett* (London: Faber and Faber, 2006).
Belsey, Catherine, *The Subject of Tragedy: Identity and Difference in English Renaissance Drama* (London: Methuen, 1985).
Benjamin, Walter, *Illuminations*, ed. Hannah Arendt (London: Pimlico, 1999).
Benjamin, Walter, *The Origin of German Tragic Drama*, trans. John Osborne (London: Verso, 1998).
Bennett, Susan, *Performing Nostalgia: Shifting Shakespeare and the Contemporary Past* (London: Routledge, 1996).
Berger, Harry, Jr, '"King Lear": The Lear Family Romance', *The Centennial Review*, 23:4 (1979).
Bernstein, J.M., *Disenchantment and Ethics* (Cambridge: Cambridge University Press, 2001).
Bernstein, J.M., *The Dialectical Imagination: A History of the Frankfurt School and the Institute for Social Research, 1923–1950* (Berkeley, Los Angeles and London: University of California Press, 1996).
Bewes, Timothy, *Reification, or, The Anxiety of Late Capitalism* (London: Verso, 2002).
Blanchot, Maurice, *The Writing of the Disaster*, trans. Ann Smock (Lincoln and London: University of Nebraska Press, 1995).
Blanton, C. D., *Epic Negation: The Dialectical Poetics of Late Modernism* (Oxford: Oxford University Press, 2005).
Bickersteth, Geoffrey, 'The Golden World of *King Lear*', *British Academy Annual Shakespeare Lectures, 1946–1951* (London: Geoffrey Cumberlege Amen House, 1951).
Bielsa, Esperanca, 'Theodor W. Adorno's Homecoming', *European Journal of Social Theory*, 19:3 (2016).
Billingham, Peter, *Edward Bond: A Critical Study* (London: Palgrave Macmillan, 2014).

Billington, Michael, '*King Lear* review – Sher shores up his place in Shakespeare royalty', *The Guardian*, <https://www.theguardian.com/stage/2016/sep/02/king-lear-review-royal-antony-sher> (accessed 30 October 2019).

Billington, Michael, '*The Gods Weep*', *The Guardian*, <https://www.theguardian.com/stage/2010/mar/18/the-gods-weep-review> (accessed 5 February 2018).

Biro, Andrew (ed.), *Critical Ecologies: The Frankfurt School and Contemporary Environmental Crises* (Toronto: University of Toronto Press, 2011).

Boltanski, Luc and Eve Chiapello, *The New Spirit of Capitalism*, trans. Gregory Elliott (London: Verso, 2017).

Bond, Edward, 'A blast at our smug theatre', *The Guardian*, <https://www.theguardian.com/stage/2015/jan/12/edward-bond-sarah-kane-blasted> (accessed 19 July 2019).

Bond, Edward, *Coffee: A Tragedy* (London: Methuen, 1996).

Bond, Edward, *Edward Bond: Letters Volume 2*, ed. Ian Stuart (Amsterdam: Harwood Academic Publishers, 1995).

Bond, Edward, *Edward Bond: Letters Volume 3*, ed. Ian Stuart (London: Routledge, 2003).

Bond, Edward, *Edward Bond: Letters Volume 4*, ed. Ian Stuart (Amsterdam: Harwood Academic Publishers, 1998).

Bond, Edward, *Edward Bond: Letters Volume 5*, ed. Ian Stuart (London: Routledge, 2001).

Bond, Edward, *Edward Bond: The Playwright Speaks*, ed. David Tuaillon (London: Bloomsbury Methuen, 2015).

Bond, Edward, *Lear* (London: Methuen, 2009).

Bond, Edward, *Plays 3: Bingo, The Fool, The Woman, Stone* (London: Methuen, 1999).

Bond, Edward, *Plays 7: Olly's Prison, Coffee, The Crime of the Twenty-First Century* (London: Methuen, 2003).

Bond, Edward, *Selections from the Notebooks of Edward Bond, Volume 1 1959–1980*, ed. Ian Stuart (London: Methuen, 2000).

Bond, Edward, *Selections from the Notebooks of Edward Bond, Volume 2 1980–1995*, ed. Ian Stuart (London: Methuen, 2000).

Bond, Edward, 'The First Word', *Edward Bond*, <http://www.edwardbond.org/Comment/comment.html> (accessed 3 May 2018).

Bond, Edward, *The Hidden Plot* (London: Methuen, 2000).

Bond, Edward, *The Chair Plays* (London: Bloomsbury Methuen, 2012).

Bond, Edward, 'The Third Crisis: The State of Future Drama', *Edward Bond*, <http://www.edwardbond.org/Comment/comment.html> (accessed 3 May 2018).

Bond, Edward, *The War Plays* (London: Methuen, 1988).

Booth, Stephen, *King Lear, Macbeth, Indefinition and Tragedy* (New Haven: Yale University Press, 1983).

Bottomore, Tom, *The Frankfurt School and Its Critics* (London: Routledge, 2002).

Bottoms, Stephens and Richard Gough (eds), 'Performing Literatures', *Performance Research*, 14:1 (2009).

Bowie, Andrew, *Adorno and the Ends of Philosophy* (Cambridge: Polity, 2013).

Bradley, A. C., *Shakespearean Tragedy* (London: Penguin, 1991).
Bradley, Lynne, *Adapting King Lear for the Stage* (Farnham and Burlington: Ashgate, 2010).
Brecht, Bertolt, *Brecht on Theatre*, ed. Marc Silberman, Tom Kuhn and Steve Giles, trans. various (London: Bloomsbury, 2019).
Brecht, Bertolt, 'On the Experimental Theatre', trans. Carl Richard Mueller, *Tulane Drama Review*, 6:1 (1961).
Brecht, Bertolt, *The Messingkauf Dialogues*, ed. and trans. John Willett (London: Bloomsbury, 2014).
Bronner, Stephen Eric and Douglas Kellner (eds), *Critical Theory and Society: A Reader* (London: Routledge, 1989).
Brook, Peter, *The Empty Space* (New York: Simon and Schuster, 1996).
Brown, Sarah and Catherine Silverstone (eds), *Tragedy in Transition* (Oxford: Blackwell, 2007).
Bruckner, Lynne and Dan Brayton (eds), *Ecocritical Shakespeare* (London: Routledge, 2011).
Bulman, James C., 'Bond, Shakespeare and the Absurd', *Modern Drama*, 29:1 (1986).
Burke, Sean, *The Death and Return of the Author: Criticism and Subjectivity in Barthes, Foucault and Derrida*, 2nd edn (Edinburgh: Edinburgh University Press, 2008).
Butler, Christopher, *Modernism: A Very Short Introduction* (Oxford: Oxford University Press, 2010).
Butler, Judith, *Giving an Account of Oneself* (New York: Fordham University Press, 2005).
Campbell, O.J., 'The Salvation of Lear', *English Literary History*, 15 (1948).
Canetti, Elias, *Crowds and Power* (Harmondsworth: Penguin, 1974).
Carney, Sean, *The Politics and Poetics of Contemporary English Tragedy* (Toronto: University of Toronto Press, 2013).
Carney, Sean, 'The Tragedy of History in Sarah Kane's *Blasted*', *Theatre Survey*, 1:2 (2005).
Carroll, William C., '"The Base Shall Top th'Legitimate": The Bedlam Beggar and the Role of Edgar in *King Lear*', *Shakespeare Quarterly*, 38:4 (1987).
Carson, Rachel, *Silent Spring* (Boston: Houghton Mifflin, 1962).
Carson, Susannah (ed.), *Shakespeare and Me* (London: OneWorld Classics, 2013).
Cavell, Stanley, *Disowning Knowledge: In Seven Plays of Shakespeare* (Cambridge: Cambridge University Press, 2003).
Cesarani, David, *Final Solution: The Fate of the Jews 1933–49* (London: Macmillan, 2016).
Chambers, Colin, *Inside the Royal Shakespeare Company: Creativity and the Institution* (London: Routledge, 2004).
Chambers, R. W., '*King Lear*', W. P. Ker Memorial Lecture, 1939 (Glasgow: Jackson Son and Co., 1940).
Chandler, David and Julian Reid, *The Neoliberal Subject: Resilience, Adaptation and Vulnerability* (London and New York: Rowman and Littlefield, 2016).
Chedgzoy, Kate, *Shakespeare's Queer Children: Sexual Politics and Contemporary Culture* (Manchester: Manchester University Press, 1995).
Chen, Chien-Cheng, 'On Edward Bond's Dramaturgy of Crisis in *The Chair*

Plays: The Dystopian Imagination and the Imagination in Dystopia', *Platform*, 10:2 (2016).

Chiari, Sophie, *Shakespeare's Representation of Weather, Climate and Environment: The Early Modern 'Fated Sky'* (Edinburgh, Edinburgh University Press, 2018).

Childs, Nicki and Jeni Walwin (eds), *A Split Second of Paradise: Live Art, Installation and Performance* (London and New York: Rivers Oram Press, 1998).

Churchill, Caryl, *Serious Money*, ed. Bill Naismith (London: Methuen, 2002).

Cohen, Derek, 'The Malignant Scapegoats of *King Lear*', *Studies in English Literature 1500-1900*, 49:2 (2009).

Cohn, Ruby, *Modern Shakespeare Offshoots* (Princeton: Princeton University Press, 1974).

Coleman, Terry, *Olivier: The Authorised Biography* (London: Bloomsbury, 2005).

Collie, Rosalie and F. T. Flahiff, *Some Facets of King Lear: Essays in Prismatic Criticism* (Toronto: University of Toronto Press, 1974).

Conrad Jackson, Joshua and Michele Gelfand, 'Could Climate Change Fuel the Rise of Right-Wing Nationalism?', *The Conversation*, <https://theconversation.com/could-climate-change-fuel-the-rise-of-right-wing-nationalism-123503> (accessed 1 October 2019).

Cook, Deborah (ed.), *Adorno: Key Concepts* (Oxford: Routledge, 2014).

Cook, Deborah, *Adorno on Nature* (London: Routledge, 2014).

Cook, Deborah, *Adorno, Habermas and the Search for a Rational Society* (London: Routledge, 2004).

Coole, Diana and Samantha Frost (eds), *New Materialisms: Ontology, Agency, and Politics* (Durham, NC and London: Duke University Press, 2010).

Coursen, Herbert, *Reading Shakespeare on Stage* (London: Associated University Presses, 1995).

Craig, Edward (ed.), *Concise Routledge Encyclopedia of Philosophy* (London and New York: Routledge, 2000).

Crawford, Ryan and Erik Vogt (eds), *Adorno and the Concept of Genocide* (Leiden and Boston: Brill Rodopi, 2014).

Croall, Jonathan, *Performing King Lear: Gielgud to Russel Beale* (London: Bloomsbury, 2015).

Crystal, David and Ben Crystal, *The Shakespeare Miscellany* (London: Penguin, 2005).

Cummings, Brian, '"Dead March": Liturgy and Mimesis in Shakespeare's Funerals', *Shakespeare*, 8:4 (2010).

Daddario, Will and Karoline Gritzner (eds), *Adorno and Performance* (Basingstoke: Palgrave Macmillan, 2014).

Danby, John F., *Shakespeare's Doctrine of Nature: A Study of King Lear* (London: Faber, 1949).

Danson, Laurence (ed.), *On 'King Lear'* (Princeton: Princeton University Press, 1981).

Davis, Belinda, Wilfried Mausbach, Martin Klimke and Carla MacDougall (eds), *Changing the World, Changing Oneself: Political Protest and Collective Identities in West Germany and the US in the 1960s and 1970s* (New York and Oxford: Berghahn Books, 2012).

Davis, David (ed.), *Edward Bond and the Dramatic Child: Edward Bond's Plays for Young People* (Stoke-on-Trent: Trentham Books, 2005).
Davies, Peter and Derek Lynch (eds), *The Routledge Companion to Fascism and the Far Right* (London and New York: Routledge, 2002).
de Montaigne, Michel, *The Complete Essays*, trans. M. A. Screech (London: Penguin, 2003).
de Vos, Laurens and Graham Saunders (eds), *Sarah Kane: In Context* (Manchester: Manchester University Press, 2010).
Delgado-Garcia, Cristina, 'Subversion, Refusal and Contingency: The Transgression of Liberal Humanist Subjectivity and Characterization in Sarah Kane's *Cleansed*, *Crave*, and *4.48 Psychosis*', *Modern Drama*, 55:2 (2012).
Derrida, Jacques, *Truth in Painting* (Chicago: University of Chicago Press, 1987).
Desmet, Christy and Sujata Iyengar, 'Adaptation, Appropriation, or What you Will', *Shakespeare*, 11:1 (2015).
Desmet, Christy and Robert Sawyer (eds), *Shakespeare and Appropriation* (London and New York: Routledge, 1999).
Dews, Peter, *Logics of Disintegration: Poststructuralist Thought and the Claims of Critical Theory* (London: Verso, 2007).
Diedrich, Antje, '"Last in a Long Line of Literary Kleptomaniacs": Intertextuality in Sarah Kane's *4.48 Psychosis*', *Modern Drama*, 56:3 (2013).
Dollimore, Jonathan, *Radical Tragedy: Religion, Ideology and Power in the Drama of Shakespeare and His Contemporaries*, 3rd edn (Basingstoke: Palgrave Macmillan, 2010).
Dollimore, Jonathan and Alan Sinfield (eds), *Political Shakespeare: Essays in Cultural Materialism* (Manchester: Manchester University Press, 1983).
Dotto, Charles Joseph Del, 'Engaging and Evading the Bard: Shakespeare, Nationalism, and British Theatrical Modernism, 1900–1964', PhD thesis (Duke University, 2010).
Duncan, Hal, *Rhapsody: Notes on Strange Fictions* (Maple Shade, NJ: Lethe Press, 2014).
Duncan-Jones, Katherine, *Shakespeare: An Ungentle Life* (London: Bloomsbury Arden, 2010).
Dupuy, Jean-Pierre, *A Short Treatise on the Metaphysics of Tsunamis*, trans. M. B. DeBevoise (East Lansing: Michigan State University Press, 2015).
Durão, Fabio Akcelrud (ed.), *Culture Industry Today* (Newcastle: Cambridge Scholars Publishing, 2010).
Eaglestone, Robert, *The Holocaust and the Postmodern* (Oxford: Oxford University Press, 2004).
Eagleton, Terry, *After Theory* (London: Penguin, 2004).
Eagleton, Terry, *Sweet Violence: The Idea of the Tragic* (London: Blackwell, 2003).
Edgar, David, *Albert Speer* (London: Nick Hern Books, 2000).
Edwards, Paul, and Jane Beckett, *Blast: Vorticism, 1914–1918* (London: Ashgate, 2000).
Egan, Gabriel, *Green Shakespeare: From Ecopolitics to Ecocriticism* (London: Routledge, 2006).
Eldon, Stuart, 'The Geopolitics of *King Lear*: Territory, Land, Earth', *Law & Literature*, 25:2 (2013).

Ellis, Erle C., *Anthropocene: A Very Short Introduction* (Oxford: Oxford University Press, 2018).
Elton, William, *King Lear and the Gods* (Lexington: The University Press of Kentucky, 1966).
Erasmus, Desiderius, *The Collected Works of Erasmus: Adages*, ed. Richard J. Schoeck and Beatrice Corrigan (Toronto: University of Toronto Press, 1982).
Erickson, Peter, *Rewriting Shakespeare, Rewriting Ourselves* (Berkeley: University of California Press, 1991).
Etchells, Tim, *Certain Fragments: Contemporary Performance and the Theatre of Forced Entertainment* (London: Routledge, 1999).
Etchells, Tim, 'Interview with Dan Rebellato, Richard Ashby and Jessica Chiba: *Table Top Shakespeare, The Complete Works*', *YouTube*, <https://www.youtube.com/watch?v=nu8C5eJc0pc> (accessed 5 September 2019).
Everett, Barbara, 'The New *King Lear*', *Critical Quarterly*, 2:4 (1960).
Feldman, Matthew and Mark Nixon, *Beckett's Literary Legacies* (Newcastle upon Tyne: Cambridge Scholars, 2007).
Fernie, Ewan, *Shakespeare for Freedom: Why the Plays Matter* (Cambridge: Cambridge University Press, 2017).
Fernie, Ewan, *The Demonic: Literature and Experience* (London: Routledge, 2013).
Finlayson, James, 'Adorno on the Ethical and the Ineffable', *European Journal of Philosophy*, 10:1 (2002).
Finlayson, James, 'Modern Art, Metaphysics and Radical Evil', *Modernism/Modernity*, 10:1 (2003).
Fischlin, Daniel and Mark Fortier (eds), *Adaptations of Shakespeare* (London and New York: Routledge, 2000).
Foakes, R. A., *Hamlet Versus Lear: Cultural Politics and Shakespeare's Art* (Cambridge: Cambridge University Press, 1993).
Foakes, R. A., '*King Lear* and the Displacement of Hamlet', *Huntington Library Quarterly*, 50:3 (1987).
Forchtner, Bernhard (ed.), *The Far Right and the Environment: Politics, Discourse and Communication* (Oxford: Routledge, 2020).
Forsdyke, Sara, *Exile, Ostracism, and Democracy: The Politics of Expulsion in Ancient Greece* (Princeton: Princeton University Press, 2005).
Foster, Hal (ed.), *Postmodern Culture* (London: Pluto Press, 1985).
Foucault, Michel, *Michel Foucault: Aesthetics, Method, and Epistemology, Volume 2*, ed. Faubion, James D and Paul Rabinow (New York: The New Press, 1994).
Foucault, Michel, '*Society Must Be Defended*': *Lectures at the Collège de France, 1975–1976*, ed. Mauro Bertani and Alessandro Fontana, trans. David Macey (London: Penguin, 2004).
Foucault, Michel, *The Birth of Biopolitics: Lectures at the Collège de France, 1978–1979*, ed. Michel Sellenart, trans. Graham Burchell (Basingstoke: Palgrave Macmillan, 2008).
Fraser, Scott, *A Politic Theatre: The Drama of David Hare* (Amsterdam and Atlanta: Rodopi, 1996).
French, William W, 'A Kind of Courage: *King Lear* at the Old Vic, London, 1940', *Theatre Topics*, 3:1 (1993).

Fukuyama, Francis, *The End of History and the Last Man* (London: Penguin, 2012).
Funke, Manuel, Moritz Schularick and Christoph Trebesch, 'Going to Extremes: Politics after Financial Crises, 1870–2014', *European Economic Review*, 88 (2016).
Gandesha, Samir, 'Enlightenment as Tragedy: Reflections on Adorno's Ethics', *Thesis Eleven*, 65:1 (2001).
Garrard, Greg (ed.), *The Oxford Handbook of Ecocriticism* (Oxford: Oxford University Press, 2014).
Gaskill, William, *A Sense of Direction: Life at the Royal Court* (London: Faber and Faber, 1988).
Genter, Robert, *Late Modernism: Art, Culture, and Politics in Cold War America* (Philadelphia: University of Pennsylvania Press, 2010).
George, Theodore D., *Tragedies of Spirit: Tracing Finitude in Hegel's Phenomenology* (New York: State University of New York Press, 2006).
Gerstenberger, Katharina and Tanja Nusser (eds), *Catastrophe and Catharsis: Perspectives on Disasters and Redemption in German Culture and Beyond* (Rochester, NY: Camden House, 2015).
Gielgud, John, *Sir John Gielgud: A Life in Letters*, ed. Richard Mangan (New York: Arcade Publishing, 2004).
Goldberg, S. L., *An Essay on King Lear* (Cambridge: Cambridge University Press, 1974).
Gordin, Michael D and G. John Ikenberry (eds), *The Age of Hiroshima* (Princeton: Princeton University Press, 2020).
Gorman, Sarah, 'Chronicles of the Indeterminate: Ordering Chaos in the Retrospectives of Forced Entertainment', *Performance Research: A Journal of the Performing Arts*, 10:1 (2014).
Grady, Hugh (ed.), *Great Shakespeareans, Volume Thirteen: Empson, Wilson, Knight, Barber, Kott* (London: Continuum, 2012).
Grady, Hugh, *Shakespeare and Impure Aesthetics* (Cambridge: Cambridge University Press, 2009).
Grady, Hugh (ed.), *Shakespeare and Modernity: Early Modern to Millennium* (London: Routledge, 2000).
Grady, Hugh, *Shakespeare's Universal Wolf: Studies in Early Modern Reification* (Oxford: Clarendon Press, 1996).
Grady, Hugh, *The Modernist Shakespeare: Critical Texts in a Material World* (Oxford: Clarendon Press, 1991).
Granville-Barker, Harley, *Preface to King Lear* (London: Nick Hern Books, 1993).
Greenblatt, Stephen, *Renaissance Self-Fashioning: From More to Shakespeare* (Chicago: University of Chicago Press, 2005).
Greenblatt, Stephen, *Shakespearean Negotiations: The Circulation of Social Energy in Renaissance England* (Berkeley and Los Angeles: University of California Press, 1988).
Gritzner, Karoline, *Adorno and Modern Theatre: The Drama of the Damaged Self in Bond, Rudkin, Barker and Kane* (Basingstoke: Palgrave Macmillan, 2015).
Gritzner, Karoline, 'Adorno and the Sublime in Live Performance', *The European Legacy*, 21:7 (2016).

Gritzner, Karoline, 'Adorno on Tragedy: Reading Catastrophe in Late Capitalist Culture', *Critical Engagements: A Journal of Criticism and Theory*, 1:2 (2007).

Gritzner, Karoline, '(Post)Modern Subjectivity and the New Expressionism: Howard Barker, Sarah Kane, and Forced Entertainment', *Contemporary Theatre Review*, 18.3 (2008).

Groves, Peter, 'Sacred Tragedy: An Exploration into the Spiritual Dimension of the Theatre of Howard Barker', PhD thesis (University of Warwick, 2014).

Habermas, Jürgen, *Moral Consciousness and Communicative Action*, trans. Christian Lenhardt and Sherry Weber Nicholson (Cambridge, MA: MIT Press, 1993).

Habermas, Jürgen, *The Philosophical Discourse of Modernity*, trans. Frederick Lawrence (Cambridge: Polity, 2007).

Haider, Asad, *Mistaken Identity: Race and Class in the Age of Trump* (London: Verso, 2018).

Halpern, Richard, *The Poetics of Primitive Accumulation: English Renaissance Culture and the Genealogy of Capital* (Ithaca and London: Cornell University Press, 1991).

Hamilton, Jennifer Mae, *This Contentious Storm: An Ecocritical and Performance History of King Lear* (London: Bloomsbury, 2017).

Hammer, Espen, *Adorno and the Political* (Oxford: Routledge, 2006).

Hammond, Philip and Edward S. Herman (eds), *Degraded Capability: The Media and the Kosovo Crisis* (London: Pluto Press, 2000).

Harding, James Martin, *Adorno and 'A Writing of the Ruins'* (New York: State University of New York Press, 1997).

Harman, Graham, *Object-Oriented Ontology: A New Theory of Everything* (London: Penguin, 2018).

Harrison, G. B., *Shakespeare's Tragedies* (London: Routledge, 1951).

Hawkes, Terence, *William Shakespeare: King Lear* (Plymouth: Northcote House Publishers, 1995).

Hawkes, Terence, *Meaning by Shakespeare* (London: Routledge, 1992).

Hawkes, Terence, *That Shakespearean Rag: Essays on a Critical Process* (London: Methuen, 1986).

Hay, Malcom and Philip Roberts, *Edward Bond: A Companion to the Plays* (London: TQ Publications, 1978).

Hayes, Peter and John K. Roth (eds), *The Oxford Handbook of Holocaust Studies* (Oxford: Oxford University Press, 2010).

Heathfield, Adrien (ed.), *The Millennium and the Marking of Time* (London: Black Dog Publishing, 2000).

Heberle, Renee J. (ed.), *Feminist Interpretations of Theodor Adorno* (Philadelphia: University of Pennsylvania Press, 2006).

Hecht, Anthony, *Selected Poems*, ed. James McClatchy (New York: Alfred Knopf, 2011).

Hegel, Georg Wilhelm Friedrich, *Aesthetics: Volume One*, trans. T. M. Knox (Oxford: Oxford University Press, 1975).

Hegel, Georg Wilhelm Friedrich, *Outlines of the Philosophy of Right*, ed. Stephen Houlgate, trans. T. M. Knox (Oxford: Oxford University Press, 2008).

Hegel, Georg Wilhelm Friedrich, *Phenomenology of Spirit*, trans. A. V. Miller (Oxford: Oxford University Press, 1977).

Hegel, Georg Wilhelm Friedrich, *Philosophy of Mind*, ed. Michael Inwood, trans. W. Wallace and A. V. Miller (Oxford: Oxford University Press, 2007).
Hegel, Georg Wilhelm Friedrich, *The Philosophy of History*, trans. J. Sibree (New York: Dover Publications, 2004).
Heijes, Coen, 'Reviews: *King Lear* by David Farr; *Antony and Cleopatra* by Michael Boyd', *Shakespeare Bulletin*, 28:4 (2010).
Heilman, Robert B., 'The Unity of "*King Lear*"', *The Sewanee Review*, 56:1 (1948).
Hellings, James, *Adorno and Art: Aesthetic Theory Contra Critical Theory* (Basingstoke: Palgrave Macmillan, 2014).
Helmling, Steven, *Adorno's Poetics of Critique* (London: Continuum, 2009).
Hemler, Judith and Florian Malzacher (eds), *Not Even a Game Anymore: The Theatre of Forced Entertainment* (Berlin: Alexander Verlag, 2012).
Hermans, Theo (ed.), *The Manipulation of Literature: Studies in Literary Translation* (Oxford: Routledge, 2014).
Heyes, Cressida, 'Identity Politics', *The Stanford Encyclopedia of Philosophy*, <https://plato.stanford.edu/archives/sum2016/entries/identity-politics/> (accessed 18 June 2020).
Higgins, John, *The first parte of the Mirour for magistrates* (London: 1574). *Early English Books Online*, <http://eebo.chadwyck.com.ezproxy01.rhul.ac.uk/search/fulltext?ACTION=ByID&ID=D20000998418730033&SOURCE=var_spell.cfg&DISPLAY=AUTHOR&WARN=N&FILE=../session/1501148434_13628> (accessed 27 July 2017).
Hirst, David, *Edward Bond* (Basingstoke: Macmillan, 1985).
Hiscock, Andrew and Lisa Hopkins (eds), *King Lear: A Critical Guide* (London: Continuum, 2011).
Hodgdon, Barbara, *The Shakespeare Trade: Performances and Appropriations* (Philadelphia: University of Pennsylvania Press, 1998).
Holbrook, Peter, 'The Left and *King Lear*', *Textual Practice*, 14:2 (2000).
Holderness, Graham (ed.), *The Shakespeare Myth* (Manchester: Manchester University Press, 1988).
Holdsworth, Nadine and Mary Luckhurst (eds), *Concise Companion to Contemporary British and Irish Drama* (Oxford: Blackwell, 2013).
Holland, Peter, *English Shakespeares: Shakespeare on the English Stage in the 1990s* (Cambridge: Cambridge University Press, 1997).
Holland, Peter (ed.) *Shakespeare Survey: Volume 55* (Cambridge: Cambridge University Press, 2002).
Holland, Peter (ed), *Shakespeare Survey: Volume 63* (Cambridge: Cambridge University Press, 2010).
Homden, Carol, *The Plays of David Hare* (Cambridge: Cambridge University Press, 1995).
Horkheimer, Max, *Critique of Instrumental Reason*, trans. Matthew Jay O'Connell et al. (London: Verso, 2012).
Horkheimer, Max, *Eclipse of Reason* (London: Bloomsbury, 2013).
Housden, Martyn, *Hans Frank: Lebensraum and the Holocaust* (Basingstoke: Palgrave Macmillan, 2003).
Huang, Alexa and Elizabeth Rivlin (eds), *Shakespeare and the Ethics of Appropriation* (New York: Palgrave Macmillan, 2013).

Hughes, Ted, *Shakespeare and the Goddess of Complete Being* (London: Faber and Faber, 1992).
Huhn, Tom and Lambert Zuidervaart (eds), *The Semblance of Subjectivity: Essays on Adorno's Aesthetic Theory* (Cambridge, MA: MIT Press, 1999).
Hunter, G. K., *Dramatic Identities and Cultural Tradition: Studies in Shakespeare and His Contemporaries* (Liverpool: Liverpool University Press, 1978).
Hutcheon, Linda, *A Theory of Adaptation*, 2nd edn (Oxford: Routledge, 2013).
Innes, Christopher, *Modern British Drama: The Twentieth Century* (Cambridge: Cambridge University Press, 2002).
Innes, Christopher, 'The Political Spectrum of Edward Bond: From Rationalism to Rhapsody', *Modern Drama*, 25:2 (1982).
Ioppolo, Grace (ed.), *A Routledge Literary Sourcebook on William Shakespeare's King Lear* (London: Routledge, 2003).
Jameson, Fredric, *A Singular Modernity* (London: Verso, 2012).
Jameson, Fredric, *Late Marxism: Adorno, or, the Persistence of the Dialectic* (London: Verso, 2007).
Jameson, Fredric, *Marxism and Form* (Princeton: Princeton University Press, 1971).
Jameson, Fredric, *Postmodernism, or, The Cultural Logic of Late Capitalism* (London: Verso, 1991).
Jarvis, Simon, *Adorno: A Critical Introduction* (London and New York: Routledge, 1998).
Jay, Martin, *Permanent Exiles: Essays on the Intellectual Migration from Germany to America* (New York: Columbia University Press, 1986).
Jones, Emrys, *Scenic Form in Shakespeare* (Oxford: Clarendon Press, 1971).
Jones, Gwilym, *Shakespeare's Storms* (Manchester: Manchester University Press, 2015).
Joughin, John (ed.), *Philosophical Shakespeares* (London: Routledge, 2000).
Kahan, Jeffrey (ed.), *King Lear: New Critical Essays* (New York and Oxford: Routledge, 2008).
Kainulainen, Maggie 'Saying Climate Change: Ethics of the Sublime and the Problem of Representation', *symploke*, 21:1–2 (2014).
Kamps, Ivo (ed), *Materialist Shakespeare: A History* (London: Verso, 1995).
Kane, Sarah, *Complete Plays* (London: Methuen, 2001).
Kant, Immanuel, *Critique of Judgement*, trans. James Creed Meredith (Oxford: Oxford University Press, 2007).
Kant, Immanuel, *Critique of Pure Reason*, trans. Norman Kemp Smith (Basingstoke: Palgrave Macmillan, 2005).
Kant, Immanuel, *Groundwork of the Metaphysics of Morals*, trans. Mary Gregor (Cambridge: Cambridge University Press, 1997).
Katafiasz, Kate, 'Drama and Desire: Edward Bond and Jacques Lacan', PhD thesis (Reading University, 2011).
Katafiasz, Kate, 'Quarrelling with Brecht: Understanding Bond's Post-Structuralist Political Aesthetic', *Studies in Theatre and Performance*, 28:3 (2008).
Kaye, Nick, 'On Objects', *Performance Research*, 23:4–5 (2018).
Keefe, Barrie, *King of England and Bastard Angel: Two Plays* (London: Methuen, 1988).

Kelly, Dennis, 'Dennis Kelly talks about *The Gods Weep*', YouTube, <https://www.youtube.com/watch?v=vnpdWqsV5CI> (accessed 4 February 2018).
Kelly, Dennis, 'Identity Crisis', *The Guardian*, <https://www.theguardian.com/stage/2008/feb/28/theatre.television> (accessed 4 February 2018).
Kelly, Dennis, *Plays One* (London: Oberon Books, 2008).
Kelly, Dennis, *Plays Two* (London: Oberon Books, 2013).
Kelly, Dennis, *The Gods Weep* (London: Oberon Books, 2010).
Kelly, Dennis and Maria Aberg, 'Dennis Kelly and Maria Aberg: *The Gods Weep*', interview with Aleks Sierz, *Theatre Voice*, <http://www.theatrevoice.com/audio-tags/aleks-sierz/> (accessed 23 August 2019).
Kennedy, Dennis, '"*King Lear*" and the Theatre', *Educational Theatre Journal*, 28:1 (1976).
Kennedy, Dennis, *Looking at Shakespeare: A Visual History of Twentieth-Century Performance*, 2nd edn (Cambridge: Cambridge University Press, 2001).
Kermode, Frank, *The Sense of an Ending: Studies in the Theory of Fiction* (Oxford: Oxford University Press, 2000).
Kettle, Arnold, *Literature and Liberation: Selected Essays*, ed. Graham Martin and W. R. Owens (Manchester: Manchester University Press, 1988).
Kettle, Arnold (ed.), *Shakespeare in a Changing World* (London: Laurence and Wishart, 1964).
Kingsley-Smith, Jane, 'Banishment in Shakespeare's Plays', PhD thesis (Birmingham: Shakespeare Institute, 1999).
Kingsley-Smith, Jane, *Shakespeare's Drama of Exile* (Basingstoke: Palgrave Macmillan, 2003).
Kipp, Lara, 'Between Excess and Subtraction: Scenographic Violence in Howard Barker's *Found in the Ground*', *Sillages Critiques*, <https://journals.openedition.org/sillagescritiques/4830?lang=en> (accessed 13 November 2019).
Klein, Naomi, *The Shock Doctrine: The Rise of Disaster Capitalism* (London: Penguin, 2007).
Knights, L.C., *Some Shakespearean Themes: And An Approach to 'Hamlet'* (Stanford: Stanford University Press, 1950).
Kott, Jan, *Shakespeare Our Contemporary* (New York: Norton, 1974).
Kott, Jan, *The Theatre of Essence* (Evanston: Northwestern University Press, 1984).
Kracauer, Siegfried, *The Mass Ornament: Weimar Essays*, trans. Thomas Y. Levin (Cambridge, MA: Harvard University Press, 1995).
Kristeva, Julia, *Powers of Horror: An Essay on Abjection*, trans. Leon S. Roudiez (New York: Columbia University Press, 1982).
Kristeva, Julia, *Strangers to Ourselves*, trans. Leon S. Roudiez (New York: Columbia University Press, 1991).
Kurosawa, Akira (dir.), *Ran* (London: WHV DVD, 2004).
Lang, Berel, *The Future of the Holocaust: Between History and Memory* (Ithaca and London: Cornell University Press, 1999).
Langer, Lawrence L., *Preempting the Holocaust* (New Haven and London: Yale University Press, 1998).
Laroque, François et al. (eds), *And That's True Too: New Essays on King Lear* (Newcastle: Cambridge Scholars Publishing, 2009).
Latour, Bruno, *Reassembling the Social: An Introduction to Actor-Network-Theory* (Oxford: Oxford University Press, 2005).

Lawrence, Sean, 'The Difficulty of Dying in *King Lear*', *English Studies in Canada*, 34:1 (2005).
Lee, Lisa Yun, *Dialectics of the Body: Corporeality in the Philosophy of T. W. Adorno* (London: Routledge, 2005).
Leggatt, Alexander, *Shakespeare in Performance: King Lear*, 2nd edn (Manchester: Manchester University Press, 2005).
Leggatt, Alexander (ed), *The Cambridge Companion to Shakespearean Comedy* (Cambridge: Cambridge University Press, 2002).
Leiblein, Leanore, 'Jan Kott, Peter Brook and *King Lear*', *Journal of Dramatic Theory and Criticism*, 1:2 (1987).
Lehman, Hans-Thies, *Postdramatic Theatre*, trans. Karen Jürs-Munby (Oxford: Routledge, 2006).
Levene, Mark and Daniele Conversi, 'Subsistence Societies, Globalisation, Climate Change and Genocide: Discourses of Vulnerability and Resilience', *The International Journal of Human Rights*, 18:3 (2014).
Lever, J. W., *The Tragedy of State* (London: Methuen, 1974).
Levi, Primo, *If This Is a Man/The Truce* (London: Abacus Books, 2013).
Levi, Primo, *The Drowned and the Saved* (London: Abacus Books, 2013).
Linley, Keith, *King Lear in Context: The Cultural Background* (London and New York: Anthem Press, 2015).
Livingstone, Rodney, Perry Anderson and Frances Mulhern (eds), *Aesthetics and Politics*, trans. various (London: Verso, 2007).
Loftis, Sonya Freeman, *Shakespeare's Surrogates: Rewriting Renaissance Drama* (London and New York: Palgrave Macmillan, 2013).
Loughnane, Rory and Edel Semple (eds), *Staged Transgression in Shakespeare's England* (New York and London: Palgrave Macmillan, 2013).
Lowenthal, David, *Shakespeare and the Good Life: Ethics and Politics in Dramatic Form* (Lanham, MD: Rowman & Littlefield, 1997).
Lukács, György, *History and Class Consciousness: Studies in Marxist Dialectics*, trans. Rodney Livingstone (Pontypool: The Merlin Press, 1971).
Lupton, Julia Reinhard, *Thinking with Shakespeare: Essays on Politics and Life* (London and Chicago: University of Chicago Press, 2011).
Lyotard, Jean-François, 'Adorno as the Devil', *Telos*, 19 (1974).
Lyotard, Jean-François, *Heidegger and "the jews"*, trans. Andreas Michel and Mark Roberts (Minneapolis: University of Minnesota Press, 1988).
Lyotard, Jean-François, *Lessons on the Analytic of the Sublime (Kant's "Critique of Judgment")*, trans. Elizabeth Rottenberg (Stanford: Stanford University Press, 1991).
Lyotard, Jean-François, *Libidinal Economy*, trans. Ian Hamilton Grant (London: Bloomsbury, 2015).
Lyotard, Jean-François, *The Differend: Phrases in Dispute* (Minneapolis: University of Minnesota Press, 1988).
Lyotard, Jean-François, *The Inhuman: Reflections on Time*, trans. Geoffrey Bennington and Rachel Bowdy (Stanford: Stanford University Press, 1988).
Lyotard, Jean-François, *The Postmodern Condition*, trans. Geoff Bennington and Brian Massumi (Manchester: Manchester University Press, 1986).
Lyotard, Jean-François, *The Postmodern Explained: Correspondence, 1982–1985*, ed. and trans. Julian Pefanis and Morgan Thomas (Minneapolis: University of Minnesota, 1997).

Mack, Maynard, *'King Lear' in Our Time* (Berkeley and Los Angeles: University of California Press, 1965).
Malm, Andreas, *The Progress of This Storm: Nature and Society in a Warming World* (London: Verso, 2018).
Mandel, Ernest, *Late Capitalism* (London: Verso, 1998).
Marcuse, Herbert, *One-Dimensional Man: Studies in the Ideology of Advanced Industrial Society*, trans. Douglas Kellner (Oxford: Routledge, 2002).
Marowitz, Charles, 'Lear Log', *Tulane Drama Review*, 8:2 (1963).
Marsden, Jean (ed.), *The Appropriation of Shakespeare: Post-Renaissance Reconstructions of the Works and Myths* (Hemel Hempstead: Harvester Wheatsheaf, 1991).
Mason, H. A., *Shakespeare's Tragedies of Love* (London: Chatto and Windus, 1970).
Massai, Sonia, 'Stage Over Study: Charles Marowitz, Edward Bond and Recent Materialist Approaches to Shakespeare', *New Theatre Quarterly*, 59 (1999).
McCarthy, Cormac, *The Road* (London: Picador, 2010).
McCullough, Christopher, *Theatre and Europe, 1957–95* (Bristol: Intellect Books, 1996).
McCumber, John, *Understanding Hegel's Mature Critique of Kant* (Stanford: Stanford University Press, 2012).
McDonald, Bradley J., 'Theodor Adorno, Alterglobalization, and Non-identity Politics', *New Political Science*, 34:3 (2012).
Meiner, Carsten and Kristin Veel (eds), *The Cultural Life of Catastrophes and Crises* (Berlin and Boston: de Gruyter, 2012).
Mentz, Steven, '"Strange Weather" in *King Lear*', *Shakespeare*, 6:2 (2010).
Meyer-Dinkgräfe, Daniel (ed.), *Consciousness, Theatre, Literature and the Arts* (Newcastle upon Tyne: Cambridge Scholars, 2006).
Miklitsch, Robert, *Roll Over Adorno: Critical Theory, Popular Culture, Audiovisual Media* (New York: State University of New York Press, 2006).
Monmouth, Geoffrey, *The History of the Kings of Britain*, trans. Lewis Thorpe (London: Penguin, 1966).
Moore, Andrew, *Shakespeare Between Machiavelli and Hobbes: Dead Body Politics* (New York and London: Lexington Books, 2016).
Morgan, Alistair, 'A Preponderance of Objects: Critical Theory and the Turn to the Object', *Adorno Studies*, 1:1 (2017).
Morgan, Alistair, 'Mere Life, Damaged Life and Ephemeral Life: Adorno and the Concept of Life', *Angelaki: Journal of the Theoretical Humanities*, 19:1 (2014).
Muir, Edwin, 'The Politics of *King Lear*', W. P. Ker Memorial Lecture, 1946 (Glasgow: Glasgow University Publications, 1947).
Muir, Kenneth, *Shakespeare's Sources: Comedies and Tragedies* (Oxford: Routledge, 2005).
Muir, Kenneth (ed.), *Shakespeare Survey: Volume 33* (Cambridge: Cambridge University Press, 1980).
Muir, Tom, 'Without Remainder: Ruins and Tombs in Shakespeare's Sonnets', *Textual Practice*, 24:1 (2009).
Mullin, Emily, 'Macready's Triumph: The Restoration of *King Lear* to the Stage', *Penn History Review*, 18:1 (2010).

Mussell, Simon, '"Pervaded by a chill": The Dialectic of Coldness in Adorno's Social Theory', *Thesis Eleven*, 117:1 (2013).

Nancy, Jean-Luc, *After Fukushima: The Equivalence of Catastrophes* (New York: Fordham University Press, 2015).

Neill, Michael and David Schalkwyk (eds), *The Oxford Handbook to Shakespearean Tragedy* (Oxford: Oxford University Press, 2016).

Nicoll, Allardyce, *Shakespeare Survey: Volume 13* (Cambridge: Cambridge University Press, 1966).

Nivalainen, Markku, 'On Thinking the Tragic with Adorno', *The European Legacy*, 21:7 (2016).

Nolan, Aoife (ed.), *Economic and Social Rights after the Global Financial Crisis* (Cambridge: Cambridge University Press, 2014).

Norland, Howard B., *Drama in Early Tudor Britain, 1485–1558* (Lincoln and London: University of Nebraska Press, 1995).

Novy, Marianne (ed.), *Cross-Cultural Performances: Difference in Women's Re-Visions of Shakespeare* (Urbana and Chicago: University of Illinois, 1993).

Novy, Marianne (ed.), *Transforming Shakespeare: Contemporary Women's Re-Visions in Literature and Performance* (Basingstoke: Macmillan, 1999).

Ogden, James and Arthur Scouten (eds), *Lear from Study to Stage: Essays in Criticism* (Madison, WI and London: Associated University Presses, 1997).

Oppo, Andrea, *Philosophical Aesthetics and Samuel Beckett* (Oxford: Peter Lang, 2008).

Palfrey, Simon, *Poor Tom: Living King Lear* (Chicago: Chicago University Press, 2014).

Pearce, Andy, 'The Development of Holocaust Consciousness in Contemporary Britain, 1979–2001', *Holocaust Studies*, 14:2 (2008).

Pendas, Devin O., *The Frankfurt Auschwitz Trial, 1963–1965: Genocide, History, and the Limits of the Law* (Cambridge: Cambridge University Press, 2006).

Pensky, Max, *The Actuality of Adorno: Critical Essays on Adorno and the Postmodern* (New York: State University of New York Press, 1997).

Peters, Jens, 'Crowd or Chorus? Howard Barker's *mise-en-scène* and the Tradition of the Chorus in the European Theatre of the Twentieth Century', *Studies in Theatre and Performance*, 32:2 (2012).

Peterson, Kaara L. and Deanne Williams (eds), *The Afterlife of Ophelia* (New York: Palgrave MacMillan, 2012).

Poole, Adrian, *Tragedy: A Very Short Introduction* (Oxford: Oxford University Press, 2005).

Postone, Moshie and Eric Santner, *Catastrophe and Meaning: The Holocaust and the Twentieth Century* (Chicago: University of Chicago Press, 2003).

Rabey, David Ian, *David Rudkin: Sacred Disobedience – An Expository Study of His Drama 1959–1996* (Oxford: Routledge, 1997).

Rabey, David Ian, *English Drama Since 1940* (Oxford: Routledge, 2014).

Rabey, David Ian, *Howard Barker: Ecstasy and Death – An Expository Study of His Drama, Theory and Production, 1988–2008* (Basingstoke: Palgrave Macmillan, 2009).

Rabey, David Ian, *Howard Barker: Politics and Desire – An Expository Study of His Drama and Poetry, 1969–1987* (Basingstoke: Macmillan, 1989).

Rabey, David Ian, *The Wye Plays* (Bristol: Intellect Books, 2004).
Rabey, David Ian and Sarah Goldingay (eds), *Howard Barker's Art of Theatre: Essays on His Plays, Poetry and Production Work* (Manchester: Manchester University Press, 2013).
Rabey, David Ian and Karoline Gritzner (eds), *Theatre of Catastrophe: New Essays in Howard Barker* (London: Oberon Books, 2006).
Rancière, Jacques, *On the Shores of Politics*, trans. Liz Heron (London and New York: Verso, 1995).
Rayman, Joshua, 'Dialectics of Exile: Adorno, Mann, and the Culture Industry', *Monatshefte*, 106:3 (2014).
Raw, Lawrence, 'People's Theatre and Shakespeare in Wartime: Donald Wolfit's *King Lear* in London and Leeds, 1944–1945', *Shakespeare*, 12:1 (2016).
Rebellato, Dan, '"And I Will Reach Out My Hand With A Kind of Infinite Slowness And Say The Perfect Thing": The Utopian Theatre of Suspect Culture', *Contemporary Theatre Review*, 13:1 (2003).
Rebellato, Dan, 'Brief Encounter: An Interview with Sarah Kane', *Dan Rebellato*, <http://www.danrebellato.co.uk/sarah-kane-interview/> (accessed 18 June 2020).
Rebellato, Dan, 'New Writing, Dennis Kelly', 'Backpages', *Contemporary Theatre Review*, 17.4 (2007).
Remshardt, Ralf, *Staging the Savage God: The Grotesque in Performance* (Carbondale: Southern Illinois University Press, 2004).
Rensmann, Lars, 'Returning from Forced Exile, Some Observations on Theodor W. Adorno's and Hannah Arendt's Experience of Postwar Germany and Their Political Theories of Totalitarianism', *Leo Baeck Institute Year Book*, 49 (2004).
Ribner, Irving, '"The Gods are Just": A Reading of *King Lear*', *Tulane Drama Review*, 2:3 (1958).
Richardson, Samuel, *Clarissa, or, The History of a Young Lady* (London: Penguin, 1985).
Rosen, Alan, *Dislocating the End: Climax, Closure, and the Invention of Genre* (Oxford: Peter Lang, 2001).
Rosenberg, Marvin, *The Masks of King Lear* (London: Associated University Press, 1975).
Roth, John K., *Ethics During and After the Holocaust: In the Shadow of Birkenau* (Basingstoke: Palgrave Macmillan, 2005).
Rudkin, David, *Afore Night Come* (London: Oberon Modern Plays, 2001).
Rudkin, David, 'Afore Night Come', *David Rudkin*, <http://www.davidrudkin.com/theatre/afore-night-come/afore-night-comep2.html> (accessed 6 July 2019).
Rudkin, David, 'An Affliction of Images: An Interview with David Rudkin', *Encore*, 11:4 (1964).
Rudkin, David, 'Burning Alone in the Dark: David Rudkin Talks to David Ian Rabey', *Planet*, 114 (1995–6).
Rudkin, David, 'Commentary', *David Rudkin*, <http://www.davidrudkin.com/more/commentary.html> (accessed 6 July 2019).
Rudkin, David, *Interrogations*, dir. Stephen Garrett (Central Independent Television, Carlton Videocassettes, 1985).
Rudkin, David, 'Mongrel Nation', *Vertigo*, 2:5 (2003).

Rudkin, David, 'On Being an Artaudian Dramatist', *Past Masters: Antonin Artaud Conference*, 8–10 November 1996 (Aberystwyth: Centre for Performance Research, 1996).
Rudkin, David, *Red Sun and Merlin Unchained* (Bristol: Intellect Books, 2011).
Rudkin, David, *The Lovesong of Alfred J. Hitchcock* (London: Oberon Modern Plays, 2014).
Rudkin, David, *The Saxon Shore* (London: Eyre Methuen, 1986).
Rudkin, David, *The Sons of Light* (London: Eyre Methuen, 1981).
Rudkin, David, '*The Sons of Light*', *David Rudkin*, <http://www.davidrudkin.com/theatre/the-sons-of-light.html> (accessed 3 February 2018).
Rudkin, David, *The Triumph of Death* (London: Eyre Methuen, 1981).
Rudkin, David, *Will's Way* (Halford: The Celandine Press, 1993).
Rumbold, Kate, 'Review of Shakespeare's *King Lear* (directed by David Farr for the Royal Shakespeare Company) at the Courtyard Theatre, Stratford-upon-Avon, 30 March 2010', *Shakespeare*, 7:2 (2010).
Ryan, Kiernan (ed.), *King Lear: Contemporary Critical Essays* (Basingstoke: Macmillan, 1993).
Ryan, Kiernan, *Shakespeare* (Basingstoke: Palgrave Macmillan, 2002).
Said, Edward, *Reflections on Exile, And Other Literary and Cultural Essays* (London: Granta Books, 2000).
Sakellaridou, Elizabeth, 'A Lover's Discourse – but Whose? Inversions of the Fascist Aesthetic in Howard Barker's *Und* and Other Recent English Plays', *European Journal of English Studies*, 7:1 (2003).
Salingar, Leo, *Shakespeare and the Traditions of Comedy* (Cambridge: Cambridge University Press, 1974).
Samuels, Diane, *Kindertransport* (London: Nick Hern Books, 2008).
Sanders, Julie, *Adaptation and Appropriation* (Oxford: Routledge, 2006).
Sanders, Wilbur, *The Dramatist and the Received Idea: Studies in Shakespeare* (Cambridge: Cambridge University Press, 1968).
Sandu, Sukhdev (ed.), *The Edge Is Where the Centre Is: David Rudkin and Penda's Fen – An Archaeology* (Brooklyn: Keegan and Cooke, 2015).
Saunders, Graham, '"A theatre of ruins": Edward Bond and Samuel Beckett, Theatrical Antagonists', *Studies in Theatre and Performance*, 25:1 (2005).
Saunders, Graham, *About Kane: The Playwright and the Work* (London: Faber and Faber, 2009).
Saunders, Graham (ed.), *British Theatre Companies 1980–1994* (London: Bloomsbury, 2015).
Saunders, Graham, 'Edward Bond and the Celebrity of Exile', *Theatre Research International*, 29:3 (2004).
Saunders, Graham, *Elizabethan and Jacobean Reappropriation in Contemporary British Drama: 'Upstart Crows'* (Basingstoke: Palgrave Macmillan, 2018).
Saunders, Graham, '"Just a word on the page and there is the drama": Sarah Kane's Theatrical Legacy', *Contemporary Theatre Review*, 13:1 (2003).
Saunders, Graham, *'Love me or kill me': Sarah Kane and the Theatre of Extremes* (Manchester: Manchester University Press, 2001).
Saunders, Graham, '"Missing Mothers and Absent Fathers": Howard Barker's *Seven Lears* and Elaine Feinstein's *Lear's Daughters*', *Modern Drama*, 42:3 (1999).

Saunders, Graham, '"Out Vile Jelly": Sarah Kane's *Blasted* and Shakespeare's *King Lear*', *New Theatre Quarterly*, 20:1 (2004).
Schweppenhäuser, Gerhard, *Theodor W. Adorno: An Introduction*, trans. James Rolleston (Durham, NC and London: Duke University Press, 2009).
Scott, Michael, *Shakespeare and the Modern Dramatist* (Basingstoke: Macmillan, 1989).
Sharples, Caroline and Olaf Jensen (eds), *Britain and the Holocaust: Remembering and Representing War and Genocide* (Basingstoke: Palgrave Macmillan, 2013).
Shaughnessy, Robert, *The Shakespeare Effect: A History of Twentieth-Century Performance* (Basingstoke: Palgrave Macmillan, 2002).
Shenton, Mark, 'Antony Sher in *King Lear*, Royal Shakespeare Theatre Review – "Physically Subdued"', *The Stage*, <https://www.thestage.co.uk/reviews/2016/antony-sher-as-king-lear-review-royal-shakespeare-theatre-physically-subdued/> (accessed 16 October 2019).
Shakespeare, William, *King Lear*, ed. R. A. Foakes (London: Methuen, 1997).
Shakespeare, William, *King Lear*, ed. Kenneth Muir (London: Methuen, 1952).
Shakespeare, William, *King Lear*, ed. Kiernan Ryan (London: Penguin, 2005).
Shakespeare, William, *King Lear: A Parallel Text Edition*, 2nd edn, ed. René Weis (Oxford: Routledge, 2013).
Shakespeare, William, *The First Quarto of King Lear*, ed. Jay L. Halio (Cambridge: Cambridge University Press, 1994).
Shakespeare, William, *The History of King Lear*, ed. Stanley Wells (Oxford: Oxford University Press, 2000).
Shakespeare, William, *The Oxford Shakespeare: The Complete Works*, ed. Stanley Wells and Gary Taylor. (Oxford: Oxford University Press, 1985).
Shakespeare, William, *The Oxford Shakespeare: The Complete Works*, 2nd edn, ed. Stanley Wells and Gary Taylor (Oxford: Oxford University Press, 2005).
Shannon, Laurie, *The Accommodated Animal: Cosmopolity in Shakespearean Locales* (London and Chicago: University of Chicago Press, 2012).
Sher, Antony, *Year of the Mad King: The Lear Diaries* (London: Nick Hern Books, 2018).
Sherman, David, *Sartre and Adorno: Dialectics of Subjectivity* (New York: State University of New York Press, 2007).
Shue, Henry, *Climate Justice, Vulnerability and Protection* (Oxford: Oxford University Press, 2014).
Sidney, Philip, *The Countesse of Pembrokes Arcadia* (London: 1590), *Early English Books Online*, <https://data-historicaltexts-jisc-ac-uk.ezproxy01.rhul.ac.uk/view?pubId=eebo-ocm17202096e&terms=New%20Arcadia&pageTerms=New%20Arcadia&pageId=eebo-ocm17202096e-106206-1> (accessed 27 July 2017).
Sierz, Aleks, *In-Yer-Face Theatre: British Drama Today* (London: Faber and Faber, 2001).
Sinfield, Alan, *Faultlines: Cultural Materialism and the Politics of Dissident Reading* (Berkeley, Los Angeles, Oxford: University of California Press, 1992).
Sinfield, Alan, '*King Lear* versus *Lear* at Stratford', *Critical Quarterly*, 24:4 (1982).

Sjoholm, Cecilia, *Kristeva and the Political* (Oxford: Routledge, 2005).
Smith, Andy and James Reynolds (eds), *Howard Barker's Theatre: Wrestling with Catastrophe* (London: Methuen, 2015).
Smith, Emma and Garrett Sullivan (eds), *The Cambridge Companion to English Renaissance Tragedy* (Cambridge: Cambridge University Press, 2010).
Smith, Leslie, 'Edward Bond's *Lear*', *Comparative Drama*, 13:1 (1979).
Smith, Peter, 'Play Review, *King Lear*, directed by Gregory Doran for RSC, Royal Shakespeare Theatre', *Cahiers Élisabéthains*, 92:1 (2017).
Smith-Howard, Alicia, *Studio Shakespeare: The Royal Shakespeare Company at The Other Place* (Aldershot: Ashgate Publishing, 2006).
Snyder, Timothy, *Black Earth: The Holocaust as History and Warning* (London: Penguin, 2015).
Soncini, Sara, '"A horror so deep only ritual can contain it": The Art of Dying in the Theatre of Sarah Kane', *Other Modernities*, 4:10 (2010).
Spencer, Benjamin, '*King Lear*: A Prophetic Tragedy', *College English*, 5:6 (1944).
Spencer, Charles, 'Admirably repulsive: Charles Spencer reviews *Blasted* at the Royal Court', *The Telegraph*, <https://www.telegraph.co.uk/culture/4722664/Admirably-repulsive.html> (accessed 4 February 2018).
Spencer, Charles, '*The Gods Weep*, RSC', *Telegraph*, <http://www.telegraph.co.uk/culture/theatre/london-shows/7472953/The-Gods-Weep-RSC-Hampstead-Theatre-review.html> (accessed 4 February 2018).
Spencer, Jenny S., *Dramatic Strategies in the Plays of Edward Bond* (Cambridge: Cambridge University Press, 1992).
Spencer, Robert, 'Thoughts from Abroad, Theodor Adorno as Postcolonial Theorist', *Culture, Theory and Critique*, 51:3 (2010).
Spencer, Theodore, *Shakespeare and the Nature of Man* (New York: Macmillan, 1942).
Spielberg, Steven (dir.), *Schindler's List* (London: DVD Universal Pictures UK, 2019).
Spinks, Jennifer and Charles Zika (eds), *Disaster, Death and the Emotions in the Shadow of the Apocalypse, 1400–1700* (Basingstoke: Palgrave Macmillan, 2016).
Spurgeon, Caroline, *Shakespeare's Imagery and What it Tells Us* (Cambridge: Cambridge University Press, 1935).
St Aubyn, Edward, *Dunbar* (London: Hogarth Press, 2017).
Steinbacher, Sybille, *Auschwitz: A History*, trans. Shaun Whiteside (London: Penguin, 2005).
Steiner, George, *In Bluebeard's Castle: Some Notes Towards the Redefinition of Culture* (New Haven: Yale University Press, 1971).
Steiner, George, *The Death of Tragedy* (New Haven: Yale University Press, 1996).
Steiner, George, '"Tragedy", Reconsidered', *New Literary History*, 35:1 (2005).
Stephenson, Heidi and Natasha Langridge (eds), *Rage and Reason: Women Playwrights on Playwriting* (London: Methuen, 1997).
Stone, Dan, *The Concentration Camp: A Short History* (Oxford: Oxford University Press, 2017).
Suk, Jan, 'Glocal Spin-Offs: Ghostings of Shakespeare in the Works of Forced

Entertainment', *Academia.edu*, <https://www.academia.edu/21331643/Glocal_Spin-Offs_Ghosting_of_Shakespeare_in_the_Works_of_Forced_Entertainment> (accessed 2 October 2019).

Sun, Emily, *Succeeding King Lear: Literature, Exposure and the Possibility of Politics* (New York: Fordham University Press, 2010).

Szondi, Peter, *An Essay on The Tragic*, trans. Paul Fleming (Stanford: Stanford University Press, 2002).

Tate, Nahum, *The History of King Lear*, ed. James Black (London: Edward Arnold, 1976).

Taneja, Preti, *We That Are Young* (Norwich: Galley Beggar Press, 2017).

Taylor, Charles and Amy Gutmann (eds), *Multiculturalism* (Princeton: Princeton University Press, 1994).

Taylor, Paul, 'The Gods Weep', *The Independent*, <http://www.independent.co.uk/arts-entertainment/theatre-dance/reviews/the-gods-weep-hampstead-theatre-london-1925376.html> (accessed 5 February 2018).

Taylor, Paul, 'The Woman Question', *The Independent*, <https://www.independent.co.uk/arts-entertainment/theatre-the-woman-question-paul-taylor-reviews-max-stafford-clarks-production-of-king-lear-at-the-1480290.html> (accessed 19 April 2019).

Taylor, Gary and Michael Warren (eds), *The Division of the Kingdoms: Shakespeare's Two Versions of King Lear* (Oxford: Oxford University Press, 1983).

Tennenhouse, Leonard, *Power on Display: The Politics of Shakespeare's Genres* (London: Routledge, 2004).

Terada, Rei, *Looking Away: Phenomenality and Dissatisfaction, Kant to Adorno* (Cambridge, MA: Harvard University Press, 2009).

Thibodeau, Martin, *Hegel and Greek Tragedy*, trans. Hans Jakob Wilhelm (New York and Plymouth: Lexington Books, 2013).

Thomson, Leslie, 'The Meaning of "Thunder and Lightning": Stage Directions and Audience Expectations', *Early Theatre*, 2 (1999).

Tomlin, Liz, 'The Politics of Catastrophe, Confrontation or Confirmation in Howard Barker's Theatre', *Modern Drama*, 43:1 (2000).

Traverso, Enzo, *Understanding the Nazi Genocide: Marxism After the Holocaust*, trans. Peter Drucker (London: Pluto Press, 1999).

Trewin, John Courtney, *Peter Brook: A Biography* (London: Penguin, 1971).

Urban, Kenneth, 'An Ethics of Catastrophe: The Theatre of Sarah Kane', *PAJ, A Journal of Performance and Art*, 23:2 (2002).

Urban, Kenneth, 'Towards a Theory of Cruel Britannia: Coolness, Cruelty, and the Nineties', *New Theatre Quarterly*, 20:4 (2004).

Weber, Max, *Political Writings*, ed. Peter Lassman, trans. Ronald Speirs (Cambridge: Cambridge University Press, 1994).

Webber, Mark J., 'Metaphorizing the Holocaust: The Ethics of Comparison', *Images*, 8:15–16 (2011).

Welch, Jack, *Jack: Straight from the Gut* (London: Headline, 2001).

Williams, Robert R, *Tragedy, Recognition, and the Death of God: Studies in Hegel and Nietzsche* (Oxford: Oxford University Press, 2012).

Wells, Stanley (ed), *Shakespeare Survey: Volume 44* (Cambridge: Cambridge University Press, 1992).

Wittreich, Joseph, *'"Image of that Horror"': History, Prophecy and the*

Apocalypse in King Lear (San Marino: University of California Press, 1984).

Wixson, Christopher, '"In Better Places": Space, Identity, and Alienation in Sarah Kane's *Blasted*', *Comparative Drama*, 39:1 (2005).

Wolfit, Donald (dir.), 'BBC Living Shakespeare: *King Lear*' (1962), *YouTube*, <https://www.youtube.com/watch?v=zNtbCKm5qn8> (accessed 14 October 2019).

Wyman, David S. (ed.), *The World Reacts to the Holocaust* (Baltimore and London: The Johns Hopkins University Press, 1996).

Zapf, Hubert, 'Two Concepts of Society in Drama: Bertolt Brecht's *The Good Woman of Setzuan* and Edward Bond's *Lear*', *Modern Drama*, 31:3 (1988).

Zimmerer, Jürgen (ed.), *Climate Change and Genocide: Environmental Violence* (London: Routledge, 2015).

Žižek, Slavoj, *The Fragile Absolute, Or, Why is the Christian Legacy Worth Fighting For?* (London: Verso, 2000).

Žižek, Slavoj, *The Parallax View* (London: MIT Press, 2006).

Index

9/11, 4, 10, 276, 288n
7/7, 10
2008 economic crash, 10, 97, 275, 277, 280–1, 296, 302, 303; *see also* credit crunch

Aberg, Maria, 289, 294n
Abramović, Marina, 269
Actor-Network Theory, 273, 275
adaptation, 12, 13–14, 15, 16
Adelman, Janet, 119
Adorno, Theodor, 5n, 23–4, **26–64**, 94, 152, 184, 203, 208, 232, 252, 292, 302
 'addendum', 45n
 aesthetics, 9, 27, 50–5; *see also* aesthetic
 'after' Auschwitz, 11, 303–4
 anti-Semitism/the other, 34–5, 48; *see also* anti-Semitism; Jews
 Auschwitz, **26–64**; *see also* Auschwitz
 on Beckett, 60–1, 247–8
 on Brecht, 53
 capitalism, 35–8
 catastrophe *see* catastrophe
 on categorical imperative (Kant), 207; *see also* new categorical imperative
 cold/coldness, 144, 147, 147n
 critiques of/postmodernism, 38–43
 Culture Industry, 36–8, 49, 53, 60–1, 127, 142, 167, 199, 268, 299
 on death, 247–8
 dialectic of enlightenment, 26–35, 40, 43, 65, 76, 144, 157, 163, 167, 222, 241
 enlightenment, as demythologising process, 29–30, 30n, 57–8
 'ephemeral life', 237, 238–9, 253, 256, 263, 298
 exile, 176–7, 178–9
 and feminism, 48n
 on *Hamlet*, 60
 on Hegel, 29, 45
 and Horkheimer, 27–38, 57, 60, 62, 73, 167, 199, 283, 297

identity politics, 47–9
identity-thinking, 30, 35, 38, 45, 47, 48, 54, 58, 190, 241, 242, 251, 300
 influence on Barker, 9, 207–8, 208n, 210, 211, 213
 influence on Bond, 157, 157n
 influence on post-war playwriting, 8, 27
 influence on Rudkin, 199–200
 instrumental reason, 29, 49, 74, 75, 134, 146, 167, 176, 197, 267, 283, 284, 287, 297
 on late capitalism, 10, 11, 36
 on late modernism, 55n
 on materialism/metaphysics, 237–9, 250n, 251–2; *see also* ephemeral life
 on morality/ethics, 205–7, 222, 229; *see also* Mündigkeit
 Mündigkeit, 206–7
 nature, 29, 32, 44, 238–9, 282–4; *see also* sublime
 on needs, 283, 283n
 negative dialectics, 45, 63, 252
 'new categorical imperative', 27, 207, 284
 non-identity, 45, 47, 49, 62, 63, 65, 95, 171, 175, 176, 177, 179, 183, 185–6, 185n, 194, 199, 202, 212, 233, 252, 283, 297–8
 and postcolonialism, 48–9n
 and queer theory, 48n
 reification, 32–3; *see also* Lukács, György; reification
 sacrifice, 62–3, 183
 'share'/'surplus', 45–6
 shudder, 54–5, 54n, 199–200, 262–3, 299–300, 301
 subject/subjectivity, 9, 43–7; *see also* subject/subjectivity
 sublime, 282–4
 suicide, 250
 totality, 29, 31, 32, 34, 36, 37–8, 41–3, 45, 46, 47, 48, 49, 50, 51, 52, 53, 54, 55, 56, 61, 63, 65, 80, 82, 83, 84, 94, 95, 121, 122, 142, 146, 167, 171,

Adorno, Theodor (*cont.*)
  174, 175, 180, 181, 183, 184, 185, 186, 187, 195, 197, 198, 202, 206, 210, 211, 212, 213, 222, 232, 233, 235, 236, 237, 238, 239, 243, 243n, 244, 245, 246, 247, 248, 251, 256, 260, 264, 266, 267, 277, 281, 282, 298, 300, 304
  tragedy, 57–64; *see also* tragedy
  aesthetic, 8, 16, 20, 24, 27, 92, 95, 102, 102n, 106, 120–1, 192
    affect, 54–5, 54n, 199–200, 201, 202, 262–3, 268, 299–300; *see also* Adorno: shudder
    autonomy of, 52–3, 56, 62, 63, 142, 183
    catastrophe/catastrophic, 9, 46, 52, 266, 270
    closure, 161
    closure, violation of, 7, 18, 51–2, 63, 84, 93, 94–5, 106, 133, 200, 202, 215, 259–60, 301
    and Enlightenment philosophy, 50
    fragmentation, 51, 192, 213, 214, 267, 269, 285, 299
    harmony, 50–1
    history of aesthetic theory, 52–3
    late modernism, 55–6, 55n
    modernism, 55, 56, 190, 240, 269
    as politically engaged, 53
    postmodern, 55–6, 128, 265
    and realism, 53
    see also Adorno: aesthetic
  Agamben, Giorgio, 9, 80, 81, 183–5, 248n
  Agee, James, 23
  Améry, Jean, 155
  Anders, Günther, 154n
  Angel-Perez, Elisabeth, 213
  Angelaki, Vicky, 276–7, 301
  Anthropocene, 132, 141
  anti-Semitism, 5, 34; *see also* Adorno: anti-Semitism/the other
  appropriation, 11–12, 14–16; *see also* Barker, Howard; Bond, Edward; Forced Entertainment; Kane, Sarah; Kelly, Dennis; Rudkin, David: on appropriation
  Archer, Jayne Elisabeth, 294
  Arendt, Hannah, 9, 107, 155–6, 169, 268
  Aristotle, 58–9, 60, 86, 204, 206–7, 208, 212, 223–4
  Artaud, Antonin, 113, 114, 189, 190, 240
  Arthur, Robin, 264
  Aryan, 5n, 48, 206
  As You Like It, 218
  astrology, 37, 73, 292n
  Atropos, 200
  Aubyn, Edward St (*Dunbar*), 304
  Auden, W. H., 111, 157n
  Auschwitz
    de-subjectification *see* subject/subjectivity: destruction of
    and environment, 135, 283–4
    as 'factory', 36, 157
    and late capitalism, 11
    as metonym, 5, 5–6n, 9, 146n, 157, 289–91
    number of deaths, 5
    and private industry, 37
    witnessing, 98, 268, 271–2
    see also catastrophe: modern
  author/authorship, 12, 13, 15, 16
  autonomy *see* subject/subjectivity

Babi Yar, 148, 244
Bacon, Francis, 73
Barker, Francis, 127
Barker, Howard, 6, 7n, 9, 15, 16, 18, 21, 23n, 25, 129, 141, 167n, 199n, 202, **203–33**, 235, 236, 240, 270, 280, 282, 299
  on appropriation, 15, 15n, 214–17
  'Art of Theatre', 216
  Brutopia, 214
  Claw, 209
  Gertrude – The Cry, 214, 216
  Golgo, 210
  Henry V in Two Parts, 214, 216
  Minna, 214
  One Afternoon on the 63rd Level of the North Face of the Pyramid of Cheops the Great, 209n
  Seven Lears, 6, 25, 129, 167n, 174n, **203–33**, 260n, 291, 295, 295n
  That Good Between Us, 209, 209n
  The Bite of the Night, 210
  The Castle, 222
  The Hang of the Gaol, 209, 209n
  The Last Supper, 210
  The Possibilities, 210
  The Wrestling School, 204
  'Theatre of Catastrophe'/'Catastrophism', 7–8, 209–14, 210n, 217, 229, 232, 233, 259–60
  (Uncle) Vanya, 214
  Victory, 222
  Women Beware Women, 214
Bauman, Zygmunt, 35
Beckett, Samuel, 8n, 55, 60–1, 109, 113, 124, 144, 146, 159, 240, 246–7, 255, 259
  on Adorno and Hamm/Hamlet, 60
  Endgame, 44, 60, 150, 246, 248, 255, 266
  Happy Days, 255
  Waiting for Godot, 124, 150, 266
  see also Adorno: on Beckett
Belsey, Catherine, 117
Benjamin, Walter, 46, 303
Bennett, Susan, 126
Bergen-Belsen (also 'Belsen'), 101, 107, 155
Berger, Harry, 119

Berlin Wall, 2, 10, 106, 145, 157, 166, 169, 212, 226
Berliner Ensemble, 146–7
Bernhard, Thomas (*Minetti*), 4n
Bernstein, J.M., 297
Bewes, Timothy, 42n
Bickersteth, Geoffrey, 100–1
Billingham, Peter, 159, 162, 164–5
Billington, Michael, 279
Black Lives Matter, 47, 243n
Blanchot, Maurice, 5n, 9
Bond, Edward, 2–3, 6, 16, 21, 23n, 24, 61n, 111, 114, 116, 141, **143–71**, 226, 235, 236, 240, 244, 255, 280, 282, 292, 301n, 304
  A Window, 165
  on appropriation, 150–1
  At the Inland Sea, 165
  Bingo, 144, **163–5**, 168, 170, 172, 288n, 295n
  Born, 165
  Coffee, 165
  Innocence, 165
  Lear, 2–3, 6, 24, 61n, 116, **144–63**, 164, 169, 170, 171, 173, 174n, 244, 277n, 287, 293
  'Lear War', 165, **167–8**
  People, 165
  'Radical Innocence', 166–70
  The Crime of the Twentieth Century, 165
  'William Shakespeare's Last Notebook', 165, **168–9**
Booth, Stephen, 87, 88, 90, 94, 256
Bosnia, 4, 25, 244, 258, 264, 270
Bowie, Andrew, 304
Bradley, A. C., 93, 98–9, 99n, 105
Bradley, David, 156
Bradley, Lynne, 23, 167n
Brecht, Bertolt, 113, 114, 124, 146, 147–8, 154, 165, 170, 209
  on *King Lear*, 150, 161n
  Roundheads and Peakheads, 147
  on Shakespearean tragic 'hero', 149
  The Resistible Rise of Arturo Ui, 283n
  on tragedy, 61, 61n, 161
  Verfremdungseffekt, 113–14, 147, 160, 160n
Brockbank, Phillip, 117
Brook, Peter, 78n, 111–15, 124, 125, 138, 139, 140, 150, 150n, 138, 188
Buchenwald, 155
Büchner, Georg, 240
Butler, Leo (*Faces in the Crowd*), 277

Callaghan, Dympna, 115
Camus, Albert, 159, 240
Canetti, Elias, 290
Carney, Sean, 255, 256n
Carson, Rachel, 138
Cartelli, Thomas, 155

Casson, Lewis, 102
catastrophe
  as aesthetic, 7–8, 9, 50–2, 55, 193, 202, 214, 266, 268, 269, 270, 275
  and autonomy, 7, 46, 81–2
  as character, 85–6
  early modern, 84–8, 93, 99n, 203, 205, 233, 266, 267, 276, 281, 283, 304
  etymology, 85
  modern, 1, 2–4, 6, 9, 10–11, 23, 24, 25, 26, 38, 41, 46, 60n, 65, 67, 72–81, 94, 95, 96, 97, 101, 102, 105, 106, 108, 109, 110, 111, 114, 123, 131, 132, 134, 141, 144, 146, 147n, 165, 166, 167, 169, 171, 198, 203, 205, 233, 266, 267, 275, 276, 281, 303, 304
  as 'sudden turn', 85, 200–1, 209, 231–2, 231n, 260–1, 280, 298–300
Caygill, Howard, 252
Chadbourn, Huw, 264
Chambers, Colin, 114
Chambers, R. W., 98, 104
Chasin, Alexandra, 49
Chekhov, Anton, 214
Chen, Chien-Cheng, 146n
Chernobyl, 4
Church, Tony, 115
Churchill, Caryl (*Serious Money*), 126–7
climate change, 4, 10, 24, 97, 132, 134–5, 136, 137, 141, 273, 275, 281, 294, 296, 302, 303
  and far right, 284n
  and sublime, 282n
Cohen, Derek, 182–3
Cohn, Ruby, 23
Cold War, 2, 10, 106, 123, 134, 147n
Coleridge, Samuel Taylor, 93
colonialism, 34, 297n
communism, 35, 108
concentration camps/camps, 1, 3, 5, 24, 25, 33, 36, 80, 81, 104, 106, 107, 108, 109, 111, 116, 122, 143, 146, 150, 151, 157, 174, 191n, 205, 206, 208, 237, 244, 264, 279, 284, 304
Conversi, Daniel, 296
Cooke, Deborah, 283–4
Cooper, Thomas, 85
coronavirus, 303
credit crunch, 276, 302, 303
Crimp, Martin, 240

Dachau, 3, 101
Danby, John F., 11, 99–100, 101–2, 106, 131–2, 141, 197
Davis, David, 169–70
de Montaigne, Michel, 86, 224
de Schutter, Olivier, 296–7
'Death of the Author', 13; *see also* author/authorship
deconstructionism, 44

Derrida, Jacques, 90n, 282, 282n
Deutsch, Michel (*John Lear*), 4n
Devine, George, 104n, 146
disaster
  capitalism, 45n
  etymology, 70n
  see also catastrophe
Dollimore, Jonathon, 14n, 117–18, 122n, 127
Donaghy, Pip, 254
Donatus, Aelius, 65, 85–6, 93
Doran, Gregory, 138–40
Dresden, 244
Duncan, Hal, 178
Dupuy, Jean-Pierre, 9, 134, 135

Eagleton, Terry, 58, 122n, 291
ecocatastrophe, 24
ecosphere, 10, 138, 275, 284, 294
Edgar, David (*Albert Speer*), 5n
Eichmann, Adolf, 107, 155–6, 156n, 156–7n, 207, 207n
Eldon, Stuart, 295
Eliot, T. S., 240
Elton, William, 98n, 105, 106
Estok, Simon C., 134
Etchells, Mark, 265, 270; *see also* Forced Entertainment: *Mark Does Lear*
Etchells, Tim *see* Forced Entertainment
Evans, Walker, 23
Everett, Barbara, 105, 106
exile, 24, 77n, 80, 82, 144n, 171, 179–91, 191n, 194–5, 198–9, 201, 202

Farr, David, 137–8, 140
Faurisson, Robert, 40n
Feinstein, Elaine, 128; *see also* Women's Theatre Group
feminism/feminist, 14, 15, 116, 122, 126, 128, 217–18, 241
Fernie, Ewan, 84, 186n
Final Solution/'Final Solution to the Jewish Question', 5n, 34, 104, 148, 155
Fischlin, Daniel, 12
Florio, John, 86
Foakes, R.A, 3, 21, 22, 79–80, 106–7, 109, 258
food, 25, 135, 136, 140; *see also* Kelly, Dennis: *The Gods Weep*
Forced Entertainment, 6, 23n, 24, 141, 171n, **264–75**
  200% & Bloody Thirsty, 268–9
  on appropriation, 265–6
  Club of No Regrets, 268n
  Dirty Work, 269
  Emmanuel Enchanted, 269
  Five Day Lear, 6, 25, **264–72**, 274, 275
  Mark Does Lear, 265, 270
  Speak Bitterness, 269
  Table Top Shakespeare: The Complete Works, 25, **272–5**

Ford, John, 240
Fordham, Hallam, 103
Fortier, Mark, 12
Foucault, Michel, 9n, 80
Frank, Hans, 101, 101n
Frankfurt Auschwitz Trials, 107
Frankfurt School, 8, 43, 47, 59, 67, 163, 176, 283n
freedom *see* autonomy; subject/subjectivity
French, William, 99, 104
Freud, Sigmund, 283
Fukushima, 4, 304
Fukuyama, Francis, 10

García, Rodrigo (*Rey Lear*), 4n
Gaskill, William, 3, 146
gender, 32, 47, 48, 118, 120, 126, 241, 242, 243
genocide, 4, 16n, 31, 33, 108, 123, 134, 169, 244, 268, 290, 296, 302
Gielgud, John, 102–4, 104n, 112, 113, 162
globalisation/global capital, 25, 41, 42, 49, 97, 169, 210, 243, 244, 274, 285, 286, 297, 303
Goldberg, S. L., 110
Goldman, Michael, 186
Goodbody, Buzz, 111, 114–16, 124n
Goodman, Lizbeth, 128
Gorman, Sarah, 269
Gould, Rupert, 137
Goya, Francisco, 284
Grady, Hugh, 82–4, 120, 121
Granville-Barker, Harley, 102–4, 102n
Gray, John, 61n
Greenblatt, Stephen, 174n, 186n
Greig, David, 255
Gritzner, Karoline, 8n, 235, 255
gulag, 38, 147
Gwilym, Mike, 115

Habermas, Jürgen, 38, 40n, 83; *see also* *King Lear*: consensus theory
Halio, Jay, 114
Hall, Peter, 124
Hamilton, Jennifer Mae, 132, 134, 137
Hamlet, 3, 60, 76, 89–90, 91, 106, 108, 113, 127, 195, 214, 220, 252
Hare, David, 124–5, 277
  The Great Exhibition, 124–5
  The Power of Yes, 277
Harman, Graham, 273
Harrison, G. B., 11, 101
Harwood, Ronald (*The Dresser*), 269
Hausner, Gideon, 156n
Hawkes, Terence, 122–3, 133
Heathfield, Adrien, 267
Hecht, Anthony, 279, 279n
Hegel, Georg Wilhelm Friedrich, 29, 45, 50, 59, 86, 212, 252
Heidegger, Martin, 252

Heijes, Coen, 137
Heilman, R. B., 98, 106
Heinemann, Margot, 80n, 89n
Hellings, James, 55
Henry IV Part Two, 86
Hicks, Greg, 137
Hickson, Ella (*Precious Little Talent*), 277
Higgins, John, 17
Himmler, Heinrich, 101
Hiroshima, 4, 104, 131–2, 154n, 244, 266, 269
Hitchcock, Alfred, 190
Hitler, Adolf, 101, 204, 244, 296, 296n
Hobbes, Thomas, 70
Hochhuth, Rolf (*The Deputy*), 112
Holbrook, Peter, 79
Holinshed, Raphael, 17
Holocaust, etymology, 13n; *see also* Auschwitz
Homden, Carol, 125
Horkheimer, Max, 31, 38, 145, 207n; *see also* Adorno: Horkheimer
Horowitz, Sara, 91n
Horton, Joanna, 289
Hullot-Kentor, Robert, 305
Hunter, G. K., 117
Hutcheon, Linda, 13
Huxley, Aldous, 240
Hytner, Nicholas, 20n, 124

Ibsen, Henrik, 240
identity politics/political identity, 14, 15, 16, 47n, 116–31, 190, 202, 218, 239–43, 244–5, 281
Innes, Christopher, 165
intertextuality, 12–13, 15, 16
Ionesco, Eugène, 113
Ireland, Kenny, 204
Irons, Jeremy, 289

Jackson, Phillip, 259
James I, 70
Jameson, Fredric, 41–3, 46–7, 49, 55–6, 55n
Jews, 4, 5n, 28n, 34–5, 38, 48, 101, 116, 148, 150, 205, 207n, 244, 244n, 269, 279, 288, 302; *see also* anti-Semitism
Johnson, Samuel, 85, 92–3
Johnstone, Oliver, 139
Joughin, John, 94–5, 120

Kafka, Franz, 55
Kahn, Coppélia, 118–19
Kane, Sarah, 6, 15, 16, 18, 19n, 21, 23n, 25, 141, 233, **234–64**, 270, 274, 299
  4.48 Psychosis, 235, 240, 244n, 289
  on appropriation, 239–45
  Blasted, 6, 19n, 25, 87, 125, **234–64**, 270, 279n, 280, 295, 295n, 298, 299n
  Crave, 235, 254n, 289
  Phaedra's Love, 235n

Kant, Immanuel, 29, 50, 156, 204, 207, 207n, 282, 282n
Keats, John, 93
Keefe, Barrie, 127
  King of England, 127, 129–31
Kelly, Dennis, 1–2, 3, 6, 15, 16, 23n, 25, 141, 264, 275, **276–302**, 303, 304
  After the End, 276
  on appropriation, 281–2
  Debris, 276
  Girls and Boys, 276
  Love and Money, 277, 289–91
  Matilda, 276
  Orphans, 276
  Osama the Hero, 276
  Pulling, 276
  The Gods Weep, 1–2, **276–302**, 303
  The Ritual Slaughter of Gorge Mastromas, 276
Kennedy, Dennis, 106
Kermode, Frank, 256–7
Kettle, Arnold, 109–10, 111, 197
King Lear, **64–95**
  absurdist interpretation of, 105–9, 111–14, 123–6, 245–8
  'bare life', 80–1, 115, 183–5, 248n; *see also* 'base life' (below)
  'base life', 65, 66, 75–9, 80, 184–5; *see also* 'bare life' (above)
  and bio-power, 80–1
  'blasted heath', as editorial intervention, 22, 181, 236n
  catastrophe (as disaster), 67–72
  catastrophe (as end of play), 84–92
  Christian interpretations of, 97–104
  and commodity-form, 76
  and concentration camps, 80–1
  and consensus theory, 82–4
  cultural materialist appropriations of, 127–31
  cultural materialist interpretations of, 116–23
  Dover 'cliff', 25, 109, 186, 236, 245–8, 249, 253, 256, 257, 261
  ecocritical interpretations of, 131–40
  Edgar/Poor Tom, 24, 65, 66, 81–3, 172–3, 173n, 177, 179–202
  ending of, 87–92: and Holocaust, 93–5, 106
  exile, 179–87
  forms of appropriation, 3–4, 16
  and *Hamlet*, 3, 108, 127
  history of appropriation, 16–17
  humanist interpretations of, 117, 123–6, 208
  hunger, 294–5
  and late capitalism, 79–80
  Marxist interpretations of, 109–11, 114–16
  'missing mother', 119, 120, 129, 130, 164n, 204, 217–18

King Lear (cont.)
  and modernity, 72–9
  pre-Holocaust criticism, 92–3
  sources/intertexts of, 17–18
  storm, 25, 66, 81, 83, 84, 97–9, 103, 110, 112, 113, 114, 117, 119, 120, 131, 132, 132n, 133, 134, 135–48, 151, 162, 163, 164, 168, 183, 188, 208–15, 219–21, 224, 236, 269, 285, 288n, 294, 299, 300
  subject-object split, 74, 74n
  and tragic freedom, 81–2
  two texts of, 19–22, 88–90, 120
  weather, 2, 134, 135, 140; *see also* storm (above)
Kingsley-Smith, Jane, 179, 198
Kipp, Lara, 203
Klein, Naomi, 45n
Knights, L.C., 108
Knowles, Richard, 21
Kosovo, 270–2
Kott, Jan, 108–9, 111–12, 113, 124, 150, 161, 162, 246–8, 261
Kozintsev, Grigori, 150n
Kracauer, Siegfried, 285n
Kristeva, Julia, 178, 199
Kurosawa, Akira (*Ran*), 280, 280n, 293, 300
Kyle, Barry, 156

Lacan, Jacques, 166
Lamb, Charles, 136–7
Langar, Lawrence, 93–4
late capitalism, 10–11, 25, 36, 42, 56, 79, 142, 157, 166, 167, 169, 174, 197, 198, 202, 210, 211, 212, 213, 235, 239, 243, 264, 266, 267, 268, 280, 281, 284, 290, 291, 298, 302, 304; *see also* Mandel, Ernest
late modernism, 55–6, 114, 142, 190, 213, 240, 263, 269
Latour, Bruno, 273
Lawrence, Sean, 256
Laysiepen, Uwe, 269
Le Provost, Nicholas, 209, 219n, 231
Lee, Yun Lisa, 176
Leech, Clifford, 117
Leggatt, Alexander, 103n, 112
Lehmann, Rosamond, 107
Lessing, Gotthold, 214
Levene, Mark, 296
Levi, Primo, 33, 66, 80
Linley, Keith, 119
Loftis, Sonya Freeman, 23
Lousley, Cheryl, 136
Lowdon, Richard, 264, 272
Lowenthal, David, 219
Lukács, György, 32, 152; *see also* reification
Lyotard, Jean-François, 9, 39–41, 40n, 43, 54, 282, 282n

Macbeth, 89, 90, 193, 236n, 286, 287, 286-7n
Mack, Maynard, 107
Macready, William Charles, 17, 93
Mahler, Gustav, 190
Malm, Andreas, 302
Mandel, Ernest, 10–11
Mann, Thomas, 39
Marcuse, Herbert, 111
Marshall, Claire, 264
Mason, H. A., 110
McCarthy, Cormac (*The Road*), 293
McDonald, James, 254, 256n
McLuskie, Katherine, 118
Megson, Chris, 281
Mengele, Josef, 155
Mentz, Stephen, 294
#MeToo, 47
Middleton, Thomas, 214
Minor, Benjamin, 119–20
Monmouth, Geoffrey, 17
More, Thomas, 214
Morgan, Alistair, 238–9
Muir, Edwin, 99, 102
Muir, Kenneth, 21, 86, 98
Munby, Jonathon, 137
Muselmann, 248, 248n
Muslim/Muslims, 248n, 302

Naden, Cathy, 264
Nagasaki, 4, 244, 269
Nancy, Jean-Luc, 303–4
Nazi ideology, 5n, 34, 34n, 36n, 48, 100, 135, 150, 156, 191n, 205–6, 287, 295–6, 296n, 297n
Neeson, Liam, 288
New Materialism, 273–5
New Right, 121, 130; *see also* Thatcher, Margaret/Thatcherism; Reagan, Ronald
Nivalainen, Marku, 64
Noble, Adrian, 123–4
Noguchi, Isamu, 105n
nuclear weapons/war, 2, 10, 90n, 106, 107, 122, 134, 138, 276, 293
Nuremberg trials, 101

Object-Orientated Ontology, 273
O'Connor, Terry, 264, 267
Ollendorf, Robert, 196
Omarska, 244
Othello, 89, 90, 91

Palfrey, Simon, 184, 196
Parr, Anthony, 134
Paster, Gail Kern, 74n
Peck, Bob, 156
Peters, Jens, 220
Picasso, Pablo, 55
populism, 281, 281n, 284n
postcolonialism, 14, 122, 297

Postone, Moshie, 49, 110
poststructuralism, 12, 20, 44, 56, 233, 265, 267
Prebble, Lucy (*Enron*), 277

queer, 14, 122, 126, 246

Rabey, David Ian, 18–19, 87n, 188n, 255
  The Back of Beyond, 18, 19n, 192n
  The Battle of Crows, 18
race, 32, 47, 48, 120, 241, 243
race theory/science, 4, 5n, 34, 34n, 48, 135, 205–6, 295–6, 296n, 297n
Rancière, Jacques, 206n
Reagan, Ronald, 121
Rebellato, Dan, 243, 276, 289
refugee, 125, 136, 140, 145, 171n, 271, 303
reification, 32–3, 36, 38, 41, 42n, 43, 52, 56, 57, 61, 62, 65, 67, 76, 77, 79, 80, 84, 121, 134, 135, 136, 141, 144, 146, 152, 155, 157, 158, 159, 169, 170, 171, 174, 176, 184, 198, 202, 227, 281, 284, 285, 285n, 286, 291, 293, 298, 299, 300, 302, 304
Ribner, Irving, 98
Richard II, 223
Richardson, Samuel, 228
Rosen, Alan, 86–7, 94
Rosenberg, Marvin, 112
Roth, John K., 205
Rousset, David, 33
Rowe, Nicholas, 181; *see also King Lear*: blasted heath
Rudkin, David, 6, 15, 16, 21, 23n, 24, 77n, 82, 141, 171, **172–202**, 220, 233, 235, 242, 246n, 252, 260, 266, 282, 299, 304
  Afore Night Come, 172, 176, 191
  on appropriation, 190–2
  Ashes, 176
  Merlin Unchained, 174, 191
  Place Prints, 172
  Red Sun, 172, 176
  'self re-authorship', 173–5
  Sovereignty Under Elizabeth, 175
  The Lovesong of Alfred J. Hitchcock, 176
  The Saxon Shore, 173n, 175, 188
  The Sons of Light, 172, 174, 188, 196
  The Triumph of Death, 172, 188, 191
  untitled Shakespeare play, 191
  Will's Way, 6, 172–3, 185n, 190, **191–201**, 191n, 246
Rumbold, Kate, 137
Rwanda, 4, 123
Ryan, Kiernan, 116, 285

sacrifice, 5n, 182–3, 191n, 195, 215, 277; *see also* Adorno: tragedy; Adorno: sacrifice
Said, Edward, 177

Sakellaridou, Elizabeth, 6
Salingar, Leo, 86
Samuels, Diane (*Kindertransport*), 5n
Sanders, Julie, 15
Sanders, Wilbur, 117
Santner, Eric, 110
Saunders, Graham, 23, 248
scapegoat, 178, 178n, 179, 183; *see also* sacrifice
Schafer, Elizabeth, 114
Schoenberg, Arnold, 55
Scott, Michael, 23
Second World War, 3, 10, 24, 28, 35, 54, 55, 97, 99, 101, 107, 111, 116, 122, 123, 134, 140, 141, 143, 266, 279, 284, 303
Serkis, Andy, 125–6, 128
sexuality, 32, 47, 48, 116, 117, 119, 120, 125, 133, 175, 190, 243
Shakespeare, William, and appropriation, 11–16, 22–3; *see also individual plays*
Shannon, Laurie, 134
Shaughnessy, Robert, 270
Shaw, George Bernard, 93
Shenton, Mark, 139
Sher, Antony, 138, 140
Shostakovich, Dmitri, 190
Sidney, Philip, 17
Sierz, Aleks, 277, 293
Sinfield, Alan, 14n, 127
Slater, Ben, 267
Smith, Peter, 140
Snyder, Timothy, 5n, 38, 135, 296n, 297n
Soncini, Sara, 255
Spencer, Benjamin, 101
Spencer, Charles, 235n, 279, 280
Spencer, Theodor, 99
Spielberg, Stephen, 288
  Schindler's List, 288–9, 288n
Spurgeon, Caroline, 101
Srebrenica, 165, 244
Stafford-Clark, Max, 125–6, 258, 259
Stalinism, 37–8, 114, 146, 146n, 226
Stampfer, J., 105–6
Steiner, George, 57n, 107
Stone, Dan, 36n
Stoppard, Tom, 113
  Rosencrantz and Guildenstern Are Dead, 113, 145n
  Rosencrantz and Guildenstern Meet King Lear, 113, 145n
subject/subjectivity
  autonomy, 7, 11, 14, 24, 25, 29, 33, 42, 43, 46–7, 49, 56, 58, 62–3, 79, 82, 133, 142, 174n, 178, 183, 185, 201, 205, 211–12, 213, 217, 222, 231, 232–3, 235, 260, 264, 266, 274, 282, 305
  destruction of, 5, 9, 24, 35, 42, 46, 141, 142, 171, 174–5, 225, 226, 281, 284, 293, 302, 304
  humanist, 43–4, 46, 48, 74n, 133, 273

subject/subjectivity (*cont.*)
  subject as object, 5, 25, 32, 36, 161, 162, 170, 286, 290, 297, 302; *see also* reification
sublime, 25, 93, 133, 143, 298, 299, 301; *see also* Adorno: sublime
Sun, Emily, 3, 32, 180
Swinburne, Algernon, 93
Syria, 140
Szondi, Peter, 58

Taneja, Preti (*We That Are Young*), 304
Tate, Nahum, 13n, 16, 17, 18, 23, 92–3, 186
  The History of King Lear, 16–17
'Tatification', 17
Taylor, Gary, 20
Taylor, Paul, 125, 279
Tennenhouse, Leonard, 71n
Terence, 85
terrorism, 4, 10, 134, 276
Thatcher, Margaret/Thatcherism, 121, 130, 198, 212
The Tempest, 231
The True Chronicle History of King Leir, 17–18, 19, 184
'Theatres of Catastrophe'/catastrophic theatre, 7–8, 8n, 11, 19, 22, 24, 27, 63, 65, 84, 87n, 95, 141–2, 172, 179, 200, 280, 304, 305
Thomas, Howard, 294
Thompson, Ayanna, 119–20
Thomson, Leslie, 135
Tillyard, E. M., 70
Tinker, Jack, 234n
Titus Andronicus, 4n, 235n
Tomlin, Liz, 211–12
totalitarianism, 35, 169
tragedy, 6, 7, 8, 18–19, 24, 27, 52, 56, 57–64, 185, 210–12, 217, 232, 256–7, 260, 276–7
  and absurdism, 60–1, 109–10, 141, 247, 255
  and affect, 63
  'after' Auschwitz, 27, 57, 59–60, 93–4, 95
  and Aristotle, 58–9, 212
  Chorus, 59, 212, 219, 231
  closure, 7, 18, 59–60, 63, 178, 237
  Culture Industry, 60–1
  'death of', 57n
  early modern, 58n
  Enlightenment philosophy, 58–9
  etymology, 73
  exile, 24, 177–9, 198
  fate, 57–8, 59, 60, 61, 149–50, 160, 162, 200
  Greek/Attic, 57–8, 200, 219
  Hegel on, 59, 212
  and humanist subject, 113, 117–20
  and modernist tradition, 56
  origin of aesthetic autonomy, 62–3, 183
  origin of subjective autonomy, 57–8, 63, 183
  sacrifice, 62–3, 183
  Shakespearean, 58, 86, 89–90, 91, 99n, 102, 117–20, 133, 215, 219
  'tragic freedom', 8, 24, 81, 248
  'tragic subject', 6, 25, 60, 61, 63, 109, 117, 118, 142, 183, 200, 201, 210, 211, 212, 282
Traverso, Enzo, 36
Trump, Donald, 171n
Turley, Richard Marggraf, 294

Urban, Ken, 259, 260–1
Ure, Joan, 128

Vietnam, 2, 107, 134
vitality curve, 286–7; *see also* Welch, Jack

Wallace, Jennifer, 177–8
Warren, Michael, 20
Weis, René, 20–1, 20n
Welch, Jack, 286; *see also* vitality curve
Wilcher, Robert, 192
Williams, Susie, 264
Wilson, Robert, 269
Wittgenstein, Ludwig, 39, 237
Wittreich, Joseph, 256
Wolfit, Donald, 265, 265n, 269
Women's Theatre Group (WTG), 127
  Lear's Daughters, 127, 128–9, 131
  see also Feinstein, Elaine
Wooster Group, 269
Wordsworth, William, 23

Yanow, Dvora, 49n

Zapf, Hubert, 152
Zimmerer, Jürgen, 296
Žižek, Slavoj, 285, 305

EU representative:
Easy Access System Europe
Mustamäe tee 50, 10621 Tallinn, Estonia
Gpsr.requests@easproject.com

www.ingramcontent.com/pod-product-compliance
Lightning Source LLC
Chambersburg PA
CBHW051557230426
43668CB00013B/1888